Prague & Czechia

North & East Bohemia p199

PRAGUE p48

South & West Bohemia p164

Moravia & Silesia p236

Mark Baker, Marc Di Duca, Becki Enright

View from Prague Castle (p56)

CONTENTS

Plan Your Trip

- The Journey Begins Here 4
- Czechia Map 6
- Our Picks 8
- Regions & Cities 22
- Itineraries 24
- When to Go 32
- Get Prepared 34
- The Food Scene 36
- The Outdoors 40

The Guide

- Prague 48
  - Prague Castle & Hradčany 54
  - Malá Strana 63
  - Staré Město 76
  - Nové Město 95
  - Žižkov & Karlín 109
  - inohrady & Vršovice 115
  - Holešovice 123
  - Bubeneč & Dejvice 132
  - Smíchov 142
  - Vyšehrad 148
  - Day Trips from Prague 154

South & West Bohemia 164
- Karlovy Vary 170
- Beyond Karlovy Vary 175
- Mariánské Lázně 178
- Beyond Mariánské Lázně 182
- Plzeň (Pilsen) 184
- Beyond Plzeň (Pilsen) 188
- Český Krumlov 190
- Beyond Český Krumlov 195

North & East Bohemia 199
- Liberec 204
- Beyond Liberec 208
- Czech Switzerland 211
- Beyond Czech Switzerland 216
- Kutná Hora 219
- Beyond Kutná Hora 223
- Litomyšl 225
- Pardubice 231

Moravia & Silesia 236
- Brno 242
- Beyona Brno 249
- Mikulov 255
- Beyond Mikulov 259
- Znojmo 262
- Olomouc 265
- Ostrava 269

Toolkit

- Arriving 276
- Money 277
- Getting Around 278
- Accommodation 280
- Family Travel 281
- LGBTIQ+ Travellers 282
- Health & Safe Travel 283
- Food, Drink & Nightlife 284
- Responsible Travel 286
- Accessible Travel 288
- Nuts & Bolts 289
- Language 290

Storybook

- A History of Czechia in 15 Places 294
- Meet the Czechs 298
- Architecture: The Battle over Communist Buildings 300
- Czech Humour: A Penchant for the Absurd 304
- Sport: Natural-Born Athletes 308
- Czech Spa Culture 312
- Industrial Relic Revival 314

Karlovy Vary (p170)

Charles Bridge (p68), Prague

PRAGUE & CZECHIA
THE JOURNEY BEGINS HERE

I'm a wanderer by nature, and there's nothing I enjoy more than meandering around the alleyways and hidden lanes of Prague's Old Town or Malá Strana. Although I've lived here for the better part of 30 years, the experience never gets old. Maybe it's the notion that I'm retracing steps that people have walked for centuries, or maybe it's simply the city's undeniable beauty. Every building, every bridge, every bend in the road feels purposefully placed by a set designer in a lush, historic drama, and for this moment in time at least, I'm the actor. Life in Prague – and Czechia generally – feels somehow easy. Not in learning the nuances of the language, perhaps, or in the ways of the culture, but in the local appreciation of simple pleasures: activities like strolling or sitting down for a coffee or beer in the shadow of 1000 years of history.

Mark Baker
@markbakerprague

Mark is based in Prague and the author of Čas proměn *(Time of Changes), a personal, Czech-language account of the period around the 1989 Velvet Revolution. He wrote the Prague chapter and the Plan Your Trip section.*

My favourite experience
is walking across Charles Bridge to feel the breeze and enjoy the sensation of space after wandering the city's closed-in, cobblestoned streets.

WHO GOES WHERE

Our writers and experts choose the places that, for them, define Prague & Czechia

The **Karlovy Vary region** (p170) is a magical place of low mountains, lonely villages, dark forests and a million stories. One of Central Europe's most sparsely populated areas sees the snow fall deep on the Krušné Mountains and the Slavkovský Forest, winter's fiery sunsets setting the ice ablaze. The temperature plummets when the sun goes down, which means it's time to find a log burner in a snug tavern to enjoy a plate of goulash and a tankard or two of the Czechs' world-beating beer.

Marc Di Duca
@marcdiduca

Marc is a travel author, translator, guide and outdoor enthusiast based in Czechia. He wrote the South & West Bohemia and North & East Bohemia chapters and the Toolkit section.

The dreamy peach-painted castle of **Mikulov** (p255) beckons from afar, its slopes winding with cobblestoned lanes and pastel palette squares in a fairytale town circled by monument topper rocks and nature reserves. It's the pop-up picture book of classical South Moravia; one you sip to in a sun-ripened haze after a hilltop hike or a two-wheeled trail, knowing that a rewarding glass of the region's vineyard harvest awaits you wherever you turn.

Becki Enright
@bordersofadventure

Becki is a writer based in Vienna, penning guidebooks and articles on culture, adventure and responsible travel. She wrote the chapter on Moravia & Silesia.

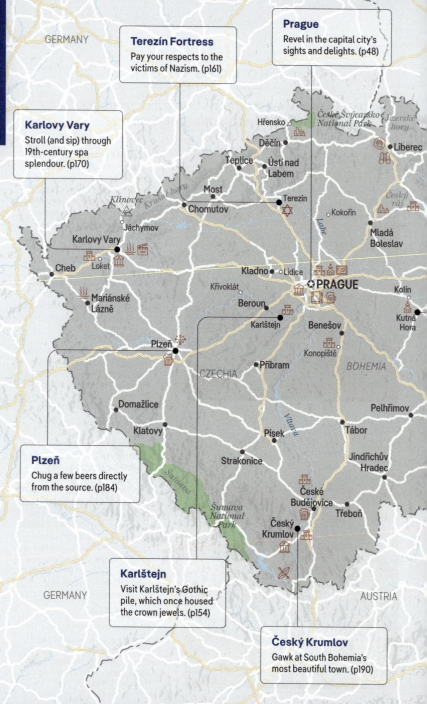

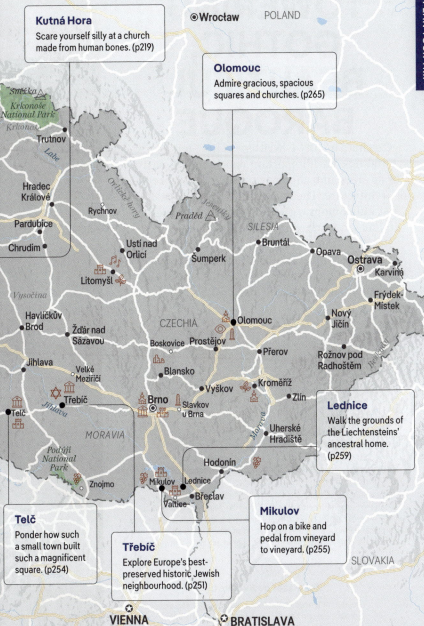

TOWERING GOTHIC, BEAUTIFUL BAROQUE

Czechia's history is written on the faces of its buildings. Each important epoch, new dynasty or advance in technology ushered in a new type of architecture. The story begins at the turn of the first millennium with heavy, round Romanesque and moves forward through the centuries to the stately Gothic town halls and cathedrals, and then to symmetrical Renaissance, dazzling baroque and beyond. To read the country's history, one need only decipher the styles.

Everyone Loves Gothic

Tall, sombre Gothic buildings recall the heady 14th century, when Emperor Charles IV was on the throne and Prague served as the capital of the Holy Roman Empire.

Razzle-Dazzle Baroque

The statues on Charles Bridge and the swirling gold and marble interiors of many churches ushered in an era of Catholic-Habsburg supremacy in the 17th century.

Renaissance Symmetry

Italian-influenced Renaissance, with its emphasis on proportion and beauty, came to Czechia in the 16th century and is strongly connected to the Reformation.

Charles Bridge (p68), Prague

BEST ARCHITECTURE EXPERIENCES

Stroll across ❶ **Charles Bridge**, a Gothic masterpiece from the 14th century. The evocative statues were added a few centuries later. (p68)

Take in Prague's beautiful ❷ **Old Town Hall**, with its tall tower and Astronomical Clock, a textbook example of Gothic architecture. (p82)

Admire ❸ **Český Krumlov's castle**, which gained its Renaissance exterior starting in the 16th century under the stewardship of the noble Rožmberk family. (p190)

Stand before Olomouc's moving ❹ **Holy Trinity Column** – said to be the biggest single baroque sculpture in all of Central Europe. (p265)

Walk and gawk at the gorgeous 19th-century spa architecture at a timeless resort like ❺ **Karlovy Vary**. (p170)

CHILLED TO THE BONE

Czechia is underrated as a spooky, downright macabre destination. Where else on earth will you find a church with an interior built entirely of human bones? If mummies are more your thing, a monastery in Brno has them splayed out on the basement floor – and the city has its own collection of human bones just down the street. The back alleys of Prague's former Jewish quarter, Josefov, is haunted by a legendary creature called the Golem.

Sanctuary of Skeletons

Kutná Hora's Sedlec Ossuary (pictured above) is home to Czechia's creepiest creation. Local woodcarver František Rint sculpted the church interior from the bones of around 40,000 people.

Blood-Curdling Brno

Brno places first for eye-popping oddities. The Capuchin Monastery (pictured above) houses several well-preserved mummies, and a nearby church is stuffed with thousands of human bones.

Prague's Jewish Quarter

The capital's former Jewish Quarter is filled with local legends going back centuries. These clearly inspired a young Franz Kafka, who considered the neighbourhood his early stomping ground.

Grave of Rabbi Loew, Old Jewish Cemetery (p90), Prague

BEST SPOOKY EXPERIENCES

Peek inside the ❶ **Sedlec Ossuary** to see garlands of skulls and femurs strung from the vaulted ceiling like an Addams Family house. (p159)

Pay respects to the 18th-century noblemen resting in eternal repose in the cellar of Brno's ❷ **Capuchin Monastery**. (p245)

Tour the crypts of Brno's ❸ **Church of St James** to see bones from 50,000 people who perished from wars and famine. (p245)

Visit the grave of Rabbi Loew at Prague's ❹ **Old Jewish Cemetery**. He's associated with the legend of the Golem, a creature made from the mud of the Vltava. (p90)

Walk along tiny ❺ **Golden Lane** at Prague Castle, where alchemists and sorcerers under Holy Roman Emperor Rudolf II plied their trades. (p56)

LOOK BEHIND THE IRON CURTAIN

Not that long ago, Czechia (as part of Czechoslovakia) was firmly locked into the Soviet-led Eastern bloc. The 1989 Velvet Revolution that overthrew communist rule and brought in playwright Václav Havel as president inspired the world. The changes since then have been profound, but here and there you can still see remains of the former authoritarian dictatorship.

BEST 'VELVET' EXPERIENCES

Descend to the cellar of ❶ **Vítkov Monument** in Prague's Žižkov to see the ghoulish laboratory where scientists tried unsuccessfully to preserve Gottwald's remains. (p112)

Peek inside the nuclear bunker below the capital's ❷ **Hotel Jalta** to look at the sophisticated surveillance equipment used to spy on hotel guests. (p101)

Take a self-guided tour of a Cold War-era nuclear fallout ❸ **bunker** in Brno built to protect the city's political elite. (p245)

Walk along ❹ **Národní třída**, where the Velvet Revolution began. The point where police first attacked demonstrators is marked by a small monument. (p297)

Feel history on ❺ **Wenceslas Square**, where thousands of protesters gathered, demanded the resignation of the communists. (p100)

Communists Declare a Coup

Communist rule came to Czechoslovakia in February 1948, when communist leader Klement Gottwald declared a takeover from the balcony of Prague's Kinský Palace on Old Town Square (pictured above).

Soviet-Led Invasion

Warsaw Pact forces, led by the Soviet Union, invaded a brotherly country in August 1968 to put down the democratic reforms known as the Prague Spring.

A 'Velvet' Revolution

On 17 November 1989, thousands rallied on Prague's central avenue, Národní, to call on communists to step down. Within a month, the regime had collapsed.

Upper Synagogue (p257), Mikulov

BEST JEWISH HERITAGE EXPERIENCES

Head to ❶ **Mikulov** to see the renovated Upper Synagogue – the only surviving synagogue in Czechia of the unique 'Polish' style. (p257)

Don a *kippah* (skullcap) and view the ancient tombstones that push through the ground like jagged teeth at Prague's ❷ **Old Jewish Cemetery**. (p90)

Visit the Moravian city of ❸ **Třebíč** to see Europe's best-preserved historic Jewish neighbourhood, a UNESCO World Heritage Site. (p251)

Pay your respects to the victims of Nazism at ❹ **Terezín**, a former Austrian military garrison used as a transit camp to Auschwitz. (p161)

Marvel at Plzeň's gigantic ❺ **synagogue**, the world's third-biggest Jewish place of worship, after Jerusalem and Budapest. (p187)

MILLENNIUM OF JEWISH HISTORY

For centuries, both Bohemia and Moravia were relatively safe havens for Jews. Prague, in particular, evolved into an important centre of Jewish life and scholarship, but towns like Mikulov and Třebíč in Moravia also developed into influential Jewish settlements. This long heritage came to a brutal end with the German Nazi occupation during WWII.

16th-Century Splendour

The vibrancy of the community, particularly in the 16th century, can be seen in Prague's Jewish Quarter, where the main synagogues and Old Jewish Cemetery have been preserved.

Remembering the Holocaust

The German occupation of WWII led to the destruction of this community. Many Jews were held at Terezín before being sent to Auschwitz-Birkenau.

STORYBOOK CASTLES

The Czechs' homeland in the middle of Europe has seen a long history of raiding tribes, conquering armies and triumphant dynasties. This turbulent past left a legacy of hundreds of castles and chateaux – everywhere there seems to be a many-turreted fortress perched above a town, or a romantic summer palace lazing amid manicured parkland. The number and variety of Czech castles is simply awe-inspiring – everything from grim Gothic ruins to majestic, baroque mansions.

Seat of the Bohemian Kingdom

Prague's enormous castle complex (pictured above) has served as the ruling centre of Bohemia, and a model for castles across the country, since around the first millennium.

Fortress Prison

Brno's ancient, foreboding Špilberk Castle (pictured above) dates from the mid-13th century, but it's best known for its role in later centuries as the cruellest prison of the Habsburg Empire.

19th-Century Bling

Many of Czechia's flashiest chateaux, particularly in South Bohemia and Moravia, were built in the 19th century by aristocratic families allied with the ruling Habsburg monarchy.

Lednice Chateau (p259)

BEST CASTLE EXPERIENCES

Tour magnificent ❶ **Prague Castle**, the world's largest castle complex by area. The grounds are breathtaking and the buildings are surrounded by parks and gardens. (p56)

Let yourself be dazzled by ❷ **Karlštejn**, once used to store the Bohemian crown jewels during the Hussite religious wars of the 15th century. (p155)

Enjoy the Renaissance spectacle of ❸ **Litomyšl**, which has one of the country's most exquisite chateaux. (p228)

Walk the lovely grounds of ❹ **Lednice Chateau**. The Liechtenstein family's ancestral home includes a lavish greenhouse and a mock minaret. (p259)

Delight your senses at ❺ **Hluboká**, an over-the-top confection of neo-Gothic frivolity modelled on Windsor Castle in England. (p196)

Prague's Old Town Square (p81)

WALKING THE COBBLES

A pretty, cobblestoned public square stands at the heart of just about every town and city in the country. Indeed, the Czech word for a plaza or open square – *náměstí* – literally means 'at the town'. Back in the Middle Ages, places were ranked in importance by the size of their squares, and Czechia has some very big – and beautiful – ones.

BEST COBBLESTONE EXPERIENCES

Enjoy the cheerful chaos of Prague's ❶ **Old Town Square**, one of the Central Europe's main marketplaces for more than 1000 years. (p81)

Take a deep breath while you take in tiny ❷ **Telč's main square**. This UNESCO-protected space is, hands down, Czechia's prettiest public plaza. (p254)

Do a circuit of ❸ **Peace Square** in Domažlice, one of the country's handsomest expanses of cobbles. (p189)

Admire Olomouc's majestic, massive ❹ **Upper and Lower Squares**, surrounded by historic buildings and blessed with a UNESCO-protected Holy Trinity Column. (p265)

See ❺ **Mikulov**'s simple, evocative square, called simply 'Náměstí', to realise squares don't need to be big to be breathtaking. (p255)

Architecture on Parade

Head straight to the central square to see just about every town's best historical architecture. It might be a Gothic town hall or a pretty row of Renaissance or baroque houses.

Main Market Square

Town squares started out as marketplaces. They remain at the heart of town life, and typically serve as scenic backdrops for festivals and holiday celebrations.

A NIGHT AT THE PUB

Spending an evening in the pub may just be Czechia's quintessential experience. The pub is more than a bar and means more than the beer – it functions as the country's collective living room. On several nights of the week, people gather to meet friends, catch up on news and enjoy a meal. Oh yeah, the beer's good too.

BEST PUB EXPERIENCES

Pair a visit to Prague Castle with a freshly poured Pilsner-Urquell at the delightfully old-school ❶ **Hostinec U Černého vola** not far away. (p61)

In Plzeň, finish off the Pilsner Urquell brewery tour with a cold one at ❷ **Na Spilce**, conveniently located within the brewery itself. (p187)

In Chodová Planá, enjoy a beer in Czechia's only cave restaurant: the ❸ **Restaurance Ve Skále**. (p183)

A České Budějovice institution, ❹ **Masné Krámy** is one of the best places to sample the city's own Budvar (Budweiser) beer. (p196)

Olomouc's ❺ **Hanácká hospoda** combines a beer hall with a storied Renaissance palace and offers classic Czech food and share platters. (p268)

Beers to the Table

In traditional pubs, waiters will often bring beers to the table without the need to order – and stop bringing them only when you say you've had enough.

Local Food

Most pubs serve food and are excellent spots to try traditional cooking. Even if a pub doesn't have a kitchen, they'll always offer beer snacks.

Literary Aspirations

Czech writer Jaroslav Hašek, author of *The Good Soldier Švejk*, wrote many books in the pub. *Švejk* practically begins with the main character swilling beers in the local saloon.

TOP OF THE HOPS

Few (apart from a small number of deluded Bavarians and Belgians) would disagree that Czech beer is the world's best. Since the invention of modern-style lager here in 1842, the locals have been famous for producing some of the finest beers one can find anywhere. These days, internationally famous local brands – like Pilsner Urquell, Staropramen and Budvar (Czech Budweiser) – have been equalled, and even surpassed, by a bunch of regional Czech beers, microbrews and craft beers.

Inventors of Modern Lager

Plzeň (Pilsen in German) is famed among beer fans worldwide as the mother of all lagers. Pilsner-style beer was invented here in 1842.

Craft-Beer Revolution

The global craft-beer trend has reached Czechia and is most pronounced in Prague and Brno, which boast several pubs that brew their own creations.

Budvar vs 'Budweiser'

Czech Budvar and US Budweiser share the same name and have been embroiled in copyright disputes for decades, but they don't remotely taste the same. Do your own comparison.

Budweiser Budvar Brewery (p195), České Budějovice

BEST BEER EXPERIENCES

Tour the temple itself. The ❶ **Pilsner Urquell Brewery** was where it all began and the highlight of the tour is a sip of the golden nectar itself. (p184)

Stop in and stand up at Brno's ❷ **Výčep Na Stojáka**, where you can choose from an array of special and microbrew beers on tap. (p246)

See where the original 'Budweiser' was born. The team at the ❸ **Budweiser Budvar Brewery** continue the more-than-a century-long tradition of brewing excellence. (p195)

Visit Prague's last surviving large-scale brewery, ❹ **Staropramen**, and discover a century of production that's still going strong. (p144)

Indulge in some home-brewed dark at ❺ **U Fleků**, a Prague institution that's been serving its own since 1499. (p108)

DON'T MISS THE WINE

Czechia is best-known for beer, but the wine's not at all bad and it's getting better every year. Southern Moravia is covered with vineyards and makers are marking out new turf for experimental wines. If you're one of those travellers who prefers the grape to hops and barley, the country has you covered.

BEST WINE EXPERIENCES

Delve beneath a courtyard in central Brno to find ❶ **Vinotéka U Tri Knižat**, a historic cellar featuring Moravian wines. (p245)

Head to Mikulov and visit ❷ **Zahrádka U Zajíce**, a lively courtyard bar off Náměstí that offers tastings from local wineries. (p258)

Hike or bike the beautiful ❸ **Mikulov Wine Trail**, which runs through vineyards, wine cellars, and castle monuments on flat roads and mildly steep hills. (p260)

Sample steel-tank- and barrel-fermented wines while touring the underground cellars at ❹ **Wine Bar Chatka** in Znojmo. (p264)

Pair a visit to Prague's ❺ **Botanical Gardens** with a meal or wine-tasting featuring locally made varietals. (p137)

Head to Moravia

Czechia's best wine comes from the southern end of its eastern province, particularly around Mikulov and Znojmo. Visit historic cellars and chic bars, or hike between vineyards.

It Started With Charles IV

In addition to building Charles Bridge and founding Charles University, Charles IV passed a raft of laws that greatly improved wine quality in the 14th century.

Mostly Whites (but Decent Reds)

The Moravian wine region is best known for quality white varietals, like Grüner Veltliner, but look out too for spicy, medium-bodied reds such as Blaufränkisch (Frankovka).

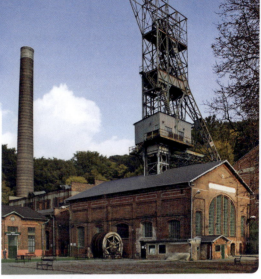

Landek Park (p271), Ostrava

BEST OFFBEAT EXPERIENCES

Descend into the museum via the sooty shafts of the former Anselm mine in Ostrava's ❶ **Landek Park**. (p271)

Marvel at the architectural ingenuity employed to secure the city's water supply in Brno's pillar-vaulted, cathedral-like ❷ **Water Tanks**. (p245)

Embark on high-adrenaline ladder climbs in the ❸ **Znojmo Underground**, a medieval braid of passageways on four levels, covering 27km. (p262)

Learn about Prague's fascinating industrial heritage in the ❹ **Old Wastewater Treatment Plant**, an industrial marvel from the early 20th century. (p139)

View the hyper-realistic paintings of the idiosyncratic Josef Váchal on the walls and ceilings of the wondrous ❺ **Portmoneum** in Litomyšl. (p225)

A LITTLE OFFBEAT

In recent years, Czechs have embraced the offbeat and created historical attractions that defy easy categorisation – and things that you could really only see or do while you're here. Want to explore miles and miles of underground medieval passageways? They have it. How about some awe-inspiring industrial-age wonders? That too.

Underground Excitement

Many Czech towns and cities are built atop labyrinthine passageways that once served as communal hiding places for when enemies came knocking.

Industrial Heritage

Ostrava has built an entire tourism infrastructure around mines and mills. Prague and Brno have also reached back in time to showcase awesome achievements of the industrial age.

Prague

MEDIEVAL METROPOLIS MEETS MODERN VIBE

Czechia's world-class capital has it all. Whole blocks of breathtaking Gothic, Renaissance, baroque and art nouveau architecture, topped by the world's largest castle complex, dazzle the senses, but don't be deceived. Prague also offers the culture and energy of a dynamic 21st-century city. Use it as a base to explore surrounding eye-catching castles and chateaux.

✪ **Prague**
p48

South & West Bohemia
p164

South & West Bohemia

SPAS, BEER AND UNESCO SITES

UNESCO-protected Český Krumlov, with its riverside setting and Renaissance castle, is in a class of its own, but the region is riddled with beautiful places. The famed 19th-century spa towns retain an old-world lustre. Beer lovers will want to see České Budějovice and, especially, Plzeň, home to Czechia's renowned Pilsner Urquell brewery.

REGIONS & CITIES

Find the places that tick all your boxes.

North & East Bohemia

SANDSTONE ROCKS AND BONE CHURCHES

The quieter lands north of Prague are popular with Czechs but don't see many international visitors. The Czech Switzerland National Park features stunning sandstone-rock formations. The perfectly preserved silver-mining town of Kutná Hora has architectural splendours and a freakish church whose interior is crafted entirely from human bones.

North & East Bohemia
p199

Moravia & Silesia
p236

Moravia & Silesia

SPLENDOUR, FOLKLORE AND VINEYARD HILLS

Mikulov, nestled in the hills of south Moravian wine country, promises hiking, biking and wine-tasting in a relaxing, bucolic setting. Bigger cities like Brno and Olomouc balance urban sophistication with captivating historic architecture. Tiny Telč hides Czechia's most wonderfully preserved town square, lined on all sides by Renaissance and baroque houses.

Prague's Old Town Square (p81)

ITINERARIES

Best of Prague & Around

Allow: 6 Days   **Distance:** 200km

From one breathtaking sight to the next, follow this leisurely exploration of Europe's prettiest capital. Take a few days to wander the city, and then leave the big lights behind for day trips to majestic Karlštejn and somber Terezín, a Nazi concentration camp and weigh station to Auschwitz.

❶ OLD TOWN ⏱ 1 DAY

Walk the back alleyways of the **Old Town** (p76) and catch the hourly spectacle of the Astronomical Clock, then climb the tower of the Old Town Hall for a wonderful view of Old Town Square.

↪ *Detour:* Tour the magnificent synagogues of the Prague Jewish Museum (p90), and don't miss the Old Jewish Cemetery (p90).

❷ CHARLES BRIDGE & MALÁ STRANA ⏱ 1 DAY

Plan an early-morning crossing of **Charles Bridge** (p68) and pause to take in the evocative statuary. Meander the quiet lanes of **Malá Strana** (p63) and Kampa Park. Admire the baroque beauty of **St Nicholas Church** (p63).

↪ *Detour:* Hike (or take the funicular) up to Petřín Hill (p66) for more magnificent views and fun stuff for the kids.

❸ PRAGUE CASTLE & HRADČANY ⏱ 1 DAY

Spend the first half of the day wandering the chambers of **Prague Castle** (p56) and visiting **St Vitus Cathedral** (p59; pictured). Splurge on the pricey admission or simply stroll the grounds (free to enter).

↪ *Detour:* Walk around the castle gardens or take a tour of nearby Strahov Monastery Library (p92), a medieval masterpiece.

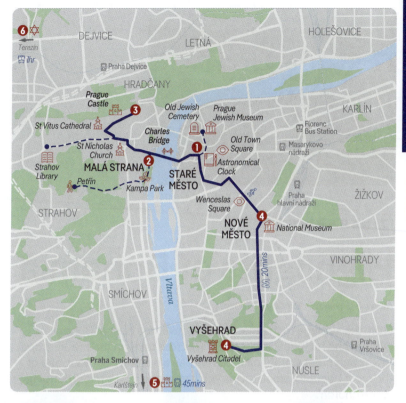

④ NOVÉ MĚSTO & VYŠEHRAD ⏱ 1 DAY

Walk Nové Město's sweeping **Wenceslas Square** (p100; pictured), with the **National Museum** (p98) at the upper end. Take the metro out to **Vyšehrad** (p148) to see the remains of Prague's 'other castle': Vyšehrad citadel.

🍴 *Detour:* Have dinner and drinks in one of the city's outlying up-and-coming neighbourhoods, like Karlín.

⑤ KARLŠTEJN ⏱ 1 DAY

Hop the train for a 45-minute ride to **Karlštejn** (p145) to tour the impressive castle, which once protected the Bohemian crown jewels. Be sure to book the tour in advance via the castle website.

🍴 *Detour:* Hike to nearby Svatý Jan pod Skalou and Beroun. From Beroun, catch the train back to Prague.

⑥ TEREZÍN ⏱ 1 DAY

An hour-long bus ride brings you to the former fortress of **Terezín** (p161) and back to a grimmer time during WWII. The Nazis transformed this garrison town into a Jewish ghetto and a bizarre, horrific showcase camp to trick the world into believing their policies were somehow 'humane'. Sadly, the ruse worked.

Karlovy Vary (p170)

ITINERARIES

Highlights of Bohemia

Allow: 8 Days   **Distance:** 400km

From the sublime to the macabre, discover the best of Bohemia's cultural and historical attractions. This tour takes in the prettiest spa towns and most vibrant cities, as well as a historic beer tour, one of the most beautiful small towns you'll ever see, and a mind-bending 'bone church'.

❶ PRAGUE ⏱ 2 DAYS

Start in **Prague** (p48) and spend a couple days exploring the Old Town and Malá Strana. Walk across Charles Bridge and climb up steep Nerudova street to pay your respects at Prague Castle. Rent a car or catch a bus from Florenc bus station for the two-hour journey to Karlovy Vary.

❷ KARLOVY VARY ⏱ 1 DAY

The gorgeous spa of **Karlovy Vary** (p170) drew celebrities from all around Europe back in the day for its unique, health-giving spring waters and elegant, 19th-century colonnades. Walk through the town's magnificent spa area.

↪ *Detour: Plan a day trip to picture-postcard Loket (p175) or explore the smaller and quieter nearby spa town of Mariánské Lázně (p178).*

❸ PLZEŇ ⏱ 1 DAY

Beer-lovers will make a bee-line to **Plzeň** (p184) to tour the brewery (pictured) where Pilsner Urquell is made and where modern lager was invented in the 19th century. Book your tour in advance over the website. Parents with kids in tow will want to pay a visit to Techmania, which is like a science fair on steroids.

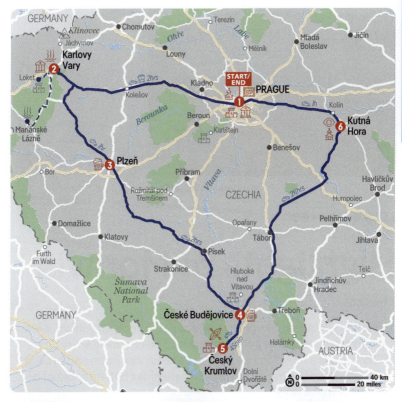

❹ ČESKÉ BUDĚJOVICE ⏱ 1 DAY

Continue the beer theme at **České Budějovice** (p195), home of the Budvar brewery and one of Central Europe's largest and prettiest town squares. From here, it's an easy 45-minute drive or train ride to UNESCO-protected Český Krumlov.

❺ ČESKÝ KRUMLOV ⏱ 2 DAYS

It's true, **Český Krumlov** (p190) rivals Prague in sheer beauty. Amble around the town's impossibly picturesque alleyways and climb up to the spectacular Renaissance pile of Krumlov Castle. Spend the second day out in nature – one option is to hire kayaks for a jaunt on the Vltava River.

❻ KUTNÁ HORA ⏱ 1 DAY

On the return to Prague, make a detour to **Kutná Hora** (p219) to take in the town's medieval opulence and to visit Czechia's oddest attraction: the 'Bone Church' in the suburb of Sedlec. The interior is sculpted from the bones of 40,000 people.

Vineyards, Mikulov (p255)

ITINERARIES

Highlights of Moravia

Allow: 7 Days   **Distance:** 300km

Slow down, relax, enjoy some wine and get to know Czechia's quieter eastern province and its colourful towns. The charming small city of Olomouc is a must. The south is covered in vineyards and cycling trails. Like Prague, Brno offers big-city amenities but attracts just a fraction of the visitors.

❶ BRNO ⏱ 2 DAYS

Start in the Moravian capital, **Brno** (p242), and take advantage of the city's excellent pubs and restaurants. Book a tour (well in advance) to see the interiors of the Villa Tugendhat. Spend a second day visiting Brno's spookier attractions, including a climb up to Špilberk Castle.

❷ OLOMOUC ⏱ 1 DAY

A former Moravian capital, **Olomouc** (p265) was known for centuries as a Catholic bastion and has the magnificent baroque Holy Trinity Column (pictured) and big churches to prove it. Be sure not to miss the string of parks and walks that surround the walls of the old town.

❸ KROMĚŘÍŽ ⏱ 1 DAY

Sleepy **Kroměříž** (p252) can be visited as a day trip from Olomouc. It's worth a stopover though to see the sumptuous baroque Archbishop's Chateau (pictured), a UNESCO heritage site, and its certifiable artistic masterpiece: Titian's *Flaying of Marsyas*.

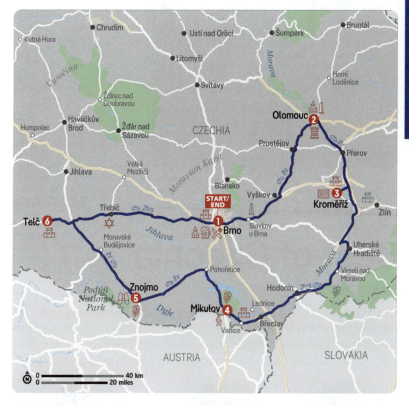

MIKULOV ⏱ 1 DAY

Stunning **Mikulov** (p255), in the heart of wine country, looks like a piece of Italy plunked down in South Moravia. Walk the cobbled main square and admire the mix of stately Renaissance and baroque buildings. Spend part of the day visiting the Liechtenstein family chateau at nearby Lednice or head to Valtice to taste some Czech wines.

ZNOJMO ⏱ 1 DAY

The wine theme carries over to pretty **Znojmo** (p262). In addition to tasting local wines, explore the extensive tunnels that run below the town and catch some beautiful vistas out over the Thaya River valley.

TELČ ⏱ 1 DAY

Unfortunately, the Renaissance jewel and UNESCO-protected town of **Telč** (p254), with Czechia's most beautiful town square, is relatively remote (but worth the effort to get here). Try to squeeze it in as a day trip from Brno or as a stopover on the return to Brno or Prague.

Prague (p48)

ITINERARIES

Best of Czechia

Allow: 7 Days   **Distance:** 400km

Czechia is small and it's possible to see the best of everything on a relatively short trip. View this itinerary as a chocolate box, a sampler for where you might want to focus on your next visit. This circuit is possible with public transport, but you'll need a car to finish in seven days.

1 PRAGUE ⏱ 2 DAYS

Two days is barely enough time to explore **Prague** (p48), Czechia's jaw-dropping capital. Focus your attention on the sights of the scenic Old Town, stroll across Charles Bridge, and then make the hike up to Prague Castle. Rent a pedal boat for some fun on the river. Be sure take advantage of the city's excellent restaurants, like Field or 420, but you'll have to reserve ahead.

2 KARLOVY VARY ⏱ 1 DAY

Spend a day in **Karlovy Vary** (p170) walking amidst the stunning 19th-century colonnades, sipping the waters and taking in the grandest of the country's spa heritage. Stretch your legs on the paths in the surrounding hills or book a memorable tour of famed Moser Glassworks.

🚗 *Detour: Karlovy Vary is a good jumping off spot for a few hours to explore the nearby Krušné Mountains and the old mining town of Jáchymov (p176).*

3 ČESKÝ KRUMLOV ⏱ 1 DAY

Prepare to be wowed. **Český Krumlov** (p190) is simply unforgettable. Stow the car as soon as possible, slip on comfortable walking shoes and hit the cobblestones. Poke around the small alleys of the old town and then make the modest climb up to the town's stunning Renaissance chateau. Check the art collection at the Egon Schiele Art Centre or the dazzling mineral display at the Moldavite Museum.

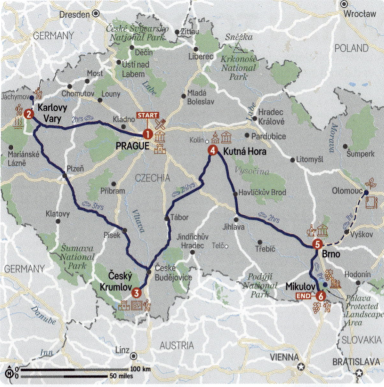

④ KUTNÁ HORA ⏱ 1 DAY

The old mining centre of **Kutná Hora** (p219) is much more interesting than it sounds. Once a rival to Prague itself in terms of wealth and influence, it's now a museum town, with a gorgeous Gothic cathedral and lots of fun mining activities. Of course, you wouldn't want to leave town without checking out arguably Czechia's most macabre attraction: the Sedlec Ossuary (pictured).

⑤ BRNO ⏱ 1 DAY

Brno (p242), Czechia's second city, oozes youthful energy, including great cafes, clubs and bars. By day, tour the city's impressive underground sites or book ahead to tour early-modern architect Mies van der Rohe's ground-breaking Villa Tugendhat.

🚗 *Detour:* Try to squeeze in an extra day to visit the pretty college town of Olomouc (p265), about an hour's drive north of Brno. Admire the gorgeous main square and parks and gardens.

⑥ MIKULOV ⏱ 1 DAY

The small border town of **Mikulov** (p255) boasts a dramatic setting amidst the wine-making hills of southern Moravia. Walk the tiny lanes, pop in here or there for a glass of wine, or spend the day out hiking the Mikulov Wine Trail.

🚗 *Detour:* Hikers will want to spend half a day exploring the Pálava Protected Landscape Area (p261; pictured) to see castle ruins and endless vineyards.

WHEN TO GO

Answer: it all depends on what you plan to do. Czechia has four distinct seasons and each offers something different.

Most visitors travel to Prague and Czechia in summer (from June through August), and it's not hard to see why. The days are long (in late June, it stays light until 10pm), the weather is sunny, and just about everything a visitor might want to do is open. Prague, though, can get uncomfortably crowded during this time. Add in the potential for a midsummer heat wave, and you have the ingredients for a less-than-optimal stay. Consider, instead, travelling in spring or autumn, when the crowds are lighter and the temperatures are cooler.

Bear in mind that some attractions, like castles and museums – particularly in smaller towns, but also some of the gardens around Prague Castle – shut down for the season from October to April.

Want a Bargain?

Prices for lodging in Prague drop considerably during the colder months from November through March – the exceptions being around the Christmas, New Year and Easter holidays.

> ### ⓘ I LIVE HERE
>
> ### AUTUMN REFLECTION
>
> **Prague-based Markéta Hradecká is a private tour guide (caputregni.cz). She spends lots of time wandering the streets of the capital city.**
>
> Autumn always brings a touch of melancholy and introspection to Prague. The late afternoon casts a long shadow over the city, and I can feel the first cold wisps of winter. On these days, I like to walk along the Vltava riverbank and contemplate the water as it flows past. Watching the water during these last golden hours can feel like an existential experience.

Beskydy Mountains, Moravia

EARLY SNOWFALL

Winter can come relatively early to higher-elevation areas. While September and October can still be warm and sunny in places like Prague and Brno, early autumn often brings the season's first snowfall to mountainous parts of the country.

Weather through the Year – Prague

JANUARY	FEBRUARY	MARCH	APRIL	MAY	JUNE
Ave. daytime max: **2°C**	Ave. daytime max: **4°C**	Ave. daytime max: **9°C**	Ave. daytime max: **19°C**	Ave. daytime max: **22°C**	Ave. daytime max: **24°C**
Days of snow/rain: 6	Days of snow/rain: 5	Days of snow/rain: 6	Days of rainfall: 9	Days of rainfall: 10	Days of rainfall: 10

HOT, HOT, HOT

Climate change is having a noticeable effect on Czechia's summer temperatures. Not that long ago, maximums rarely exceeded 30°C. Now, 30°C days are common and the thermometer occasionally reaches as high as 35°C.

Major Festivals

The **Prague Spring International Music Festival** (festival.cz) is the high point of the cultural calendar. It starts on 12 May, the anniversary of Czech composer Bedřich Smetana's death, with a rousing rendition of his symphony *Má vlast (My Country)* at Prague's Municipal House (p85).
🌼 **May**

The biggest cultural event in South Bohemia, Český Krumlov's **Five-Petalled Rose Festival** (p192), is a medieval bash of swordfights, puppeteers, music and tons of food and drink. 🌼 **June**

Book ahead for Ostrava's **Colours of Ostrava** (p273; colours.cz) music festival, when 40,000 fans fill the former ironworks at Dolní Vítkovice for four days.
☀️ **July**

In a nation of cinephiles, Czechia's most prestigious cinematic celebratio is the **Karlovy Vary International Film Festival** (p172). The event attracts international and local film stars and plays against a backdrop of steep hills and gorgeous 19th-century spa architecture.
☀️ **July**

MULLED WINE IN WINTER

Czech Martina Sulková manages social media accounts for a large data company in Prague.

The winter holidays here can be magical. I love the Christmas markets, and especially the cups of mulled wine you find everywhere (even hipster cafes serve it now). The mood quiets down after New Year's. That's when I head to the cinema or outdoors on a ski adventure. This time of year is perfect for a visit to the fairy tale town of Český Krumlov to bask in the old-world feeling.

Skiing, Šumava Mountains (p188)

Local & Quirkier Events

On 6 January, **Three Kings' Day** marks the formal end of the Christmas season. Czechs celebrate with carol-singing, bell-ringing and gifts to the poor.
❄️ **January**

Once banned by the communists, the annual carnival, **Masopust**, involves street parties, fireworks and concerts. Celebrations start on the Friday before Shrove Tuesday (aka Mardi Gras).
❄️ **February**

Each spring, people around Czechia gather (often on hilltops) to light bonfires in an annual ritual called **Burning of the Witches** (*Pálení čarodějnic*).
🌿 **30 April**

On the night of 5 December, the eve of **St Nicholas Day**, people around the country dress up as the saint, or as an angel or (scary-looking) devil to hand out treats to children who have been good. (Bad kids get a piece of coal!)
❄️ **December**

PRAGUE SPRING

Spring truly is a glorious season in Prague and around the country. April, in particular, is an eye-catching month. That's when the first trees start to bud, and Czechia's parks and gardens explode in riotous pinks and yellows.

JULY	AUGUST	SEPTEMBER	OCTOBER	NOVEMBER	DECEMBER
Ave. daytime max: **24°C**	Ave. daytime max: **24°C**	Ave. daytime max: **19°C**	Ave. daytime max: **13°C**	Ave. daytime max: **7°C**	Ave. daytime max: **3°C**
Days of rainfall: 10	Days of rainfall: 10	Days of rainfall: 7	Days of rainfall: 6	Days of snow/rain: 6	Days of snow/rain: 6

GET PREPARED FOR PRAGUE & CZECHIA

Useful things to load in your bag, your ears and your brain

Clothes

Layers Czechia's weather can be impossible to predict. Wherever you go, summers can be stiflingly hot or unseasonably cool. Even on hot days, evening temperatures can drop to the point where you'll need a pullover or jacket outdoors. Winters can be cold or extremely cold, especially in higher-elevation areas.

Shoes A trip to Czechia invariably means lots of walking. Many historic areas, including much of central Prague, are covered in cobblestones. Flat, comfortable shoes are much better than heels. Pack hiking boots if you plan on hitting the trails.

Manners

Czechs can be formal with strangers. Shake hands on first meeting. Use the more formal *dobrý den* instead of the casual *ahoj* to say hello.

Take your shoes off when entering someone's home. Always check your socks for holes before heading out.

Bring a small gift if you're invited to a party. A bottle of wine or a small bouquet of flowers makes a nice gesture.

Dressing up Casual clothes are fine for most occasions, but men should bring along a nice jacket and women a dress or skirt if there are plans to attend a concert, opera or theatre performance.

READ

The Glass Room (Simon Mawer; 2009) Entertaining look at Brno life in the interwar years of the 20th century.

The Book of Laughter and Forgetting (Milan Kundera; 1979) Tragicomic aspects of life in communist Czechoslovakia.

The Trial (Franz Kafka; 1925) Classic Kafka tale about bureaucracy, which seemed to foretell communist-era horrors.

I Served the King of England (Bohumil Hrabal; 1983) Odd tales from Nazi-occupied Prague from Czechia's favourite author.

Words

Ahoj (*uh*-hoy) It's true. Landlocked Czechs use this common aquatic (or pirate) greeting as the most common way to say 'hello'. It's informal, though, and only used between friends. When addressing a stranger or to show respect, say **'dobrý den'** (*doh*-bree den), 'good day'. You'll also hear **'čau'** (chow) – the Czech equivalent of 'ciao'. It's used both to say hello and goodbye (again, only between friends).

Na shledanou (nuh-skhle-duh-noh) is the way Czechs say 'goodbye'. Handy when leaving a shop or store, where it's considered good manners to let everyone know you're going.

Děkuji (*dye*-ku-yi) means 'thank you'.

Prosím (*pro*-seem) is Czech for 'please'.

Ano/ne (*uh*-no/ne) means 'yes'/'no'. In conversation, Czechs often shorten 'ano' to simply 'no', which can create confusion.

Promiňte (*pro*-min-te) means 'excuse me'. It's handy if you accidentally bump into someone or need to attract someone's attention.

Pivo (*pee*-voh) means 'beer'. To order one in a bar, say **'jedno pivo, prosím'** (*jed*-no *pee*-voh *pro*-seem), literally 'one beer, please'.

Na zdraví! (nah zdrah-vee) means 'cheers!' Don't forget to look the person in the eye as you raise your glass.

Jídelní lístek (*jee*-del-nee *lee*-steck) or simply **'lístek'** is how to ask for a 'menu' in a restaurant. 'Menu' is understood, but can also refer to the 'daily special'.

Nerozumím (ne-ro-zu-meem) means 'I don't understand' – probably another word that will come in very handy.

WATCH

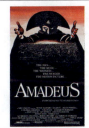

Closely Watched Trains (Jiří Menzel; 1966) Brilliant adaptation of WWII classic that put the Czech New Wave on the international radar.

Loves of a Blonde (Miloš Forman; 1965) Bittersweet 1960s love story between a naive factory girl and her Prague beau.

Kolya (Jan Svěrák; 1996) Heartwarming, Oscar-winning tale of an ageing Czech bachelor and a cute Russian kid.

Cosy Dens (Jan Hřebejk; 1999) Czech directors have yet to make the definitive film about communism, but this comedy comes close. A Christmas classic.

Amadeus (Miloš Forman; 1985; pictured) Prague stands in for Vienna in this Oscar-winning tale of Mozart.

LISTEN

Prayer for Marta (Marta Kubišová; 1969) This moving ballad became the informal anthem of the 1989 Velvet Revolution.

O' Brother, Shut the Door (Karel Kryl; 1969) Echoes the hopelessness that many Czechoslovaks felt after the 1968 Warsaw Pact invasion.

Trezor (Karel Gott; 1965) One of an endless number of sappy hits by the Czech crooner extraordinaire, who passed away in 2019.

Čtyři slunce (Vypsaná fiXa; 2012) Punk rockers with surreal lyrics from Pardubice who formed in 1995 and are still going strong.

Pork goulash

THE FOOD SCENE

Czech food is classic meat-and-dumpling fare, which can be immensely satisfying when prepared well.

Cuisine in Czechia, even when it is served in restaurants, always has a distinctive home-made quality. The classic pairings – braised beef with gravy and dumplings, or roast pork and sauerkraut – feel like they came straight from the family kitchen. While the dishes appear simple on the surface, the sauces, soups and stews can hide complexity. Sunday afternoon dinners often involve hours of preparation.

Czech food is part of the Central European family and resembles German and Austrian cooking. The mains revolve around meat, with pork being the most common. Beef, chicken and duck are popular too. Czechs are avid hunters and enjoy game, so scan restaurant menus for more exotic options featuring rabbit, venison or boar.

Let your waiter choose the proper side. The correct pairings appear to be etched in stone and rarely vary. If a main is served with gravy, then *knedlíky* (bread dumplings) are the usual go-to. For 'dry' dishes (without gravy), choose a potato or vegetable. Wash it down with a local beer (or two).

Home Staples

The typical Czech spice rack will have all the usual suspects, plus local faves like paprika, dill, marjoram and caraway seeds (a must for making goulash). Home-cooked meals invariably begin with soup. These are usually made with pork or beef and feature whatever root vegetable looks good at the market, like fennel, leek, onion, celery root, carrot or beetroot.

Best Czech Dishes	VEPŘO KNEDLO ZELO	SVÍČKOVÁ NA SMETANĚ	GULÁŠ
	Roast pork with bread dumplings and sauerkraut. Use the dumplings to soak up the gravy.	Marinated roast beef, served in cream sauce and garnished with lemon and cranberries.	A stew of beef or pork in a tomato, onion and paprika gravy.

Eggs, flour and breadcrumbs are essentials for making *řízek* – schnitzels of chicken or veal pounded out flat, crumbed and fried. Flour is frequently used to thicken soups and sauces (gluten-free diners take note). It's also an essential ingredient for making beloved *knedlíky*, big bread dumplings that take on the flavour of whatever sauce they're paired with. (Indeed, the whole point of dumplings is to mop up gravy, so don't butter them like a piece of bread – unless you want to drive your server crazy.)

Most locals buy their bread at the shop, though traditional home bakers favour darker flours and season their loaves with caraway or rye. Czechs love cakes and pastries, and local kitchens will always have powdered sugar, walnuts, poppy seed and fresh fruit for baking. On the dessert menu, look out for delicious fruit dumplings or *buchty*, a type of Czech bun made from sweet yeast dough and filled with poppy seed, curd cheese or jam.

Restaurant Revolution

Under communism, the local restaurant scene was stifled for decades. Menus were standardised and quality suffered accordingly. Most places offered only a handful of traditional dishes (if you were lucky), like roast pork, goulash, stewed cabbage or fried cheese.

In the past few years, chefs have reached deeper into the traditional Czech playbook and resurfaced older, more interesting recipes. The classics have been given a modern refresh and choices have widened

FOOD & WINE FESTIVALS

Prague Festival of Micro-Brewers

Gastronomic Festival of MD Rettigová *(gastroslavnosti.cz; May)* A tribute to the author of one of the country's first cookbooks and a celebration of traditional Czech cooking. Held in Litomyšl.

Prague Festival of Micro-Brewers *(minipivo.cz; Jun)* Small-scale brewers and craft-beer makers from around the country – and the people who love their beers – descend on the grounds of Prague Castle.

Prague Burgerfest *(burgerfest.cz; Sep)* This annual celebration of burgers and beer at the city's Výstaviště exhibition grounds is one of the capital's most popular food festivals.

Znojmo Wine Festival *(znojemskevinobrani.cz; Sep)* Czechia's premier wine festival is much more than wine, with music, parades and street theatre.

St Martin's Day On 11 November each year, restaurants around the country put out the white linens to serve sumptuous meals built around roast goose.

Czech schnitzel

VEPŘOVÝ ŘÍZEK	SMAŽENÝ SÝR	KULAJDA	BRAMBORÁK	KAPR
Czech schnitzel; thin fillet of pork coated in breadcrumbs and fried.	A wedge of cheese that's breaded and fried to perfection.	Hearty soup made of sour cream, potatoes, dill, mushrooms and egg.	Filling, savoury pancake made from shredded potatoes, flour and garlic.	Pond-raised carp, often served breaded and fried.

Street food, Prague

to include more game dishes, like duck, rabbit or fallow deer, as well as mains like trout or carp, steak tartare or beef cheeks. These days, you never really know what you're going to see on the menu, and that's a welcome change.

Foreign Influences

In the past three decades, the local dining scene has opened itself up to influences from around the world. Pizza and pasta, of course, are ubiquitous, but the local craft burger scene is huge too. Czechs love sushi; steakhouses, Indian restaurants, Mexican places and tapas joints are thriving. In short, you always have options, particularly in the bigger cities.

One surprise many travellers don't see coming: the local Vietnamese community is big (going back to communist times). That means you will nearly always find restaurants that serve convincing renditions of classic Vietnamese dishes like *pho* (a hearty noodle soup).

Farm Fresh & Sustainable

Along with this influx of international foods has come a new emphasis on farm-fresh sourcing and sustainability. Many restaurants now make a point of using only Czech-sourced meats and mains, and emphasising seasonality in choosing which fruits and vegetables to pair with their meals. Michelin-starred Field, in Prague, and the nationwide chain Ambiente, which runs the popular Lokál chain of pubs, has led the way in using quality local ingredients. Restaurants around the country have followed suit.

Vegetarians & Vegans

The number of vegetarian and vegan restaurants sprouting up around Prague, Brno and other large cities continues to grow every year. We've listed many of our our favourites in this guide. In addition, a growing number of places are abiding by European Union recommendations to list food allergies on menus, making it easier than ever to choose items that are meat- or animal-free, or to avoid common allergies, like shellfish, peanuts, dairy or gluten.

Alas, the last holdouts appear to be traditional pubs. Here, your options will likely be limited. The best bets for going meat-free at the pub are to opt for a salad or the ubiquitous (yet often excellent) fried cheese (*smažený sýr*), usually served with a dollop of cranberry and/or tartar sauce.

Local Specialities

Dare to Try

Drštková polévka Tripe soup, favoured in pubs and school canteens.

Olomoucké tvarůžky Pungent Czech cheese that tastes better than it smells.

Koprová omáčka Dill sauce served over dumplings.

Utopence Fat, pickled sausages served in pubs and known as 'drowned men'.

Beer Snacks & Street Food

Klobásy Spicy pork or beef sausages that are a great accompaniment to beer.

Chlebíčky Open sandwiches, often with ham, cheese, sliced egg and mayonnaise.

Nakládaný hermelín Pickled and marinated soft cheese, similar to Camembert, served in pubs.

Trdelník Chimney cakes made from rolled dough and served with sugar or ice cream. Despite claims to the contrary, these cakes have little to do with Czech traditions.

Utopence

Párky Frankfurters served with mustard on rye bread or stuffed in a roll.

Desserts & Sweets

Ovocné knedlíky Flour dumplings, stuffed with berries, plums or apricots, with a drizzle of butter and a sprinkle of sugar.

Palačinky/lívance Pancakes topped with jam.

Jablkový závin Apple strudel, usually served with a dollop of whipped cream.

Koláč Sweet pastries, filled with fruit or poppy seed.

Zmrzlina Ice cream; available as soft-serve or scoops in a variety of flavours.

MEALS OF A LIFETIME

Long Story Short (p268) In central Olomouc, this former military bakery has been converted into an upmarket contemporary eatery.

Pension Kladská (p183) A true gem, one of the country's top restaurants, tucked away amidst the splendours of the Slavkovský Forest.

Krčma v Šatlavské (p193) Book this one ahead of your trip. An atmospheric medieval setting featuring delicious grilled meats.

Vinobona Wine & Bistro (p62) Tiny, romantic spot on Nový Svět near Prague Castle that has delicious tasting menus in a secluded setting.

420 Restuarant (p85) Directly across from Prague's Astronomical Clock but feels like a find. You won't soon forget the original baroque statues. Book ahead.

THE YEAR IN FOOD

Spring

Easter brings painted eggs, baked meats, cakes and breads. Sweet *mazanec* bread (pictured) is made with raisins and almonds, while *beránek* cake is baked in the shape of a lamb.

Summer

The first fruits of the season – strawberries and wild cherries – are soon followed by plums, apricots, pears and watermelon. Czechs are enthusiastic grillers, so look out for barbecues featuring pork, chicken and sausages (pictured).

Autumn

Mushroom pickers head to the woods in early autumn. Wine festivals take place throughout September and October. St Martin's Day, on 11 November, is celebrated with young wine and roast goose (pictured).

Winter

Czechs are keen picklers, so there's no shortage of preserved mushrooms, gherkins and cherries in winter. Carnival season in February occasionally involves a pig slaughter, (pictured) with buckets of pork fat and garlicky blood sausage.

Pravčicka Brana (p213)

THE OUTDOORS

Czechia, with its varied landscapes – including mountainous areas in the north of Bohemia – and seasonal, Central European climate, is perfect for outdoor activities year-round.

Czechs love to be active and spend time outdoors. As soon as the snow melts, you'll find people are stiding along mountain trails, traversing steep gorges, zipping along cycle paths, rolling over river rapids, climbing foreboding rock faces and floating peacefully on lakes and reservoirs. And just as the last of the autumn rays dip below the horizon, the skiers, snowboarders and skaters come out once again to carve up the slopes and cut up the ponds.

Walking & Hiking

With a network of some 40,000km of well-marked hiking trails, Czechia is superbly equipped for walking or hiking. There are routes to suit every taste, from one or two hours to one or two months. The way-marked, colour-coded trails are clearly indicated on KČT (Klub českých turistů – Czech Hiking Club) hiking maps.

For the most dramatic landscapes head to Northern Bohemia. The Czech Switzerland National Park (České Švýcarsko), in the north of the country, features gargantuan stone towers, cliffs, rock fingers, arches and caves that often rise vertically from the trails and surrounding forests. Most visitors only walk long enough to see the Pravčická brána *(Pravčická Gate),* Europe's largest natural stone arch, but there are countless other options that take in the dramatic natural beauty. We've outlined a classic Czech Switzerland loop (p213) that

Popular Sports

SWIMMING
Swimming season runs from June through August. Find a clean and popular swimming lake at the **Brno Reservoir** (p246).

CAVING
Czechia is honeycombed with dramatic caves; the best are in the **Moravian Karst**, north of Brno (p249).

RAFTING & CANOEING
Head south along the Vltava to **Český Krumlov** (p190), where outfitters run relaxing floats and more ambitious trips.

🌿 FAMILY ADVENTURES

Splash around under waterfalls, on slides, and in heated outdoor pools and hot tubs at **Aquaforum** (p176) in Františkovy Lázně.

Treat the little ones to a gentle, guided horse ride at the **Bohemium miniature park** (p180) in Mariánské Lázně and don't miss the impressive recreations of the country's most-important sites.

Climb Prague's **Petřín Hill** (or ride the funicular; p66) to find a whole range of hilltop diversions, including an impressive lookout tower and some mirror maze fun for younger kids.

Take in a football (soccer) match at Sparta's **Letná Stadium** (p141) or go native to see local faves FC Bohemians 1905 play in **Vršovice** (p122).

Ride a boat through Punkva Cave (p249) in the Moravian Karst; a weird-and-wonderful experience for all ages.

---

starts and ends in Hřensko and passes through all the best-known sights in the national park.

Far less visited than the Czech Switzerland National Park, the Labské Pískovce Protected Area (p217), west of Děčín, is a wonderful place to escape the day-tripping crowds and tour groups with some parts that are no less idyllic than the more celebrated national park.

Not to be outdone by either, the Český Ráj protected landscape (p209) is a fairy-tale place to explore. The hills are dotted with the ruins of old castles that weave among a maze of sandstone 'rock towns' and basalt volcanic fingers. The park gradually ascends into the foothills of the much-higher Krkonoše Mountains.

Trails in Moravia tend to be gentler, but offer awe-inspiring vistas as well. The Pálava Protected Landscape Area and UNESCO Biosphere Reserve (p261) features white limestone plateaus, centuries-old castle ruins, sloping vineyards and the famed Pálava hills.

The 63-sq-km Podyjí National Park (p264), Moravia's only national park, follows the meandering Dyje River on a route from Znojmo Castle to the hilltop chateau in Vranov nad Dyjí. The park combines vineyards and forest reserves and features rare species, including oaks, orchids, butterflies and woodpeckers. A scenic introduction is the hike to Šobes, one of Czechia's oldest vineyards (p264), but we've outlined some other great walks as well.

Several long-distance European footpaths pass through Czechia. Route E8 runs near the southern border. The E10 traverses the country from north to south. The Czech Trail *(Cesta Českem; stezkaceskem.cz)* is a multistage path that covers the entire circumference of the country.

BEST SPOTS
For the best outdoor spots and routes, see map on pp44-5.

Český Ráj (p209)

ROCK CLIMBING
Czechs are inveterate climbers. A good place to try is at Svatošské skály, near **Loket** (p175), on the Ohře River.

RUNNING
Running and jogging have taken off in a big way; virtually any trail that can be hiked can be run (with care) as well. The Prague marathon is held each year in May.

FISHING
The rivers of South Bohemia and Moravia are popular with local fishers, though you'll need a permit. Try your luck on the lakes around **Telč** (p254).

GOLF
Golf has become increasingly popular the past decade; find **a beautiful, historic course** (p181) in Mariánské Lázně.

Mountains & High-Altitude Walks

Czechia is surrounded by relatively low-lying mountains that boast higher-elevation routes with classic mountain landscapes. These require a bit more exertion, but usually not special skills or gear.

The Krkonoše Mountains *(Giant Mountains)* feature Mt Sněžka, the country's highest peak at 1602m. There are several ways to approach Sněžka (all requiring only a medium level of fitness), including an especially scenic 10km trek that passes through Výrovka and Luční bouda (p208). Of course, you can always opt to ride the cable car. Once on top, follow the pretty, red-marked ridge path or take a blue-marked trail to Špindlerův Mlýn through the White Elbe river valley.

The Bohemian peaks offer several other relatively gentle but no less rewarding climbs. Mt Plechý in the Šumava Mountains (p188) features superb views out across neighbouring countries. We've also marked out a hiking loop through the highest parts of the pretty Krušné Mountains that starts and ends in Jáchymov (p176).

It's not exactly high altitude, but it's certainly worth climbing up Ostrava's Mound Ema *(Halda Ema; p271)*, a 315m-high slag heap that's remarkably still smouldering from underground combustion. Locals regard the 'Ostrava Volcano' as a prime lookout spot over the city, especially at sunset.

Cycling

One of the best ways to see the country is by bike. Mountain- and gravel-biking have taken off in a big way, and Czechia is crisscrossed by dozens of marked cycling paths *(cyklotrasy)*. Big cities like Prague and Brno are building out their local networks. The trails sometimes follow roads (suitable for road cyclists), though many deviate along forest paths or open fields and are better tackled with wider tyres. Ask before heading out. Cycling maps are widely available.

Moravian wine country, particularly around Mikulov, Valtice and Lednice, is particularly popular for cyclists. Scenic, marked trails make it easy to pair a day on the bike with stops at local wineries. The Mikulov Wine Trail runs 82km through vineyards, wine cellars, and castle monuments and connects to UNESCO heritage sites in both Valtice and Lednice (p259).

For long-distance rides, the 456km Greenways Prague-Vienna Trail *(prague viennagreenways.org)* links the two capital cities and follows a mix of roads and trails. A 240km-long route links Prague to Dresden (in Germany), along the Vltava and Elbe rivers. The path is still under construction in spots. Cycle paths also link up with the Europe-wide network of trails, Euro Velo *(eurovelo.org)*. Three sections pass through Czechia: EV4 runs west-east via Prague and Brno; EV7 north-south through Prague and on to Berlin; and EV9 north-south via Olomouc and Brno to Vienna or Poland.

Skiing & Winter Sports

It's not the Alps, but skiing and snowboarding in Czechia are extremely popular and relatively inexpensive. If you're travelling during ski season (December–March), see p43 for our tips on how best to enjoy winter sports.

River Cruising

Prague is the place for getting out on the river. Operators run all kinds of themed cruises on the Vltava (p107). Choose from standard hour-long floats to slightly longer trips from the centre of the city out to Prague Zoo (p140) or even day-long adventures to the town of Mělník (p158), where the Vltava and Elbe rivers meet.

For something more offbeat, the Labská Plavební company runs small boats between Děčín and Dresden (Drážďany in Czech) via Hřensko, Bad Schandau, Königstein and Pillnitz (p217). Even if you're not up for a longer cruise, the mini-cruise to Hřensko passes through the pretty Elbe Valley, with its sandstone cliffs and pastel houses.

It's not a river cruise per se, but Brno offers its own picturesque water-based fun (p246). From April to October, passenger boats cross the Brno Reservoir and cruise upstream on a narrow stretch of the Svratka to one of Moravia's oldest castles, pretty Veveří Castle from the late 12th-century.

Klínovec ski resort (p176)

HOW TO... Enjoy Winter Sports in Czechia

Czechia may not be the first place most think of when they are looking for a winter sports destination, but this largely mountainous country has lots of under-the-radar snow fun to be had, especially if you are into less-obvious activities such as cross-country skiing and winter hiking. If you want to teach the kids to slither on powder, the Czech mountains have tens of low-key slopes where little ones can learn. The season lasts from late December to early April.

Downhill Skiing

The Krkonoše resorts (p208) of Harrachov, Pec pod Sněžkou and Špindlerův Mlýn are the stars of the Czech skiing scene, with the full range of hire centres, apres-ski options and luxury accommodation available. But there are tens of other slopes and resorts across the north of the country and the Šumava.

Klínovec (p176) is the largest centre in the Krušné Mountains, while Špičák and Zadov rule the Šumava (p188). Deštné is the top resort in the Orlické Mountains; Bedřichov is the place to snap on skis in the Jizerské Mountains.

Ski passes cost from 500Kč to 1,300Kč depending on the facilities and size of resort. For gear hire, add another 800–3000Kč.

Cross-Country Skiing

Cross-country skiing (*běžkování* in Czech) is a hugely popular sport. When the downhill slopes were closed during the Covid pandemic, half the country seemed to head for the cross-country skiing trails. Great places for a day out on the *stopa* (the grooves in the snow formed by a special snow plough) include the Jizerské Mountains, the Krušné Mountains (p177), the Highlands Region and the Slavkovský Forest (p182). Hire costs very little and winter-only refreshment kiosks punctuate the trails which are often marked out by the Czech Hiking Club.

Other Winter Activities

Snowshoeing has gained popularity in recent years, as has snow hiking. With snow guaranteed in the mountains from December to March, Czech kids are good skaters and sledgers. Ice hockey matches on frozen lakes are a common sight though skate-hire options can be hard to find in the wild. Of course, wherever you can ski, you can also snowboard.

BEST RESORTS FOR...

Downhill Skiing
The country's best overall ski area is the Krkonoše Mountains (p208) in north Bohemia, at Špindlerův Mlýn, Pec pod Sněžkou and Harrachov.

Cross-Country Skiing
Look for ranges with lower peaks and gentler terrain. These include Šumava (p188) and Krušné Mountains (p177) in Bohemia and the Beskydy and Jeseníky mountains in Moravia.

Beginners
Single-slope resorts in the Krušné Mountains (p177) and the slopes on Mt Ještěd (p206) are ideal for first-timers.

Families
The Klínovec ski resort (p176), the Krkonoše resorts (p208) and the tiny ski centres in the Krušné Mountains (p177) are best for families with tots.

ACTION AREAS

Where to find Czechia's best outdoor activities.

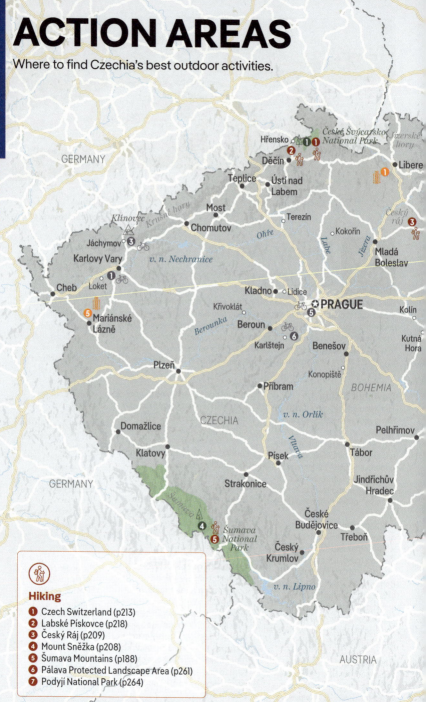

Hiking
1. Czech Switzerland (p213)
2. Labské Pískovce (p218)
3. Český Ráj (p209)
4. Mount Sněžka (p208)
5. Šumava Mountains (p188)
6. Pálava Protected Landscape Area (p261)
7. Podyjí National Park (p264)

THE GUIDE

PRAGUE & CZECHIA

THE GUIDE

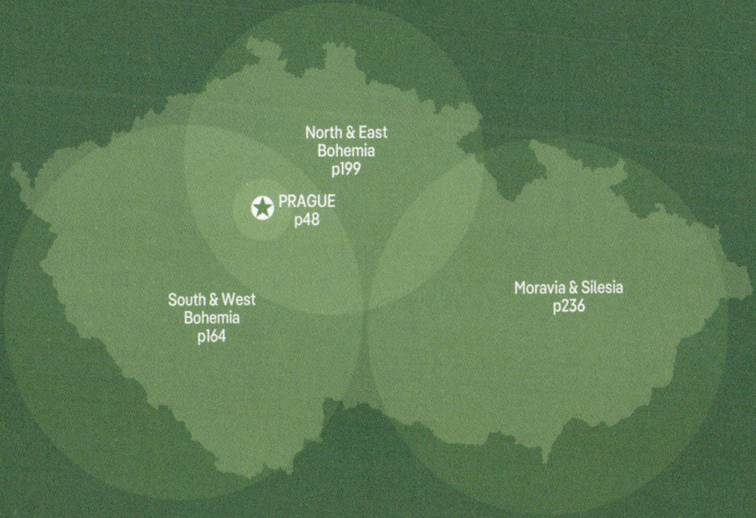

North & East Bohemia
p199

★ PRAGUE
p48

South & West Bohemia
p164

Moravia & Silesia
p236

Chapters in this section are organised by hubs and their surrounding areas. We see the hub as your base in the destination, where you'll find unique experiences, local insights, insider tips and expert recommendations. It's also your gateway to the surrounding area, where you'll see what and how much you can do from there.

Prague's Old Town Square (p81)
ALEX_MASTRO/SHUTTERSTOCK ©

Researched by Mark Baker

Prague

MEDIEVAL METROPOLIS MEETS MODERN VIBE

Czechia's capital city is a living textbook of European history – and much more.

THE MAIN AREAS

PRAGUE CASTLE & HRADČANY
Regal and refined.
p54

MALÁ STRANA
Lesser is more.
p63

STARÉ MĚSTO (OLD TOWN)
The heart of Prague.
p76

NOVÉ MĚSTO (NEW TOWN)
Prague's commercial area.
p95

ŽIŽKOV & KARLÍN
Hillside pubs, riverside revival.
p109

VINOHRADY & VRŠOVICE
Regal and rowdy.
p115

HOLEŠOVICE
Art and street vibe.
p123

BUBENEČ & DEJVICE
Villas, parks and gardens.
p132

SMÍCHOV
Prague's beer quarter.
p142

VYŠEHRAD
Prague's 'other' castle.
p148

DAY TRIPS FROM PRAGUE
Beautiful castles, contemporary history.
p154

The ups and downs of centuries past, of empires, wars, plagues and prosperity, are etched into the city's soul like the lines that are carved onto the facades of its Gothic towers and Renaissance palaces. Some 35 years ago, Prague re-emerged on the European stage after languishing for years under communism, and the world was agog. Those years trapped behind the Iron Curtain left Prague looking neglected and rundown, but it was obvious the city's rich history and intrinsic beauty – the hypnotic, visual tension between Charles Bridge and Prague Castle – had survived intact.

In the years since the fall of communism, as the scaffolding was pulled down from the faces of rehabbed buildings, the number of visitors to the city has exploded. Indeed, Prague became so popular that in recent years the city had sadly found itself – along with places like Venice and Amsterdam – as one of Europe's leading poster children for over-tourism. The authorities are aware of the issues and the mayor's office has promised big changes for tourism going forward, including positioning Prague less as a destination for raucous pubs and cheap beer, and more for the city's appealing cultural amenities, museums and parks.

They will have their work cut out for them. Prague remains immensely popular. Part of the city's enduring appeal owes something to the whimsical nature of the 1989 Velvet Revolution itself that installed a playwright, Václav Havel, as the first president of the newly liberated country. An even bigger part of the city's attraction might be its own storybook mystique: the dramatic way the floodlit twin towers of the Týn Church rise behind Old Town Square like something from *Grimms' Fairy Tales*, or the play of shadows on the back streets of the Old Town after dark. A little over a century ago, these same streets inspired the darker sensibilities of writers such as Franz Kafka.

For places to stay in Prague, see p162

THE GUIDE

PRAGUE

View from Prague Castle (p56)

Find Your Way

Prague has an excellent integrated public transport system of metro lines, trams, buses and night trams, but when it comes to moving around the relatively compact historic neighbourhoods of Staré Město (Old Town), Malá Strana and Prague Castle, it's more convenient – and more scenic – to travel by foot.

Holešovice
p123

Žižkov & Karlín
p109

National Monument on Vítkov Hill

Praha Holešovice

Praha Holešovice zastávka

Trade Fair Palace

Masarykovo nádraží

Bubeneč & Dejvice
p132

National Technical Museum

Convent of St Agnes

Prague Jewish Museum

Old Town Square

Staré Město (Old Town)
p76

Klementinum

Charles Bridge

Praha Dejvice

Prague Castle

Prague Castle & Hradčany
p54

St Vitus Cathedral

THE GUIDE
PRAGUE

Map labels

- Church of the Most Sacred Heart of Our Lord
- Praha hlavní nádraží
- Praha Vršovice
- Vinohrady & Vršovice p115
- Mucha Museum
- Wenceslas Square
- Nové Město (New Town) p95
- National Museum
- Vyšehrad p148
- Vyšehrad Cementery
- Praha Smíchov
- Smíchov p142
- Malá Strana p63
- Petřín

WALK
The historic core is compact and flat (though the trek to Prague Castle involves a climb) and walking is the best way to get around. Much of Staré Město and Malá Strana is paved with cobblestones, so sneakers or comfortable walking shoes work best.

TRAM
Use trams to cover shorter distances or to reach Prague Castle (and spare the climb). Tram 22 is known as the 'tourist' line as it runs through many historic areas, including Prague Castle and Malá Strana, before heading out to pretty and lively Vinohrady.

FROM THE AIRPORT
Trolleybus 59 runs regularly from the airport to metro stop Nádraží Veleslavín (Line A, green line) to catch the metro to the centre. The Airport Express (AE) bus ferries passengers between the airport and main train station at 30-minute intervals. Bus and trolleybus services run daily from around 5am to 11pm.

METRO
Prague's efficient metro is handy for covering long distances in a short amount of time. Several stops on Line A (green line) are useful for reaching sights around Staré Město, Malá Strana and central Wenceslas Square. Line C serves the main train station, Hlavní nádraží.

Plan Your Days

Three days is ideal for taking in Prague's historical sweep at a leisurely pace. Put on comfortable shoes, get ready to walk (over) 10,000 steps a day, and prepare to be dazzled.

Astronomical clock (p82)

Day 1

Morning
● Start the exploration in **Staré Město** (Old Town, p76), with the hourly chiming of the **Astronomical Clock** (p82), then wander through the **Old Town Square** (p81), taking in the array of architectural styles and the spires of the **Church of Our Lady Before Týn** (p82).

Afternoon
● Spend the afternoon exploring the buildings of the **Prague Jewish Museum** (p90). For art lovers, the nearby **Convent of St Agnes** (p80) holds a valuable collection of medieval art.

Evening
● Return to Old Town Square and follow the alleyways for a first glimpse at stunning **Charles Bridge** (p68) and **Prague Castle** (p56) in the backdrop. Enjoy dinner at **420 Restaurant** (p85).

You'll Also Want To...

Get out of the centre and see the rest of the city without the tourists, stop in at a pub and check out some ice hockey.

KNOCK ONE BACK AT THE PUB
The quintessential Prague experience. One classic pub, **Hostinec U Černého vola** (p61), is located temptingly close to Prague Castle.

CATCH SOME ICE HOCKEY
The Czech Extraliga is one of the most competitive hockey leagues in the world and features Prague's **HC Sparta Praha** (p131).

SAMPLE REAL CZECH FOOD
Hearty and delicious, like a home-cooked meal. Go the whole nine yards, with traditional steak tartare at **Kuchyň** (p62) or roast duck at **Hostinec na Výtoni** (p105).

Day 2

Morning
- Get an early start and return to the Staré Město side of **Charles Bridge** (p68) for the crossing over to pretty Malá Strana. Spend the morning exploring the quaint backstreets and **Kampa Park** (p72). Stop for lunch at **Café Savoy** (p70) before hiking up to **Prague Castle** (p56).

Afternoon
- Visiting the Castle complex and **St Vitus Cathedral** (p59) will easily take the rest of the day. Don't miss the **Royal Garden** (p58) on the castle's northern side.

Evening
- Spend the evening strolling the pretty lanes of **Hradčany** (p62) and reward yourself with traditional Czech food (and home-brewed beer) at the **Klášterní Pivovar Strahov** (p61).

Day 3

Morning
- Start with coffee at **Kavárna Slavia** (p93), with a view of **Prague Castle** (p56). Check at the **National Theatre** (p105) to see if any last-minute tickets are available to the opera or ballet. From here, walk up Národní třída to historic **Wenceslas Square** (p100).

Afternoon
- Pop into the **National Museum** (p98) to admire the interiors. Lunch at **Čestr** (p105) before taking the metro to **Vyšehrad** (p148) to admire the former fortress and visit the **graves of Dvořak and Mucha** (p150).

Evening
- Spend the evening outside the centre. Book a table at **Výčep** (p122) in Vinohrady for a modern take on Czech cooking and relax on '**JZP**' (p119).

VISIT A FARMERS MARKET
On Saturdays in warm weather, the entire city turns out to stock up on groceries and hobnob. Find a good market at **Náplavka** (p107).

ATTEND A CLASSICAL CONCERT
Composers Dvořák and Smetana are national heroes, and opulent concert halls like the **Rudolfinum** (p76) often feature them on their programme.

KICK BACK IN A PRETTY PARK
Prague is surprisingly green, and the city's most beautiful park is the former royal hunting grounds **Stromovka** (p138), in Bubeneč.

GET OUT ON THE RIVER
Several outfitters organise boating tours on the Vltava but renting a pedal-boat on **Slovanský ostrov** (p107) (an island) can be fun too.

Prague Castle & Hradčany

REGAL AND REFINED

GETTING AROUND

Most visitors come to Hradčany by walking up steep Nerudova street from Malá Strana. An alternative route that takes you directly to the castle's entry gate (also steep), begins at Malostranské náměstí. Climb tiny Zámecká street and then turn left on Zámecké schody, the 'castle steps'. Keep walking up until you alight on the large square in front of the castle. To spare the climbs, tram 22 conveniently stops just outside the castle gates.

☑ TOP TIP

Away from the crowds of Prague Castle, the Hradčany neighbourhood is one of prettiest and least-visited parts of the city. Leave time to stroll the cobbled backstreets of this historic quarter at your leisure and admire the elegant chateaux that once belonged to Bohemia's most powerful families.

The hilltop neighbourhood of Hradčany, home to Prague Castle, retains a whiff of exclusivity centuries after the emperors and kings who once lived here have gone. Years ago, noble families competed for access to the rulers and built grand chateaux around the castle. Those opulent piles are still here, many converted to museums and government offices. Hradčany's relative tranquillity comes as a breath of fresh air after the hustle and bustle of Old Town Square and Charles Bridge.

Most visitors come here for Prague Castle and St Vitus Cathedral, though there are several other interesting places to see. The Loreta Church is a baroque, 17th-century pilgrimage site modelled on Santa Casa in the Holy Lands. Strahov Monastery has been here since at least 1140; the monks' adjoining library is one of the most beautiful in Europe.

Scattered among the incredible palaces are pubs, restaurants and breathtaking views out over Malá Strana and the Old Town.

Take in the Old Masters

Two impressive collections of European paintings

The area around Prague Castle is home to not one, but two impressive art museums – situated across the street from each other – that focus largely on European masters from the 15th to the 18th centuries. Both are worth visiting, but the dilemma arises when you've only got time for one. The imposing **Schwarzenberg Palace** *(ngprague.cz; adult/child 250/140Kč)*, built in north Italian Renaissance style by the noble Lobkowicz family in 1567 and sporting a neo-Renaissance sgraffito exterior, is more impressive when it comes to household names. The collection here features works from artists such as Lucas Cranach, Albrecht Dürer, El Greco, Hans Holbein, Rembrandt and Rubens.

continued on p61

THE GUIDE

PRAGUE PRAGUE CASTLE & HRADČANY

HIGHLIGHTS
1. Prague Castle
2. St Vitus Cathedral

SIGHTS
3. Archbishop's Palace
4. Ball-Game House
5. Basilica of St George
6. Černín Palace
7. Golden Lane
8. Great South Tower of St Vitus Cathedral
9. Lobkowicz Palace
10. Loreta
11. Nový Svět Quarter
12. Old Royal Palace
13. Plečnik Viewpoint
14. Prague Castle Picture Gallery
15. Riding School
16. Royal Garden
17. Schwarzenberg Palace
18. Šternberg Palace
19. Story of Prague Castle
20. Strahov Library
21. Strahov Monastery
22. Summer Palace

SLEEPING
23. Hotel Monastery
24. Romantik Hotel U Raka

EATING
25. Kuchyň
26. Malý Buddha
27. U Zavěšenýho Kafe
28. Vinobona Wine & Bistro

DRINKING & NIGHTLIFE
29. Hostinec U Černého Vola
30. Kavárna Nový Svět
31. Klášterní Pivovar Strahov
32. Lobkowicz Palace Café

INFORMATION
33. Castle Information Centre

Old Royal Palace courtyard

TOP EXPERIENCE

Prague Castle

Looming high above the Vltava River, Prague Castle *(Pražský hrad)*, with its serried ranks of spires and palaces, dominates the city centre. Within its walls lies a fascinating collection of historic buildings, museums and galleries: home to some of Czechia's greatest artistic and cultural treasures. The grounds of the Castle complex are free to enter, though to see the interiors (including adjoining St Vitus Cathedral) requires an admission ticket.

DON'T MISS

- Old Royal Palace
- Vladislav Hall
- Story of Prague Castle
- Plečnik Viewpoint
- Golden Lane
- Basilica of St George
- Lobkowicz Palace
- Royal Garden

Admire the Entryway

Most visitors enter the castle complex through the main gate on **Hradčany Square** (Hradčanské náměstí). The entry is flanked by huge, baroque statues of battling Titans (1767–70) that dwarf the castle guards standing below. The changing of the guard takes place every hour on the hour, but the longest and most impressive display is at noon, when banners are exchanged while a brass band plays various fanfares.

Practicalities
Scan this QR code for prices and opening hours.

Prague Castle Picture Gallery

This impressive **picture gallery** *(hrad.cz; adult/child 200/150Kč)*, built up by Emperor Rudolf II and situated in the castle's second courtyard on entering, could have been so much grander had it not been for Swedish soldiers looting much of it in 1648. No matter, the collection has been beefed up over the years and includes valuable works by Cranach, Holbein, Rubens, Tintoretto and Titian. Admission is not included in the main castle-entry ticket.

The Old Royal Palace

The **Old Royal Palace**, situated in the castle's third courtyard, is one of the oldest surviving parts of the castle, dating from 1135, and the high point for most visitors.

Don't miss the **Vladislav Hall** (Vladislavský sál), which is famous for its beautiful, late-Gothic vaulted ceiling (1493–1502) designed by Benedikt Rejt. Though more than 500 years old, the flowing, interwoven lines of the vaults have an almost art-nouveau feel, in contrast to the rectilinear form of the Renaissance windows. The vast hall was used for banquets, councils and coronations, and for indoor jousting tournaments - hence the **Riders' Staircase** (Jezdecké schody), through an arch on the northern side, designed to admit a knight on horseback.

A door in the hall's southwestern corner leads to the former offices of the **Bohemian Chancellery** (České kanceláře). On 23 May 1618, in the second room, Protestant nobles rebelling against the Bohemian Estates and the Habsburg emperor threw two of his councillors and their secretary out of the window. They survived, as their fall was broken by the dung-filled moat, but this Second Defenestration of Prague sparked the Thirty Years' War.

Story of Prague Castle

The **Story of Prague Castle** museum, located in the Gothic vaults beneath the Old Royal Palace, ranks alongside the **Lobkowicz Palace** (p58) as one of the most interesting collections in the castle complex. It traces 1000 years of castle history, from the building of the first wooden palisade to the present day, illustrated by models of the site at various stages.

The exhibits include the grave of a 9th-century warrior discovered in the castle grounds, the helmet and chain mail worn by St Wenceslas, and a replica of the gold crown of St Wenceslas, which was made for Charles IV in 1346.

Basilica of St George

Just beyond St Vitus Cathedral and hiding behind a brick-red, baroque facade, the **Basilica of St George** is Czechia's best-preserved Romanesque basilica. The church was established in the 10th century by Vratislav I (the father of St Wenceslas). What you see today is mostly the result of more-recent restorations. The austerity of the Romanesque

---

TICKETS & PRACTICAL INFO

The main Prague Castle ticket includes entry to the Old Royal Palace as well as the Basilica of St George, Golden Lane and St Vitus Cathedral. Note an extra ticket is required to see the Story of Prague Castle exhibition and the Prague Castle Picture Gallery. Buy tickets online at **Ticketportal** *(ticketportal.cz)* or at the **castle information centre**.

DON'T MISS THIS VIEW

In the 1920s, President Tomáš Masaryk hired Slovene architect Jože Plečnik to renovate the castle; Plečnik modernised the complex and added obelisks and decorative elements. His greatest contribution is the spectacular observation platform, **Plečnik Viewpoint** *(free)*, on the castle's southern side. To find it, look for the Bull Staircase (Býčí schodiště) in the third courtyard opposite the south entrance to St Vitus Cathedral. The viewpoint is open April–October.

> **TOP TIPS**
>
> - Time your visit for the top of the hour to see an impressive changing-of-the-guard at the main gate.
>
> - Bring your passport for occasional identity checks.
>
> - Castle tickets are valid for two days. Each attraction can be entered only once.
>
> - The castle grounds are open from 6am to 10pm. Although the historic buildings are closed, an early-morning or late-evening stroll through the courtyards (minus the daytime crowds) is wonderfully atmospheric.
>
> - Classical music concerts are staged daily at 1pm at the Lobkowicz Palace. Buy tickets *(550Kč)* online at *prague-castle-concert.cz* or at the palace ticket office.

nave is relieved by a baroque double staircase leading to the apse, where fragments of 12th-century frescoes survive. In front of the stairs lie the tombs of Prince Boleslav II (d 997) and Prince Vratislav I (d 921). The arch beneath the stairs allows a glimpse of the 12th-century crypt; Přemysl kings are buried here.

Kafka's House on Golden Lane

While strolling the castle grounds, nip down this colourful **Golden Lane** that runs along the castle's northern wall. The impossibly tiny cottages here were built in the 16th century for the sharpshooters of the castle guard but were later used by goldsmiths. In the 19th and early 20th centuries, they were occupied by artists, including writer Franz Kafka, who stayed at his sister's house at number 22 from 1916 to 1917.

Fascinating Lobkowicz Palace

The 16th-century **Lobkowicz Palace** *(lobkowicz.cz; adult/child 340/270Kč)* houses a private museum that shows off the Lobkowicz family's priceless paintings, furniture and musical memorabilia. The tour includes an audio guide narrated by the owner William Lobkowicz and his family. Highlights include paintings by Cranach, Brueghel the Elder, Canaletto and Piranesi, original musical scores annotated by Mozart, Beethoven and Haydn, and an impressive collection of musical instruments.

Explore the Royal Garden

To reach the **Royal Garden** *(free)*, follow the gate on the northern side of the castle's second courtyard that leads to the Powder Bridge, which spans an even wilder piece of green called Stag Moat.

The Royal Garden started life as a classic Renaissance garden, built by Ferdinand I in 1534. It's graced by several gorgeous Renaissance follies that feel forgotten amid the trees. The most beautiful of the buildings is the 1569 **Ball-Game House**, a masterpiece of Renaissance sgraffito where the Habsburgs once played a primitive version of badminton. To the east is the **Summer Palace** or Belvedere (1538–60), the most authentic Italian Renaissance building outside Italy, while to the west is the former **Riding School** (1695).

TOP EXPERIENCE

St Vitus Cathedral

Built over a time span of almost 600 years, St Vitus Cathedral is one of the most richly endowed cathedrals in central Europe. It is pivotal to the country's cultural life, housing treasures that range from the tombs of St Wenceslas and Charles IV, to the baroque silver tomb of St John of Nepomuk, and the ornate Chapel of St Wenceslas.

DON'T MISS

Stained-glass window by Alfons Mucha

South window

Royal Mausoleum

Tomb of St John of Nepomuk

Chapel of St Wenceslas

The Crypt

Golden Gate

Great South Tower

Enter the Cathedral

The massive nave is a crowd-pleaser. It's flooded with colour from stained-glass windows created by eminent Czech artists of the early 20th century – note the one by **Alfons Mucha** in the third chapel on the northern side, which depicts the lives of Sts Cyril and Methodius (1909).

Walk up to the crossing, where the nave and transept meet, which is dominated by the colourful **south window** (1938) by Max Švabinský depicting the Last Judgment. In the north transept, beneath the baroque organ, are three carved wooden doors decorated with reliefs of Bohemian saints, with smaller panels beneath each saint depicting their martyrdom – look on the lower left side of the left-

Practicalities
Scan this QR code for prices and opening hours.

> **CATHEDRAL'S LONG HISTORY**
>
> Emperor Charles IV laid the foundation stone in 1344 on the site of a 10th-century Romanesque rotunda. Architect Matthias of Arras began work on the church but died eight years later. His German successor, Peter Parler, built much of the eastern part, but it remained unfinished. In the 19th century a concerted effort was made to complete the project and it was consecrated in 1929.

> **TOP TIPS**
>
> ● You can briefly enter the western end of the nave for free, without a ticket.
>
> ● Arrive early in the day to avoid the long lines to enter the cathedral.
>
> ● St Vitus is still a working church. Attend mass at 7am *(Mon-Sat)* and at 8.30am and 10am *(Sun)*.
>
> ● Organised groups of pilgrims can visit the cathedral free of charge. Make an appointment to visit at least three days in advance at katedrala@efara.cz.
>
> ● Find an excellent 3-D virtual tour of the cathedral, including views of the crypts, on the cathedral website *(katedralasvatehovita.cz)*.

hand door for St Vitus being tortured in a cauldron of boiling oil. Next to him is the martyrdom of St Wenceslas, while his treacherous brother Boleslav drives a spear into his back.

Go Deeper Into the Church

The eastern end of the cathedral is capped with graceful late-Gothic vaulting dating from the 14th century, and ringed by side chapels. In the centre, opposite the pulpit, lies the ornate **Royal Mausoleum** (1571–89) with its cold marble effigies of Archduke Ferdinand I, Archduchess Anna Jagellonská and their son, Maximilián II.

Rounding the far end of the ambulatory, you'll pass the tomb of St Vitus – a patron saint of Bohemia. Further round is the spectacular, baroque silver tomb of **St John of Nepomuk**, its draped canopy supported by a squadron of silver angels (the tomb contains 2 tonnes of silver). The nearby **Wallenstein Chapel** contains the worn grave slabs of cathedral architects Matthias of Arras and Peter Parler.

The crypt (closed to the public) contains sarcophagi with the remains of Czech rulers, including Charles IV, Wenceslas IV, George of Poděbrady and Rudolf II.

See the Chapel of St Wenceslas

The biggest and most beautiful of the cathedral's numerous side chapels is Peter Parler's **Chapel of St Wenceslas**. Its walls are adorned with gilded panels containing polished slabs of semiprecious stones. Wall paintings from the early 16th century depict scenes from the life of the Czechs' patron saint, while older frescoes show scenes from the life of Christ.

Gawk at the Golden Gate

Back outside, the cathedral's south entrance is known as the **Golden Gate** (Zlatá brána), an elegant, triple-arched Gothic porch designed by Peter Parler. Above is a mosaic of the Last Judgment (1370–71) – on the left, the godly are raised into Heaven by angels; on the right, sinners are cast down into Hell by demons; and in the centre, Christ reigns in glory with saints Procopius, Sigismund, Vitus, Wenceslas, Ludmila and Adalbert below. Beneath them, Charles IV and his wife kneel in prayer.

Climb the Great South Tower

The cathedral's bell **tower** *(adult/child 200/150Kč)* was left unfinished in the 15th century; its soaring Gothic lines are capped by a Renaissance gallery added in the late 16th century, and a bulging spire that dates from the 1770s. You can climb the 297 steps to the top for excellent views – the entrance is outside the cathedral in Prague Castle's Third Courtyard (admission not included with Prague Castle tour tickets).

continued from p54

The stately baroque **Šternberg Palace** *(ngprague.cz; adult/child 180/100Kč)* dates from the turn of the 18th century and originally served as a base for one of Bohemia's most powerful noble families. The museum's treasures include a rare collection of Russian Christian icons, and early Italian paintings from the 14th and 15th centuries that formerly belonged to Austrian Archduke Franz Ferdinand. There's also an impressive grouping of Dutch and Flemish masters. The dealbreaker might be the palace's hidden baroque garden (open from May to September) at the back.

See the Loreta
A dazzling palace of pilgrimage

The **Loreta** *(loreta.cz; adult/child 230/160Kč)* religious complex, built to serve as a place of pilgrimage, originated from the 17th-century Counter-Reformation, when the Catholic Church was trying to win back converts to the fold. It was originally conceived to dazzle the masses and still does today. Among the highlights are a replica of the 'Santa Casa' (Holy House) of the Holy Lands, at the centre of the complex. Behind the Santa Casa, find the Church of the Nativity of Our Lord, built in 1737 to a design by Christoph Dientzenhofer. The unusual Chapel of Our Lady of Sorrows, at the corner of the courtyard, features a crucified bearded lady: St Starosta. The treasury is a bastion of religious bling centred on a 90cm-tall 'Prague Sun', made of silver and gold and studded with thousands of diamonds.

The World's Prettiest Library?
Tour the Strahov library

Tucked away in a quiet corner of Hradčany, the **Strahov Monastery** *(strahovskyklaster.cz; library tours adult/child 150/80Kč)* for the Premonstratensian order has stood here since 1140, when it was founded by Duke Vladislav II. The present monastery buildings, completed in the 17th and 18th centuries, were used until the communist government closed them down and imprisoned most of the monks; they returned in 1990. Inside the main gate is the 1612 Church of St Roch, now a picture gallery, and the Church of the Assumption of Our Lady. Mozart is said to have played the organ here.

However, the biggest attraction is the complex's magnificent **library**. Guided tours allow you to peer into the library's two

EARLY STORY OF HRADČANY

Hradčany got its first royal residents in the 9th century. A ducal palace was built here to accommodate the early ruling Přemyslid dynasty. The 12th century saw significant expansion. A grander ducal palace was completed.

In 1140, the Premonstratensian Monastery was founded in Strahov. In the 14th century, Emperor Charles IV rebuilt the castle to more properly represent Prague's status as seat of the Holy Roman Empire. He also embarked on construction of St Vitus Cathedral.

In 1541, a tragic fire engulfed the district and damaged many buildings, including the castle and cathedral. Yet the fire created large, empty lots that eventually gave way to today's mega-palaces, including the **Schwarzenberg Palace** (p54) and the **Archbishop's Palace**.

Very good home-brewed beers.

 DRINKING NEAR PRAGUE CASTLE: OUR PICKS

| **Hostinec U Černého Vola:** Rough-and-tumble, authentically Czech pub stands a stone's throw from the gates of Prague Castle. *10am-10pm* | **Lobkowicz Palace Café:** The best pit stop for drinks and light meals within the Prague Castle complex. Superb views from back balcony. *10am-6pm* | **Kavárna Novy Svět:** Welcoming cafe with pretty views off the back terrace. Excellent coffees and sweets. *10am-8pm Tue-Sun* | **Klášterní Pivovar Strahov:** Convivial pub near Strahov Monastery serves its own St Norbert beers – and very good Czech food. *10am-10pm* |

Loreta (p61)

>
>
> **ANOTHER PRAGUE DEFENESTRATION?**
>
> The stern-looking **Černín Palace** (home to the Czech Foreign Ministry, closed to the public) hides a scintillating communist-era mystery that remains unsolved to this day.
>
> In February 1948, the Czechoslovak Communist Party, backed by the Soviet Union, seized power in a coup. The new leaders quickly installed high-ranking communists in positions of power, but left Jan Masaryk – the son of Czechoslovakia's first president Tomáš Garrigue Masaryk – in office as foreign minister. He was the only noncommunist in the new government.
>
> A few weeks later, Masaryk fell to his death from one of the palace's upper windows. The official report ruled his death a suicide, though speculation remains widespread he was murdered, perhaps by the Soviet KGB.

baroque halls. The stunning interior of the 2-storey 'Philosophy Hall' features floor-to-ceiling walnut shelving. The feeling of height here is accentuated by a grandiose ceiling fresco. The older 'Theology Hall' is even more breathtaking. The low, curved ceiling is thickly encrusted in ornate baroque stucco work and decorated with painted cartouches. The lobby contains an 18th-century 'Cabinet of Curiosities' displaying the grotesquely shrivelled remains of sharks, turtles and other sea creatures. As you enter the corridor, look left to find a facsimile of the library's most prized possession, the Strahov Evangeliary, a 9th-century codex in a gem-studded 12th-century binding.

Wander Quiet Nový Svět
Have the city to yourself

Head to the lovely, lonely quarter of the **Nový Svět Quarter** *(New World; free)* to escape the crowds and find some headspace. The diminutive cottages that line this curving cobbled street, north of the Loreta, date from the 16th century and once housed members of the castle staff. Today, many have been restored and painted in pastel shades. Danish astronomer Tycho Brahe once lived at Nový Svět 1.

Order the original 'steak tartare'.

 EATING NEAR PRAGUE CASTLE: OUR PICKS

Malý Buddha: Quirky tearoom offers traditional temple menu. Vietnamese soups and Chinese rice dishes, many vegetarian. *11am-9pm Tue-Sun* €

Vinobona Wine & Bistro: Tiny, romantic spot; perfect for breakfast/lunch. Dress smartly for pricier dinner tasting menu. *9am-3pm, 6pm-10pm Thu-Mon* €€€

Kuchyň: Book well in advance to secure one of the popular terrace tables. Excellent Czech standards. *11.30am-11pm* €€

U Zavěšeného Kafe: Beloved by locals, this delightful cafe sports a playful interior and good-value Czech cooking. *11am-midnight* €

Malá Strana

LESSER IS MORE

Visitors are often surprised to discover that Malá Strana – 'Lesser Quarter' – in some ways is grander and more beautiful than Staré Město (Old Town). In the 17th and 18th centuries, many noble families built their sumptuous Renaissance and baroque palaces and plotted out spacious gardens here.

Malá Strana certainly feels much quieter and more relaxed. The neighbourhood is home to some top sights, including the beautiful baroque Church of St Nicholas, the elegant Wallenstein and Vrtbov Garden, and other pretty, aristocratic gardens. The best way to explore the quarter is to amble along the cobblestoned backstreets, or through Kampa Park along the river, and admire the many handsome buildings and tiny squares.

Malá Strana's western boundary is formed by the steep ridge of the Petřín Gardens. Climb (or ride a funicular) to the top to a lookout tower that bears an intentional resemblance to the Eiffel Tower, and a host of diverting, kid-friendly amusements.

Admire Grand St Nicholas

Prague's favourite church

Praguers generally have a love-hate affair with baroque architecture. Many residents find it too 'over the top', too much bling. Everyone, though, loves **St Nicholas Church** *(Kostel svatého Mikuláše; stnicholas.cz; adult/child 140/80Kč)*; its big green dome can be seen from just about anywhere in the centre. (The cupola makes it easy to distinguish from the city's other **Church of St Nicholas** (p84) on Old Town Square.)

The building was begun by famed baroque architect Christoph Dientzenhofer; his son Kilian continued the work and Anselmo Lurago finished the job in 1755. Mozart himself tickled the ivories on the 2500-pipe organ in 1787 and was honoured with a requiem mass here on 14 December 1791.

GETTING AROUND

The grandest way of accessing Malá Strana, like kings of yore, is to walk across Charles Bridge (which we've included here within the Malá Strana neighbourhood). Several trams, including 9, 12, 20, 22 and 23, stop at the quarter's main square, Malostranské náměstí. The area is serviced by metro Line A (green line), stop 'Malostranská'. Once in Malá Strana, the distances are short and you can walk everywhere.

☑ TOP TIP

Try to get off the well-worn Mostecká and Nerudova streets and explore the quarter's lovely, peaceful parks and side alleys. The gorgeous Wallenstein Gardens are free to enter, but note that many of the best parks and gardens are closed from October to April.

continued on p70

HIGHLIGHTS
1. Charles Bridge
2. Petřín

SIGHTS
3. Bretfeld Palace
4. *Crucifix*
5. Czech Museum of Music
6. Franz Kafka Museum
7. House at the Three Fiddles
8. House of the Golden Horseshoe
9. House of the Two Suns
10. Hunger Wall
11. Infant Jesus of Prague
12. John Lennon Peace Wall
13. Kampa Park
14. Karel Hynek Mácha
15. Karel Zeman Museum
16. Kunsthalle
17. Loreta
18. Malá Strana Bridge Tower
19. Memorial to the Victims of Communism
20. Mirror Maze
21. Museum Kampa
22. Museum of Prague Ghosts & Legends
23. Old Town Bridge Tower
24. Palace Gardens Beneath Prague Castle
25. Petřín Funicular Railway
26. Petřín Lookout Tower
27. Petřín Rose Garden
28. *Proudy* (David Černý sculpture)
29. *Quo Vadis* (David Černý sculpture)
30. St Francis Xavier
31. St John of Nepomuk House
32. St John of Nepomuk Statue
33. St Nicholas Church
34. Štefánik Observatory
35. Vision of St Luitgard
36. Vojan Gardens
37. Vrtbov Garden
38. Wallenstein Garden
39. Wallenstein Palace

SLEEPING
40. Aria Hotel
41. Dům U Velké Boty
42. Golden Well Hotel
43. Little Quarter Hostel

EATING
44. Café Savoy
45. Ichnusa Botega Bistro
46. Lokál U Bílé kuželky
47. Pork's
48. Restaurant Nebozízek
49. Terasa U Zlaté Studně
50. U Modré Kachničky
51. Vegan's Prague

DRINKING & NIGHTLIFE
52. Blue Light
53. Cukrkávalimonáda
54. IF Café – Werich Villa
55. Kellyxír Alchemical Pub
56. Klub Újezd
57. Malostranská Beseda
58. Mlýnská Kavárna
59. Nightmare Horror Bar
60. U Hrocha
61. U Malého Glena
62. U Svatého Tomáše

SHOPPING
63. Amadea
64. Artěl
65. Orel & Friends
66. Shakespeare & Son

View from Petřín

TOP EXPERIENCE

Petřín

The 318m-high Petřín is one of Prague's largest green spaces. It's great for quiet, tree-shaded walks and fine views over the 'city of a hundred spires' from the observation deck of a highly convincing Eiffel Tower wannabe. There were once vineyards here, and a quarry that provided the stone for most of Prague's Romanesque and Gothic buildings.

DON'T MISS

- Petřín Funicular
- Hike with incredible views
- Karel Hynek Mácha statue
- Rose Garden
- Observatory
- Petřín Lookout Tower
- Mirror Maze

Ride the Funicular Railway...

This tiny railway has been trundling up Petřín since 1891. The **funicular railway** *(dpp.cz; single fare 60Kč)* now uses modern coaches that move back and forth on 510m of track, though it still numbers among the city's most popular attractions. The ride is an easy way to add a little adventure to summiting the hill (and saves a hefty 20-minute climb). The funicular runs every 10 minutes (every 15 minutes November to March) from a base station at Újezd to near the Petřín

Practicalities
Scan this QR code for prices and opening hours.

Lookout Tower, with a stop in between at Nebozízek. Buy single, one-way fares at ticketing machines located at both the base and upper stations.

...Or Climb the Hill

The funicular is fun (especially for kids), but most Praguers opt for the slow, pretty climb along meandering trails and up through a changing landscape of orchards and tree cover. The walk is particularly lovely in April or early May to catch the first budding flowers on the trees. The ascent takes 20 minutes of moderate, occasionally breathy exertion. There's no direct path to the summit; the best plan is simply to keep moving uphill.

Once at the Summit

Once on top, take a moment to appreciate the hill and summit. Just south of the upper funicular station, there's a tended **rose garden** *(free)* with some 12,000 roses (and plenty of benches to relax on). While sitting here, ponder the fact that once upon a time this hill was draped with vineyards. It was also a major part of Prague's fortification system. Look down toward the city to see the long stone barrier, the **Hunger Wall**, that cuts along the middle of Petřín. The wall was constructed in 1362 under Emperor Charles IV to protect Prague from invasion; the name comes from the fact that it was built by the city's poor in return for food.

Not far from the rose garden, the small **Štefánik Observatory** *(planetum.cz; adult/child 90/70Kč)* has stood here since the 1920s. Check the website for scheduled public viewings of the daytime and nighttime skies, as well as a permanent exhibition on astronomy.

Lookout Tower & Mirror Maze

Walk north of the funicular's upper station to find the **Petřín Lookout Tower** *(adult/child 220/150Kč)*, a 60m-high Eiffel Tower lookalike (though much smaller at a ratio of 1:5) built by members of the Czech Hikers Club in 1891 for the Prague Jubilee. The resemblance to the Eiffel Tower is intentional. The club's members were apparently wowed by the Paris tower and wanted to put one here too. Climb the tower's 299 steps (or take the lift) for some of the best views in the city – on clear days you can see all the way to the forests of Central Bohemia to the southwest.

Just near the lookout tower is a **Mirror Maze** *(adult/child 120/80Kč)* that was also built for the 1891 exposition. Younger children will get a kick out of the distorting funhouse mirrors and labyrinth. There's also a diorama of the 1648 battle between Praguers and Swedes on Charles Bridge, though few of the kids take any notice of this.

'LOVERS' DAY'

Petřín comes into its own on 1 May when Prague residents celebrate an informal 'Lovers' Day'. Tradition says young couples must meet and kiss at the statue of **Karel Hynek Mácha** (1810–36), a famous Czech writer whose poem *Máj* explores the tragedy of unfulfilled love. The space is undeniably romantic and couples kiss here all the time (no need to wait until 1 May).

TOP TIPS

● The funicular's midway stop, Nebozízek, has a good Czech **restaurant** (p71).

● Or before heading up, stop at a bakery or market to gather picnic fare. There are lots of benches and places to spread a blanket.

● Save on the funicular fare by purchasing a transport pass *(24/72hr, 120/330Kč)*; valid on all metros, trams, buses and the funicular.

● Look out for cheaper combined tickets that are good for the lookout tower, mirror maze and observatory.

● A pretty path leads north across the meadow all the way to Prague Castle and Hradčany.

TOP EXPERIENCE

Charles Bridge

Who knew a bridge could ever be this beautiful or that mounting 30 baroque statues along its edges might elevate a handsome Gothic structure into a public work of art? Charles Bridge *(Karlův most, free)* is a world-class attraction. One of the signature Prague enjoyments is emerging from the Old Town onto a sunny bridge filled with busking musicians and people from around the world.

DON'T MISS

- Old Town Bridge Tower
- Busking musicians
- Crucifix
- Statue of St Francis Xavier
- Statue of St John of Nepomuk
- Statue of the Vision of St Luitgard
- Malá Strana Bridge Tower

A Little History

Charles Bridge began life in 1357 when Emperor Charles IV commissioned Peter Parler (architect of St Vitus Cathedral) to replace the older, 12th-century 'Judith Bridge', which had been washed away by floods in 1342. The new bridge was completed in 1390. It took Charles' name only in the 19th century – before that it was known simply as 'Kamenný most' (Stone Bridge).

The statues came three centuries later, when the bridge's first monument, the **Crucifix** near the eastern end, was mounted in 1657. The invocation in Hebrew reads: 'Holy, holy, holy Lord' (funded by the fine of a Jew who had mocked it in 1696). The first statue – the Jesuits' 1683 tribute to **St John of Nepomuk** – inspired other Catholic orders, and over the next 30 years a score more went up. Not everyone loved the new statues at the time, which some viewed as Catholic overreach to mark out new territory.

Climb the Towers

Perched at the eastern end of Charles Bridge in Staré Město, the elegant, late-14th-century **Old Town Bridge Tower** *(prague.eu; adult/child 190/130Kč)* was built not only as a fortification, but also as a triumphal arch marking the entrance to the Old Town. Like the bridge itself, the tower was designed by Peter Parler and incorporates many symbolic elements. While the tower houses a small exhibition about the bridge, the main justification for the admission fee is the amazing view from up top of the busy bridge below.

There are actually two towers at the Malá Strana end of Charles Bridge. The lower one was originally part of the long-gone 12th-century Judith Bridge, while the taller one was built in the mid-15th century in imitation of the Staré Město tower. The taller **Malá Strana Bridge Tower** *(prague.eu; adult/child 190/130Kč)* is open to the public and houses a small exhibit on the tower's history but, like its Staré Město counterpart, the main attraction is the view from the top.

Rub St John of Nepomuk

The bridge is home to a stunning array of 30 valuable baroque statues (though some have now been replaced by replicas). The most famous figure is the monument to **St John of Nepomuk**. According to the legend at the base of the statue, King Wenceslas IV had him trussed up in armour and thrown off the bridge in 1393 for refusing to divulge the queen's confessions (he was her priest). The stars in his halo allegedly followed his corpse down the river. Tradition says if you rub the bronze plaque, you'll one day return to Prague. A bronze cross set in the parapet between statues 17 and 19 marks the point where he was thrown off.

The other statues depict prominent saints at the end of the 17th and early-18th centuries. Art historians consider the statue of **St Francis Xavier** (1711), by the baroque master Ferdinand Maxmilián Brokoff, to be the most valuable. The **Vision of St Luitgard** (1710) is another contender. This monument depicts Christ appearing before a blind saint and allowing her to kiss his wounds.

INFLUENCE OF THE CHURCH

The statues on Charles Bridge played an important propaganda role during the 17th century. In the aftermath of the Thirty Years' War (1618–48), the ruling Habsburg dynasty was trying to rebuild the Catholic Church in the Czech lands. The statues of saints were intended to impress and dazzle the laypeople, at least in part to convince them to rejoin the church.

TOP TIPS

● It's a cliché, but to have this lovely bridge to yourself you have to get up very early in the morning.

● If you climb just one Prague tower during your stay, make it the Old Town Bridge Tower.

● Pickpockets may be around, so keep your purse or wallet safe.

● Return at sunset to catch the sun's last rays illuminating the Old Town.

● Find two beautiful bridge photo-op spots on the Old Town side: one at the Karlovy lázně tram stop, the other at the small plaza next to the Old Town Bridge Tower.

continued from p63

Take the stairs up to the gallery to see Karel Škréta's emotive, 17th-century *Passion Cycle* paintings. On the ceiling, Johann Kracker's 1770 *Apotheosis of St Nicholas* is Europe's largest fresco. (Clever trompe l'oeil techniques mean the painting merges almost seamlessly with the architecture.)

Instead of touring the church, a better option might be to hear a classical concert here. The swirling, hypnotic interiors, the pillars and statuary delight the eyes and more than compensate for any minor acoustic flaws the chamber might have as a music venue. Find a concert programme on the church website.

You can also climb the 215 steps up the **bell tower** *(adult/child 140/80Kč)*, though the views here are not quite as good as the nearby **Old Town Bridge Tower** (p69). During the communist era, the Czechoslovak secret police used the tower to spy on the nearby American embassy. On the way up, you can still see a white, cast-iron urinal installed for use by the watchers.

Learn About Franz Kafka
Connecting the author and city

Franz Kafka is arguably Prague's most famous native son. The German-Jewish author was born here in 1883, and Prague obviously played an important role as the setting for much of his work (though Prague is rarely – if ever – mentioned in the books and stories). That said, the rather dry **Franz Kafka Museum** *(kafkamuseum.cz; adult/child 300/220Kč)* is directed more at true fans than the general public. Exhibits explore the complex relationship between the author and his birth city through letters, photographs, period newspapers and publications.

A Museum Devoted to Music
Mozart's grand piano

Czechia's capital is a city of music and this 17th-century baroque monastery building provides a beautiful setting for the **Czech Museum of Music** *(nm.cz; adult/child 140/100Kč)*. The permanent exhibition, entitled 'Man–Instrument–Music', explores the relationship between people and musical instruments, and showcases an incredible collection of violins, guitars, lutes, trumpets, flutes and harmonicas. Highlights include a grand piano played by Mozart in 1787, and the

THE HOUSE SIGNS OF NERUDOVA

Steep Nerudova street leads from Malá Strana to Prague Castle. It has a long, rich history – much of it written on the playful symbols that adorn the fronts of the houses.

The **House at the Three Fiddles** (Nerudova 12) once belonged, fittingly, to a family of violin-makers.

St John of Nepomuk House (No 18) is adorned with an image of the patron saint himself.

Bretfeld Palace (No 33) was a social hotspot, entertaining the likes of Mozart and Casanova.

The **House of the Golden Horseshoe** (No 34) is named after St Wenceslas' horse, allegedly shod with gold.

Czech writer and journalist Jan Neruda, after whom the street is named, lived at the **House of the Two Suns** (No 47) from 1845 to 1857.

 EATING IN MALÁ STRANA: OUR PICKS

Good for a romantic splurge.

Terasa U Zlaté Studně: Perched atop a Renaissance mansion close to the castle, 'The Golden Well' has truly fine dining. *noon-4pm, 6-11pm €€€*

Ichnusa Botega Bistro: Superb Italian food and wines ferried to Prague directly from the owner's homeland of Sardinia. *11am-10pm €€*

Café Savoy: Elegant Viennese-style coffeehouse, with terrific Czech specialities and homemade desserts. *8am-10pm Mon-Fri, from 9am Sat & Sun €€*

U Modré Kachničky: This feels like an old-fashioned hunting lodge, with quiet, candlelit nooks. The traditional roast duck is very good. *noon-11pm €€€*

Infant Jesus of Prague

woodwind instruments of the 16th-century Rožmberk Court Ensemble. The exhibits are brought to life by recordings played using the actual instruments on display.

Honour the Infant Jesus
Wax object of adoration

Prague is underrated as a place of religious pilgrimage. There's the **Loreta** near Prague Castle, of course, and this even more-popular place of holy pursuit: the Church of Our Lady Victorious and its world-famous wax figurine, the **Infant Jesus of Prague** *(pragjesu.cz; free)*. The 47cm-tall figure of baby Jesus is both an object of veneration and a curiosity. It was brought here from Spain in 1556. It's said to have protected Prague from the plague and the Thirty Years' War. An 18th-century German prior, ES Stephano, wrote about the miracles and kicked off what became a worldwide cult.

The small museum tells the story of the Infant Jesus and shows off the figurine's beautiful robes, acquired over the years from benefactors both rich and poor.

HUMAN COSTS OF COMMUNISM

The more than 40 years (1948–89) of communist rule in Czechoslovakia exacted a staggering human cost on the population that every year seems to slip further and further into memory.

In total, some 205,000 people were arrested, nearly 171,000 were driven into exile, around 250 people were executed, some 4500 people died in prison, and more than 300 people were shot while trying to flee across the border.

These shocking statistics are listed on the bronze strip in front of the **Memorial to the Victims of Communism** (at the western end of Vítězná street). The sculpture consists of seven human figures (controversially, all are male) in progressive stages of disintegration, descending a staggered slope.

Definitely opt for the pork knuckle.

 EATING IN MALÁ STRANA: OUR PICKS

Restaurant Nebozízek: Handy midway stop on the Petřín funicular. Eclectic menu of international/Czech dishes. *noon-11pm* €€

Lokál U Bílé kuželky: Malá Strana branch of popular national chain with traditional Czech food and excellent Pilsner Urquell beer. *11am-11pm* €€

Vegan's Prague: Beneath the Renaissance beams, enjoy curries, veggie burgers and meat-and-dairy-free versions of Czech faves. *11.30am-9pm* €

Pork's: The name says it all... massive plate-sized pork knuckle served with mustard, horseradish and sauerkraut. Book in advance. *noon-11.30pm* €€

MALÁ STRANA PRAGUE — THE GUIDE

BEST SPOTS FOR EVENING FUN

Malostranská Beseda (malostranska-beseda.cz): Four-storey entertainment palace with fabled music club on 2nd floor. Lively roster of Czech acts old and new.

U Malého Glena (malyglen.cz): American-owned 'Little Glen's' has been around since 1995. Local jazz or blues bands play nightly in the cellar.

Blue Light (bluelightbar.cz): High-octane party bar only really starts to jump in the wee hours.

Klub Újezd (klubujezd.cz): Not quite the legendary nightspot it was in the 1990s, but a great place for a drink. Occasional live music shows and exhibitions.

Mlýnská Kavárna (facebook.com/kavarna.mlynska): Favourite evening hangout for local celebs and journalists, including occasionally artist David Černý.

Museum Kampa

Drop by the Museum Kampa
Old mill showcases modern art

The **Museum Kampa** (museumkampa.cz; adult/concession 350/190Kč), located in splendid **Kampa Park**, is frequently bypassed by visitors who may not even realise the museum is there. The permanent collection will appeal especially to lovers of modern art from the early 20th century. Look for the bronzes by Cubist sculptor Otto Gutfreund and paintings by the celebrated Czech master František Kupka. The most impressive canvas is Kupka's *Cathedral*, a pleated mass of blue and red diagonals. The museum also hosts high-quality temporary exhibitions.

Meet Ghosts & Monsters
Horror-themed museum and pubs

Tidy, cute Malá Strana hides a more-ghoulish underbelly. Start off at the fascinating **Museum of Prague Ghosts and Legends** (*Muzeum pražských pověstí a strašidel; mysteriapragensia.cz; adult/child 190/140Kc*) to learn all about the city's scary mysteries. The museum is built on two levels. The 12th-century basement is stuffed with ghosts.

DRINKING IN MALÁ STRANA: OUR PICKS

Ideal spot to rest weary legs.

U Svatého Tomáše: Beer-lovers around the city rejoiced in 2024 when this historic pub reopened after being closed for many years. *4pm-11pm Wed-Sun*

U Hrocha: Popular watering hole hasn't changed much since the days of the people's republic. Beloved by staff from nearby British embassy. *noon-11.30pm*

IF Café – Werich Villa: Always crowded Kampa Park cafe features excellent homemade cakes and very good breakfasts. *8.30am-7.30pm*

Cukrkávalimonáda: Cute cafe–bistro combining minimalist 21st-century styling with impressive Renaissance-era painted timber roof beams. *9am-7pm*

The main floor features interactive storytelling. Kids will love it.

Keep the monster theme rolling with a drink at the **Nightmare Horror Bar** *(nightmare-bar.com; 4pm–2am)*, a basement space dedicated to horror films that's part-camp, part-scary and absolutely fascinating. Another drinks bar, the **Kellyxír Alchemical Pub** *(mysteriapragensia.cz; 1pm–11pm)*, plays on the alchemy theme. Look out for signature cocktails, where drinks come to the table bubbling and smoking. It's fun.

Chill at the Lennon Peace Wall
Colourful graffiti wall

Long before street art was cool, Prague had its own **John Lennon Peace Wall** *(Velkopřevorské náměstí; free)*, a place where people could express themselves through imagery and spray paint. The wall began life under the former communist regime, following the death of John Lennon on 8 December 1980. The Beatles' singer became a pacifist hero, and someone painted an image of Lennon on a wall in this secluded square. Despite repeated coats of whitewash, the secret police never managed to keep it clean, and the wall evolved into a symbol of resistance.

These days, the Lennon Wall has long lost any ideological potency, though tourists still come to scrawl messages on the wall, and buskers hang out to sing and soak up the lingering counterculture vibe.

Two Guys Peeing in Public
Another David Černý shocker

Don't leave Malá Strana without checking out what might be David Černý's most ridiculous (and shocking) public-art installation. **Proudy** *('Streams'; davidcerny.cz; free)* is a saucy, animatronic sculpture of two guys urinating in a puddle that's shaped like Czechia. We're not sure if the artist is poking fun at Czechs' relatively lax restrictions on public urination or maybe a penchant for national self-loathing. Whatever, it's definitely amusing.

Malá Strana is home to a second, more-serious Černý artwork, though it's not open to the public. **Quo Vadis** *(free)* depicts a bronze Trabant (East German car) on four legs. It's a tribute to thousands of East Germans who fled communism and came to Prague in late 1989, before being granted asylum (and leaving their cars behind). It's locked in the garden of the **German Embassy** (Vlašská 19) and only visible through a fence behind the embassy.

BEST SPOTS FOR PICKING UP SOUVENIRS

Orel & Friends *(orelandfriends.cz)*: Authentic, locally made souvenirs, including tablecloths made using the UNESCO-listed *modrotisk* (blue-print) technique.

Artěl *(artelglass.com)*: Traditional Bohemian glassmaking meets modern design in this stylish shop founded by US designer Karen Feldman.

Shakespeare & Sons *(shakes.cz)*: English-language bookshop with extensive range of translated Czech titles and books on Central European history.

Amadea *(amadea.cz)*: Czechia's woodworking tradition is brought to visitors courtesy of Amadea, whose artisans in northeast Bohemia create delicate jewellery, toys, chopping boards, Christmas decorations and heaps more.

SEE MORE DAVID ČERNÝ

David Černý's street art, statues and installations can be found all over Prague. Other statues worth seeking out include **Kůň** (p103) (Horse) at the Lucerna Palace, and **K** (p103), Černý's giant, mesmerising rotating bust of Franz Kafka. Both are in Nové Město.

Check Out Kunsthalle
High-end contemporary art space

The **Kunsthalle** *(adult/child 290/180Kč)* exhibition space first opened in 2022, repurposing what had formerly served as an electricity substation. Since then, the curators have put together a series of demanding, eclectic exhibitions featuring the country's best-known contemporary artists. Check the website to see what's on.

Underrated Karel Zeman Museum
Family-fun animation and film effects

Bohemia-born film director Karel Zeman (1910–89) was a pioneer of special effects, though his work remains little known outside his home country. Movie buffs will want to pop into the **Karel Zeman Museum** *(muzeumkarlazemana.cz; adult/child 300/190Kč)* to see some of the tricks and techniques he perfected. Many exhibits allow for hands-on interaction and are perfect for kids.

Zeman's inventive use of animation and matte paintings combined with live action – seen in films like Czech cult classics *Journey to the Beginning of Time* (Cesta do pravěku; 1955) and *The Fabulous Baron Munchausen* (Baron Prášil; 1962) – influenced more-famous directors, including George Lucas, Tim Burton and Terry Gilliam.

Lavish Wallenstein Palace & Gardens
Home to a wannabe emperor

In his day, in the early 17th century, the Habsburg general Albrecht of Wallenstein (1583–1634) was a larger-than-life figure and rival to the emperors and kings who depended on his wealth to fund their war-making aims. The enormous **Wallenstein Palace** *(senat.cz; free)* – now home to the Czech Senate (the parliament's upper chamber) – was intended to rival Prague Castle itself and stands as a testament to the man's wealth and immense ego. Access for the general public is limited (normally Saturdays April–October, 9am–4pm), but check the website for an updated schedule. The ceiling fresco in the Baroque Hall shows Wallenstein as a warrior at the reins of a chariot, while the unusual oval Audience Hall has a fresco of Vulcan at work in his forge.

Even if you don't tour the palace itself, take a look at the extraordinary **garden** *(senat.cz; free)* behind the palace – an immense, unexpected oasis. The garden was created in late-Renaissance style in the 17th century. Aside from ponds, statues and peaceful, manicured greenery, the garden features a huge loggia decorated with scenes from the Trojan Wars. This is flanked on one side by an enormous fake stalactite grotto – as was the fashion back in the day. The gardens are open daily from April to October.

UNMISSABLE GARDENS OF MALÁ STRANA

Bonita Rhoads, an American who has lived in Prague for 20 years, is cofounder of Insight Cities *(insightcities.com)*.

These are my all-time favourite gardens in Malá Strana: **Vrtbov Garden** is often overlooked by visitors; the walled-in baroque landscaping here gives a luminous glimpse into the life of the nobility. Climb to the top courtyard for panoramic views of the Old Town and Prague Castle.

The **Wallenstein Garden** (p74) is hidden from view. Wander through the gate to find albino peacocks, mannerist statues, mythical fountains and tragic family histories spanning 400 years.

Travellers, alas, also often frequently miss the **Palace Gardens Beneath Prague Castle**. These are meticulously maintained terraced gardens that climb the hills below Prague Castle.

TOUR THE GARDENS OF MALÁ STRANA

This ramble hits the district's most important parks and gardens. Note many gardens are closed from October to April, but the walk is also fun during winter.

START	END	LENGTH
Malostranská metro	Vrtbov Garden	2.5km; 1½ hours

Exit ❶ **Malostranská metro station** and head west along Valdštejnská to the ❷ **Palace Gardens beneath Prague Castle** (p74). After exploring the gardens, return to Valdštejnská and turn right, then left into ❸ **Wallenstein Palace** (p74) and through the courtyard to the Wallenstein Garden. Head for its northeastern corner and leave through the gate beside Malostranská metro station. Turn right on Klárov and continue along U Lužického semináře. A gate on the right leads to the ❹ **Vojan Gardens**, a peaceful corner inhabited by a big peacock.

Continue along U Lužického semináře then left across the little bridge over the Čertovka stream. Pass under Charles Bridge and through the picturesque square of Na Kampě into ❺ **Kampa Park** (p72), one of the city's favourite chill-out zones.

Retrace your steps and bear left along Hroznová, which leads to a bridge over the Čertovka beside a waterwheel. Find the tiny cobbled square with the ❻ **John Lennon Peace Wall** (p73) to your right. The far end of the square curves right, past the severe Gothic towers of the Church of Our Lady Below the Chain. Turn left opposite the church and bear right along Prokopská; cross busy Karmelitská and turn right.

Find an alley on your left that leads to another pretty green space, the ❼ **Vrtbov Garden** (p74).

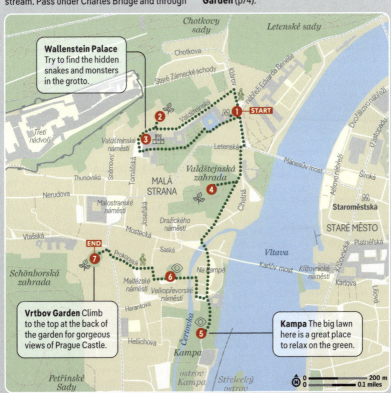

Wallenstein Palace Try to find the hidden snakes and monsters in the grotto.

Vrtbov Garden Climb to the top at the back of the garden for gorgeous views of Prague Castle.

Kampa The big lawn here is a great place to relax on the green.

Staré Město (Old Town)

THE HEART OF PRAGUE

GETTING AROUND

Much of Staré Město, including Old Town Square, is closed to cars, so walking is not just the best, but sometimes the only way of getting around. The closest metro station to Old Town Square is Staroměstská (Line A, green line). Metro stations Můstek (on lines A and B) and Náměstí Republiky (Line B, yellow line) are located a short walk away. Trams 2, 17 and 18 bring you to within a couple blocks of Old Town Square. Trams 6, 8, 15 and 26 stop at Dlouhá třída, close to the Convent of St Agnes.

☑ TOP TIP

To escape the crowds, try to get off heavily travelled pedestrianised streets like Karlova and Celetná in favour of quieter backstreets. Try as best you can to ignore the dubious cannabis shops, *trdelník* (chimney cake) vendors, and Thai massage parlours to see the area's underlying medieval beauty.

Staré Město, Prague's Old Town, has been the city's beating heart for more than 1000 years. The grand buildings, churches and squares, the Old Town Hall and Astronomical Clock, and the Church of Our Lady Before Týn stand as testimony to the growing wealth and influence over the centuries of Prague's merchants and artisans. This splendour came to rival that of the emperors, kings and noble families on the other side of the river. Centuries ago, the Old Town was protected by high walls, moats and grand gates. The path of the former moat still defines Staré Město's borders and can be traced along Na příkopě and Národní streets. Of the former gates, only the Powder Tower survives.

The best way to take in Staré Město's sights is simply to wander at will. The street plan appears to have little logic at all; perfect for getting lost in.

Tour Two Historic Spaces
The Estates Theatre and Rudolfinum

Staré Město is home to two beautiful, historic spaces for the performing arts, and both offer guided tours. The colourful neoclassical **Estates Theatre** (MAP P78; *narodni-divadlo.cz; tours adult/child 260/160Kč*), from 1783, incredibly hosted Mozart himself for the premiere of his opera *Don Giovanni* on 29 October 1787. The theatre was originally patronised by upper-class German citizens and thus came to be called the Estates Theatre – the Estates being the traditional nobility. These days it serves as part of the National Theatre's (p105) family of dramatic venues and makes an unforgettable setting for a piece of theatre or the occasional concert of baroque music. Book tours over the website.

The grand 1884 **Rudolfinum** (MAP P88; *rudolfinum.cz; tours adult/child 250/125Kč*), designed by architects Josef Schulz and Josef Zítek, is considered one of Prague's finest neo-Renaissance buildings. It served as the seat of the Czechoslovak Parliament between the two world wars, and as

Estates Theatre

the administrative offices of the occupying Nazis during WWII. These days, it's home to the Czech Philharmonic Orchestra, and the impressive **Dvořák Hall** is one Prague's great venues for listening to classical music. Arrange tours at least a couple of weeks in advance by email at prohlidky@ceskafilharmonie.cz.

Visit the Museum of Decorative Arts
Vintage glass and priceless tapestries

The graceful **Museum of Decorative Arts** (MAP P88; *upm.cz; adult/child 350/180Kč*) is packed with vintage Czech glassware, furniture, tapestries and period clothing. The museum began in 1900 as part of a Europe-wide Arts and Crafts movement to encourage a return to the aesthetic values sacrificed to the Industrial Revolution. The permanent exhibition 'Art. Life. Art for Life' focuses on the role of design and applied arts from the Middle Ages to the current day. One of the treats of a visit to the museum is the view out over the Old Jewish Cemetery (p90) from the back window. The museum also has a cute cafe and garden.

continued on p85

OLD TOWN'S HIDDEN NOOKS

Veronika Primm, lifelong Praguer and travel writer *(TravelGeekery.com)*

I'm still captivated by our Old Town. Even after years here, I still get blissfully lost in Old Town's hidden nooks, stumbling upon tucked-away courtyards and little details I might have previously missed. I seek out quieter corners, like my favourite haunt: the area around Haštalské Square to the Convent of St Agnes (p80) is perfect for peaceful wandering. Here, time seems to slow down, and you can almost hear echoes of centuries past. For a livelier vibe, I head to bustling Dlouhá Street. Whether you're seeking tranquillity or excitement, Prague Old Town's labyrinthine streets never fail to deliver the magic. I can recommend it to everybody.

🍴 EATING IN STARÉ MĚSTO: OUR PICKS

Good spot for a traditional schnitzel or roast pork.

MAPS P78 & P88

Field: Michelin-starred spot features farm-fresh ingredients, minimalist design and unfussy attitude. Book in advance. *11am-2.30pm & 6-10.30pm* €€€

Lehká Hlava: The emphasis is on healthy, fresh vegetarian and vegan dishes, often with an international theme. *noon-11pm* €

Lokál: Excellent beer and Czech comfort food in a modern take on a communist-era canteen. Book ahead. *11am-midnight Mon-Sat, to 10pm Sun* €€

SmetanaQ Café & Bistro: From top breakfasts to ambitious mains, like Asian pork belly and Slovak-style *halušky* (dumplings). *9am-9pm* €€

STARÉ MĚSTO (OLD TOWN) PRAGUE

STARÉ MĚSTO - EAST

HIGHLIGHTS
1. Convent of St Agnes
2. Old Town Square

SIGHTS
3. Astronomical Clock
4. Church of Our Lady Before Týn
5. Church of St James
6. Church of St Nicholas
7. Estates Theatre
8. Granovský Palace
9. House at the Minute
10. House at the Stone Bell
11. House of the Black Madonna
12. Jan Hus statue
13. Kinský Palace
14. Marian Column
15. Municipal House
16. Old Town Hall
17. Plisner Urquell Experience
18. Powder Gate
19. Smetana Hall
20. Spanish Synagogue
21. Týn Courtyard

SLEEPING
22. Design Hotel Josef

EATING
23. 420 Restaurant
24. Field
25. Kolacherie
26. Lokál
27. Mincovna
28. Naše Maso
29. V Kolkovně

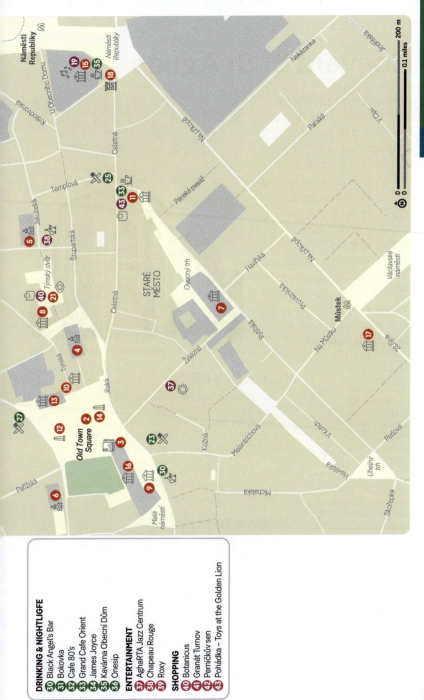

TOP EXPERIENCE

Convent of St Agnes

In the northeastern corner of Staré Město, the former Convent of St Agnes *(ngprague.cz; adult/child 250/140Kč)* holds the National Gallery's priceless collection of medieval and early Renaissance art (1200–1550): glowing Gothic altar paintings and polychrome religious sculptures. The building is considered Prague's oldest surviving example of Gothic architecture and has a fascinating history itself.

TOP TIPS

- Don't miss the renovated gardens – perfect for taking a break or taking in the occasional outdoor concert.

- The gallery is fully wheelchair-accessible and has a unique tactile presentation of 12 casts of medieval sculptures with explanatory text in Braille.

Practicalities
Scan this QR code for prices and opening hours.

Monastery's Origins

In 1234 the Franciscan Order of the Poor Clares was founded by Přemysl King Wenceslas I, who made his sister Agnes (Anežka) the first abbess. In the 16th century, the convent was handed over to the Dominicans, and after Habsburg Emperor Joseph II dissolved the monasteries in the 18th century, it became a squatters' paradise. The complex was restored and renovated in the 1980s. Agnes went on to become beatified in the 19th century and was canonised as 'St Agnes of Bohemia' in 1989.

Medieval Treasures

The highlights of the permanent collection include dozens of paintings, images and altarpieces from the late-Gothic and early-Renaissance, and are drawn in part from the collections of John of Bohemia (1296–1346) and his son, Emperor Charles IV (1316–78). Look for notable painters and sculptors: Master Theodoric, the Master of the Třeboň Altarpiece (and the magnificent triptych itself) and the Master of the Krumlov Madonna (from around 1400).

In addition to the art gallery, visit the French Gothic Church of the Holy Saviour, which contains the tombs of St Agnes herself and Wenceslas I's Queen Kunigunde of Hohenstaufen.

TOP EXPERIENCE

Old Town Square

One of Europe's most beautiful and busiest urban spaces, the Old Town Square (Staroměstské náměstí, or *Staromák* for short) has been Prague's principal public square since the 10th century, and was its main marketplace until the beginning of the 20th century. Today it's where all tourists converge, some coming from Charles Bridge, others from the start of the Royal Way (p93).

DON'T MISS

- Old Town Hall Tower
- Astronomical Clock
- Statue of Jan Hus
- Marian Column
- Church of Our Lady Before Týn
- Church of St Nicholas
- House at the Stone Bell

Take In the Square

Before exploring, take a moment to familiarise yourself with the buildings surrounding this colourful, lively square. These include the 14th-century **Old Town Hall**, presided over by a tall Gothic tower and splendid **Astronomical Clock**. The most dramatic structure on the square is the twin-spired **Church of Our Lady Before Týn**, across the way, which stands incongruously behind a row of baroque facades. The 14th-century **House at the Stone Bell** is considered the square's oldest building. This solemn Gothic structure shares the same block with the attention-grabbing, late-baroque **Kinský Palace** from 1765, with its riotous, pinkish facade. Find another important church, the baroque **Church of St Nicholas**, wedged into the northwestern corner.

Old Town Hall & Astronomical Clock

The most important building, **Old Town Hall** *(staromestskaradnicepraha.cz; tower adult/child 300/200Kč)*, was founded in 1338 to serve as Staré Město's independent seat of government. These days it no longer has a formal governing function, and is used mostly for wedding ceremonies. The building houses a branch of the tourist information office and a giftshop.

The admission system to enter and tour the town hall is complicated and prices quickly add up. The main admission ticket includes only entry to the tower, which affords dramatic views of the square below. You can climb stairs or take the lift (the latter, though, requires a 100Kč surcharge). The family ticket *(650Kč)*, for two adults and up to four children, takes some of the sting out the tower admission. If you'd like to see the historic interiors, including the council chambers, Gothic chapel and Romanesque and Gothic cellars beneath the building, you'll have to plump for an add-on guided tour *(per person 150Kč)*. Tours in English are conducted daily. Tour times are listed at the ticket counter.

The building's main attraction is the **Astronomical Clock** *(free)* on its south-facing exterior. On the hour, from 9am to 9pm, spectators are treated to a 45-second mechanised marionette display straight out of the Middle Ages. The four figures beside the clock represent the deepest civic anxieties of 15th-century Praguers: 'Vanity' (with a mirror), 'Greed' (with a moneybag), 'Death' (the skeleton) and 'Pagan Invasion' (represented by a Turk). On the hour, 'Death' rings a bell and inverts his hourglass, and the 12 Apostles parade past the windows above the clock, nodding to the crowd. At the end, a rooster crows and the hour is rung.

Before leaving the Old Town Hall, take a moment to examine the jagged edges of the eastern edge of the building. This wing once ran northward along the square but was tragically destroyed by Nazi gunfire at the end of WWII. The wing was never rebuilt. You'll also find a plaque here commemorating an earlier tragic event. The plaque lists the names of 27 Protestant nobles who were beheaded here by the victorious Austrian Habsburgs in 1621 after the Battle of Bílá Hora (White Mountain); the white crosses on the ground mark where the deed was done.

Church of Our Lady Before Týn

The distinctive twin Gothic spires make the **Týn Church** *(tyn.cz; suggested donation 40Kč)* an unmistakable landmark. Like something out of a 15th-century fairy tale, they loom over the square, decorated with a golden image of the Virgin Mary made in the 1620s using the melted-down Hussite chalice that previously adorned the church.

Though impressively Gothic on the outside, the church's interior is smothered in heavy baroque. Two of the most interesting features are the main altar with its *Virgin and the Holy Trinity* by baroque painter Karel Škréta, and the

---

HISTORY OF THE ASTRONOMICAL CLOCK

Built in 1490 by a master clockmaker named Hanuš, the Astronomical Clock was a scientific feat in its day – even after various renovations, it remains a paradigm of antique technology. The upper dial, the astrolabe, depicts the time in various forms and the movement of heavenly bodies through the sky. The lower dial, the calendar, shows the day of the year.

TOP TIPS

● The most romantic time to visit the square is after dark, when the medieval buildings are beautifully illuminated.

● Avoid the temptation of dining directly on or near Old Town Square. With some notable exceptions, many restaurants, regrettably, are tourist traps.

● Check out the giftshop in the Old Town Hall for some humorous and creative souvenirs.

● Arrive a few minutes before the top of the hour to position yourself for a good view of the Astronomical Clock.

● There are lively food and craft stalls in Old Town Square around major holidays like Christmas and Easter.

tomb of Tycho Brahe, the Danish astronomer who was one of Rudolf II's most illustrious court scientists. (He died in 1601 of a burst bladder following a royal drinking session.) Find the entrance to the church through the arcades at Staroměstské náměstí 14/604.

House at the Stone Bell

During restoration in the 1980s, a baroque stucco facade was stripped away from the elegant medieval **House at the Stone Bell** *(ghmp.cz; admission according to exhibition)*, next to the Týn Church, to reveal the original 14th-century Gothic stonework. The stone bell that gives the building its name is on the corner. Inside the building, two restored Gothic chapels now serve as branches of the Prague City Gallery *(ghmp.cz)*, with changing exhibits of modern and contemporary art.

Statues of Jan Hus & Mary

Two pieces of statuary in the middle of the square are integral to this public space. Praguers love the dramatic art-nouveau depiction of Czech religious reformer **Jan Hus** by Ladislav Šaloun. The statue was unveiled on 6 July 1915, the 500th anniversary of Hus' death at the stake as a purported heretic.

The newer **Marian Column** was installed in 2020, and it's fair to say locals haven't quite warmed up to it yet. The column replaced a baroque original that had stood on this spot for centuries and which was pulled down by anti-Habsburg Czech nationalists at the end of WWI.

> **PRAGUE MERIDIAN**
>
> Look at the ground in the middle of the square to find the 'Prague Meridian'. This was added in the 17th century to give Praguers an easy way to tell time. The strip was placed near the **Marian Column** (p83) so that at high noon the column's shadow would fall directly on the meridian. The strip still works with the new column, but it's now a few minutes off.

Jan Hus memorial

HISTORY-MAKING BALCONY

Look closely at the balcony of the **Kinský Palace**. This was where communist leader Klement Gottwald proclaimed communist rule in Czechoslovakia in February 1948. The moment is recalled in Milan Kundera's *Book of Laughter & Forgetting*, where he describes a famous photograph of Gottwald standing on the balcony. During the speech, one of Gottwald's deputies, Vlado Clementis, offered him a fur cap to keep warm. Four years later, during the political purges, Clementis was unjustly charged with treason, hanged and subsequently airbrushed from all official photos. As Kundera wryly observed: "All that remained of Clementis was the cap on Gottwald's head."

Church of St Nicholas

Church of St Nicholas

This baroque wedding-cake-style **Church of St Nicholas** (*svmikulas.cz; concerts from 300Kč*) in the far northwestern corner of Old Town Square was built in the 1730s by Kilian Dientzenhofer (not to be confused with the Dientzenhofers' masterpiece of the same name in Malá Strana (p63)). The church was built on top of a much older house of worship dedicated to St Nicholas from the 13th century. Originally, the church was wedged behind the Old Town Hall's north-running eastern wing (destroyed by the retreating Nazi soldiers in May 1945). The church is frequently used as a venue for chamber concerts, and you can take a tour that includes its splendid baroque interior 30 minutes before concerts begin.

Worth Searching Out

In addition to the colourful assembly of mainly baroque buildings along the square's perimeter, look out for some truly unique features. Just left of the main entrance to Old Town Hall, the ornate **House at the Minute** (*dům U minuty*) is an arcaded building covered with Renaissance sgraffito. Franz Kafka lived here (1889–96) as a child just before the building was bought by the town council.

At Staroměstské náměstí 17, look for a plaque commemorating Albert Einstein's time in Prague from 1911 to 1912. The plaque marks the former residence of socialite Berta Fanta, who ran a remarkable weekly salon in her drawing room that must have been the talk of the town. The memorial reads:

Here in this salon of Mrs. Berta Fanta, Albert Einstein, professor at Prague University in 1911 to 1912, founder of the theory of relativity, Nobel prize winner, played the violin and met his friends, famous writers, Max Brod and Franz Kafka.

continued from p77

Shrivelled Arm on the Wall?
The deceptive Church of St James

The Gothic **Church of St James** (MAP P78; *praha.minorite.cz; free*) holds lots of surprises. The first is its size. From the outside, this 14th-century church looks deceptively small. It's only on the inside where its true girth takes shape. St James started out as a Minorite monastery and got a baroque facelift in the 18th century. In the midst of the gilt and stucco, the interior holds another surprising find. On the western wall (look right as you enter) hangs a shrivelled human arm. Legend claims that when a thief tried to steal the jewels from the statue of the Virgin, the Virgin grabbed his wrist in an iron grip and his arm had to be lopped off. The large organ is used for recitals.

Admire Art-Nouveau Elegance
Tour the Municipal House

Just near the Powder Tower, you can't miss Prague's most exuberantly art-nouveau building. The **Municipal House** (MAP P78; *Obecní dům; obecnidum.cz; guided tours adult/child 320/270Kč; free to enter*) was a labour of love, with every detail of its design and decoration carefully considered, and every painting and sculpture loaded with symbolism.

The building was built between 1906 and 1912. It was a lavish joint effort by around 30 leading Czech artists of the day, including Alfons Mucha. The origins were part of the Czech national revival and meant to showcase the abilities of Czech – as opposed to Austrian or German – artists. The site of the building is significant. This was the home of the former Royal Court, the seat of Bohemia's kings from 1383 to 1483, which was demolished at the end of the 19th century.

While the building looks almost too pretty to enter, don't be afraid to walk in. The building's purpose was always to serve as a place of recreation for city residents. The ground floor holds both a grand cafe and an unspeakably opulent restaurant. Walk downstairs to find an ornately decorated Czech pub and an early-20th-century rendition of an American-style cocktail bar. The Municipal House is home to **Smetana Hall** (MAP P78), Prague's biggest classical concert hall, with seating for 1200.

Guided tours in English can be booked over the website or at the venue box office. The highlight of the tour is the octagonal Lord Mayor's Hall, the windows of which overlook the main

BEST VENUES FOR CLASSICAL MUSIC

Rudolfinum *(rudolfinum.cz; standing tickets from 200Kč)*: Gorgeous neo-Renaissance building with Dvořák Hall (p77), home of the Czech Philharmonic Orchestra. The season runs September–June.

Smetana Hall *(fok.cz; tickets from 400Kč)*: Centrepiece stage of the Municipal House and home of the Prague Symphony Orchestra.

Church of St James *(praha.minorite.cz; free)*: Features a splendid pipe organ. Pop in on Sunday mornings at 10am for a free organ recital.

Church of St Nicholas *(svmikulas.cz; tickets from 300Kč)*: Chamber concerts here are visually splendid (though acoustically average).

Estates Theatre *(narodni-divadlo.cz; tickets from 400Kč)*: Branch of the National Theatre hosts occasional baroque music concerts.

Line up for excellent burgers.

🍴 EATING IN STARÉ MĚSTO: OUR PICKS — MAP P78

420 Restaurant: Opulent dining room with baroque statues. Traditional Czech dishes given fusion upgrade. Book ahead. *11.30am-10.30pm* €€€

Mincovna: Best of an average bunch of restaurants on Old Town Square. Decent pork knee, schnitzels and duck. *11.30am-11pm* €€

Naše Maso: Tiny butcher with stand-up tables at the forefront of Prague's rush to embrace the foodie philosophy of locally sourced meat. *11am-10pm* €€

V Kolkovně: Operated by Pilsner Urquell Brewery. Stylish, modern take on traditional Prague pub; fancy-ish versions of classic Czech dishes. *11am-midnight* €€

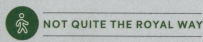

NOT QUITE THE ROYAL WAY

This relaxing walk takes you through the centre of the Old Town while avoiding some of the more crowded streets.

START	END	LENGTH
Powder Gate	Charles Bridge	1.5km, 45 minutes

Start at the ❶ **Powder Gate** (p87), one of the old entryways into the Old Town, and set off along busy Celetná to the Cubist museum ❷ **House of the Black Madonna** (p87). Turn right into the enclosed passage at Celetná 17 and then straight along Malá Štupartská to the deceptively massive ❸ **Church of St James** (p85). Peek inside the church and then find the passage opposite the church that leads to the ❹ **Týn Courtyard** (p87), an enclosed piazza with a Renaissance loggia. Exit at the far end and proceed straight along a small lane. Emerge onto ❺ **Old Town Square** (p81).

Enjoy the square's atmosphere and then continue past the Old Town Hall to reach Malé náměstí (Little Square), dominated by the highly decorated facade of the historic hardware store ❻ **VJ Rott Building** (No 3). From here, follow Linhartská street to Mariánské náměstí and Prague's New City Hall. Nip into the ❼ **Municipal Library** to see an interesting book-tower sculpture by artist Matej Krén.

Find the main gate of the former Jesuit college at the ❽ **Klementinum** (p92). Go through and turn left. Continue through a triple arch and turn right to pass through quiet courtyards and emerge into crowds at ❾ **Charles Bridge** (p68).

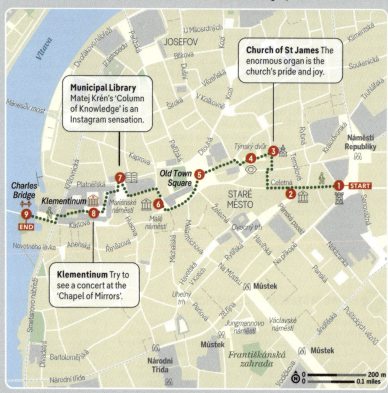

entrance. Every aspect of its decoration was designed by Alfons Mucha, who also painted the superbly moody murals that adorn the walls and ceiling.

Learn about 'Cubist' Design
Fabulous 'House of the Black Madonna'

Among Prague's early-modern designers, Cubism was regarded as not only a painting technique, but also a thorough-going design approach that could be applied equally to architecture and industrial style. The **House of the Black Madonna** (MAP P78; *upm.cz; adult/child 150/80Kč*) showcases the Museum of Decorative Arts' wide-ranging collection of Cubist furniture, ceramics and glassware. The exhibitions are fittingly housed in Josef Gočár's eye-catching Cubist building. Don't miss the arresting interiors of the adjoining Cubist cafe: the Grand Cafe Orient (p93).

CUBISM ON THE CANVAS

After you've taken in the Cubist architecture and design at the Museum of Czech Cubism, head over to the National Gallery's **Trade Fair Palace** (p126) in Holešovice to see how Czech painters applied Cubist techniques to the canvas.

Climb the Powder Gate
Surviving medieval entryway

Back in the day, Prague's Old Town was surrounded by walls and moats, and could only be accessed through one of 13 town gates. The splendour of the 65m-tall **Powder Gate** (MAP P78; *prague.eu; tower adult/child 190/130Kč*), which dates from 1475 and marks the start of the royal route, gives us an idea of the grand scope of those old entryways.

The Powder Gate remained unfinished until the 19th century; neo-Gothic architect Josef Mocker put the final touches to the building in 1886. The 'powder' part of the name comes from the gate's function in the 18th century as a gunpowder store. The Gothic interior houses a few information panels about the tower's construction – the main attraction is the view from the top.

Explore the Týn Courtyard
Once keeper of the customs duties

The small lane that runs to the left of the Church of Our Lady Týn leads to the **Týn Courtyard** (MAP P78; *free*), a medieval caravanserai: a fortified hotel, trading centre and customs office for visiting foreign merchants. Now attractively renovated, the space houses shops, restaurants and hotels. The courtyard is still often referred to by its German name: *Ungelt* (meaning 'customs duty'). The origins of the courtyard may date back as far as the 11th century and it was busiest and most prosperous in the 14th century during the reign of Charles IV.

The most valuable building is the 16th-century **Granovsky Palace** (MAP P78), sporting an elegant Renaissance loggia, and sgraffito and painted decorations depicting biblical and mythological scenes.

THE UBIQUITOUS 'TRDELNÍK'

We don't want to harsh your mellow, or in this case your chimney cake, but the dozens of stands around the Old Town selling 'Traditional Czech Trdelník' are trying to put one over on you. There's little evidence that these grilled cylinder cakes – sprinkled with sugar or cinnamon and sometimes stuffed with ice cream – have all that much to do with Czech tradition. Of course, try one if you'd like (they're not bad). If you're looking for true Czech desserts, though, try the *koláče* (round pastries with fruit or poppy seeds) at **Kolacherie** or the Bohemian gingerbread at **Perníčkův sen** (Gingerbread Dream). This is the only place in Prague for Bohemian *sakrajda*: gingerbread strudel stuffed with plum jam and walnuts.

STARÉ MĚSTO - WEST

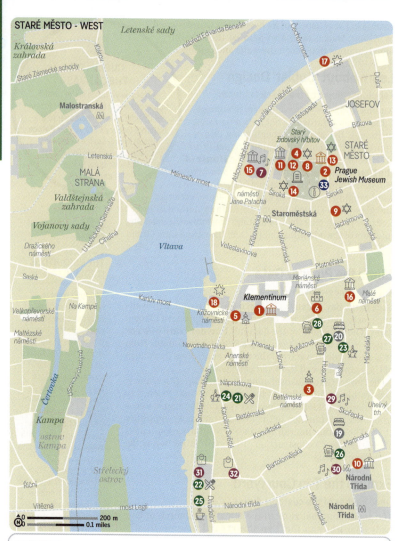

HIGHLIGHTS
1. Klementinum
2. Prague Jewish Museum

SIGHTS
3. Bethlehem Chapel
4. Ceremonial Hall
5. Church of the Holy Saviour
6. Clam-Gallas Palace
7. Dvořák Hall
8. Klaus Synagogue
9. Maisel Synagogue
10. Museum of Bricks
11. Museum of Decorative Arts
12. Old Jewish Cemetery
13. Old-New Synagogue
14. Pinkas Synagogue
15. Rudolfinum
16. VJ Rott Building

ACTIVITES
17. Prague Boats
18. Prague Venice

SLEEPING
19. Ahoy! Hostel
20. Dominican

EATING
21. Lehká Hlava
22. SmetanaQ Café & Bistro

DRINKING & NIGHTLIFE
23. Absintherie
24. Hemingway Bar
25. Kavárna Slavia
26. U Medvídků
27. U Tří Růží
28. U Zlatého Tygra

ENTERTAINMENT
29. Jazz Republic
30. Vagon

SHOPPING
31. Deelive
32. Kavka

INFORMATION
33. Museum Reservation Centre

Museum of Bricks

Loads & Loads of Legos
Prague's Museum of Bricks

Prague's Old Town can be a feast for the eyes, but it can be something of a slog for younger kids. The **Museum of Bricks** (MAP P88; *museumofbricks.cz; adult/child 285/190Kč*) claims to have the largest private collection of Lego models in the world, with a play area at the end where kids can build stuff from Lego, and a shop selling almost every set going. According to the organisers, the museum houses something like 3000 unique models, which are composed of more than 1 million Lego bricks. That should impress the little ones.

Learn More about Jan Hus
Hus's Bethlehem Chapel

The rather plain-looking **Bethlehem Chapel** (MAP P88; *bethlehemchapel.eu; adult/child 60/30Kč*) hides what's in effect a national cultural monument. This was the birthplace of the Hussite cause, and Jan Hus preached here from 1402 to 1412. Every year on the night of 5 July, the eve of the anniversary of Hus' burning at the stake in 1415, a memorial is held with speeches and bell-ringing.

In the 18th century, the original chapel was torn down, and much of what survives is a reconstruction based on old drawings, descriptions and traces of the original work. An explanatory text in English is available at the chapel entrance.

continued on p93

BEST PLACES FOR ROCK OR JAZZ

Roxy (roxy.cz): In ramshackle shell of an art-deco cinema. Nurtured the indie end of Prague's club spectrum for three decades.

Vagon (vagon.cz): Live rock virtually every night, from Pink Floyd and Led Zep tribute bands to classic Czech rockers.

AghaRTA Jazz Centrum (agharta.cz): Intimate jazz cellar hosts local musicians as well as occasional gigs by leading international artists.

Jazz Republic (jazzrepublic.cz): Relaxed club stages all kinds of live music, including rock, blues and reggae, as well as jazz. Book seats over the website.

Chapeau Rouge (chapeaurouge.cz): Anything-goes bar with a regular pro-gramme of visiting DJs, slasher rock bands and everything else.

 DRINKING IN STARÉ MĚSTO: BEST FOR WINE & COCKTAILS

| **Bokovka:** Crumbling, atmospheric cellar bar and a great place to sample the best Czech wines. *4pm-midnight.* | **Black Angel's Bar:** Cosy cluster of mirrored bars, chesterfields and lamps recreates the atmosphere of a 1930s cocktail bar. *5pm-3am* | **Hemingway Bar:** Snug, sophisticated hideaway with leather benches and flickering candlelight. Book ahead. *5pm-1am* | **Cafe '80s:** Raucous, retro 1980s cocktail bar on the Old Town's busiest street for late-night drinking and carousing. *5pm-4am* |

TOP EXPERIENCE

Prague Jewish Museum

The Prague Jewish Museum isn't simply one museum, but a grouping of historic synagogues and an ancient burial ground. The holdings constitute possibly the world's biggest collection of sacred Jewish artefacts, many rescued from synagogues destroyed by Nazi Germany during WWII. The crumbling Old Jewish Cemetery is a must. The weatherworn headstones mark just a fraction of the thousands buried here.

DON'T MISS

Old Jewish Cemetery

Graves of Mordechai Maisel and Rabbi Loew

Old-New Synagogue

Pinkas Synagogue

Maisel Synagogue

Spanish Synagogue

Klaus Synagogue

Ceremonial Hall

Old Jewish Cemetery

The highly evocative, unforgettable **Old Jewish Cemetery** is Europe's oldest surviving Jewish graveyard. Founded in the early 15th century, it has a palpable atmosphere of mourning, even after more than two centuries of disuse (it was closed in 1787). Around 12,000 crumbling stones (some brought from other, long-gone cemeteries) are heaped together, but beneath them are tens of thousands of graves, piled in layers because of a lack of space.

The most prominent graves, marked by pairs of marble tablets with a 'roof' between them, are near the main gate; among them are the graves of 16th-century benefactor and

Practicalities
Scan this QR code for prices and opening hours.

community leader Mordechai Maisel and the fabled Rabbi Loew. The oldest stone (now replaced by a replica) is that of Avigdor Karo, a chief rabbi and court poet to Wenceslas IV, who died in 1439. Most stones bear the name of the deceased and his or her father, the date of death (and sometimes of burial) and poetic texts. Elaborate markers from the 17th and 18th centuries are carved with bas-reliefs, some of them indicating the deceased's occupation – look out for a pair of hands marking the grave of a pianist.

Old-New Synagogue

Completed around 1270, the **Old-New Synagogue** is Europe's oldest working synagogue and one of Prague's earliest Gothic buildings. Around the central chamber are an entry hall, a winter prayer hall and the room from which women watch the men-only services. The interior, with a pulpit surrounded by a 15th-century wrought-iron grill, looks much as it would have 500 years ago.

The 17th-century scriptures on the walls were recovered from beneath a later 'restoration'. On the eastern wall is the Holy Ark that holds the Torah scrolls. In a glass case at the rear, little light bulbs beside the names of the prominent deceased are lit on their death days.

Children of Terezín

The handsome **Pinkas Synagogue**, built in 1535 and used for worship until 1941, is a highlight for many visitors. After WWII the synagogue was converted into a memorial, with wall after wall inscribed with the names, birth dates and dates of disappearance of the 77,297 Czech victims of the Nazis. The space also contains a moving collection of paintings and drawings by children held in **Terezín Fortress** (p161).

History of Jews in Bohemia

Two synagogues are home to a long exhibition on the history of Jews in Bohemia and Moravia. The exhibition begins in the neo-Gothic **Maisel Synagogue**, where artefacts such as ceremonial silver, textiles, prints and books tell this history from the 10th to the 18th centuries.

About two blocks east of the Maisel, the highly ornate, Moorish-style **Spanish Synagogue** picks up this history in the 19th and 20th centuries.

Religious Rituals

Two other structures, the **Klaus Synagogue** and the **Ceremonial Hall**, for years have displayed objects used in Jewish worship and tradition, including family ceremonies and the rites associated with birth, circumcision, bar mitzvah and marriage. As this guide was being researched, the Jewish Museum announced plans to introduce new permanent exhibitions here. Check the website to see what's on during your visit.

VISITING THE MUSEUM

One basic admission ticket allows entry to all of the main monuments, including the Old-New Synagogue. Buy tickets on the museum website or at the **Museum Reservation Centre** *(Maiselova 15)*.

Some individual synagogues also have ticket windows. Several local agencies, including the museum itself, offer guided tours of the museum. Enquire about the museum's tours via email at IRC@jewishmuseum.cz.

TOP TIPS

● Men must cover their heads before entering the Old-New Synagogue. Bring a hat or buy a paper yarmulke at the entrance.

● Holders of the **Prague Visitor Pass** *(praguevisitorpass.eu)* are entitled to free admission.

● If you're pressed for time, the highlights are the Old Jewish Cemetery and the Old-New Synagogue.

● Try to visit the Old Jewish Cemetery early or late in the day in order to avoid the crowds.

TOP EXPERIENCE

Klementinum

The Klementinum (prague.eu; guided tour adult/concession 300/200Kč) is a sprawling complex of beautiful baroque halls that once housed the 17th-century college of the all-powerful Jesuit order. Guided tours explore the lavish Library Hall, the Meridian Hall, the 68m-tall Astronomical Tower and the uber-baroque Chapel of Mirrors.

Library Hall

Here Come the Jesuits

The Jesuit order came to Prague in the 16th century to boost the power of the Roman Catholic Church. For their base, they selected this choice piece of real estate and set to work on the **Church of the Holy Saviour**, the flagship of the Counter-Reformation. The church's sooty stone saints glare down at trams and tourists on Křížovnické náměstí below.

Another Beautiful Library

In addition to the Strahov Monastery library (p61), Prague has a second candidate for 'World's Prettiest Library'. The baroque Library Hall (1727) is magnificently decorated with ornate gilded carvings and a ceiling fresco depicting the Temple of Wisdom. It houses thousands of volumes dating back to 1600. The Meridian Hall was used to determine the time of day, using a beam of sunlight cast through a hole in the wall.

Astronomical Tower & Chapel of Mirrors

Climb the **Astronomical Tower** for fascinating views out over the Old Town. The tower served as an observatory until the 1930s; it now houses 18th-century astronomical instruments. The Chapel of Mirrors is a confection of gilded stucco, marbled columns, fancy frescoes and ceiling mirrors – baroque on steroids.

TOP TIPS

● Try to catch a classical concert at the Chapel of Mirrors. Check the website (bohemianconcerts.com) to see what's on.

● St Clement's Cathedral, within the complex, serves as a Byzantine Catholic chapel. Conservatively dressed visitors are welcome to attend the services.

Practicalities
Scan this QR code for opening hours, ticket information and tour times.

continued from p89

Interactive Beer-Drinking Adventure
Pilsner Urquell Experience

One of Prague's newest attractions (opened in 2023) and ideal for a rainy day, the hypermodern, interactive **Pilsner Urquell Experience** (MAP P78; *pilsnerexperience.com; from adult/child 549/350Kc*) is dedicated to telling the story of the world's first modern lager from 1843: Pilsner Urquell. Depending on the experience, you'll get to taste several beers, learn about the production techniques and how to do the perfect pour (at the 'Tapping School'). Great for groups.

Encounter an Enormous Baroque Palace
Architecture and artistry of Clam-Gallas Palace

The **Clam-Gallas Palace** (MAP P88; *clam-gallas.cz; self-guided tours adult/child 180/80Kč*) is a tour de force of Baroque bravado – both inside and out. The enormous building was designed by Viennese court architect Johann Bernhard Fischer von Erlach in 1713; the interiors are decorated with countless sculptures and frescoes depicting scenes of ancient mythology. It's well worth a peek inside. Both guided and self-guided (with audio guides) tours are available. In summer, the hushed courtyard is used to host concerts and evening film screenings (check the website). There's a pretty cafe on-site as well when you need to take a break.

Cruise the Vltava
A day (or night) on the water

Several tour-boat operators run daytime and evening cruises up and down the Vltava. Some are paired with live jazz or dance music, others with dinner and drinks, and some are just sightseeing excursions. **Prague Boats** (MAP P88; *prague-boats.cz, 1hr cruises adult/child 450/300Kč*) runs a variety of popular cruises from March to October. Check the website to see if something appeals. Most boats tie up at the embankment just below Čech Bridge (Čechův most) at the northern end of Pařížská street. **Prague Venice** (MAP P88; *prague-venice.cz; adult/child 550/350Kč*) runs entertaining 45-minute cruises in small boats under the hidden arches of Charles Bridge and along the Čertovka stream near Kampa Park (p72). Buy tickets via the website or find touts standing at either end of Charles Bridge.

IN THE FOOTSTEPS OF KINGS

The **Royal Way** (Královská cesta) was the former processional route followed by the Bohemian kings on their way to St Vitus Cathedral for coronation.

The first king to ride the route was the Habsburg ruler Albert II, in 1438; the last was Emperor Ferdinand I of Austria, in 1836. The coronation route ran right through the heart of Staré Město.

It began at the Powder Gate. From here, the route followed Celetná to Old Town Square and the adjacent Little Square (Malé náměstí). From the squares, the route traced Karlova street to Charles Bridge and then across to Malá Strana.

On the Malá Strana side, the coronation route proceeded along Mostecká street to Malostranské náměstí before climbing up Nerudova to Prague Castle.

Touristy but too pretty to pass up.

DRINKING IN STARÉ MĚSTO: BEST FOR COFFEE — MAPS P78 & P88

Kavárna Slavia: Famous old Prague cafes. Art-deco elegance, with big windows over the river. *8am-midnight Mon-Fri, from 9am-Sat & Sun*

Grand Cafe Orient: Good coffee and cakes, but most come to Prague's only Cubist cafe (from 1912) to admire the unique styling. *9am-10pm Mon-Fri, from 10am Sat & Sun*

Onesip: Classic espresso bar and roaster. Excellent flat whites and award-winning cappuccinos. *8am-6pm*

Kavárna Obecní Dům: Spectacular cafe in opulent Municipal House offers the opportunity to sip your coffee amid art-nouveau splendour. *8am-10pm*

BEST FOR BUYING SOUVENIRS

Kavka (kavkabook.cz): The best place in Prague to pick up books on Czech art and photography.

Botanicus (botanicus.cz): Natural health and beauty products, including scented soaps, herbal bath oils and shampoos, made from organic herbs and plants.

Deelive (deelive.cz): This airy, minimalistic gallery-shop presents carefully selected items from Czech designers, predominantly interior-design pieces, jewellery and clothing.

Pohádka – Toys at the Golden Lion (eshop.ceskehracky.com): Highly visible toyshop on Celetná street, where the focus is on traditional Czech toys.

Granát Turnov (granat.cz): Rings, bracelets and necklaces featuring authentic, locally sourced Czech garnets in beautiful settings.

Absintherie

Taste the Green Fairy
The art of imbibing absinthe

Prague isn't only about beer. In the past three decades, the city has become a hub for absinthe – the allegedly hallucinatory 'green fairy' cocktail of 1920s' Paris fame. It's legal to buy and imbibe in Czechia, but not every place pours a quality drink. You can't go wrong at **Absintherie** (MAP P88; *absintherie.cz; 1pm-1am)*, which offers absinthe-based cocktails and shooters. Fancy **Hemingway Bar** (MAP P88; *hemingwaybar.cz; 5pm-1am)* offers a wide selection of absinthe brands and knowledgeable staff, but you'll have to book in advance.

English-language pub quizzes Monday nights.

 DRINKING IN STARÉ MĚSTO: BEST PUBS — MAPS P78 & P88

U Zlatého Tygra: The 'Golden Tiger' is a classic pub and a Prague legend, but carefully protected by locals (don't come in large groups). *3-11pm*

U Tří Růží: The 'Three Roses' offers six of its own beers on tap and has been at the forefront of the movement to revive local brewpubs. *11am-11pm*

U Medvídků: Traditional pub serving Czech Budvar beer, plus some of its own home-brew, and very good Czech food. *11.30am-11pm*

James Joyce: Join English speakers at this Prague original, a friendly Irish pub with a rarity in the city's bars – an open fire. *11am-12.30am*

Nové Město (New Town)

PRAGUE'S COMMERCIAL CENTRE

The busy streets in Prague's main commercial area are where Prague starts to feel like a real city (and less like a living museum). Nové Město translates as 'New Town', but there's little 'new' about it. It was laid out by Emperor Charles IV in the mid-14th century to alleviate overcrowding in Staré Město. Nové Město hugs the borders of Staré Město in a wide arc that traces the former walls and moats of the Old Town from Revoluční (east of Old Town Square) along pedestrianised Na Příkopě and out along the main avenue of Národní třída, south of Staré Město. It's a sprawling quarter that lacks a true neighbourhood feel.

That said, Nové Město is home to some of Prague's most interesting sights as well as excellent restaurants, pubs and theatres. It's also home to the city's most important public gathering area, Wenceslas Square.

Rainy-Day Family Fun
Museums dedicated to senses, fun and film

Keep these family-friendly attractions in mind if you catch a freak heatwave or rainy day. The **Museum of the Senses** *(muzeumsmyslu.cz; adult/child 350/250Kč)* bamboozles visitors with optical illusions and is a surefire winner with kids and young teens. Budget an hour and go in the morning to avoid the crowds. The **House of Fun** *(houseoffunprague.cz; free to enter, games priced separately)* is an enormous game room spread out over several spaces. Find 150 arcade games plus mini-golf and lots of other attractions. There's a big food court and a pretty rooftop bar and restaurant: **Fly Vista** *(flyvista.cz; 8am-midnight)*. The **National Film Museum** *(nafilm.org; adult/child 190/140Kč)* isn't really dedicated to the world of Czech film. It's more of an interactive space that examines how films are made. Tech-minded little ones will love building their own holograms or trying their hand at animation.

continued on p103

GETTING AROUND

Wenceslas Square is the quarter's main hub and is well-served by metro. On the square's lower (northern) end, lines A (green) and B (yellow) intersect at Můstek station, once the site of a small bridge that connected Nové Město and Staré Město. At the top of the square, lines A and C (red) cross at Muzeum station. The area around the Můstek metro station as well as Na Příkopě and Wenceslas Square are mostly restricted from car traffic, which makes them popular strolling territory.

☑ TOP TIP

Prague is amid a city-wide renovation boom that began after the COVID-19 pandemic and is expected to last until 2027 at the earliest. Nowhere is this more obvious than in Nové Město, especially around Wenceslas Square. It shouldn't significantly affect your visit, but expect to see lots of scaffolding, bulldozers, etc.

HIGHLIGHTS
1. Mucha Museum
2. National Museum
3. Wenceslas Square

SIGHTS
4. *Butterflies* (David Černý sculpture)
5. Church of Our Lady of the Snows
6. Church of Sts Cyril & Methodius
7. Cubist Lamp Post
8. Dancing House
9. Dvořák Museum
10. Franciscan Garden
11. Grand Hotel Evropa
12. Hotel Jalta Nuclear Bunker
13. Jan Palach Memorial
14. Jubilee (Jerusalem) Synagogue
15. *K* (David Černý sculpture)
16. *Kůň* (David Černý sculpture)
17. Lindt Building
18. Melantrich Building
19. Mucha Foundation Museum
20. Museum of Communism
21. Museum of the Senses
22. National Film Museum
23. National Theatre
24. New Town Hall
25. Old Town Hall
26. Palác Koruna
27. Slovanský ostrov
28. St Wenceslas Statue
29. Střelecký ostrov
30. Velvet Revolution Memorial
31. Wiehl House

SLEEPING
32. Almanac X Alcron Hotel
33. Boutique Hotel 16 – U Sv. Kateřiny
34. Icon Hotel
35. Mosaic House
36. Sophie's Hostel

EATING
37. Čestr
38. Fly Vista
39. Garden's
40. Kantýna

DRINKING & NIGHTLIFE
41. Alcron Bar
42. Cafe Louvre
43. Cukrárna Myšák
44. EMA Espresso Bar
45. Globe Bookstore & Café
46. Hoffa
47. Pivovar Národní
48. Q Cafe
49. U Fleků
50. U Pinkasů
51. U Šumavy
52. Vinograf

ENTERTAINMENT
53. Duplex
54. House of Fun Prague
55. Lucerna Music Bar
56. Prague State Opera
57. Reduta Jazz Club

SHOPPING
58. Lucerna Palace

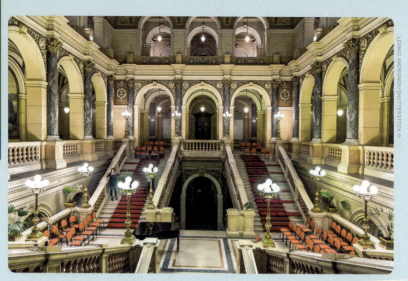

Main Hall

TOP EXPERIENCE

National Museum

Looming high above Wenceslas Square is the neo-Renaissance bulk of the National Museum, designed in the 1880s as an architectural symbol of the Czech National Revival. The museum's magnificent interior is a shrine to the cultural history of Czechia. The permanent exhibitions highlight the 'miracles of evolution' and the history of the Czech lands from the 8th to the 20th century.

DON'T MISS
- Entrance Hall
- History Exhibition
- Halls of Minerals
- Miracles of Evolution
- Pantheon
- Dome
- Children's Museum
- History of the 20th Century

Interiors & Entry Hall

For many people, simply the chance to glimpse inside this beautifully restored building is the main reason for a visit. The building's architectural style is neo-Renaissance, a 19th-century revivalist style that incorporated design elements from buildings built during the 16th-century European Renaissance. Here, that means, first of all, the elegant entry stairway, as well as plenty of marble everywhere, dazzling frescoes and interior 'loggias'. These are intricately carved open-air balconies or porches marked by an arch. Don't miss the beautifully

Practicalities
Scan this QR code for prices and opening hours.

decorated glass ceilings and views up to the cupola. This latter is accessible via a lift and affords great views over the square below. The 'pantheon' on the 2nd floor – with busts of famous Czech creators and intellectuals – fulfils the building's intention of highlighting Czech (as opposed to German or Austrian) contributions to the arts and sciences.

Centuries of History

The bulk of the holdings on the main floor are given over to history of the Czechs, from the Slavic tribe's early emergence in the 8th century to the start of the 20th century (the 'Museum of the 20th Century' in the 'new' building picks up the story from here). Some 2000 objects are on display, so the best strategy here is simply to pick a period – perhaps the medieval period and birth of the Bohemian kingdom, or the Renaissance and Counter-Reformation (16th and early 17th centuries), or the 19th century – and focus your attention there.

Gemstones & Dinosaurs

The National Museum is arguably strongest when it comes to the geology and natural-history exhibits. The 'Hall of Minerals' draws on the mineral-collecting passions of an early aristocrat, Count Kašpar Šternberg (1761–1838), and shows off some 4000 different gemstones, minerals and unique rocks. The nearby 'Hall of Meteorites' highlights both celestial objects that found their way to earth, and earthen rocks that were shaped and altered by meteorite impaction. The 'Windows into Prehistory' features recreations of the world's earliest creatures, including (naturally) dinosaurs. A newer collection, the 'Miracles of Evolution', dazzles with lifelike models of exotic animals, like enormous whales and giant squids.

The 'New' Building

Across the road from the historic building, the National Museum's 'new' building (or 'annex') forms part of the museum (linked via an underground passage) and is home to two leading attractions. The 'Children's Museum', on the building's 2nd level, is aimed at kids older than four years of age (accompanied by their parents). Three big halls filled with interactive games and attractions. Entry to this museum is limited to 90 minutes and requires a separate entry ticket. Reserve a 90-minute time slot in advance over the website. The 'Museum of the 20th Century', on the new building's 3rd level, narrates the gripping events of the 20th century, during which Czechoslovakia was born as a nation, suffered occupation at the hands of Nazi Germany, and later fell under the domination of the Soviet Union. It's part-gripping and part-bewildering to anyone who's not already familiar with this history.

MISTAKEN IDENTITY

The front of the National Museum is so impressive that invading Russian troops in August 1968 mistook the building for Czechoslovakia's parliament and riddled the facade with bullets. For years afterwards, the bullet marks endured as a memorial to that tragic invasion. The facade was renovated in the 2010s, but you can still see bullet impressions if you look closely enough.

TOP TIPS

● Buy tickets up to 30 days in advance over the museum website.

● Use the website to purchase Children's Museum tickets and to reserve your visiting times.

● The museum's holdings are immense. To avoid the burnout, pick out a few sections in advance and focus your attention there.

● Instead of eating at the museum's cafeteria, plan a meal at Čestr (p105), a high-quality steakhouse located toward the back of the museum's 'new' building.

● The museum's two buildings are connected via an underground passageway. You don't have to leave the building to move between the two.

TOP EXPERIENCE

Wenceslas Square

For centuries, Nové Město has been dominated by sloping Wenceslas Square (Václavské náměstí). This long rectangle started life as a horse market, but eventually evolved into the heart of Prague's commercial life. It's dominated at the top by the massive National Museum (p98) and along the sides by a patchwork of hotels, restaurants, hidden shopping passages and memorials to epic historic events.

DON'T MISS

St Wenceslas Statue

Memorial to Victims of Communism

Melantrich Building

Hotel Jalta Nuclear Bunker

Hotel Evropa

Wiehl House

Koruna Palace

Statues & Memorials

The upper (southeastern) end of the square is home to possibly Prague's best-known statue: Josef Myslbek's 1912 equestrian statue of **St Wenceslas**, the 10th-century pacifist Duke of Bohemia and the 'Good King Wenceslas' of Christmas carol fame. Flanked by other patron saints of Bohemia – Prokop, Adalbert, Agnes and Ludmila – he has been plastered with posters and bunting at every one of the square's historical moments.

A few metres below the statue, find a more-modest memorial – often covered in flowers – to the 'Victims of Communism', with images of two students who gave their lives to protest the 1968 Soviet-led invasion of Czechoslovakia. In January 1969, student Jan Palach set fire to himself and later died from his burns. He quickly became a national hero. A month later, a second student, Jan Zajíc, immolated himself near here as well. The exact spot where **Palach** fell stands just in front of the National Museum and is marked by a cross.

Site of Epic Events

Wenceslas Square has witnessed a great deal of Czech history. In 1848, during the revolutionary anti-Habsburg upheavals of that year, a giant mass was held here. In 1918, at the end of WWI, thousands gathered to celebrate the creation of the newly independent Czechoslovakia from the ruins of the old Austro-Hungarian Empire.

For many Czechs (and Slovaks), Wenceslas Square will forever be linked to the 1989 Velvet Revolution. Not far from the square, on Národní street, find a **memorial** to the spot where demonstrators and riot police first clashed on 17 November. In the days afterwards, angry citizens gathered on the square night after night to protest and cheer on the efforts of dissident leader Václav Havel. Look carefully at the **Melantrich Building** (Václavské náměstí 36) to find a small balcony. This was the historic perch from where Havel and popular reform politician Alexander Dubček famously greeted hundreds of thousands of demonstrators in the square below.

Historical Architecture

The square is surrounded by important buildings representative of late-19th- and early-20th-century architectural styles. The **Wiehl House** (Václavské náměstí 34) from 1896 has a gorgeous facade decorated with neo-Renaissance murals by top Czech artist Mikuláš Aleš and others. Look for art nouveau at the newly remodelled (and dazzling) **Grand Hotel Evropa** (Václavské náměstí 25) and the **Palác Koruna** (Václavské náměstí 1), topped with a crown of pearls. The **Lindt Building** (Václavské náměstí 4), designed by Ludvík Kysela in 1927, is one of Czechia's earliest examples of functionalist architecture.

Visit a Nuclear Bunker

One of the square's great secrets is this communist-era nuclear shelter that's hidden far beneath the 1950s **Hotel Jalta** (hoteljalta.com; adult/child 400/330Kč). The bunker is accessible to the public by guided tour. The highlight is the chilling communications room, which was used to listen in on the telephone calls and rooms of important hotel guests (including many foreign journalists in the runup to the 1989 revolution). Reserve tour spots on the hotel's website; look for 'fallout shelter'.

EXPLORE LUCERNA PALACE

Find the entrance to **Lucerna Palace**, an elegant 1920s-era shopping arcade, just next to Václavské náměstí 36. It's a beautiful throwback space, with an arthouse theatre, vintage cafe, music club and lots of delightful old camera and photography shops (and lots of other shops as well). It's also home to David Černý's weird, shocking hanging-horse installation, *Kůň* (p103).

TOP TIPS

- Avoid the square at night (after 10pm), when it takes on a sleazier aspect (particularly toward the upper end).

- The square is home to dozens of cafes that are fine for a quick coffee. The restaurants, though, tend to be overly touristy and mediocre.

- The St Wenceslas statue on the square's upper end is a handy meet-up spot. Locals often say 'meet you at the horse'. This is where they mean.

- If you have tired legs, take the metro (lines A or C) to Muzeum (instead of Můstek) to save yourself an uphill walk.

TOP EXPERIENCE

Mucha Museum

Alfons Mucha (1860–1939) is a Moravian-born international success story. The Mucha Museum shows off the artist's sensuous art-nouveau posters, paintings and decorative panels, as well as sketches, photographs and other memorabilia. Even if you don't immediately recognise his name, you've no doubt seen many of Mucha's trademark Slavic maidens in various guises.

Parisian Posters

Mucha first made his name and cemented his reputation in the 1890s in Paris as a poster illustrator. His muse was the legendary actress Sarah Bernhardt. The museum is strong on this part of Mucha's work, particularly the groundbreaking poster of Bernhardt in the role of 'Gismonda'.

Czech Illustrations

Mucha was an ardent defender of Slavic identity and much of his work in the 1910s highlights the styles and customs of his native Moravia. Look at his famous illustration *Princess Hyacinth*, which starred a popular actress at the time, Andula Sedláčková.

Epic Paintings

In addition to being a skilled illustrator and stylist, Mucha was a highly talented painter, as seen here in the section devoted to paintings. Mucha would go on to create 20 larger-than-life paintings known as the 'Slav Epic' (1910–28). That collection was still looking for a permanent exhibition space as this book was being researched.

Another Mucha Museum

In 2025, a separate **Mucha Foundation Museum** *(muchafoundation.org)* opened nearby with more on the life of the artist and featuring original artwork from the Mucha family.

TOP TIPS

● The giftshop is a gold mine of posters and book collections of Mucha's art.

● When touring the Municipal House, don't miss Mucha's work on the interiors.

● See more Mucha at St Vitus Cathedral, where he painted the stained glass.

Practicalities
Scan this QR code for opening hours, ticket information and tour times.

continued from p95

Kafka's Head on a Swivel
And other installations by artist David Černý

Nové Město is home to three of Czech artist David Černý's *(davidcerny.cz)* most-popular installations. Don't leave Prague without checking out **K**, a giant, rotating bust of Franz Kafka. The bust gives a mesmerising show, as Kafka's face rhythmically dissolves and re-emerges. Find it in the courtyard of a shopping centre above the Národní třída metro station (line B). Just around the corner, on the facade of the **House of Fun**, find Černý's newest installation (2024): ***Butterflies***. The two WWII-era RAF Spitfire fighter planes hanging here recall the role of British-based Czech fighter pilots in defeating Nazi Germany. The **Lucerna Palace** shopping arcade is home to Černý's oddest installation: ***Kůň*** (Horse). A giant dead horse – with St Wenceslas sitting astride – hangs from the marbled atrium. It's a wryly amusing counterpart to the more-imposing equestrian statue of St Wenceslas in nearby Wenceslas Square. The installations are free to view.

Learn About Communism
A peek behind the Iron Curtain

The privately run **Museum of Communism** *(muzeum komunismu.cz; adult/child 380/290Kč)* tells the story of Czechoslovakia's years behind the Iron Curtain with photos, words and a fascinating and varied collection of...well...stuff. The empty shops, corruption, fear and doublespeak of life in socialist Czechoslovakia are well conveyed, and there are rare photos of the Stalin monument that once stood on Letná (p127).

Admire the 'Dancing House'
Eye-catching modern architecture

One of Prague's best-known modern buildings is the eye-catching **Dancing House** *(Tančící dům; free to view)*, along the Vltava's Rašínovo embankment. The building was designed in 1996 by architects Vlado Milunić and Frank Gehry. The curved lines of the narrow-waisted glass tower clutched against its more upright and formal partner led to it being christened the 'Fred & Ginger' building, after the legendary dancing duo. The Dancing House is home to a cocktail bar and **hotel** *(dancinghousehotel.com; €€)* with great views. Come back at night to find the building bathed in colourful lighting.

FUTURE PLANS FOR WENCESLAS SQUARE

Ever since 1989, Prague's urban planners have been working overtime to reverse the destructive public-works projects carried out by the former communist government. Arguably the most egregious of these was the building of the main highway (called the *magistrale*) that runs between the National Museum and Wenceslas Square and regrettably cuts the space in two.

Maybe the project that Praguers are looking forward to most of all, though, is the conversion of Wenceslas Square into a car-free, parklike oasis. The project calls for the planting of hundreds of trees and even restoring regular tram service to the square by 2027. Construction crews have been on the job since 2023.

 DRINKING IN NOVÉ MĚSTO: BEST FOR COFFEE

Cukrárna Myšák: Historic confectionery from 1911, with top-notch traditional cakes and sweets, breakfasts and coffee. *8am-7pm Mon-Fri, from 9am Sat & Sun*

EMA Espresso Bar: Serves fine artisanal coffee in a cool, white, high-ceilinged, art-gallery-like space, with a communal table. *8am-6pm Mon-Fri, from 10am Sat & Sun*

Cafe Louvre: Old-school, Viennese-style grand cafe, as popular as in the early 1900s, frequented by Kafka and Einstein. *8am-11.30pm Mon-Fri, from 9am Sat & Sun*

Globe Bookstore & Café: Popular, expat-run shop. Decent coffee, English books, American-style brunch, open mic and quiz nights. *10am-11pm Mon-Fri, 9.30am-12.30am Sat, 9.30am-10.30pm Sun*

POKE AROUND WENCESLAS SQUARE

This relaxed stroll around Wenceslas Square hits the square's high – and some of its hidden – points.

START	END	LENGTH
Statue of St Wenceslas	Wenceslas Square	1.5km; 45 minutes

Begin at the ❶ **Statue of St Wenceslas** (p100). A flowerbed downhill from the statue contains a Memorial to the Victims of Communism. Wander the middle of the square, admiring the impressive buildings, such as the ❷ **Grand Hotel Evropa** (p101) (No 25). Opposite (at No 36) is the ❸ **Melantrich Building** (p101), where the death of communism was pronounced by Alexander Dubček and Václav Havel in November 1989.

Walk into Pasáž Rokoko (near No 36). It leads to the central atrium of the ❹ **Lucerna Palace** (p101), dominated by David Černý's *Kůň* (p103). Exit Lucerna Palace onto Vodičkova, and bear right across the street to enter ❺ **Světozor arcade**, with a beautiful stained-glass window advertising Tesla radios, dating from the late 1940s.

At the far end of the arcade, turn left into the ❻ **Franciscan Garden** (p108), a hidden oasis of peace. Exit diagonally opposite into Jungmannovo náměstí and go past the arch leading to the ❼ **Church of Our Lady of the Snows** – once meant to be the grandest church in Prague, but never completed.

Keep to the right to find what must be the only ❽ **Cubist Lamp Post** in the world, dating from 1915. Turn left here and then right through the arcade at the **Lindt Building** (p101) to re-emerge at the bottom of ❾ **Wenceslas Square** (p100).

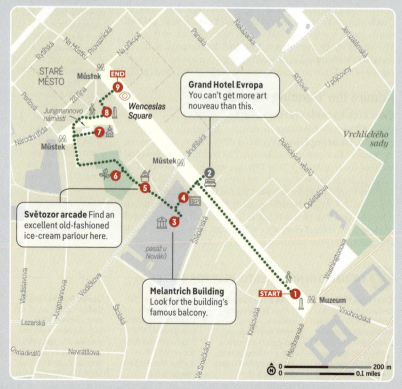

Tour the National Theatre
See inside Czechia's leading stage

The **National Theatre** *(narodni-divadlo.cz; tour adult/child 260/160Kč)* is the city's most prestigious venue for dramatic works as well as opera and dance. Check out the website ahead of your visit for the current programme. What many visitors may not know is that it's also possible to book a guided tour of the storied building itself. Tours run for the 50 minutes and visit the most important rooms of this neo-Renaissance flagship of the 19th century Czech National Revival. Architect Josef Zítek's masterpiece was funded entirely by private donations from across the land and the building was decorated inside and out by a roll call of prominent Czech artists. It burned down within weeks of its 1881 opening but, incredibly, was funded again and restored in less than two years.

Best-Known Czech Composer
Visit the Dvořák Museum

The **Dvořák Museum** *(nm.cz; adult/child 70/50Kč)* is dedicated to the life and work of Czech composer Antonín Dvořák and is probably only really for diehard fans. The museum is set in the Vila Amerika, a French-style, baroque summerhouse designed in the 1720s by the baroque master Kilian Dientzenhofer. Special concerts of Dvořák's music are occasionally staged here between May and October.

Climb the New Town Hall Tower
Prague's 'first' defenestration

Admittedly, while the **New Town Hall** *(nrpraha.cz; adult/child 60/40Kč)* has been around for several centuries (built in the late 14th century), it's not nearly as picturesque as the rival **Old Town Hall** (p82). The building's historical high (or low?) point came in 1419, when two of King Wenceslas IV's Catholic councillors were flung to their deaths by followers of the Hussite preacher Jan Želivský. That event sparked the bloody Hussite Wars that

ANOTHER TRAGIC DEFENESTRATION
Prague's other defenestration, sometimes called the 'Second Defenestration', took place in 1618 at **Prague Castle** (p56). Like this first window-pushing, this one also ignited a catastrophic European war.

HISTORY-MAKING NEW TOWN

When Nové Město (New Town) was laid out in the 14th century, it was one of the most important urban-planning projects of medieval Europe. The town was the brainchild of Emperor Charles IV, who wanted to build a city whose size was commensurate with its leading role within the Holy Roman Empire. When the New Town was finished in 1378, Prague became the third-largest city by area in Europe.

Nové Město's design incorporated enormous town squares, such as today's Wenceslas Square and even-larger Charles Square (Karlovo náměstí). The new settlement was open to anyone. Lots were parcelled out tax-free for 12 years, provided that the new owner would begin building a stone house on the land within 18 months.

If you only have duck once, make it here.

 EATING IN NOVÉ MĚSTO: OUR PICKS

Kantýna: Choose your own piece of meat for the chefs to prepare, and enjoy in an opulent former bank building. *11.30am-11pm* €€

Čestr: Splurge-worthy steakhouse behind 'New Building' of the National Museum. Pair a meal with visiting the museum or State Opera. *noon-11pm* €€€

Garden's: A passage opposite the entrance to the Lucerna Palace leads to a secret garden. Book ahead. *11am-10pm Mon-Sat, to 8pm Sun* €€

Hostinec na Výtoni: Picturesque inn by the river doing duck dishes better than anyone else in town. *11.30am-11pm* €€

Paratroopers memorial, Church of Sts Cyril & Methodius

STORY OF THE PARATROOPERS

During the German occupation in WWII, Britain secretly trained a team of Czechoslovak paratroopers to assassinate the local Nazi leader, Reinhard Heydrich. On 27 May 1942, two paratroopers, Jan Kubiš and Jozef Gabčík, attacked Heydrich as he rode in his official car through Prague's Libeň district – he later died from his wounds. The Nazis reacted to the assassination with a frenzied wave of terror, which included the annihilation of the Czech village where the assassination took place, **Lidice** (p156).

The and five co-conspirators and two assassins fled but were betrayed in their hiding place in the **Church of Sts Cyril & Methodius** (p106), now the National Memorial to the Heroes of the Heydrich Terror. All seven died in the ensuing siege.

would last a century, and gave the word 'defenestration' a lasting political meaning. Visitors can see the opulent Gothic Hall of Justice – the site of the defenestration – and climb the 221 steps (no lift) to the top of the tower.

Honour the 'Paratroopers'

National Memorial to the Heroes of the Heydrich Terror

The **Church of Sts Cyril & Methodius** *(vhu.cz; free)* houses a moving memorial to the seven Czechoslovak paratroopers who were involved in the assassination of German Reichsprotektor Reinhard Heydrich in 1942, with an exhibit and video about Nazi persecution of the Czechs.

The paratroopers hid in the church's crypt for three weeks after the killing, until their hiding place was betrayed. Three paratroopers were killed in the ensuing fight; the other four

Friendly sommeliers help you choose.

 DRINKING IN NOVÉ MĚSTO: BEST FOR WINE & COCKTAILS

Hoffa: Crowded cocktail bar with sleek, functional decor. Overlooks Senovážné náměstí's fountain. Great cocktails. *11am-2am Mon-Fri, from 6pm Sat*

Q Cafe: Low-key LBGTIQ+-friendly drinks bar attracts a youthful clientele. *3pm-2am*

Alcron Bar: Enjoy high-end cocktails in a gorgeous, jazz-age, art-deco-inflected space inside the Almanac X Alcron Prague hotel. *2pm-midnight*

Vinograf: Appealingly modern wine bar with knowledgeable staff – a great place to discover Moravian wines. *11.30am-midnight Mon-Sat*

took their own lives. In the crypt itself, note the bullet marks and shrapnel scars on the walls, and signs of the paratroopers' last desperate efforts to dig an escape tunnel to the sewer under the street. The memorial is open 9am–5pm, Tuesday–Sunday.

Hang Out at Náplavka
Lively riverbank and farmers market

Praguers have rediscovered the Nové Město waterfront in recent years. The most popular spot is **Náplavka** *(farmarsketrziste.cz; free)*, which starts below the Dancing House (p103) and runs for 2km south to the Výtoň tram stop. Saturday is the most popular day when farmers set up stalls along the river. The market runs from 8am to 3pm. That said, any nice evening in summer brings out thousands of revellers to sit along the banks and relax with a wine or beer.

Explore the Vltava Islands
Find peace from the madding crowds

The quickest way to escape the crowds in this busy part of the city is to walk out to one of the islands floating just offshore in the Vltava. Beautiful **Slovanský ostrov** *(Slav Island; free)* has been magnificently manicured and has an extensive playground at the southern end. From April to October, hire a **pedalboat** *(per hr 300Kč)* for some self-propelled fun out on the water. Rental companies operate daily from 11am to 10pm. Pack a lunch and a bottle of wine to celebrate once you're out on the water. **Střelecký ostrov** *(Marksmen's Island; free)* is bigger and more peaceful. Bring a drink, find a bench and stare out into the water.

Go Cycling Along the River
A few hours on the bike

One of the city's most scenic (and flattest) cycling routes begins in Nové Město and follows the Vltava River south for at least 20km. Find the trail, signposted as the A2, along the embankment just below the Dancing House (p103). The trail doesn't require any special cycling skill. Plan on around four hours out-and-back. Rent bikes at **Praha Bike** *(prahabike.cz; from 400Kč per 3hr rental)* or from local bike-share operator **Rekola** *(rekola.cz; 35Kč per 30 min)*; download the app and look for stands with pink bikes.

Newest (Old) Museum in the City
Newly refurbished Prague City Museum

The **Prague City Museum** *(muzeumprahy.cz)* was still closed at the time of research but set to reopen in 2025 amid much fanfare after a long renovation. Check the website for the current status, open hours and admission prices. This underrated museum is devoted to the history of Prague, from prehistoric times to the 20th century (exhibits are signposted in English as well as Czech).

BEST FOR A FUN NIGHT OUT

State Opera *(narodni-divadlo.cz)*: Prague's preeminent venue for opera is heavy on traditional Italian opera at a very high standard.

National Theatre *(narodni-divadlo.cz)*: Performs virtually anything, from Czech opera to avant-garde dance.

Reduta Jazz Club *(redutajazzclub.cz)*: Smartly dressed patrons squeeze into tiered seats and lounges to soak up the big-band, swing and Dixieland.

Lucerna Music Bar *(musicbar.cz)*: Host all kinds of live rock bands – from Czech superstars to visiting indie rockers from around the world.

Duplex *(duplex.cz)*: Visiting live DJs, several rooms, rooftop chillout zone. Often considered the best dance club in town.

LESS 'NEW' BUT VIBRANT

Eva Brejlová was born and raised in Prague and leads tour guides for Eating Prague (eatingeurope.com/prague).

To our guests, I love to say how Prague's New Town is less 'new' than it seems. When Charles IV founded New Town in 1348, it was the largest building site in Europe.

New Town is a vibrant part of the city but if you walk on **Wenceslas Square** (p100), you can still visualise the medieval square as its original purpose: a horse market. It's also full of 'passages' – intricate systems of covered shortcuts with cafes, restaurants and theatres.

The most famous is **Lucerna Palace** (p101). New Town also has a 'tranquil oasis': the **Franciscan Garden**, with some pretty rose bushes.

Jubilee Synagogue

Among the many intriguing exhibits certain to reappear is Antonín Langweil's astonishing 1:480 scale model of Prague as it looked from 1826 to 1834. The display is most rewarding after you get to know Prague a bit, as you can spot the changes. Look at St Vitus Cathedral, for example, still only half-finished.

Be Wowed by the Jubilee Synagogue

Lavish Moorish facade

Tucked down a side street near the main train station, the colourful Moorish facade of the **Jubilee Synagogue** (synagogue.cz; adult/child 150/100Kč), also called the Jerusalem Synagogue, practically jumps off the street. The building dates from 1906; note the names of the donors on the stained-glass windows. Peek inside to find an exhibition of photographs and films charting the post-WWII history of Prague's Jewish community.

 DRINKING IN NOVÉ MĚSTO: BEST PUBS — *Touristy but worth it for the beer.*

U Šumavy: Authentic Czech pub – handsome drinking room; decent food, excellent beers on tap. *11am-11pm Mon-Fri, from noon Sat & Sun*	**Pivovar Národní:** Lots of seating here makes this a good choice. Ambitious, delicious list of craft beers, good grilled dishes. *11am-11:30pm*	**U Pinkasů:** Legendary pub often overrun with visitors. Try for an outdoor table behind the pub, fronting the Church of Our Lady of the Snows. *10am-10.30pm*	**U Fleků:** Ancient pub and Prague institution. Often busy with tour groups, but purists go for excellent home-brewed dark beer. *10am-11pm*

Žižkov & Karlín

HILLSIDE PUBS, RIVERSIDE REVIVAL

Many a night has been spent – and lost – at a Žižkov pub. This hilly, traditionally working-class quarter, east of the centre, is easily Prague's rowdiest neighbourhood, with only a few tourist attractions. It is a place to unwind after a long day of sightseeing. Many of the steep streets are filled with pubs that haven't changed much since the quarter's heyday 100 years ago. To Žižkov's south and east are two important cemeteries, including the New Jewish Cemetery, Franz Kafka's final resting place.

The adjacent riverfront district of Karlín, north of the National Monument, is connected to Žižkov via a long pedestrian tunnel. Like other neighbourhoods along the Vltava, Karlín was flooded in 2002 and has since been rebuilding. The transformation has been nothing short of miraculous. It's now one of Prague's most sought-after residential neighbourhoods, with lovely art-nouveau buildings housing dozens of good restaurants, cafes, pubs and wine bars.

GETTING AROUND

There are no metro stations in Žižkov, though several stations on metro Line A (green line), including Jiřího z Poděbrad, Flora and Želivského, pass within walking distance. Trams 5, 9, 15 and 26 run through Žižkov.

Karlín lies on metro line B (yellow line), stations Florenc and Křižíkova. The quarter is accessible by trams 3, 8 and 24. Žižkov and Karlín are linked by a narrow pedestrian tunnel that runs from Husitská street on the Žižkov side to Pernerova street in Karlín.

Find Kafka's Grave
The author's final resting place

Pay your respects to famed writer and Prague native Franz Kafka at the **New Jewish Cemetery** *(kehilaprag.cz; free)*. To find Kafka's evocative, Cubist-style **grave-marker**, follow the main avenue east, turn right at row 21, then left at the wall. You'll also find a small plaque to commemorate Kafka's sisters. Many visitors choose to make the pilgrimage on 3 June, the anniversary of Kafka's death.

The cemetery is easy to reach by metro Line A (green line): stop Želivského. Note that male visitors to the cemetery should cover their heads (yarmulkes are available). The cemetery is open 9am–4pm Sunday–Thursday, to 2pm Friday.

☑ TOP TIP

Both Karlín and Žižkov offer good evening options. Karlín tends to be stronger on restaurants; Žižkov for pubs and bars (though Karlín has plenty of these too). The Karlín riverfront and the **HolKa pedestrian bridge** (p131) are popular spots for strolling and enjoying the river.

HIGHLIGHTS
1. National Monument on Vítkov Hill

SIGHTS
2. Army Museum
3. Forum Karlín
4. Jan Palach's grave
5. Jan Žižka statue
6. Kafka's grave
7. New Jewish Cemetery
8. Olšany Cemetery
9. Palác Akropolis
10. TV Tower

ACTIVITIES
11. Žižkov Highline

SLEEPING
12. Botanique Hotel
13. Brix Hostel
14. Hotel Fitzgerald
15. Hotel Mucha
16. Hotel Royal Prague

EATING
17. Eska
18. Lokál Hamburk
19. Nejen Bistro
20. Proti Proudu

21. The Tavern

DRINKING & NIGHTLIFE
22. Bukowski's
23. Dva Kohouti
24. Etapa
25. Můj Šálek Kávy
26. Přístav 18600
27. U Houdků
28. U Sadu
29. U Vystřeleného oka
30. Veltlin

ENTERTAINMENT
31. Kasárna Karlín

 DRINKING IN ŽIŽKOV: BEST WATERING HOLES

Gets rowdy after midnight.

U Vystřeleného oka: A wild bohemian hostelry with a raucous Friday-night atmosphere where just about anything goes. *4.30pm-1am Mon-Sat*

U Sadu: Popular, slightly upscale (compared to rest of this list) pub, with its very own 'Sádek' beer. *8am-4am Tue-Sat, to 2am Sun & Mon*

U Houdků: Classic boozer on pub-strewn Bořivojova street. Decent Czech food and a secluded summertime beer garden. *11am-midnight*

Bukowski's: More 'dive' than cocktail bar, but beloved for its debauched rep and generous closing times. *7pm-3am*

Gawk at Žižkov TV Tower
Complete with crawling giant babies

Prague's tallest landmark – and either its ugliest or its most futuristic feature – is the 216m-tall **TV Tower** *(towerpark.cz; adult/child 300/230Kč)*, erected between 1985 and 1992. The tower's original purpose allegedly was to jam incoming anti-communist broadcasts from Radio Free Europe and the BBC, but it quickly became obsolete. The 93m-high observation decks are fitted out with comfortable sofas and futuristic hanging armchairs. There's also a cafe and restaurant at the 66m level, and even a luxury one-room hotel.

More eye-catching than its architecture may well be the giant crawling babies that appear to be exploring the outside of the tower – an installation called *Miminka* (1999) by artist David Černý. Perhaps the installation represents our own childlike dependence on technology?

Catch Some Live Music
Enjoy the legendary clubs

Žižkov and Karlín both have excellent venues for catching a live show. **Palác Akropolis** *(palacakropolis.cz)* is a former theatre that's been transformed into a labyrinthine, sticky-floored shrine to alternative music and drama. Its various performance spaces host a smorgasbord of musical and cultural events, from DJs and string quartets to local rock gods and visiting talent. **Forum Karlín** *(forumkarlin.cz)* is a spacious, thoroughly modern concert hall that attracts the best international bands on tour in Central Europe. Check the websites to see a programme.

Explore the Army Museum
Dazzling, distracting collection of weapons

The **Army Museum** *(Armádní muzeum; vhu.cz; free)* has had a thoroughgoing renovation but remains a niche attraction of interest mainly to military buffs. The exhibitions of weapons, guns and other artefacts are divided into seven historical periods, running from the 18th century to the present day, and presented over four busy floors. Pick up a map at the door and focus on the periods and exhibitions that correspond to your own interests.

Prague's Largest Cemetery
Sprawling and lovely Olšany cemetery

Prague's main burial ground, **Olšany Cemetery** *(hrbitovy.cz; free)*, lacks the arresting beauty of the Vyšehrad Cemetery (p150) or the star power of the New Jewish Cemetery (p109), but it is peaceful and pretty. It was founded in 1680 to handle increased deaths during a plague epidemic. The most prominent grave belongs to **Jan Palach**, the student who set

INDEPENDENCE-MINDED ŽIŽKOV

Žižkov takes its name from legendary Hussite military leader Jan Žižka, now immortalised on horseback atop **Vítkov Hill** (p112). Žižka's peasant army won a decisive battle near here against the forces of the Holy Roman Empire on 14 July 1420.

Prior to 1922, Žižkov was an independent city. As a traditionally working-class area, Žižkov enjoyed a reputation for left-wing revolutionary fervour – well before the communist takeover of 1948.

After the fall of communism, Žižkov became known mainly for its grungy nightlife. While it's slowly cleaning itself up, the neighbourhood still offers some of the most authentic pub-crawl experiences in Prague. Be prepared for sticky floors and wall-to-wall noise.

THE TRAGEDY OF JAN PALACH

The **site** (p101) where student Jan Palach set himself ablaze to protest the 1968 Warsaw Pact invasion is located at the top of Wenceslas Square – it is designated by a cross on the pavement.

TOP EXPERIENCE

National Monument on Vítkov Hill

Žižkov's main tourist attraction is visible from all across the city (and we're not talking about the TV Tower). The district's prominent Vítkov Hill is home to one of the world's largest equestrian statues – of 15th-century Hussite general (and Czech hero) Jan Žižka. It's also the location of a sleek National Monument that celebrates Czechoslovak statehood and hides some bizarre communist-era secrets.

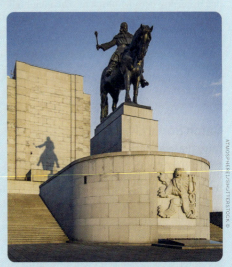

Hail to the Heroes!

The monument was originally conceived in the 1930s as a tribute to the heroes of newly independent Czechoslovakia, but was used first by the occupying Nazis in the 1940s and later by Czechoslovakia's own communist leaders to serve their propaganda ends. The interior is a startling extravaganza of polished art-deco marble, gilt and mosaics. The structure is so distinctive that the directors of Netflix's 2022 blockbuster *The Gray Man* even used it as a stand-in for a dictator's mega-palace in Azerbaijan.

Fascinating or Gruesome?

The most grimly fascinating part of the building is the Frankenstein-like laboratory on the lower level. It was here, following the death of Czechoslovak communist leader Klement Gottwald in 1953, where scientists battled in vain to prevent Gottwald's corpse from decomposing. The original plan was to preserve his body in state – not unlike Lenin at Moscow's Lenin Mausoleum. Gottwald's body was placed on display by day and lowered into the white-tiled crypt here each night for a frantic round of maintenance and repair. He was eventually removed and buried in Prague's Olšany Cemetery (p111).

TOP TIPS

● The main entry ticket allows access to the entire building, including museum, Gottwald laboratory and a Memorial to the Unknown Soldier.

● Find a small cafe on the top floor for refreshments.

● The upper-level space offers panoramic views out over neighbouring Žižkov and the Žižkov TV Tower.

Olšany Cemetery (p111)

himself on fire in January 1969 to protest the 1968 Soviet-led invasion. To find Palach's grave, enter the main gate on Vinohradská and turn right – it's 50m along on the left.

Walk the Žižkov 'Highline'
Žižkov from the back side

It's not quite New York City's more-famous highline, but this former elevated railway line has been transformed into a popular recreation trail for walkers, cyclists and rollerbladers. Pick up the **Žižkov Highline** *(free)* at an overpass on the western end of Seifertova street and follow it eastward as it runs behind some colourful Žižkov townhouses all the way to the pedestrian tunnel that leads to Karlín. The trail passes below the National Monument on Vítkov Hill (p112). The highline also runs behind a popular Žižkov pub, U Vystřeleného oka (p110).

AN INSIDER'S SCOOP ON ŽIŽKOV

Lori Wyant, an American who has lived in Vinohrady for almost three decades, co-owns and operates **The Tavern** (p122).

In the early 1990s, I lived in Žižkov, then known for having the smokiest, seediest pubs in town. Today Žižkov 2.0 has more wine bars, cafes, galleries and funky clothing shops than dive bars.

Additionally, city planners have developed peaceful stretches of urban greenery and scenic bike routes, and have rallied to protect the area's bucolic gardening zones.

The **Žižkov Highline** (p113), a multiuse pedestrian path, winds around the base of the **National Monument** (p112) through old vineyards, where you can experience a greener side of Prague – and you might even wander across some old-school Žižkov pubs along the way!

The speciality 'Potatoes in Ash' is better than it sounds.

 EATING IN KARLÍN: OUR PICKS

Nejen Bistro: Super steaks, ribs and burgers. Softly illuminated dining room feels even cosier in evenings. *11am-11pm Mon-Fri, noon-10pm Sat* €€

Proti Proudu: One of best loved bistros and cafes. All-day breakfasts and sandwiches. Limited seating. *8.30am-10pm Mon-Fri, 9am-6pm Sat* €€

Lokál Hamburk: Updated take on a traditional Czech pub is arguably Karlín's most popular gathering spot. *11am-10.30pm* €€

Eska: Artisanal bakery and industrial-chic restaurant. Great breakfasts – like locally sourced ham and soft-boiled eggs. *8am-11.30pm Mon-Fri, from 9am Sat & Sun* €€

HolKa pedestrian bridge

KARLÍN SUCCESS STORY

Of all of Prague's outlying neighbourhoods, Karlín is the area that has changed most since the 1989 fall of communism. Starting in 19th and early-20th centuries, the neighbourhood had been characterised by a mix of industrial lofts and warehouses, sprinkled about with pretty art-nouveau houses. In the run-up to 1989, Karlín had fallen into disrepair and neglect.

The catalyst for change was the 2002 Prague flood. Low-level Karlín was inundated and laid waste. Since those days, the neighbourhood has benefitted greatly from a dedicated clean-up and rebuilding effort. The result – astonishingly for Prague residents – has been Karlín's rebirth as one of the city's most-desirable and attractive residential areas.

Chill Out at Kasárna Karlín
Military barracks turned culture centre

For a taste of Karlín's growing cultural aspirations, drop by the **Kasárna Karlín** *(kasarnakarlin.cz; 1-11.30pm Mon-Fri, from 10am Sat & Sun; free)*, a popular hangout set in a former military barracks. Depending on the day, catch an outdoor film, concert, art exhibition or maybe a sports competition. There's also a children's playground and unique cafe located in a former swimming pool.

Drink & Cross the River
Karlín by the water

Karlín has rediscovered its riverfront, and the district's shady embankment is a pretty spot to relax over a beer. In warm weather, shaggy **Přístav 18600** *(18600.cz; noon-10.30pm May-Sep)* serves as an impromptu, open-air beer garden, with a couple of beer kiosks and a few scattered tables and oversized pieces of concrete to sit on. After a beer or two, follow the path west and walk over the HolKa pedestrian bridge (p131) to Šťávnice Island and further on to Holešovice Market (p131). The crossing and views out over the river are especially pretty at sunset.

DRINKING IN KARLÍN: OUR PICKS

Dva Kohouti: Excellent craft brews from local brewer Matuška and big shared outdoor drinking terrace. *3pm-1am Mon-Fri, from noon Sat & Sun*

Etapa: Relaxed neighbourhood coffee shop. Speciality coffees and daily all-vegetarian brunch. Good for gluten-free. *9am-5pm*

Můj Šálek Kávy: 'My Cup of Coffee' uses speciality 'Doubleshot' beans. Good breakfasts and lunches too. *9am-9pm Mon-Sat, 10am-6pm Sun*

Veltlin: Fun and friendly wine bar. Clued-up staff give an easy introduction to less-frequented corners of the oenophile atlas. *5-11pm Mon-Sat*

Vinohrady & Vršovice

REGAL AND ROWDY

Centuries before Czechia was famous for beer, Prague was widely known for its wine, and much of it was grown here in Vinohrady ('vineyards'), now an upscale residential neighbourhood. Some vineyards can still be seen in the pretty hillside park, Havlíčkovy sady. The rows of elegant 19th- and early-20th-century apartment buildings here, along handsome treelined streets, are home to some of Prague's most-prosperous citizens. This concentration of wealth helps support many excellent restaurants and cafes. Vinohrady is also the heart of Prague's LGBTIQ+ community and home to gay-friendly clubs and bars.

The adjacent quarter of Vršovice, south and east, is a mixed industrial and residential neighbourhood that has gained new life in recent years as a party 'hood, particularly along narrow Krymská street, near the area's boundary with Vinohrady. On weekend nights you'll find revellers standing outside bars and clubs while clutching a beer or cocktail and enjoying the evening air.

Pretty Rieger Gardens
Beer and sunset photo-ops

The spacious **Rieger Gardens** *(Riegrovy Sady; free)* are modelled on a classic 19th-century English garden and the area is a favourite among residents for strolling, jogging or simply walking the family dog. The park encloses a cosy **beer garden** that's open 4pm–midnight, May to September. The high-altitude bluff towards the back of the park affords astonishing photo-ops of the Old Town and Prague Castle in the distance. It's especially pretty at sunset with Prague Castle in the distant backdrop.

continued on p119

GETTING AROUND

Vinohrady is easy to reach from the centre by metro. Line A (green line) stops at both of the quarter's main commercial hubs: Náměstí Míru and Jiřího z Poděbrad. Tram 11 conveniently runs between Muzeum, at the top of Wenceslas Square, to Jiřího z Poděbrad and beyond. Tram 22, sometimes called the 'tourist' tram because its circuit passes several important sights, stops at Náměstí Míru before continuing on to Vršovice. Tram lines 4, 10 and 16 also service Vršovice.

☑ **TOP TIP**

Vinohrady is a great neighbourhood to leave the crowds behind and go local. Favourite activities of residents here include catching a sunset over Prague Castle in the distance from Rieger Gardens or hitting the farmers market at Jiřího z Poděbrad and following up with a coffee at a nearby cafe.

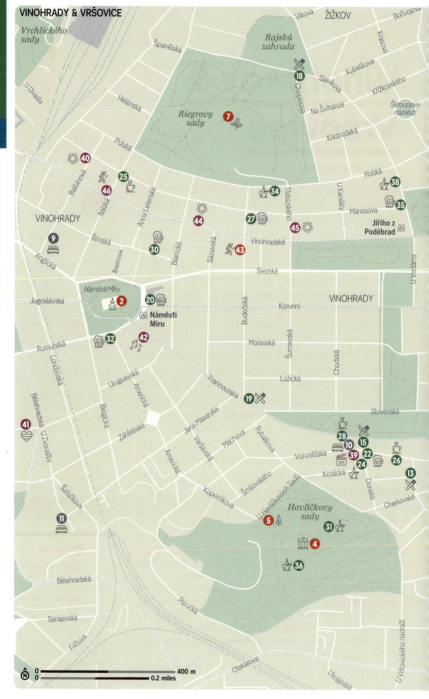

HIGHLIGHTS
1. Church of the Most Sacred Heart of Our Lord

SIGHTS
2. Church of Saint Ludmila
3. Ďolíček Stadium
4. Gröbe Villa
5. Havlíček Gardens
6. Jiřího z Poděbrad Square
7. Rieger Gardens
8. TV Tower

SLEEPING
9. Arkada
10. Czech Inn
11. Le Palais Hotel

EATING
12. Cafe Jen
13. Cafe Sladkovský
14. El Camino Tapas Restaurant
15. Jam and Co.
16. Kro Kitchen
17. La Farma
18. The Tavern
19. U Bulínů
20. Vinohradský Parlament
21. Výčep

DRINKING & NIGHTLIFE
22. Bad Flash Bar
23. Beer Geek
24. Café Bar Pilotů
25. Café Kaaba
26. Cafe V Lese
27. Hospoda U Benyho
28. Kavárna Šlágr
29. Le Caveau
30. Ossegg
31. Pavilon Grébovka
32. Prague Beer Museum
33. Ráno Kavu Večer Víno
34. Saints
35. U Růžového Sadu
36. Viniční Altán
37. Vinohradský Pivovar
38. Vinotéka Noelka

ENTERTAINMENT
39. Kino Pilotů
40. Le Clan
41. Piano Bar
42. Retro Cocktail & Music Bar
43. Royal Theatre
44. Techtle Mechtle
45. Termix
45. Tresor Club

TOP EXPERIENCE

Church of the Most Sacred Heart of Our Lord

The striking Church of the Most Sacred Heart of Our Lord dominates Vinohrady's liveliest square, Jiřího z Poděbrad. The church, finished in 1932, is arguably Prague's most-original piece of 20th-century architecture. Fans of early-modern architecture might recognise the hand of Slovenian master Jože Plečnik, best-known for decorating his home capital of Ljubljana with dozens of signature, UNESCO-protected bridges and buildings.

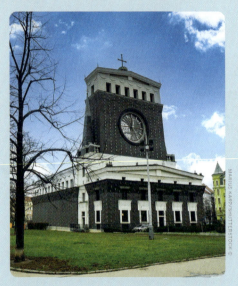

Oversized Clock Tower

Like all of Plečnik's creations, the appearance of the church is both highly modern and yet also evokes classical elements, including the three oversized portals at the front facade. The overall design of the church is said to be based on early-Christian structures. The shape recalls the outlines of a large boat – perhaps Noah's Ark (you'll have to squint pretty hard to see the resemblance). The church's signature element is its enormous clock tower, featuring a clock face diameter of nearly 8m. It's topped with a 3m copper dome and 4m-high cross.

Minimalist Interiors

The stark interiors are just as eye-catching. The main altar, crafted from white marble, is dominated by a statue of Christ as well as the figures of six Czech patron saints (St John of Nepomuk, St Agnes, St Adalbert, St Wenceslaus, St Ludmila and St Procopius). The lack of a pulpit is intentional and marks the church as a piece of modern architecture. The church is normally closed to the public, but opens for sightseers a half hour before mass times and stays open 30 minutes after mass is over.

TOP TIPS

● Jiřího z Poděbrad square was undergoing thoroughgoing renovation at the time of research, and access to the church might be restricted during your visit.

● Check the website for mass times or special events to get a glimpse of the interior.

Practicalities
Scan this QR code for service times.

continued from p115

Drink & Dine on 'JZP'
Farmers market, cafes and people-watching

Always-active **Jiřího z Poděbrad Square** – *Jiřák* to Czechs and shortened (for pronunciation purposes) by non-Czech speakers to simply 'JZP' – is dominated by the starkly modern **Church of the Most Sacred Heart of Our Lord** (p118). The square hosts a popular daytime farmers market that runs Wednesday to Saturday.

JZP is surrounded by dozens of cafes, bars and trendy restaurants. French cafe **Le Caveau** *(broz-d.cz)* is perfect to relax in with coffee or French wine. It also has delicious pastries, sandwiches and cheeses. **Kro Kitchen's** *(krokitchen. cz)* rotisserie chicken makes for an ideal lunch, with a great bakery next door. **Beer Geek** *(beergeek.cz)* has 32 taps and specialises in local craft beers. **U Růžového Sadu** *(uruzovehosadu.cz)* is a classic Czech pub, directly across from the Jiřího z Poděbrad metro station.

Party on Krymská Street
A taste of Vršovice nightlife

On weekend nights, many Praguers decamp to Vršovice's hilly Krymská street for a night of drinking and carousing. Try **Café V Lese** *(cafevlese.cz; 4pm-2am Mon-Sat, to midnight Sun)* for live music. The arthouse cinema **Kino Pilotů** *(kinopilotu.cz)* is a great place to catch an offbeat film, and then repair to the cosy, adjoining **Café Bar Pilotů** *(facebook.com/cafebarpilotu; 7pm-1am)* for an aftershow drink. **Bad Flash Bar** *(badflash-krymska.cz; 5pm-1am)* serves a dozen craft beers on tap.

Don't Forget Vinohrady's Pubs
The land of microbrews and craft beers

The neighbourhood's name may translate as 'vineyards', but Vinohrady also has excellent pubs and microbrewers. Both popular **Vinohradský Pivovar** *(vinohradskypivovar.cz; 11am-midnight Mon-Sat, to 10pm Sun)* and **Ossegg** *(praha.ossegg. com; 11am-11pm)* brew their own and serve good Czech food. Náměstí Míru's **Prague Beer Museum** *(praguebeermuseum. cz; Noon-1am)* keeps 30 different beers on tap. Across the street, **Vinohradský Parlament** *(vinohradskyparlament.cz; 11.30am-11pm)* toes the line between classic pub and upscale

BEST LATE-NIGHT CLUBS

Le Clan *(leclan.cz):*
Afterparty club. DJs on two floors, lots of bars and myriad rooms with people partying until dawn.

Techtle Mechtle *(techtle-mechtle.cz):*
Popular dance club and cocktail bar attracting local celebs and the hoi-polloi. Arrive early for a table.

Tresor Club *(tresorclub.cz):*
Special Latin, salsa and other themed dance nights on a weekly basis.

Retro Cocktail & Music Bar *(retrococktailbar.cz):*
Disco, concerts, cocktail bar and flashy restaurant. Not much 'retro' but plenty of contemporary hip-hop and dance.

Royal Theatre *(leroyal.cz):*
Gorgeous 1930s throwback in a former cinema repurposed as cabaret, burlesque and party spot.

Order the Větrník, a Czech profiterole.

 DRINKING IN VINOHRADY: BEST CAFES & BARS

| Café Kaaba: Stylish cafe-bar with retro furniture and pastel-coloured decor. *8am-midnight Mon-Fri, from 9am Sat, 10am Sun* | Vinotéka Noelka: Do like the locals and stop over at this busy *vinothèque* for a glass or two. Great selection of Czech wines. *11am-7.30pm* | Hospoda U Benyho: Old dessert shop revamped as retro Czech pub. Unbeatable goulash, matched with perfectly poured Pilsner. *4-10pm* | Kavárna Šlágr: Old-fashioned bakery–cafe with a big pastry counter; feels like stepping back into the last century. *9am-7pm* |

PRAGUE'S WINE HISTORY

Andrea Kotašková, born in Vinohrady, is the owner of Wine Travel in Czech *(wine travelinczech.com)*.

The first written documents about wine culture in Prague date from the 11th century. The earliest vineyards in Prague were located below **Petřín** (p66). At the time, wine was used primarily for liturgical purposes.

The great boom in wine production came in the 14th century with the reign of Emperor Charles IV. Prague was the leading city of the Holy Roman Empire at that time and Charles reasoned that the city should have the wine quality to match its status.

Charles issued several wine laws and brought to Bohemia varietals from Burgundy, including grapes like Pinot Noir, that are still popular today.

---

restaurant. **U Bulínů** *(restauraceubulinu.cz; 11am-11pm)* pairs a classic pub with delicious traditional cooking.

Hike & 'Wine' at Grébovka
Enjoy Vinohrady's actual vineyards

Havlíček Gardens *(Havlíčkovy sady; free),* known as 'Grébovka' by residents, occupies a steep hillside at the southern end of Americká street. The park was inspired by Italian neo-Renaissance design and it's a small piece of paradise, with hidden grottoes, fountains, big rocks and finely manicured ponds. The garden at the **Gröbe Villa** *(villagrebovka.cz; garden free)* has stunning vistas and two nearby venues for sampling wine: **Pavilon Grébovka** *(pavilongrebovka.cz; 10am-10pm)* and **Viniční Altán** *(altangrebovka.cz; noon-10pm)*, a wooden gazebo overlooking the vineyard.

Go Dancing at Termix
Gay-friendly Vinohrady

Vinohrady has evolved into the informal epicentre of Prague's LGBTIQ+ community, and the ever-lively **Termix** *(clubtermix.cz; 10pm-6am Wed-Sat)* dance club is a good place to experience the energy and vitality. Weekend nights draw a mixed crowd of gay and straight partiers. Termix is within easy walking distance of the **Saints** *(praguesaints.cz; 7pm-1am Sun-Thu, to 2am Fri & Sat)*, a convivial bar and good entrée to the local scene for newcomers. **Piano Bar** *(piano-bar.cz; 5-10pm)* is another welcoming Vinohrady spot and features regular drag shows, karaoke nights and bingo.

Admire the Church of Saint Ludmila
Spiritual heart of Vinohrady

For Praguers, the beautiful, Gothic-revival **Church of Saint Ludmila** (Kostel sv Ludmily; *ludmila vinohrady.cz; free),* on central Náměstí Míru, symbolises the heart of Vinohrady. The church was built between 1888 and 1892, based on plans by the Czech Gothic uber-enthusiast, Josef Mocker –

THE FIRST CZECH SAINT
The Church of Saint Ludmila is named after the first Czech saint. She's the grandmother of Bohemian patron saint St Wenceslas and plays an important role in the legend of Prague's founding at **Vyšehrad** (p148).

 EATING & DRINKING IN VRŠOVICE: OUR PICKS

Ráno Kavu Večer Víno: Tiny wine bar with the best wines and prosecco by the glass at drinker-friendly prices. *5-11pm Wed-Sat* €

Jam and Co: Asian cuisine with European flavours, focusing on fresh ingredients. White-brick walls and clean design. *11am-11pm* €€

Café Sladkovský: In late afternoon, a quiet spot for tapas, burgers, falafel; by night, more of a party vibe. *4.30pm-midnight Mon-Sat, from 11am Sun* €€

Very good brunches.
Cafe Jen: Inviting bakery and cafe, good-value breakfasts and friendly vibe. Prepare to queue Saturday mornings. *7.30am-6pm Mon-Fri, 8.30am-3pm Sat* €

AMBLE AMID STATELY VINOHRADY

This aimless ramble will take you past Vinohrady's stateliest villas and prettiest parks.

START	END	LENGTH
Náměstí Míru	Rieger Gardens	3km; two to three hours

Leafy **1 Náměstí Míru** (Peace Square) is the lively heart of Vinohrady. Head south along Americká. At the end of the street, the rocky hillside park **2 Havlíček Gardens** (p120) (Havlíčkovy sady) marks the border between Vinohrady and Vršovice. Look for signs to the **3 Viniční Altán** (p120) wine garden, with tastings and light bites.

From here, retrace your steps through the park, back to the street U Havlíčkových Sadů. Follow this to the right and make a left onto Rybalkova. At Máchova turn right, crossing Francouzská onto Šumavská, and make a right at Lužická. Cut through a small park and onto Hradešínská.

Hradešínská has some of the most beautiful villas in the city. The most famous is at **4 Hradešínská 6**, built by early-modern architect Jan Kotěra in 1908. Turn left at Chorvatská and left again onto Dykova, then right onto Řípská, with a distant view of Žižkov's **TV Tower** (p111).

Řípská takes you to busy Vinohradská and the **5 Church of the Most Sacred Heart of Our Lord** (p118) at Jiřího z Poděbrad square. Find Slavíkova and follow it to Polská. Walk left onto Polská for another row of handsome townhouses. Take a right onto Chopinova. The entrance to **6 Rieger Gardens** (p115) (Riegrovy sady) is opposite Na Švihance.

'ROYAL VINOHRADY'

Ever since the fields and vineyards running east of Wenceslas Square were laid out for housing in the 19th century, there's been a certain 'cachet' to living in 'Královské Vinohrady' ('Royal Vinohrady' – how the district appears on old maps and still occasionally used today).

As it expanded, the district traditionally attracted well-to-do families and white-collar workers, including a large Jewish population. Indeed, Vinohrady was home to a giant synagogue, which stood on Sázavská street from 1896 until 1951.

The area fell into neglect under communism, but since 1989 has blossomed into one of the city's premier residential neighbourhoods, with trendy restaurants and cute coffeeshops competing for customers on nearly every corner.

Church of Saint Ludmila (p120)

who helped to give Prague its nickname as 'City of 100 Spires'. The square in front of the main entrance is home to the city's most-festive Christmas market outside of Old Town Square. The market runs from early December to New Year's Day.

Cheer for the Home Team(s)
FC Bohemians 1905 and SK Slavia

Catching a **FC Bohemians 1905** *(bohemians.cz; tickets from 200Kč)* match is considered the quintessential Vršovice experience. Maybe it's the club's perpetual underdog role, but 'Bohemka' are the rogues of the Czech First League. The team plays home matches at intimate (5000-seat) **Doliček Stadium**. Vršovice's 'other' club, **SK Slavia Praha** *(slavia.cz; tickets from 200Kč)*, is bigger and more successful. They play home matches at **Fortuna Aréna**. Football season runs from August to May; consult the team websites for schedules. Purchase tickets online or at the stadium box office before matches.

EATING IN VINOHRADY: OUR PICKS

The perfect splurge choice.

Výčep: Highly rated gastropub offers updated takes on classic Czech dishes. Reservations recommended. *11am-11pm* €€

The Tavern: Great for burgers, pulled pork and other comfort foods; vegetarian-friendly. Excellent weekend brunches, speciality cocktails. *11.30am-10pm* €

La Farma: Perfect lunch/dinner choice – mix of authentic Czech favourites/international dishes. *11am-10pm Mon-Fri, from noon Sat* €€

El Camino Tapas Restaurant: Prague's best tapas and Spanish food. Reserve in advance. *5pm-midnight Mon-Fri, noon-3pm, 5pm-midnight Sat* €€€

Holešovice

ART AND STREET VIBE

Historically working-class Holešovice, with abandoned factories and lofts, has recast itself as the city's contemporary-arts hub. Building on the National Gallery's superb collection at the Trade Fair Palace, a smattering of edgy galleries have opened up, playing off the district's grittiness. Holešovice has also emerged as the epicentre of hip design in Prague, with many boutiques around central Milady Horákové street.

Holešovice is essentially two distinct districts, separated by an old railway line. The more prosperous western half is a rapidly gentrifying residential neighbourhood of late 19th-century townhouses, anchored by the Trade Fair Palace art museum and National Technical Museum. This is also home to Letná Gardens on a high ridge over the Vltava. The scruffier eastern half is filled with old factories, many now converted to design studios and loft residences. The mood here is edgier, with late-night clubs like Cross Club and the always interesting DOX Centre for Contemporary Art.

Catch an Exhibition at DOX

Eye-opening art museum

The **DOX Centre for Contemporary Art** *(dox.cz; adult/child 280/130Kč)*, occupying a former factory in the eastern part of Holešovice, stands at the heart of the neighbourhood's artistic ambitions. Shows here highlight a wide range of media, including video, sculpture, photography, sound and painting. There's a decent cafe and excellent bookshop that's heavy on art and architecture. Don't miss the 'Gulliver Airship', a giant wooden zeppelin that has been perched atop the building since 2016. It's worth a peek inside, as well as snapping a few photos from outside on the street.

continued on p127

GETTING AROUND

Holešovice is situated across the river from Staré Město (Old Town) and Nové Město (New Town). To access Letná Park from Staré Město, follow Pařížská street north, cross Čechův bridge and then climb the stairs. Holešovice is served by metro line C (red line): both Vltavská and Nádraží Holešovice stations. Strossmayerovo náměstí is an important tram junction (lines 1, 6, 8, 12, 17, 25, 26). To reach Holešovice Market, ride tram 1, 12, or 25 to stop 'Holešovická tržnice'.

☑ TOP TIP

Holešovice is great to stretch your legs. After you've explored the busy main street, Milady Horákové, walk a couple blocks south to the Letná Gardens and its relaxing beer garden. In the eastern part of Holešovice, stroll the pretty HolKa pedestrian bridge, which crosses the river over to Karlín.

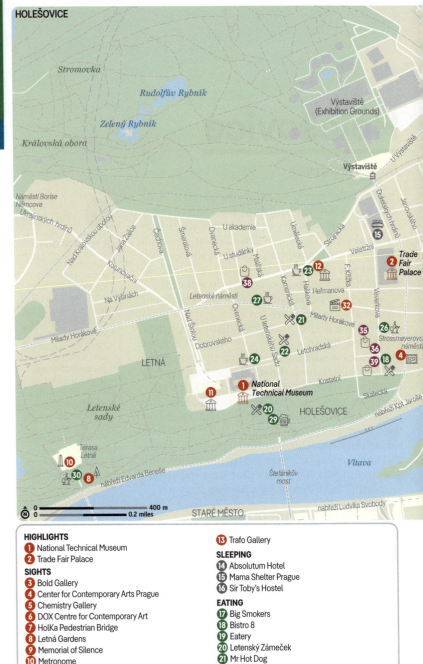

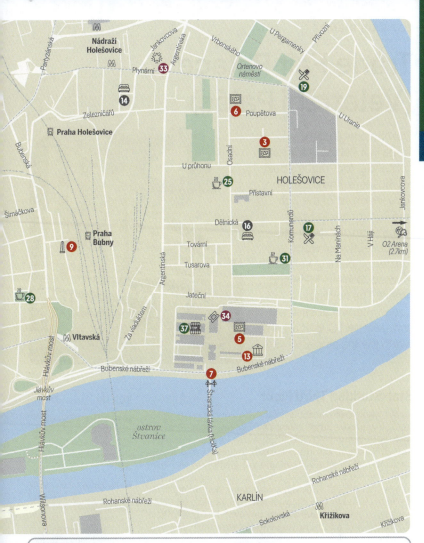

DRINKING & NIGHTLIFE
23 Cafe Hrnek
24 Café Letka
25 Cafe Osada
26 Cobra
27 Erhartova Cukrárna
28 Kavárna Liberál
29 Letná Beer Garden
30 Stalin
31 Vnitroblock

ENTERTAINMENT
32 Bio Oko
33 Cross Club
34 Jatka 78

SHOPPING
35 Charaktery Design Store
36 Helena Dařbujánová
37 Holešovice Market
38 Kuràž
39 PageFive

TOP EXPERIENCE

Trade Fair Palace (Veletržní Palác)

The National Gallery's Trade Fair Palace is a strong contender for Prague's best art museum. The collection focuses on art of the 19th and 20th centuries and features an unexpectedly rich collection of world masters, including Van Gogh, Picasso, Schiele, Klimt and others. The holdings of Czech interwar abstract, surrealist and Cubist art are worth the trip alone.

Star-Studded Third Floor

Most visitors head straight for the 3rd floor to enjoy works from an impressive array of household names of late-19th- and early-20th-century art, including works by French masters Monet, Gauguin, Cézanne, Picasso, Delacroix and Rodin. Look out for Gauguin's *Flight* and Van Gogh's *Green Wheat Field*. The 3rd floor is also home to a stunning assembly of interwar (1918–38) Czech art. Standouts here include the geometric works by Czech master František Kupka, and Cubist paintings, ceramics and design by several artists – these paintings show an interesting parallel with the concurrent art scene in Paris.

Don't Miss the Fourth Floor

Not to be outdone by the 3rd floor, the museum's 4th floor is another tour de force, featuring breathtaking landscapes and portraiture of what the curators here have called the 'long 19th century' (running from 1796 to 1918). Look out for major works by well-known painters, such as Gustav Klimt, Egon Schiele and Edvard Munch, to list only a few. Two highlights take on distinctly feminine themes: Klimt's luscious, vibrantly hued *Virgin* and Schiele's much darker, foreboding *Pregnant Woman and Death*.

TOP TIP

- Built in 1928, this was Prague's first functionalist building and the largest structure of its kind in the world.

- The ground-floor cafe is a great place to relax over beer or coffee.

- For 680Kč, buy a combined-entry ticket for all of the National Gallery collections in Prague.

Practicalities
Scan this QR code for service times.

continued from p123

Do Some Window-Shopping
Home to trendy boutiques

In the past few years, dozens of small shops, designer-paper sellers, booksellers and boutiques have popped up in the western end of Holešovice. The most fruitful hunting grounds run along the main street, Milady Horákové, and lively side streets like Veverkova, Františka Křížka and Kamenická. It's fun to poke around. Some of our favourites include **Charaktery Design Store** *(charaktery.cz; 11am-7pm Mon-Fri)*, a collective that turns out exquisitely formed jewellery and accessories. **Kuràž** *(kuraz.cz; 11am-7pm Mon-Fri, to 4pm Sat)* features clothing and accessories from young Czech and Slovak designers. **PageFive** *(pagefive.com; 11am-7pm Mon-Fri, to 4pm Sat)* has a colourful, offbeat collection of books and prints. **Helena Dařbujánová** *(helenadarbujanova.cz; Noon-7pm Mon-Fri, 1-5pm Sat)* is an independent Czech furniture designer who makes elegant retro-inspired pieces.

Visit Letná Gardens
Rocky bluff with gorgeous views

The **Letná Gardens** *(Letenské Sady)* trace a rocky bluff above the Vltava on the opposite side of the river from Staré Město (Old Town). The views from up here are, well, sublime. The park is popular as a place to walk, jog, rollerblade and bike. We've outlined our own walking tour (p130). Towards the western end of the gardens, a giant, creaking metronome (p127) stands atop a high hill. This marks the spot where an imposing 15m statue of Soviet leader Josef Stalin stood from 1955 until 1962. In summer, an open-air music club, appropriately called 'Stalin', draws crowds to hang out on the steps and listen to (often) electronic music.

Contemplate the 'Gate of Infinity'
Holocaust deportation site

From October 1941 until the end of WWII, the occupying Germans used Holešovice's Praha-Bubny train station as the main departure point for transporting Prague's Jewish population to the ghetto fortress at Terezín (Theresienstadt) (p161). From there, many Jews were eventually transported to Auschwitz-Birkenau or to the ghetto in the Polish city of Łódź. More than 45,000 Jews passed through here.

PRAGUE'S STALIN STATUE

The odd, open-air **metronome** that marks time on a high plateau in Letná Gardens also marks one of most notorious statues that ever stood in this city of many statues. From 1955 to 1962, this plinth was home to the world's largest (15m) statue of former Soviet dictator Josef Stalin. The statue was conceived after WWII as a symbol of Czechoslovakia's devotion to the occupying Soviet Union. But by the time the statue was unveiled, Stalin's memory had been disgraced in his homeland. The statue was dynamited out of existence just seven years later in a massive detonation (estimated at 800kg of explosives). Shock waves from the blast broke windows across the Old Town.

 EATING IN WESTERN HOLEŠOVICE: OUR PICKS

Legendary sliders and onion rings.

Bistro 8: Welcoming, vegan-friendly space with all-day breakfasts, lunch specials, good coffee. *8am-7pm Mon-Fri, 10am-3pm Sat & Sun* €

Letenský zámeček: Upscale dining on a terrace adjacent to the Letná Beer Garden. Book in advance. *11am-11pm* €€

Peperoncino: Insider's choice for good Italian cooking. Beautiful, bucolic garden in summer. Reservations recommended. *11am-10pm* €€

Mr Hot Dog: Holds local cult status for gourmet hot dogs. Sliders (mini hamburgers) and cheese fries hit the spot, too. *11.30am-10pm* €

TOP EXPERIENCE

National Technical Museum

Prague's National Technical Museum is a dazzling presentation of Czechia's industrial heritage over the decades and a surprising no-brainer, family-friendly attraction. Little kids will love the main hall, filled with life-sized trains, planes, cars and motorcycles. Older kids (and adults) will enjoy the more technical, hands-on displays of astronomy, photography, printing and other scientific and industrial fields.

TOP TIP

- The 600Kč 'family ticket' includes two adults and up to four kids (aged 6–15).

- Pair a visit to the **Letná Beer Garden** (p129), across the road from the main entrance.

- The **National Museum of Agriculture**, next door, has fun tractor rides for kids and a pretty rooftop terrace.

Practicalities
Scan this QR code for service times.

Planes, Trains & Automobiles

The 'Transportation Hall' on the main floor is by far the museum's most popular attraction and features an amazing collection of historic planes, trains, automobiles and motorcycles that are close enough to touch. The highlights here include the first automobile manufactured in the Czech lands, a 'Tatra 80' model limousine from 1935 that was used by Czechoslovak President TG Masaryk and a Spitfire fighter plane from WWII that was used by Czech pilots, based in Great Britain, for raids over Nazi Germany.

What Else To See

Separate halls scattered throughout the rest of the building are devoted to drier displays of Czech industrial prowess in fields like photography, printing, household design, architecture and astronomy. There's no point in trying to see it all. The best strategy is to follow your nose, depending on your interests. Astronomy buffs will want to see Jost Bürgi's sextant from the late 16th century. This instrument was used by Johannes Kepler, the top mathematician of Emperor Rudolf II, in forming his laws of planetary motion. The 'Intercamera' exhibition teaches the principles of colour photography.

Gate of Infinity

To mark these tragic deportations, the **Memorial of Silence** *(pamatnikticha.cz; free)* consists of a 20m section of railway track aimed toward the sky – the *Gate of Infinity* – by sculptor Aleš Veselý to recall the biblical story of Jacob's Ladder. The site is home to frequent exhibitions on the Holocaust.

Cold Brew in the Open Air
Prague's best beer garden?

Budget an afternoon or evening to hang out at the **Letná Beer Garden** *(letenskyzamecek.cz, free)*, one of Prague's signature warm-weather (May to September) watering holes. Line up with everyone else at a small beer-dispensing kiosk to buy a half-litre of Gambrinus, served in returnable plastic cups. Find a nearby picnic table, relax with a mix of tourists and locals. On warm nights, in high summer, the kiosk stays open until around midnight.

> **BEER GARDENS**
> After you've had a few at Letná's beer garden, check out its crosstown rival in Vinohrady, where **Rieger Gardens** (p115) has a quieter open-air garden that locals say might be even better.

BEST EVENING ENTERTAINMENT

Jatka 78 *(jatka78.cz)*: Alternative art space housed in a former slaughterhouse in Holešovice Market (p131), stages performances from dance to circus and acrobatics.

Cross Club *(crossclub.cz)*: Industrial club: the setting is a factory zone with a must-see maze of gadgets, shafts, cranks and pipes.

Bio Oko *(biooko.net)*: Repertory cinema showing a varied programme of underground films, selections from film festivals, documentaries and global classics.

Kavárna Liberál *(facebook.com/kavarnaliberal)*: By day, a quiet spot for coffee; evenings bring out a more pub-like feel, with occasional live bands.

Stalin *(stalinletna.cz)*: From May to September, an open-air venue for electronic music and happenings.

DRINKING IN WESTERN HOLEŠOVICE: OUR PICKS

Cafe Letka: Beautifully ornate coffeehouse stands just a few steps away from Letná Gardens. *8am-11pm Mon-Fri, from 9am Sat & Sun*

Cobra: Combination cocktail bar and decent restaurant stands at the heart of hip Holešovice. *11.30am-1am Mon-Fri, to 2am Sat*

Erhartova Cukrárna: Stylish 1930s-era cafe and sweetshop draws a mixed crowd to cakes, pastries, homemade ice cream. *10am-7pm*

Cafe Hrnek: Neighbourhood favourite for relaxing over coffee or enjoying one of the city's best brunches. *8am-6pm Mon-Fri, from 10am Sat & Sun*

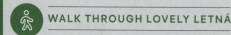

WALK THROUGH LOVELY LETNÁ

High-altitude Letná Gardens offers breathtaking views over Prague's Old Town and the Vltava River. This walk hits the best spots for photo ops.

START	END	LENGTH
Chotkovy sady tram stop	Expo '58 Restaurant	2km; one hour

Catch tram 2, 12, 18 or 20 to the ❶ **Chotkovy sady** stop, find a green footbridge and cross it in the direction of Prague Castle; here you'll find a stone grotto dedicated to the novelist ❷ **Julius Zeyer**. There are park benches nearby with superb views over Malá Strana and Prague Castle.

Retrace your steps across the footbridge and head east. Follow the path, which bears right, then detour to visit the ❸ **Hanavský pavilón**, a delightful piece of 1891 art-nouveau architecture. The pretty pond to the left was added in 2022 to enhance the park's natural beauty. Continue along the top of the bluff to a purpose-built ❹ **viewing spot** with gorgeous views over the Vltava. A little further on, find a monumental stepped terrace topped by a giant, creaking ❺ **metronome** (p127). The area, known as 'Stalin', gets its name from a giant Stalin statue that once stood here.

Continue east, hugging the ridge, to arrive at one of the city's most popular summertime watering holes, the ❻ **Letná Beer Garden** (p129). Letná Gardens extends another 300m eastward. About 100m east of the beer garden stands an architectural curiosity, the retro-futuristic ❼ **Expo '58 Restaurant**. Built for the 1958 Brussels World Exposition, the restaurant now houses corporate offices.

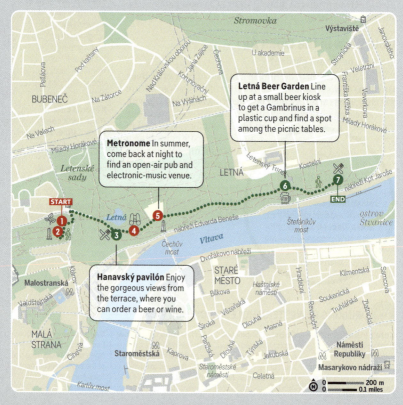

Head to Holešovice Market
Food market and budding cultural space

Holešovice Market (Holešovická tržnice; *holesovickatrznice.cz*), in the eastern part of Holešovice, functioned for years as the city's main market. In the 1990s and early 2000s, it fell on hard times, but now the complex is in the throes of major renovation. It's home to alternative theatre Jatka 78 (p129) as well as a couple of noteworthy art galleries. Saturdays are the liveliest days. The market is home to a decent food hall (in Building 22) and a very good Vietnamese restaurant, **Tràng An** *(Building 5; facebook.com/asijskebistropodosmickou; 10am-8pm Mon-Sat, €)*.

Walk Across the River
The 'HolKa' pedestrian bridge

In 2023, Prague city officials finally made good on a long promise to build a footbridge linking eastern Holešovice to the district of Karlín across the river. Indeed, the **HolKa pedestrian bridge** has been a tour de force, an uncommonly graceful bridge that's quickly become one of the city's most popular promenades. On the Holešovice side, the bridge begins just in front of the Holešovice Market (p131). From here, you can walk over to Štvánice island in the Vltava and then continue on to Karlín. Štvánice is a cool spot to throw down a blanket or simply admire the river views (which can be otherworldly at sunset). Once on the Karlín side, meander over to Přístav 18600 (p114) for a break and a cold beer.

Catch Some Ice Hockey
See the action on ice

From September through April, **O2 Arena** *(o2arena.cz; tickets from 200Kč)*, 5km east of Holešovice in the district of Libeň, is home ice for the leading local hockey club, HC Sparta Praha. Quality of play is high and the Czech Extraliga, the country's top hockey league, is arguably the most competitive national league outside of North America's NHL. Find a schedule and buy tickets online at Ticketportal *(ticketportal.cz)*. The arena is located on metro line B (yellow line), Českomoravská stop.

MANIA FOR HOCKEY

Czechs generally excel at (and love) ice hockey. Read more about the country's unbridled passion for this sport in the 'Natural-Born Athletes' essay (p308).

BEST ART GALLERIES

Chemistry Gallery *(thechemistry.art)*: Eclectic photos and paintings from local artists. Located in Hall 40 of the Holešovice market.

Trafo Gallery *(trafogallery.cz)*: Focuses on contemporary Czech and international artists. Hosts six exhibitions per year. Situated in Hall 14 of the Holešovice market.

Bold Gallery *(boldgallery.art)*: Represents the best up-and-coming Czech and regional artists. Check the website for events and shows.

Center for Contemporary Arts Prague *(cca.fcca.cz)*: Gallery and residence to support contemporary fine art. The courtyard has a delightful, tucked-away cafe.

Polansky Gallery *(polanskygallery.com)*: Represents leading Czech artists. See the website for a current list of talent and upcoming exhibitions.

EATING & DRINKING IN EASTERN HOLEŠOVICE: OUR PICKS

Eatery: Best restaurant in Holešovice. Sophisticated space; local, seasonal dishes from open kitchen. *11.30am-2.30pm & 5.30-10pm Tue-Fri, 5.30-10pm Sat €€*

Big Smokers: Informal, American-style smoker. Excellent brisket, pulled pork, homemade sausages. Occasional taco nights. *11am-10pm Tue-Sat, to 6pm Sun €€*

Cafe Osada: Fresh-roasted coffees, extended-hour breakfasts, and a lovely hidden courtyard to enjoy. *8am-8pm Mon-Fri, 9am-4pm Sat & Sun €*

Vnitroblock: Hidden in back of an industrial building, this part sneaker store, part industrial-style cafe, is the coolest daytime hangout. *Good for Wi-Fi and remote work. 9am-10pm €*

Bubeneč & Dejvice

VILLAS, PARKS AND GARDENS

GETTING AROUND

Both Bubeneč and Dejvice are easily reachable by metro line A (green line), to stations Hradčanská and Dejvická. Both neighbourhoods are well-served by tram. Lines 1, 8, 12, 25 and 26 run to busy Letenské náměstí – from where it's an easy walk to Stromovka Park. Dejvice's main commercial hub at Vítězné náměstí (Victory Square) is served by trams 8, 18, 20 and 26. Reach the Výstaviště Exhibition Grounds via trams 12 and 17. Walk to the Prague Zoo or travel by bus 112 from Nádraží Holešovice metro station (line C).

✓ TOP TIP

Leave time to explore the hilly, winegrowing area north of Stromovka Park and across the Vltava River. Troja, as the area is called, is home to the Prague Zoo, Troja Chateau and the remote-feeling Botanical Gardens, with its exotic plants and opportunities to taste some local wines.

After navigating the congested central parts of the city, a trip to the outlying neighbourhoods of Bubeneč and Dejvice, north of the centre, feels like a breath of fresh air. Both are prosperous residential areas laid out in the 19th and early 20th centuries. You'll find beautiful parkland, perfect for hikes and walks, as well as stunning villas.

Bubeneč is home to Stromovka Park, the city's largest and prettiest piece of nature, hugging the Vltava's southern bank. Adjoining Stromovka, the Výstaviště exhibition grounds – built for the 1891 Prague Jubilee – look neglected, though they hold an interesting branch of the National Museum and the city's largest aquarium. Across the river, north of Stromovka, you'll find the Prague Zoo, Troja Chateau and the beautiful Prague Botanical Gardens. Further west, in Dejvice, marked hiking trails follow Šárka creek (a tributary of the Vltava) all the way out to Divoká Šárka, a striking piece of urban wilderness.

Communist-Era Palace
Glimpse the grand Hotel International

Budding Cold War historians have a real treat in store. Dejvice's **Hotel International** *(hotelint.cz; Koulova 15)* is one of the best-surviving examples in Prague of early-1950s 'Socialist-Realist' architecture, inspired by the Soviet Union. The style was intentionally ostentatious to glorify the communist state and demonstrate the power of its rulers. This hotel was a gift from Stalin and modelled on a soaring tower of Moscow University, down to the Soviet-style star on top of the spire. Note the impressive sil-houette, the 88m-tall tower, beautiful external mosaics, and impressive interior. It's still a functioning

LOVE IT OR HATE IT

Czechs have a love-hate affair with communist-era buildings like the Hotel International. To read more about a controversy that seems to get more heated every year, see 'The Battle over Communist Buildings' essay (p300).

Villa Müller

hotel (p163), though the rooms are not as elegant as the lobby.

Outrageous Troja Chateau
Indulge in some baroque bling

Across the Vltava from Stromovka (accessible via footbridge), the delightful **Troja Chateau** (Trojský Zámek; *ghmp.cz; adult/child 200/90Kč*) was originally conceived as a Roman-style suburban villa. It was designed in baroque in the 17th century by French architect Jean Baptiste Mathey for the noble Šternberg family. The permanent exhibition is devoted to the interior furnishings of the chateau and shows off the lavish chambers and frescoes. The Prague City Gallery also uses the chateau as a venue for exhibitions. The grounds are free to enter, and the baroque stone giants in the winding French garden make for some beautiful photographs.

Tour the Villa Müller
Masterpiece of early-modern architecture

Fans of modern architecture will enjoy a visit to the **Villa Müller** *(muzeumprahy.cz; adult/child 400/250Kč)*, a masterpiece of design, located just west of Dejvice in the upscale district of Střešovice. It was built in 1930 for construction entrepreneur František Müller, and drafted by the Brno-born architect Adolf Loos. The clean-cut, ultramodern exterior contrasts with the polished wood, leather and oriental rugs of the classically decorated interior. Admission is by guided tour, booked in advance online or by phone (224 312 012).

FIND ANOTHER ADOLF LOOS

The modern master architect Adolf Loos had a hand in designing several villas in and around Prague over the years. One of his most impressive works, and the last to be completed during his lifetime, is the 1932 **Villa Winternitz** (p146) in Smíchov.

continued on p137

A STROLL THROUGH STROMOVKA

Wander through the historic Výstaviště exhibition grounds and across the northern bend of the Vltava River to Troja Chateau, Prague Zoo and the Botanical Gardens.

START	END	LENGTH
Industrial Palace	Prague Zoo	3km; two hours

Catch tram 12 or 17 to Výstaviště tram stop at the front of the exhibition grounds. Most structures date from 1891, when Prague hosted a world jubilee. Proceed through the gates (entry is normally free) to find the massive ❶ **Industrial Palace** (Průmyslový Palác). Part of the Industrial Palace was undergoing repairs during research and may not be open to the public.

In front of the palace to the right, find the ❷ **Lapidárium** (p137), a museum of some of the city's finest sculptures. These include several original statues from Charles Bridge. The same building holds Prague's biggest aquarium, ❸ **Mořský Svět** (p138).

Retrace your steps back to the entrance of Výstaviště and follow the path to the right of the tram stop, passing the ❹ **Prague Planetarium** as you enter the former royal hunting ground, Stromovka. From here, wander through Stromovka at your leisure, heading vaguely west and north through meadows and flower gardens.

Following the signs to 'Troja' and 'Zoo', walk under a railway line. From here, climb some steps to enter Emperor's Island (Císařský ostrov); the road leads to a bridge over the Vltava. At this point, it's a short walk to ❺ **Troja Chateau** (p133) and ❻ **Prague Zoo** (p140). The Botanical Gardens (p137) is a 10-minute walk north of here.

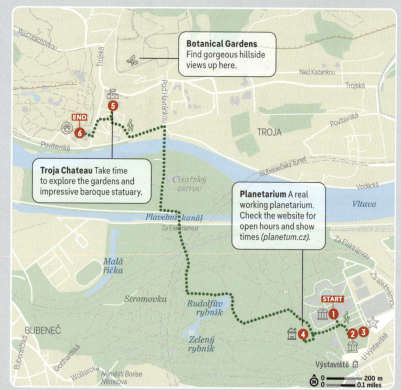

continued from p133

Beautiful Botanical Gardens
Butterflies, bonsai trees and wine

The gently rolling hills across the Vltava River, north of Stromovka, create an idyllic setting for the sprawling **Prague Botanical Gardens** *(botanicka.cz; adult/child 180/120Kč)*, one of Prague's most under-appreciated attractions. There's something for every budding botanist, including the S-shaped 'Fata Morgana' greenhouse, which features free-range butterflies, a small aquarium and rare plants from Latin America, Australia and Africa. A smallish Japanese garden holds an impressive display of bonsai and other plants. Trails run here and there, with breathtaking views over the Vltava River valley.

Vineyards climb up the south-facing hillside, and the gardens have begun a promising side business in wine tourism. Wannabe sommeliers can test their olfactory skills at 20 scent casks that have been built into a specially marked 'Wine Trail'; buy bottles of local wine at the giftshop. Pair a visit to the gardens with a gourmet meal and winetasting at **Salabka** *(salabka.cz, Noon-11pm Wed-Sat, €€)*. **Wine Travel in Czech** *(winetravelinczech.com)* has guided tours of the area, including a multi-flight tasting in an old-fashioned wine cellar.

Catch a Show at Výstaviště
Prague's quirky exhibition grounds

The **Výstaviště Exhibition Grounds** *(navystavisti.cz; free to enter)*, adjacent to Stromovka Park, defy easy description. The grounds were planned out for the 1891 Prague Jubilee to celebrate the city's cultural and industrial progress. These days, the area feels neglected, though some faded grandeur can still be seen in the enormous **Industrial Palace** that stands at the centre. The grounds are used to hold open-air concerts, festivals, food fairs and other events (including a brutal 'World Hot Chili Pepper' eating contest in 2023). Find a complete programme on the website.

Aside from hosting events, Výstaviště has a couple of permanent attractions. The National Gallery's **Lapidárium** *(nm.cz; adult/child 70/50Kč)* houses some original baroque statues that once stood on Charles Bridge. For travellers with

WHY I LOVE BUBENEČ

Mark Baker, Lonely Planet writer

Bubeneč is quiet, but that's how I like it. My apartment is close to Stromovka Park and I often walk there, but my favourite activity is to stroll the residential streets and admire the stylish, oversized villas and mansions. Bubeneč grew wealthy in the early-20th century as the neighbourhood of choice for newly rich robber barons and bankers. The villas here reflect the various architectural styles of the time: art-nouveau, functionalist and a distinctive Czech style called Rondo-Cubism.

To see the splendour, gawk at the **US ambassador's residence** *(ul Ronalda Reagana 3)*, a 65-room palace built by industrialist Otto Petschek in the early 1930s. If anything, the **Russian Embassy** *(ul Ukrajinských hrdinů 36)* is even grander.

 DRINKING IN BUBENEČ & DEJVICE: OUR PICKS

Kavárna Alibi: Lively coffeehouse packed with students. Perfect spot for a coffee/good book. *9am-midnight Mon-Fri, from 2pm Sat & Sun*

Pivní Jistota: Traditional pub favouring smaller craft producers. Check the chalkboard to see what's on tap. *3-11.30pm Mon-Sat*

Potrvá: Relaxing cafe for quiet reflection during the day or catch occasional live music and open-mic nights in the evening. *3pm-midnight*

Kabinet: Old-school cafe set in a leafy residential patch of Bubeneč. Good for beer too. *3pm-10pm Mon-Fri*

STROMOVKA: RUDOLF II'S PLAYGROUND

The creation of Stromovka Park is inextricably tied to Holy Roman Emperor Rudolf II (1552-1612). It was Rudolf who first conceived of installing artificial fishponds in the park and who led a massively expensive and technologically advanced (for the time) project to realise that dream. Part of the project was to build a 1km-long tunnel running from the Vltava River, under today's Letná Gardens (p127), and ultimately into Stromovka, his private hunting ground.

Construction of the tunnel was carried out (1584-93) and entailed workers hewing channels through solid rock. The tunnel still exists (closed to the public). Marked entryways to the tunnel (bearing Rudolf's seal) can still be seen at various points around Stromovka.

Stromovka Park

kids, **Mořský Svět** (morskysvet.cz; adult/child 440/280Kč) claims the largest water tank in the country, with a capacity of 100,000L. Some 4500 living species of fish and sea creatures are on display, with a good (and suitably scary) set of sharks.

Relax at Stromovka Park
Hunting ground turned urban paradise

Strolling the long oval corso at the centre of **Stromovka Park** has been a popular pastime for Prague residents going back generations. Stromovka was established in the 13th century as a royal hunting preserve, and it's still sometimes called the *Královská obora* (Royal Hunting Ground). Emperor Rudolf II had rare trees planted here and built several fishponds.

Stromovka was badly damaged by flooding that struck the city in 2002, and in the two decades since, enchanting new ponds, bridges and flowerbeds have been added. Enter the park from the Výstaviště exhibition grounds or from Letenské náměstí (follow Čechova třída north to a ridge overlooking the park and then walk down).

Hike in 'Divoká Šárka'
Stunning rocks and nature
Divoká Šárka *(free)*, west of Dejvice, is one of the city's wildest and most remote nature parks. The area is best known for its unique landscape of barren rocks and hills at its western end, but it actually goes on for kilometres through forests and valleys along the Šárka Creek (Šárecký potok). The easiest way to access the park is by tram; lines 20 and 26 from Vítězné náměstí bring you to the park's edge ('Divoká Šárka' stop). Return by tram or, for a longer outing, find a red-marked trail that runs for about 7km all the way to the suburb of Podbaba, where the creek empties into the Vltava. Once at the river, look for the tower of the Hotel International (with a star on top). Head towards the hotel to find tram 8 or 18 for the return to Vítězné náměstí and Dejvická metro station (Line A).

Forage at the Market
A little Saturday-morning fun
From March to November, get out of bed early on a Saturday morning to join the crowds at the **Dejvice Farmers Market** *(trhynakulataku.cz; free)*, spread out across a grassy field adjacent to Dejvická metro station (Line A). The market runs 8am–2pm and the mood is more akin to a carnival than a market. Sure, there's lots of fresh fruits and vegetables, but there's also live music and plenty of food-truck fare, like tacos and burgers, to munch on.

Explore the Historic Sewers
Preserved wastewater-treatment plant
Prague's **Old Wastewater Treatment Plant** *(staracistirna.cz; tours adult/child 280/170Kč)* was an industrial wonder when it was built at the start of the 20th century. These days, it no longer functions as a working sewage plant, but the halls, chimneys, mills and reservoirs have been beautifully preserved as a piece of industrial heritage. Guided tours (English tours available), four times daily on weekends and holidays, explore the underground spaces and explain how the machinery once worked. Find tour times and book tickets on the website. Wear sturdy shoes and warm clothing (even in summer) as the rooms get chilly. To reach the plant, take tram 8 or 18 to the end station (stop: Nádraží Podbaba) and walk about 10 minutes.

THE MYTH OF DIVOKÁ ŠÁRKA

The Divoká Šárka nature park has an unusual name. It translates literally as 'Wild Šárka' (Šárka being a woman's name). The name comes from the mythical warrior 'Šárka', who is said to have thrown herself off a cliff here after the death of her lover and enemy, the handsome warrior 'Ctirad'. Depending on which version of the legend you prefer, Šárka either seduced and then murdered Ctirad (and committed suicide afterwards to avoid capture), or fell in love with Ctirad and then failed to protect him (and killed herself out of grief and guilt).

Whatever the truth is, the area is perfect for spreading out a picnic blanket. In summer, there's an unheated swimming pool (with icy cold water) and a number of pubs.

Order the buchta – a traditional Czech sweet bun.

 DRINKING IN BUBENEČ & DEJVICE: BEST FOR COFFEE

Alchymista: The hidden back garden is the real draw here, though the cakes and pastries are some of the city's finest. *1pm-7.30pm*

Kavárna Pod Lipami: Coffee and snacks served under the graceful linden trees of pretty Čechova street. *8am-8pm Mon-Fri, from 9am Sat & Sun*

Kafemat: Hole-in-the-wall serving some of Dejvice's best coffee. Order at the bar or grab your cup to go. *8am-5pm Mon-Fri, 9am-3pm Sat & Sun*

Šodó Bistro: Delicious homemade cakes and sweets, breakfast sets and light lunch bites. Book in advance. *8am-7pm Mon-Fri, from 9am Sat & Sun*

PRITYKIN_NIKITA/SHUTTERSTOCK ©

PRAGUE'S HEROIC SEAL

In some ways, Prague is still emotionally recovering from the tragic, once-in-a-100-year flood of 2002 that pushed the Vltava River far over its banks, particularly along the Troja side of the river, near the Prague Zoo.

The floods inundated the zoo's lower stretches, and a number of animals, including an elephant, a hippopotamus and a gorilla, were tragically lost. One of the saddest stories to arise during those days concerned a popular seal named 'Gaston'.

In the early days of the flooding, Prague residents rallied around news that Gaston had managed to escape the disaster and was swimming downriver on his way to Germany. Indeed, he made it all the way to Dresden, only to die of exhaustion once he got there.

Prague's Terrific Zoo
See giraffes, gorillas and rare horses

Rarely is the connection so strong between a city and its **zoo** (zoopraha.cz; adult/child 330/250Kč) than it is in Prague. Most families visit at least once during the summer season (time your own visit for a weekday, when it might be slightly less crowded). This emotional affinity was forged in the tragic 2002 Prague flood, which struck the zoo hard and, regrettably, cost many animals their lives. Over the past two decades, officials invested greatly to improve the grounds and animal safety.

The zoo has sizable collections of giraffes and gorillas, but pride of place probably goes to a herd of rare horses. The attractions also include a miniature cable car and a big play area.

To reach the zoo, take bus 112 from metro stop Nádraží Holešovice (Line C). If time is no issue, we've outlined a 30-minute walk (p136) to the zoo from the Výstaviště exhibition

EATING IN BUBENEČ & DEJVICE: OUR PICKS

Lovely setting on the edge of the park.

Kavárna Místo: Creative concoctions from locally sourced ingredients served in a minimalist setting. *9am-9pm Mon-Sat, from 10am Sun* €

Bistro à Table: Welcoming, family-run French restaurant in the heart of Dejvice. Local favourite. Excellent table wines. *11am-11pm Mon-Sat* €€

Dejvická 34: Brings fine dining to the neighbourhood by giving gourmet treatment to popular Czech dishes. *Noon-3pm, 4.30-11pm* €€€

Lokál Nad Stromovkou: Excellent Czech cooking and Pilsner beer, served on a ridge overlooking Stromovka Park. *11.30am-11pm* €€

Prague Zoo

grounds through Stromovka Park. From April to October, **Prague Steamboats** *(praguesteamboats.com; return adult/child 390/230Kč)* also operates daily river cruises out to the zoo that depart from Rašín Embankment in Nové Město.

Check Out Some Footie
Cheer on the home side

Hometown football (soccer) faves – and reigning (2023–24) Czech First League champions – **AC Sparta Praha** play home matches in Bubeneč at the 20,000-seat **Letná Stadium** (Epet Aréna; *sparta.cz; tickets from 400Kč*). This stadium also often serves as home pitch for Czechia in international matches and friendlies. Matches are usually played on weekends and the season runs from August to May. Buy tickets on the team website or at the stadium box office on game day. **Automat Matuška** *(automatmatuska.cz; 11am-midnight, €€)*, near the Hradčanská metro/tram stop, features local-brewer Matuška's craft beers and is a great place to be pre-game or enjoy a beer and bite after the match.

THE SECRETS OF BUBENEČ

Many of the fine homes of Bubeneč were built in the latter part of the 19th and early-20th centuries as mansions for Prague's newly rich industrial classes.

During the Nazi occupation (1939–45) many of the original owners were rousted and their homes confiscated to serve as plum residences for the local Nazi elite, including high-ranking officials of the SS and Gestapo.

Not to be outdone, during the communist period (1948–89), these same villas became the manors of choice for high-ranking party officials. The proximity of foreign embassies here at the time served as a backdrop to the Cold War and the area was a playground for spies from both sides of the Iron Curtain.

 DRINKING IN BUBENEČ & DEJVICE: BEST PUBS

Na Slamníku: Two handsome dining rooms and a roaring fire. Pilsner Urquell and local Únětice beer are served, plus very good food. *11.30am-11pm €€*

Na Urale: Popular neighbourhood pub, with plenty of pavement tables, on Bubeneč's quiet Puškinovo náměstí. *11am-10pm €€*

U Veverky: People come here not so much for the beer but for the excellent Czech home cooking. Book ahead for dinner. *11am-11.30pm €€*

Kulaťák: Local branch of a Pilsner Urquell-run pub chain. High-quality beer and Czech meals in a spiffed-up but authentic atmosphere. *11am-11pm €€*

Smíchov

PRAGUE'S BEER QUARTER

Working-class Smíchov, south of Malá Strana, is renowned for beer. It is home to the big Staropramen Brewery (and beer tours), and the pubs here still feel raucous and unvarnished in a way they no longer do in more-gentrified parts of the city. Yet it has almost no tourist vibe, and not much in the way of historic architecture. Most of the buildings date from the last half of the 19th or early-20th centuries, when the quarter was still largely industrial.

But don't just visit Smichov for the beer tours. As the district has evolved, better and more-varied restaurants have sprouted up. The presence of places like MeetFactory for alternative music, Jazz Dock for jazz, and Švandovo Divadlo for theatre has put Smichov firmly on Prague's cultural map. Each year the Smíchov Embankment along the Vltava River adds new places to eat, drink, stroll and admire the busy city centre across the water.

Catch a Happening at MeetFactory
Artist David Černý's experimental space

David Černý's **MeetFactory** *(meetfactory.cz; admission 100Kč)* is a remarkable project that unites artists from around the world to live and create in an abandoned factory south of Smíchov train station (Smíchovské Nádraží). Head here to catch almost anything, including art exhibitions, happenings, film screenings, theatrical performances and indie music concerts. Check the website to see what's on before making the long trip out. MeetFactory is not very easy to find. Take tram 4, 5, 12 or 20 to the Lihovar stop and walk across the bridge over some railway tracks. It's the big factory building with giant red cars hanging on the exterior.

See More of David Černý's Work
Musoleum – a self-described 'museum/mausoleum'

Fans of Czech installation artist David Černý – creator of epic Prague works like *Miminka*, the crawling babies on the Žižkov TV Tower (p111) and *K* (p103), the rotating bust of Franz Kafka – will want to visit the **Musoleum** *(musoleum.cz; adult/child 300/220Kč)*, dedicated to Černý's entire opus. The exhibition space, occupying five floors of a former distillery,

GETTING AROUND

Smíchov is easily accessible via major transport lines. Metro line B (yellow line) serves both Anděl, close to most of the area's main sights, restaurants, pubs and hotels, and the Smíchov train station (Smíchovské Nádraží). The busy quarter around the Anděl metro station is crisscrossed by tram lines (4, 5, 7, 9, 10, 12, 16, and 20) that run to all parts of the city. Trams 4, 5, 12 or 20 head south from Anděl to reach both David Černý's **MeetFactory** (p142) and his **Musoleum** (p142).

☑ TOP TIP

The **Nový Smíchov** *(9am-9pm)* shopping centre, with a large grocery, is handy for buying provisions. The **Smíchov embankment** along the Vltava is quieter and prettier than more-popular Náplavka across the river. The area around the Anděl metro station has several excellent **hotels** (p163) and good transit links to the centre.

SIGHTS
1. *Brownnosers* (David Černý sculpture)
2. Futura Gallery
3. Smíchov Embankment
4. Staropramen Brewery
5. Villa Winternitz

SLEEPING
6. Hotel Julian
7. Red & Blue Design Hotel
8. Vienna House by Windham Andel's

EATING
9. Lokal Blok
10. Manifesto Market
11. Na Verandách

12. U Bílého lva
13. Zlatý Klas

DRINKING & NIGHTLIFE
14. ALE Bar
15. Andělský Pivovar
16. Hospoda U Buldoka
17. Kavárna Co Hledá Jméno
18. Pitchers

ENTERTAINMENT
19. Jazz Dock
20. Švandovo Divadlo

SHOPPING
21. Nový Smíchov

Awesome breakfast options too. Book ahead.

 DRINKING IN SMÍCHOV: OUR PICKS

ALE Bar: Tucked-away temple dedicated to craft beers. Ambitious line-up of best local brews/imports on tap most nights. *4pm-11pm Mon-Sat*

Pitchers: Welcoming riverside pub and gallery and one of the best places to relax on the Smíchov Embankment. *3pm-midnight*

Andělský Pivovar: Thoroughly renovated space – big tables, brick drinking cellar. Own homemade brews and updated bar-food menu. *11am-10pm*

Kavárna Co Hledá Jméno: Popular cafe for coffee and chilling. Arguably has the city's best weekend brunches. *8am-8pm*

BEST DAVID ČERNÝ ART INSTALLATIONS

Kůň: Wryly amusing counterpart to the equestrian statue of St Wenceslas in Wenceslas Square.

K: Mesmerising giant rotating bust of Franz Kafka formed from 39 tonnes of mirrored stainless steel.

Proudy: Saucy animatronic sculpture of two guys peeing in a puddle shaped like Czechia.

Quo Vadis: Bronze Trabant (East German car) on four human legs recalls the 4000 East Germans who sought freedom at the then-West German embassy in 1989.

Butterflies: Installed in 2024, this work celebrates the Czechoslovak fighter pilots who served with the British RAF squadrons during WWII.

Staropramen Brewery

show off the artist's work over the past nearly four decades and include installations that have never been exhibited in public before. Pair a visit to the Musoleum with Černý's nearby MeetFactory (p142).

True fans of Černy's work will want to see his other Smíchov installation, *Brownnosers*, though in recent years, the work has not been easy to visit. It's situated in the garden of the **Futura Gallery** *(Holečkova 49)*, but the gallery was closed as this guide was being researched and it wasn't immediately clear when or if it would reopen. *Brownnosers* is one of Černý's most overtly political creations. The work shows former Czech president Václav Klaus and artist Milan Knížák feeding each other human waste, and can be viewed by climbing a ladder and peering through the backsides of the two figures.

Tour the Staropramen Brewery

Prague's big hometown brewery

Smíchov's **Staropramen Brewery** *(centrumstaropramen. cz; tours from 300Kč)* is the city's last-remaining major commercial brewery, though local microbrewers have stepped up the pace to fill the void, and Praguers themselves tend to favour other labels. Unlike similar big brewery tours in cities

 EATING IN SMÍCHOV: OUR PICKS

Fresh beer on tap from the brewery.

Manifesto Market: Open-air venue for something quick and easy; everything from food-truck faves to high-end meals. Card only. *11am-10pm* €

Zlatý Klas: Pub and restaurant with Czech roast pork, goulash and fried chicken breast in a kitsch but comfortable space. *11am-11pm* €€

Na Verandách: Popular pub situated within Staropramen Brewery complex. Excellent beer. Menu of ribs, burgers and chicken. *11am-11pm* €€

Lokal Blok: A raucous restaurant with decent Czech and Mexican food plus a state-of-the-art climbing wall. *11am-midnight Mon-Sat* €€

like Plzeň and České Budějovice, this 50-minute circuit feels more like a museum stop than an actual factory visit, although you do get to sample several very good beers along the way. The presentation focuses on the 150-plus years of tradition at the brewery. See the website for tour times or check them on the door. It usually offers several English tours per day.

Relax Along the Embankment
Riverside drinks and views

The **Smíchov Embankment** (*Hořejší nabřeží*), a quiet stretch along the Vltava, defined roughly as the riverbank running south of Vltavská street until Pivovarská street, keeps getting better and better. The area got going a few years ago in response to Nové Město's larger and more popular Náplavka (p107) on the other side. In many ways, though, Smíchov's version is superior. It's admittedly smaller, though it feels quieter and more refined.

Several pubs and restaurants put out open-air tables in nice weather, and the views up to the Vyšehrad Fortress (p153) are impressive. From March to October, a small river ferry (requiring a standard tram or metro ticket or day pass to ride) connects the embankment to the Výtoň tram stop in Nové Město on the other side of the Vltava.

Enjoy Theatre at Švandovo Divadlo
Czech drama with English subtitles

Czechs have a storied tradition in theatrical arts, though visitors don't often get the chance to appreciate this, as performances are in Czech language. The **Švandovo Divadlo** (*svandovodivadlo.cz; tickets from 380Kč*) gets props for its commitment to performing or subtitling some productions in English to allow access to international audiences. The programme leans toward contemporary comedy and drama. It also hosts occasional live music and dance, as well as regular 'stage talks' – unscripted discussions with noted personalities. Check the website for performances that are 'English-friendly' or have 'English subtitles'.

City's Best Jazz Club
Jazz Dock on the river

Prague has had a love affair with jazz going back to the 1920s – and especially during the 1950s and 1960s. Most of the city's jazz clubs are dark cellar affairs, and this above-ground riverside club is a definite step up. **Jazz Dock** (*jazzdock.cz; tickets from 200Kč*) sports clean, modern decor and a decidedly romantic view out over the Vltava. It draws some of the best local talent and international acts in jazz, blues, swing and pop. Shows normally begin at 9pm, and it's possible to pair a show with dinner and drinks. Check the programme and book a table in advance on the venue website.

COMPETING BREWERY TOURS

The Staropramen Brewery tour is fine for starters, but the best guided tour of this kind in Czechia is undoubtedly at the **Pilsner Urquell Brewery** (p184) in Plzeň.

A LITTLE ABOUT SMÍCHOV

Smíchov is easily Prague's most economically varied district. For years it was a relatively depressed industrial backwater, home to Prague's largest Roma community. At the same time, the hills south and west of the Anděl metro station had some of the city's swankiest villas, like the Villa Winternitz (p146).

These days, those jarring contrasts are seen especially in the commercial area around the Anděl metro station. It's filled with gleaming office towers, the vast Nový Smíchov shopping centre (p142), the Staropramen Brewery (p144) and some of the hottest boutique hotels – but to the south, down the road near the Smíchovské Nádraží train station, some of that old poverty and neglect start to set in again.

STAROPRAMEN'S WORLDWIDE REP

Staropramen is arguably the best-known Czech beer outside of the country – a fact that surprises locals. It's owned by mega US brewer Molson Coors and aggressively marketed around the world. What's so puzzling, though, is that in terms of local reputation, Staropramen has always come in well behind Pilsner Urquell and Budvar (Budweiser).

That opinion may well be outdated. It's true that after the 1989 anti-communist revolution, standards at Staropramen slipped. In the 1990s, you never knew what you were going to get from glass to glass.

In more recent years, beer quality has greatly improved. Staropramen's unfiltered and dark options hold their own. Beer preferences, of course, are subjective.

Villa Winternitz

Early-Modern Mansion Masterpiece
A walk through Villa Winternitz

The fully restored 1932 **Villa Winternitz** *(loosovavila.cz; adult/child 180/100Kč)*, the work of architects Adolf Loos and Karel Lhota, is a must for fans of early-modern and functionalist architecture. Indeed, Brno-born Loos (1870–1933) is often considered one of the fathers of stripped-down, spare-looking modern architecture. It was Loos who coined the concept 'ornament and crime'. By this he meant that ornamentation is based on fads that change over time and inevitably make a building look outdated.

This villa marks the architect's last design to be fully realised during his lifetime, and Loos' ideas of *raumplan* – minimalist design, lighting, use of quality materials and interior spacing – are on full display here.

The Winternitz family was forced to abandon the villa in 1941 during the Nazi occupation, and the house was later returned to the owner's descendants. The villa is open to visitors noon–6pm, Sunday–Wednesday. Alternatively, 70-minute guided tours in Czech *(per person 280Kč)* are offered on Saturdays and Sundays and can be booked on the website. Request an English tour in advance by email: loosovavila@gmail.com.

IMPROMPTU SMÍCHOV PUB CRAWL

As the site of the city's last-standing big national brewery, Smíchov is all about beer and a natural 'hood to conduct an extended pub crawl.

START	END	LENGTH
Zlatý Klas	Na Verandách	2km; 3 hours

This tour only scratches the surface of Smíchov's drinking possibilities. Feel free to branch off to other places as the mood strikes.

Start off at one of the neighbourhood's favourite old-school pubs, ❶ **Zlatý Klas** (p144). Here, beer is stored in big tanks, called *tankové pivo*, which is intended to keep it fresher. The traditional pub food is good, making this a sensible spot to line your stomach.

From here, head east along Plzeňská. This street and a parallel street, Na Bělidle, mark out the area's heartland of pubs. ❷ **U Bílého lva**, an uber-traditional Czech drinking spot, has been around since 1883. Everything feels authentic, down to the hardwood benches and shiny taps at the bar. From here, make your way over to ❸ **Andělský Pivovar** (p143), which offers a contrast to the older, classic pubs. It is an airy, renovated space that makes its own very good craft beers.

Just around the corner, nip in for a quick one at classic sports bar ❹ **Hospoda U Buldoka**. There's a drink-till-you-drop vibe here, but pace yourself. There's still one more pub to try. Head south on Nádražní a few blocks to sample beer direct from the Staropramen Brewery (p144) at ❺ **Na Verandách** (p144).

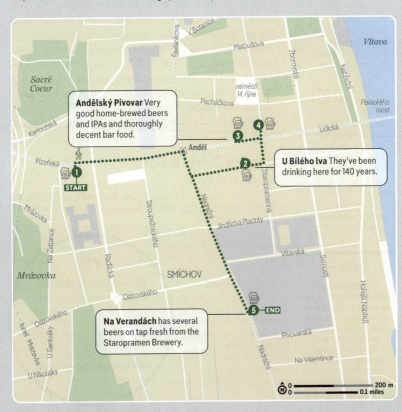

Vyšehrad

PRAGUE'S 'OTHER' CASTLE

GETTING AROUND

The former fortress and scattered ruins of Vyšehrad lie 2km south of the centre. If time is short, grab metro line C (red line) south of the centre to Vyšehrad station; from here walk 200m west to the **Tábor Gate**, the entryway to the complex. If you've got more time and want to stretch your legs a little, walk uphill along Vratislavova from the Výtoň tram stop near the Vltava River. Once you are within the fortress itself, distances are short, the sights are signposted and everything is easily walkable.

☑ TOP TIP

The **Vyšehrad Info Center** sells maps as well as soft drinks, light food and souvenirs. Check the main Vyšehrad website *(praha-vysehrad.cz)* for special guided tours that explore the complex's legends and darkest interiors.

A jaunt out to Vyšehrad is a trip back in time. This is one of Prague's oldest areas and deeply rooted in local legend. An early chieftain named Krok, in the 7th century, is said to have chosen this high bluff over the river to build his castle (the name Vyšehrad means 'upper castle'). And it was from here where his daughter Libuše prophesied that a great city would one day rise in the Vltava River valley. The earliest rulers of the Bohemian kingdom, in the 11th century, actually did make their home here, but they eventually relocated to Prague Castle on the other side of the river.

Sadly, those old castles and royal palaces are long gone. What's left is a clutch of historic buildings, including the city's most prestigious cemetery, a baroque fortress, and stretches of beautiful parkland, with arresting views over the city below. The complex is free to enter, though some buildings charge an entry fee at the door.

Prague's Oldest Building

Rotunda of St Martin

The simple, dignified 11th-century **Rotunda of St Martin** *(praha-vysehrad.cz; free)* is regarded as Prague's oldest-surviving building.

The rotunda's position here is testament to Vyšehrad's importance during the time of the early Bohemian kingdoms. The structure's thick walls and high, narrow windows are classic elements of Romanesque (pre-Gothic) architecture. The door and frescoes, though, were added much

ROMANESQUE IS RARE

Romanesque buildings, like the Rotunda of St Martin, which date back nearly 1000 years, are relatively rare in Prague. One of the finest examples of a surviving Romanesque structure is the **Basilica of St George** (p57) at Prague Castle.

later, during renovations carried out around 1880. During the bloody 17th century, when Vyšehrad served as a military fortress, the rotunda was used to store gunpowder.

The rotunda is normally closed to visitors, but the tiny interior can be viewed during mass times that are usually posted on the door.

Picnic on the Green

Drink and dine amid the statues

Vyšehrad's big grassy lawn is one of Prague's favourite spots to bring a food basket, drop a blanket and simply chill. There's lots of green up here, but most people prefer to relax in the sculpture garden, sitting amid a series of historic statues, including one of Vyšehrad heroes **Libuše and Přemysl**, created by Czech sculptor Josef Václav Myslbek 1889–97. For something fancier, **Bystro Cafe** *(bystrocafe.cz; 10am-10pm)* offers a full range of pre-prepared picnic baskets that you order in advance over the website and pick up at the cafe. You'll pay a 1000Kč deposit (for the glasses, silverware and basket) that you get back on return.

HIGHLIGHTS
1 Vyšehrad Cemetery

SIGHTS
2 Baroque Fortress
3 Basilica of Sts Peter & Paul
4 Gothic Cellar
5 Leopold Gate
6 Libuše and Přemysl statue
7 Peak Gate
8 Rotunda of St Martin
9 Tábor Gate

EATING
10 Bystro Cafe
11 Rio's Vyšehrad

DRINKING & NIGHTLIFE
12 Na Hradbách
13 U Kroka

ENTERTAINMENT
14 Letní scéna

INFORMATION
15 Vyšehrad Information Center

TOP EXPERIENCE

Vyšehrad Cemetery

Much like London's Highgate or Paris' Père Lachaise, Vyšehrad Cemetery *(free)* is more than a burial ground. The cemetery was conceived in the mid-19th century as a place to honour the very best Czech composers, writers, poets and artists of their day. The grounds themselves are lovely; many tombstones are works of art themselves, created in daring, eye-catching Cubist and art-nouveau styles.

TOP TIPS

- The cemetery is free to enter and wander at will.
- Find a list of famous graves and their locations posted at the door.
- The real fun here is simply walking the rows and locating the names.

Practicalities
Scan this QR code for opening hours and additional tour options.

Spot the Household Names

Vyšehrad Cemetery is the final resting place for dozens of Czech luminaries, including many names that will be familiar to visitors who might not otherwise know much about Czech culture. Some of the famous graves here include the composers Antonín Dvořák and Bedřich Smetana, as well as the art-nouveau artist and illustrator Alfons Mucha and artist Max Švabinský (and many others). Dvořák's grave is marked by a striking bust of the composer – the work of sculptor Ladislav Šaloun, the artist who created the Jan Hus monument in Old Town Square.

Don't Miss the 'Slavín'

The eastern end of the cemetery is dominated by the 'Slavín' (Pantheon), designed by Antonín Wiehl in the 1890s to feature noteworthy Czech writers and artists. The names may not be quite as renowned worldwide as in the general cemetery (though Mucha is interred here); they nevertheless demonstrate the importance Czech culture has attached to artistic achievement. In addition to Mucha, the pantheon holds the remains of Cubist architect Josef Gočár, opera singer Ema Destinnová, sculptor Bohumil Kafka, creator of the giant equestrian statue of Jan Žižka at the National Monument at Vítkov, and many others.

Check Out Vyšehrad's Basilica
Former rival to St Vitus

Vyšehrad's stately Gothic-spired **Basilica of Sts Peter & Paul** *(bazilika.kkvys.cz; adult/child 130/70Kč)* looms over the skyline and plays an analogous – though lower-key – role to Prague Castle's St Vitus as a royal cathedral (without, of course, any castle to attach to). The structure was built and rebuilt several times over the centuries. Like nearly everything here, the basilica suffered greatly from neglect and damage during the wars of the 15th and 17th centuries. Its arresting twin spires date from the 19th century and an architectural craze that gripped Prague at the time known as 'neo-Gothic'. The interior is richly decorated with ornamental art-nouveau wall paintings.

Pass Through Leopold Gate
The old royal entryway

The Vyšehrad complex, when approaching from the metro station, is marked by a series of impressive gates. Beyond the initial Tábor Gate, continue on to the more impressive 17th-century **Leopold Gate** *(praha-vysehrad.cz; free)*, a minor baroque masterpiece that recalls a time when this area was an important defence fortress for the ruling Habsburg empire. It has a central passageway for vehicles and two side corridors for pedestrians. Between these two main gates, note the only remnants of an earlier 14th-century Gothic gate, the '**Peak Gate**' (in Czech, *Špička brána*).

Peer into Gothic Cellars
What's left of the Royal Palace

The restored **Gothic Cellar** *(praha-vysehrad.cz; adult/child 120/80Kč)* here was once part of a four-chamber palace complex (other parts of the palace may have held a chapel and dining room) built here by Emperor Charles IV in the 14th century. The palace is long gone, but the cellars are used to house a permanent (rather dry) exhibition on the history and legends of Vyšehrad. The various display panels describe Vyšehrad's transition over the centuries from royal residence to fortress to tourist attraction. The high points are the relics on display from early pre-Slavic civilisations.

THE MYTH OF LIBUŠE

Fittingly for a country that embraces mystery, the origins of Prague are shrouded in a fairy tale that began here on Vyšehrad. Princess Libuše, the daughter of early ruler Krok, is said to have stood on this hill one day in the 8th century and predicted a glorious city would one day rise where she stood. According to the legend, Libuše needed to find a strong suitor who could yield sturdy heirs to the Bohemian throne. Passing over a field of eligible royal bachelors, she selected a simple ploughman: Přemysl. She chose well. The Přemysl dynasty would go on to rule for 400 years. In the 9th century, Přemysl prince Bořivoj selected an outcropping across the river in Prague's Hradčany district to build Prague Castle, the dynasty's seat.

Very good traditional dinner option.

 EATING & DRINKING IN VYŠEHRAD: OUR PICKS

Rio's Vyšehrad: Elegant outdoor dining in nice weather, located just opposite the beautiful Basilica of Sts Peter & Paul. *10am-10pm* €€

Bystro Cafe (p149): Pretty terrace makes for an ideal spot to linger over a casual coffee, beer or a light-bite breakfast or lunch. *10am-9pm* €

Na Hradbách: Hip beer garden with 3rd-gen coffees, craft beers and occasional live music. *noon-midnight* €

U Kroka: Classic Czech pub that delivers on not just good beer but excellent food too. Book in advance. *11.30am-11pm* €€

A STROLL AROUND VYŠEHRAD CITADEL

Walk the lovely grounds of this high-altitude park and learn something of Prague's earliest history.

START	END	LENGTH
Tábor Gate	Gothic Cellar	2km; two hours

Vyšehrad spreads out over gracious parkland and is best explored on a leisurely stroll. This walk hits the major sights and shows off pretty vistas. From Vyšehrad metro station, walk west 200m to ❶ **Tábor Gate** (p148). From here, continue through ❷ **Leopold Gate** (p151). Once inside the fortress proper, bear right to the ❸ **Rotunda of St Martin** (p148), a solemn relic that has been standing here for 1000 years.

Continue along the main path to the fortress' northern ramparts for stunning views over Prague. Look out for signs to the 'Brick Gate and Casements' to see the former ❹ **Baroque Fortress** (p153). From here, walk west and bear right to the fortress' northwestern corner, which holds ❺ **Letní Scéna**, a summer amphitheatre with dramatic views.

Trace the western wall to reach the impressive ❻ **Basilica of Sts Peter & Paul** (p151). Just near the church is the evocative ❼ **Vyšehrad Cemetery** (p150), the final resting place of Czech luminaries from the 19th and 20th centuries. From the cathedral and cemetery, walk south to a large park. A path leads to the ❽ **Gothic Cellar** (p151) and permanent exhibition on Vyšehrad's history.

Reward yourself with a meal at Rio's Vyšehrad (p151) or grab a beer at trendy Na Hradbách (p151).

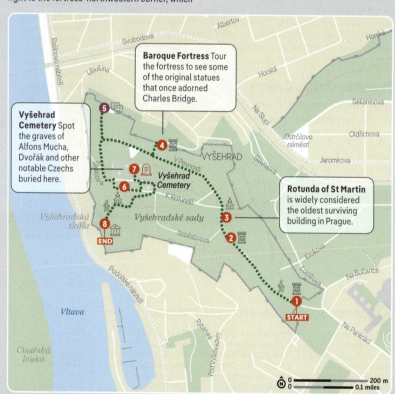

Baroque Fortress Tour the fortress to see some of the original statues that once adorned Charles Bridge.

Vyšehrad Cemetery Spot the graves of Alfons Mucha, Dvořák and other notable Czechs buried here.

Rotunda of St Martin is widely considered the oldest surviving building in Prague.

Gorlice Hall

Tour the Baroque Fortress
Spooky passageways, Charles Bridge statues

Most of Vyšehrad's surviving buildings, including this former **baroque fortress** *(praha-vysehrad.cz; tour adult/child 170/120Kč)* – known on maps as the 'Brick Gate and Casements' – date from later centuries, when the ruling Habsburg dynasty used the fortress to protect Prague against Prussian and French encroachment.

A guided 30-minute tour takes visitors through an elaborate system of vaulted brick tunnels within the ramparts. The highlight is the large, barrel-vaulted Gorlice Hall, where troops would muster without being seen by the enemy. Now, the space is home to several original baroque statues from Charles Bridge.

>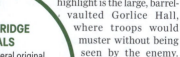
>
> **CHARLES BRIDGE ORIGINALS**
>
> Over the years, several original statues on **Charles Bridge** (p27) have been moved indoors to protect them from the elements. A few found a permanent home within the confines of the **Baroque Fortress**. Find others at the **Lapidarium** (p137) in Bubeneč.

AWESOME 'ALTERNATIVE UNIVERSE'

David Humphreys and Melissa Joulwan, Prague-based Americans, host a books-and-travel podcast, 'Strong Sense of Place' *(strong senseofplace.com)*.

The first time we climbed the stairs to Vyšehrad, a string quartet appeared through a stone arch and began to play Mozart. Then we turned a corner and discovered a cafe selling ice cream. We felt like we'd stumbled into an alternative universe where everything was awesome. Our affection for Prague's 'other castle' has only increased since then. It's our favourite spot to take an early morning walk, enjoy a picnic, and gaze at Prague Castle across the river. It doesn't hurt that myths and eerie legends are attached to every cobblestone, brick, monument and statue.

Day Trips from Prague

Castle-topped crags and pretty landscape parks share space with unassuming villages that tell tales straight out of the history books.

Places
Karlštejn p154
Průhonice p156
Lidice p156
Benešov p157
Křivoklát p158
Mělník p158
Kokořín p160

Prague is surrounded by rolling hills, river valleys, open fields and scattered woodlands. Thousand-year-old castles and wondrous landscape parks lie just an hour or so in any direction. Castle lovers will be spoiled for choice. Many visitors take the 40-minute train ride to Karlštejn to see the grand Gothic pile that used to hold the crown jewels. There's lot of contemporary history too. During WWII, the occupying Germans transformed an Austrian military garrison into the infamous 'Theresienstadt' Jewish ghetto at Terezín. Visitors can still walk the grim streets and learn of the awful events. A lesser-known memorial to another WWII tragedy, at Lidice, is about half an hour from Prague.

GETTING AROUND

While a car affords more freedom to visit the area around Prague, with some preplanning, most of the destinations here are accessible by bus or train. Many places have decent restaurants but may not offer much in the way of overnight accommodation. We've listed a few places to stay (p163), but some destinations are best explored as a day trip from Prague. Get an early start if the plan is to return the same day.

Karlštejn
TIME FROM PRAGUE: **40 MINS**

Bike out to Karlštejn
Most visitors take the train out to pretty Karlštejn village to take in impressive **Karlštejn Castle** (p155), but the village is close enough to Prague to reach by bike for cyclists of at least moderate ability. The path includes a few climbs, but generally passes through secluded woods and along quiet streams as well as the Vltava and Berounka rivers. The journey takes from three to four hours each way and is best done as part of a guided excursion. Several outfitters run a Karlštejn cycling outing. **Praha Bike** (*prahabike.cz; per person from 1600Kč*) offers a guided tour; **City Bike's** (*citybike-prague.com; per person from 790Kč*) Karlštejn trip is self-guided. Book over the websites.

Hike the Karlštejn Woods
It's easy to combine a visit to **Karlštejn Castle** (p155) with an invigorating three- to four-hour hike in the woods. The hike is moderately difficult, with some climbs, but doesn't demand any specialised skills. Get an early start at Prague's main train station. Instead of buying a ticket to Karlštejn, purchase a ticket for the next town over: **Beroun**. Walk out of the Beroun train station and look for a red-marked hiking trail. This is the path that eventually brings you to Karlštejn, about 15km away.

TOP EXPERIENCE

Karlštejn Castle

When you've had your fill of Prague, one fun, easy day-trip is to catch the train out to Karlštejn, 35km southwest of the capital, to see magnificent Karlštejn Castle. Treat yourself to a guided tour of the interior of the medieval fortress – which wouldn't look at all out of place on Disney World's Main Street – and then stroll through the charming little town that surrounds the structure.

Take the 'Basic' Tour of the Castle

Two main guided tours of the castle are available, but most visitors opt for the shorter, hourlong 'basic' tour. This option admittedly omits some of the more-impressive interiors, but provides a good overall introduction. You'll get glimpses into the Knight's Hall – still daubed with the coats-of-arms and names of the knight-vassals – as well as views of Charles IV's bedchamber, the Audience Hall and the Jewel House. Note that this tour option runs year-round and does not require advance booking.

Dive Deeper into the Castle Interiors

Real castle aficionados should opt for the longer 'exclusive' tour *(adult/child from 640/510Kč)*. Bear in mind that this option – which runs to 100 minutes – is only offered from May to October and must be reserved in advance. The reward is the chance to see the most valuable chambers, including the castle's star attraction: the exquisite Chapel of the Holy Cross, with its walls and vaulted ceiling adorned with thousands of polished semiprecious stones set in gilt stucco in the form of crosses. Note that kids might find the information overload a little dull.

TOP TIPS

● Karlštejn is an easy 40-minute train ride from Prague's Main Station.

● Wear comfy shoes and prepare to hike. The walk from the station to the castle is steep.

● The exclusive castle tour requires a prior reservation by phone (777 464 726) or e-mail: rezervace.karlstejn@npu.cz.

Practicalities
Scan this QR code for tour information and prices.

THE HISTORY OF KARLŠTEJN CASTLE

Karlštejn Castle was conceived by Holy Roman Emperor Charles IV in the 14th century to serve as a hideaway for the Bohemian crown jewels. Run by an appointed burgrave, the castle was surrounded by a network of landowning knights, who came to the castle's aid whenever enemies moved against it. Karlštejn was again used to shelter the royal valuables during the destructive Hussite Wars of the 15th century. Afterwards, the castle fell into disrepair, as its defences were regarded at the time as being outmoded. Considerable restoration work in the late 19th century returned the castle to its former glory. One of the main architects was Josef Mocker, the king of Prague's neo-Gothic architectural craze.

The hike itself is surprisingly varied. After passing through humdrum outskirts of Beroun, descend into the quiet woods. For part of the walk, the path parallels a long, sloping waterfall. The highlight of the hike is the small village of **Svatý Jan pod Skalou**, a picturesque place with a few outbuildings and an evocative chapel and cemetery. After an hour or so from here, you will alight onto a meadow and the towers of Karlštejn Castle round into view. Visit the castle or relax at one of the many restaurants in town and reward your efforts with a beer and hot meal. Take the train back to Prague from Karlštejn station.

Průhonice
TIME FROM PRAGUE: **60 MINS**

See pretty Průhonice Chateau and Park

Elegant **Průhonice Chateau** *(pruhonickypark.cz; adult/child 140/90Kč)* and the surrounding English-style park, in the southern Prague suburb of Průhonice, are considered a constituent part of Prague's UNESCO World Heritage designation. The town is an easy day trip from the capital. The original chateau complex dates to the 13th century but has been built and rebuilt several times over the years to today's majestic, 19th-century neo-Renaissance residence. After visiting the chateau, stroll the gardens and grab a coffee or bite at **Caffé Castello Průhonice** *(caffecastello.cz; 10am-8pm)*. To get to Průhonice, take metro Line C (red line) to Opatov station and transfer to bus 357 or 363.

Lidice
TIME FROM PRAGUE: **1 HR**

Pay respects at the Lidice Memorial

About 20km northwest of Prague, accessible by public transport, the **Lidice Memorial and Museum** *(lidice-memorial.cz; adult/child 150/70Kč)* recalls the tragic events that took place here in 1942 during WWII. The occupying Nazis senselessly razed the village that stood here in retaliation for the assassination by Czechoslovak paratroopers of Nazi leader Reinhard Heydrich. The Nazis murdered the village's 200 men and sent the women and children to ghettos and concentration camps in Nazi-occupied Poland. The solemn exhibitions tell the story, and the adjoining rose garden is particularly moving and beautiful in springtime. To reach Lidice, take metro Line A (green line) to Nádraží Veleslavín and board bus 300 or 322.

FATE OF THE PARATROOPERS

Lidice paid the ultimate price for the Czechoslovak action to assassinate Reinhard Heydrich. The **Church of Sts Cyril & Methodius** (p106) in Nové Město is filled with information on the operation.

Konopiště Château

Benešov
TIME FROM PRAGUE: 1 HR

Tour Archduke Franz Ferdinand's estate

The name of Archduke Franz Ferdinand d'Este is well known to history buffs. It was his famous assassination, along with his Czech wife Žofia Chotková, in Sarajevo in June 1914 that triggered WWI. But what's not so well known is that the heir to Austro-Hungarian throne actually made his home here, at **Konopiště Château** *(zamek-konopiste.cz)*, near Benešov, 50km south of Prague. A tour of the castle presents the chance to take in historic Gothic architecture dating back to the 13th century and to learn more about the habits and eccentricities of this ill-fated heir – particularly his twin obsessions with hunting and the cult of St George.

The chateau, dominated by large cylindrical towers, and the gardens are immediately impressive, but the interiors border on bizarre. Franz Ferdinand acquired the building in 1887, and after renovating the structure and installing all the latest technology – including electricity, central heating, flush toilets, showers and a lift – he began decorating his home with hunting trophies. His game books record that he shot about 300,000 creatures; a whopping 100,000 animal trophies are said to adorn the walls. The archduke's collection of art and artefacts relating to St George amounts to 3750 items. You'll need a full day to make the most of a visit here.

FAVOURITE SPOTS TO EXPLORE AROUND PRAGUE

Kateřina H Pavlitová is a communications professional, who lives on the outskirts of Prague.

A short bus ride from the Opatov metro stop brings you to **Průhonice** (p156), with its extensive English park and local chateau. It's especially lovely in spring when the rhododendrons are in bloom.

Berounka River, southwest of Prague, has stunning limestone rock formations, a verdant river valley and hills covered by deep woods. There are many hiking and biking options. I recommend the 15km hike from Karlštejn to the picturesque village of Svatý Jan pod Skalou (p156) to Beroun along the red trail. In Beroun, reward yourself at the Blackdog Bar & Grill (p157) restaurant with burgers and regional beers.

American-style burgers and fries.

🍴 EATING NEAR KARLŠTEJN: OUR PICKS

Restaurace Pod Dračí Skálou: Appealing Karlštejn country inn; outdoor tables, barbecue grill. *11am–10pm Mon–Sat, to 8pm Sun* €

Karlštejn 34: Well-done Asian fusion menu of Vietnamese and Korean favourites. *11am–6pm Fri–Tue* €€

U Adama: Traditional Czech food with terrace dining (served near a cosy fireplace in cold weather) in Karlštejn. *10am–6pm Tue–Sun* €€

Blackdog Bar & Grill: In Beroun, well-prepared steaks, barbecued meats, burgers and burritos at popular restaurant. *11am–10pm* €€

GETTING TO MĚLNÍK

Mělník makes an easy day trip by bus from Prague. Plan on taking the chateau tour in the morning, followed by lunch and then a stroll around the other sites – they're all bunched up close together. The terrace on the far side of the chateau has superb views across the water to the confluence of the Vltava and Labe (Elbe) rivers.

Buses run to Mělník from the bus stop outside Prague's Ládví metro station (Line C, red line); buy your ticket from the driver. The ride takes about 45 minutes. Alternatively, the Prague Steamboat Co (p160) runs an all-day Vltava River cruise from Prague to Mělník and returns on selected dates from May to September.

Entry to the chateau is by guided tour, with several tours on offer. All of the tours take around an hour. Tour 3 is probably the most interesting, but requires an advance reservation over the castle website *(zamek-konopiste.cz; tour adult/child 420/340Kč)*. This circuit focuses on the private apartments used by the archduke and his family, which have been restored from photographs to appear as they looked when the state took possession of the chateau in 1921. Don't miss the chance to walk around the pretty gardens. The best way to reach Konopiště is by train from Prague's main station to Benešov u Prahy, and then walk about 2km to the chateau. There are a couple of decent restaurants within walking distance from the chateau.

Křivoklát
TIME FROM PRAGUE: **60 MINS**

Gothic splendour and royal dungeons

Remote, foreboding **Křivoklát Castle** *(hrad-krivoklat.cz)*, tucked deep in the woods about 40km southwest of Prague, is one of the area's spookiest castles, yet sees relatively few international visitors. The castle is set amid the sprawling Křivoklátsko Protected Landscape Area, a UNESCO-listed biosphere that covers the highlands on both sides of the Berounka River. The surrounding nature once served as a royal hunting ground.

Learn about and book tours over the castle website or buy tickets at the castle ticket window. Visitors can opt for either a 'shorter' 60-minute tour *(adult/child 240/190Kč)* or an 80-minute 'longer' tour *(adult/child 340/270Kč)*. Both include the most important sights: the second castle courtyard, royal hall, prison and dungeon. The longer tour adds the library, picture gallery, museum and lapidarium (where some distinguished stone monuments are displayed).

Křivoklát is easiest to reach by car, but is also accessible by train from Prague's main station; most services require a change in Beroun. Note that the castle is located about a 15-minute walk from Křivoklát station. The area is surrounded by a pretty landscape park and there are a couple of decent places to eat (and a small hotel) nearby.

Mělník
TIME FROM PRAGUE: **45 MINS**

Tour and tasting at Mělník Chateau

Unlike most places in Bohemia, where beer is king, the small city of Mělník, about 30km north of Prague, prides itself on wine, and a visit to **Mělník Château** *(lobkowicz-melnik.cz;*

Great lunch pick on a chateau visit.

EATING IN KŘIVOKLÁT & KONOPIŠTĚ: OUR PICKS

Restaurace pod Hradem: Decent Czech cooking at the best of a small number of places near Křivoklát Castle. *11am-10pm Fri-Sun* €

Restaurant Na Bejkárná: In Benešov, 2km northeast of Konopiště Chateau. Above-average pork steaks, chicken and pasta. *11am-11pm* €€

Hotel Sýkora Křivoklát: Handsomely renovated hotel restaurant specialising in Czech cooking. Just below Křivoklát Castle. *11am-9.30pm* €€

Stará Myslivna: Walking distance from Konopiště Chateau. Old-fashioned Czech restaurant in 19th-century gamekeeper's lodge. *11am-9pm* €€

Mělník Château

adult/child 190/120Kč) includes a chance to sample some of the local vintage. The vines in the small vineyard below the old town are supposedly descendants of the first vines introduced to Bohemia, by Emperor Charles IV in the 14th century. The chateau itself sprawls over a rocky promontory surrounded by the flat Central Bohemian plains. The dramatic setting is amplified by stunning views over the confluence of Czechia's two most important rivers, the Vltava and Labe (Elbe). The chateau was acquired by the noble Lobkowicz family in 1739 and opened to the public in 1992. You can wander through the former living quarters, which are crowded with a rich collection of baroque furniture and 17th- and 18th-century paintings, on a self-guided tour with English text. A separate tour descends to the 14th-century wine cellars for the tasting sessions.

Incredible church-top views

Next to Mělník Château, 15th-century **Church of Sts Peter & Paul** *(adult/child 50/30Kč)* sports a Gothic exterior and baroque furnishings. Climb to the top of the tower for superlative views. The church crypt holds an **ossuary** *(adult/child 50/30Kč)* packed with the bones of around 15,000 people. The space feels even more visceral and claustrophobic than the better-known **Sedlec Ossuary** in Kutná Hora.

FATEFUL ASSASSINATION

Austrian Archduke Franz Ferdinand d'Este, nephew of Habsburg Emperor Franz Joseph I and heir-apparent to the Austro-Hungarian throne, will go down in history as perhaps the most-fateful figure of the 20th century. After all, it was his assassination in Sarajevo on 28 June 1914 that triggered the bloodbath of WWI and all that followed.

At the time, Franz Ferdinand and his Czech wife, Žofia Chotková, had been on an official visit to Bosnia, then a province of Austria-Hungary. Both Franz Ferdinand and his wife were shot to death by a young separatist, Gavrilo Princip, after an earlier assassination attempt by bombing that day had failed.

 EATING IN MĚLNÍK & KOKOŘÍN: OUR PICKS

Němý Medvěd: Mělník's go-to for burgers, fries and craft beers in an informal, family-friendly setting. 11am-10pm €€

Pobuda: Lifesaver cafe and restaurant; one of the few refreshment options near Kokořín Castle. 11am-8pm €€

Kafe Mělník ve Věži: Freshly roasted coffee and light bites within Mělník's distinctive Gothic 'Prague Gate' (Pražská brána). 10am-8pm €

Restaurace na Hradbách: In central Mělník, good Czech comfort and comfy outdoor seating in warm weather. 11am-10pm €€

Kokořín Castle

KŘIVOKLÁT CASTLE'S ORIGINS

The castle's origins date back to the 12th century and the earliest years of the Bohemian kingdom. It features spectacular Gothic interiors, the Royal Hall (which is second in significance only to Prague Castle's Vladislav Hall), a black kitchen, an immense library, and a prison and dungeon system that over the years held some famous prisoners. One of the towers here was allegedly used to imprison the English occultist and alchemist Edward Kelly, who was arrested in 1591 on the orders of Emperor Rudolf II himself for failing to turn base metals into gold.

Sail the river to Mělník

Most visitors to Mělník drive or travel by bus, but it's also possible to hop on a boat in Prague and float all the way here along the Vltava River. Several boat operators in Prague offer out-and-back cruises. The day typically takes around 15 hours, which includes a couple of hours of sightseeing in Mělník. The **Prague Steamboat Co** (*praguesteamboats.com; return adult/child 990/590Kč*) has a once-monthly voyage during summer that includes meals and unlimited drinks. Some highlights include passing through locks along the river, glancing out at the prominent, 460m-high Říp Mountain, seeing the confluence of the Vltava and Elbe rivers, and of course touring Mělník. Cruises depart Prague from Rašínovo embankment (Rašínovo nábřeží), located in Nové Město between the Palacký and Jirásek bridges. Check the website for departure times and prices, and to book tickets.

Kokořín

TIME FROM PRAGUE: **60 MINS**

See dramatic Kokořín Castle

About 10km northeast of Mělník, the 14th-century **Kokořín Castle** (Hrad Kokořín; *hrad-kokorin.cz; basic tour adult/child 120/90Kč*) features large sandstone ramparts and a solemn tower that really does feel straight out of a fairy tale. The castle was badly damaged in the 15th-century Hussite religious wars and stood as a romantic ruin for nearly 500 years, until it was purchased and refurbished in the early 20th century. The castle is open to the public via guided tour. It's surrounded by a stunning landscape park that's marked by steep sandstone rocks and canyons. There are several hiking trails, and a road makes the park accessible to cars and cyclists.

 EATING NEAR TEREZÍN: OUR PICKS

Bistro u Vlčáků: Passable hot dogs, burgers, tortillas and salads within Terezín's main fortress. *9am-5pm* €

Radniční sklípek: Well-done Czech classics in a deep-cellar dining room on nearby Litoměřice's main square. *11am-11pm* €€

Biskupský Pivovar: Popular restaurant and mini-brewery in Litoměřice makes its own very good unfiltered beer. *11am-10pm* €€

Káva s párou: Great for coffees, cakes, sandwiches and snacks (gluten-free options) in Litoměřice's former railway station. *10am-8pm* €

TOP EXPERIENCE

Terezín Fortress

The Terezín Fortress (Theresienstadt), a former Austrian military garrison, is Czechia's most-important Holocaust-remembrance site, and remains largely unchanged from those days. Visitors can stroll the melancholy grounds, where during WWII the occupying Germans transformed the fortress into a holding ghetto and transit camp. Some 150,000 people, mostly Jews, eventually passed through here, many en route to Nazi-run death camps in Poland.

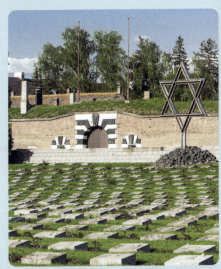

Lesser Fortress

Learn Terezín's Horrific Story

The Nazis infamously transformed Terezín into a showcase camp in order to fool international observers into thinking Germany's antisemitic policies were somehow 'humane'. Official visitors to the fortress, including representatives of the International Red Cross, were told that Terezín was a Jewish 'refuge', where Jews had their own administration, banks, shops, cafes and schools, as well as a thriving cultural life. This outrageous charade, sadly, completely fooled the observers.

Stroll the Main Fortress

The main sights are spread out over several buildings within the main fortress of the original 18th-century Austrian garrison. Highlights include the **Ghetto Museum**, which showcases wartime life inside the Terezín ghetto, and the former **Magdeburg Barracks** (200m south at Tyršova 204), which served as the seat of the Jewish 'Town Council'.

Don't Miss the 'Small Fortress'

A separate **Lesser Fortress**, east of the Main Fortress, was used by the Gestapo during the war as a POW camp and holding facility for political prisoners. You can tour the former guard offices and prison cells, including the execution site where some 2600 prisoners lost their lives. Watch a short documentary film (English subtitles) on the fortress's sad history.

TOP TIPS

● Regular buses from Prague depart from the Nádraží Holešovice metro station (Line C, red line).

● Several companies offer guided excursions to Terezín, including **Wittmann Tours** (wittmann-tours.com).

● Pack lunch before visiting, as there are few decent restaurants in Terezín.

Practicalities
Scan this QR code for prices and further information.

Places We Love to Stay

€ Budget   €€ Midrange   €€€ Top End

Prague Castle & Hradčany   p54

Hotel Monastery €€ Set in a 17th-century townhouse, the rooms here have been given a bright, modern makeover, complete with polished wood floors and dashes of colour from bedspreads and sofas. Quiet, parklike setting near Strahov Monastery.

Romantik Hotel U Raka €€€ Timber cottage with six low-ceilinged doubles tucked away in a remote corner of the picturesque Nový Svět quarter. Timber beams, wood floors and red-brick fireplaces. Book well in advance.

Malá Strana   p63

Little Quarter Hostel € Gleamingly clean and perched halfway between Charles Bridge and Prague Castle. Try to book early.

Dům U Velké Boty €€ The quaint 'House at the Big Boot' is set on a quiet square, just five minutes' walk from the castle and Charles Bridge.

Golden Well Hotel €€€ A secluded, elegant Renaissance house that is a popular choice for honeymooners in Prague.

Aria Hotel €€€ Five-star luxury. Each room sports a musical theme and the rooftop views are phenomenal.

Staré Město   p76

Ahoy! Hostel € A pleasant, welcoming and peaceful hostel (definitely not for the pub-crawl crowd), with eager-to-please staff.

Design Hotel Josef €€ The work of London-based Czech architect Eva Jiřičná; the minimalist theme is evident in the stark white lobby with glass spiral staircase.

Dominican €€€ Housed in the former monastery of St Giles, this luxury hotel is bursting with character and is full of delightful period details.

Nové Město (New Town)   p95

Sophie's Hostel € Chic step up from a typical hostel; contemporary style, with oak-veneer floors and stark, minimalist decor. Book way in advance.

Icon Hotel €€ Pretty much everything in this gorgeous boutique hotel on a hidden alleyway behind Wenceslas Square has a designer stamp on it.

Boutique Hotel 16 – U Sv. Kateřiny €€ Cosy, family-run affair, occupying a tranquil nook. The back rooms offer views onto a peaceful, terraced garden.

Mosaic House €€ Modern, clean and eye-catching, fully in keeping with the hotel's 1930s' functionalist design ethos. Great location, just a short walk from the Vltava riverbank.

Almanac X Alcron Hotel €€€ Glamorous old-school hotel from the 1930s, just off Wenceslas Square and still sporting many of the original art-deco marble-and-glass fittings.

Žižkov & Karlín   p109

Brix Hostel € Enthusiastic Žižkov hostel focused on making your stay enjoyable, from a warm welcome to the custom-built bunks and clean, modern bathrooms. The hostel's bar is open pretty much 24/7, and is a great place to make new acquaintances.

Hotel Royal Prague €€ Affordable, upscale, modern hotel – suitable for business or leisure travellers – feels perfectly in sync with Karlín's quick rise as one of Prague's nicest and most energetic neighbourhoods.

Hotel Mucha €€ A historic facade hides a deceptively stylish, modern hotel. Convenient location, just a short walk from Florenc metro station.

Botanique Hotel €€€ A full makeover – using plenty of white cottons and lighter-tone woods – has given the rooms here a fresh, natural feel.

Hotel Fitzgerald €€€ Handsome boutique hotel with elegant rooms, chic in-house cocktail bar and good location, close to Karlín's nightspots.

Vinohrady & Vršovice   p115

Czech Inn € Functions as both a hostel and boutique hotel, with a youthful vibe and lots of flash industrial design. The location is just off of Vršovice's party strip, though the hotel's location is quiet.

Arkada €€ Small hotel in an upscale residential area offers an attractive combination of style, comfort and location. The rooms are well-appointed, with a retro-1930s feel that fits the style of the building.

Le Palais Hotel €€€
Housed in a gorgeous belle-époque building from the 19th century that's been lovingly restored, complete with original floor mosaics, period fireplaces, marble staircases and painted ceilings.

Holešovice p123

Sir Toby's Hostel € Set in a refurbished apartment building with a spacious kitchen and common room. Offerings include all-female rooms; the bigger dorms are some of the cheapest in Prague.

Mama Shelter Prague €€
The Prague outpost of the fun French design-hotel chain Mama Shelter is full of loud, clashing patterns and modern flair – which you may not expect from the exterior of a grey, blocky communist-era building.

Absolutum Hotel €€ Eye-catching boutique across from Nádraží Holešovice metro station. The industrial setting wouldn't win a beauty contest, but the hotel compensates with smartly designed rooms, a wellness centre and an excellent restaurant.

Bubeneč & Dejvice p132

Hotel International €€
Impressive communist-era pile built in the 1950s, complete with Soviet-style star atop the tower. Best for history or architecture buffs.

Art Hotel €€ Small, well-managed hotel in a quiet neighbourhood behind the Sparta Praha football stadium. Sleek, modern styling throughout, with contemporary Czech art displayed in the lobby.

Smíchov p142

Red & Blue Design Hotel €€
Well-tended designer boutique set in a smartly renovated 19th-century townhouse.

Vienna House by Wyndham Andel's €€ Artful, contemporary hotel with minimalist decor. The location is a short walk from Anděl metro station.

Hotel Julian €€ Small, elegant hotel in a quiet location, just south of Malá Strana, sports a lovely rooftop terrace.

Beyond Prague p148

Pension Konopiště € Good-value pension within easy walking distance of Konopiště Château.

Hotel Sýkora Křivoklát €
Clean, nicely renovated, modern and practically across the street from Křivoklát Castle.

U Adama € Homely, family-run pension with a good restaurant and well-located in the heart of Karlštejn.

Hotel U Rytíře €€ Tastefully renovated apartment rentals in Mělník's historic centre. Friendly hosts and excellent breakfasts.

Parkhotel €€ Decent for a night; one of the few acceptable sleeping options in quiet Terezín.

Hotel Mlýn Karlštejn €€
Clean, bright, romantic choice for anyone planning to stay over in Karlštejn.

Hotel Karlštejn & Spa €€€
Enjoy Karlštejn in style, wallowing in the pool or spa, with pretty views up to the castle.

Romantik Hotel U Raka

Researched by Marc Di Duca

South & West Bohemia

SPAS, BEER AND UNESCO SITES

The western and southern regions contain some of the country's most famous places of interest.

Taking up most of the Czech lands west of Prague, Bohemia's south and west share many things. UNESCO listings pepper the landscape, from the medieval resplendence of Český Krumlov to the mines of the Krušné Mountains. The aroma of hops drifts in the air: Plzeň's brewing traditions are based on Bohemia's crystal-clear water, and Saaz hops – grown between Rakovník and Žatec – are said to be the best in the world. What links the south and west physically are endless forests and mountains, the Krušné Range in the north linked to the Šumava in the south by an unbroken string of virtually uninhabited, thickly forested peaks and valleys, ideal for backcountry hiking and mountain biking.

The spas of the Karlovy Vary (Carlsbad) region form the second most popular attraction in the country after Prague, with hundreds of thousands arriving each year to take the cure. With its hot thermal water and luxury spa area, Karlovy Vary is essential viewing, while Mariánské Lázně offers a more understated and relaxing experience. The three main spas here (little Františkovy Lázně completing the trio) were listed by UNESCO in 2021 as World Cultural Heritage Sites.

Other highlights in this incredibly varied wedge of central Europe include the folk traditions of the Chodsko region, spectacular castles at Loket, Český Krumlov and Bečov, and one of the country's best attractions for kids, Plzeň's Techmania.

THE MAIN AREAS

KARLOVY VARY
The country's biggest spa town.
p170

MARIÁNSKÉ LÁZNĚ
Exquisite spa town at altitude.
p178

PLZEŇ (PILSEN)
Bohemia's hop-infused second city.
p184

ČESKÝ KRUMLOV
Astonishingly quaint, UNESCO-listed town.
p190

For places to stay in South & West Bohemia, see p197

THE GUIDE

SOUTH & WEST BOHEMIA

Left: Krušné Mountains (p176); Above: Karlovy Vary (p170)

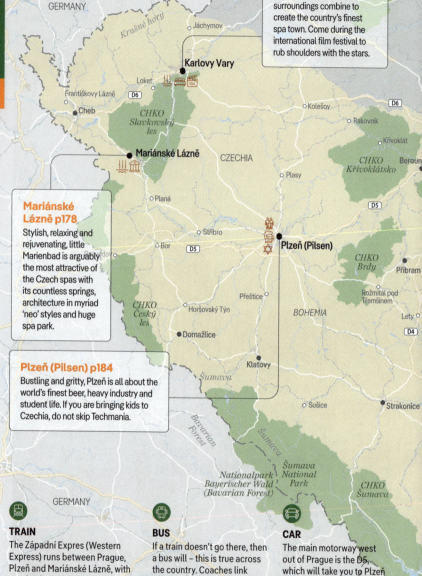

Karlovy Vary p170
Hot spas and exquisite natural surroundings combine to create the country's finest spa town. Come during the international film festival to rub shoulders with the stars.

Mariánské Lázně p178
Stylish, relaxing and rejuvenating, little Marienbad is arguably the most attractive of the Czech spas with its countless springs, architecture in myriad 'neo' styles and huge spa park.

Plzeň (Pilsen) p184
Bustling and gritty, Plzeň is all about the world's finest beer, heavy industry and student life. If you are bringing kids to Czechia, do not skip Techmania.

TRAIN
The Západní Expres (Western Express) runs between Prague, Plzeň and Mariánské Lázně, with another branch going out to Domažlice. Karlovy Vary is linked to Plzeň, Prague and Mariánské Lázně direct. Train is the way to reach České Budějovice, but not Český Krumlov.

BUS
If a train doesn't go there, then a bus will – this is true across the country. Coaches link Prague with every major town in the region, and local bus companies connect towns to each other. Rare is the bus that runs on Saturday afternoon or Sunday.

CAR
The main motorway west out of Prague is the D5, which will take you to Plzeň and almost to the spas. The permanently-under-construction D6 will one day link the capital to Karlovy Vary. The main route south is the slow, unfinished D3.

Find Your Way

The south and west constitute a large part of the Czech lands but have no fear – transport links are good here and you'll have no problem reaching even the remotest of villages and trailheads.

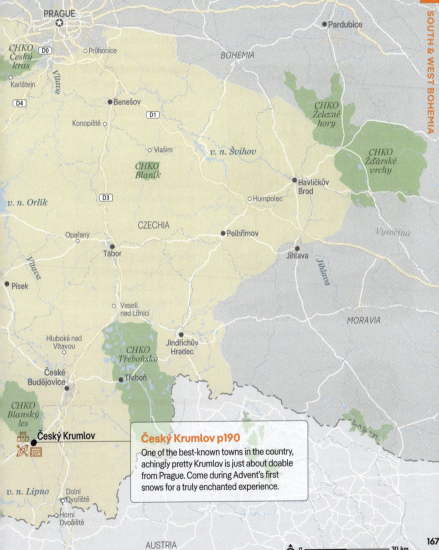

Český Krumlov p190
One of the best-known towns in the country, achingly pretty Krumlov is just about doable from Prague. Come during Advent's first snows for a truly enchanted experience.

Plan Your Time

The south and west are definitely all about finding a base and striking out from there to explore the surrounding area.

Moser glassworks (p170)

A Day Trip from Prague

Morning

Karlovy Vary (p170) has the most to offer on a (longish) day trip from Prague. Start early from Prague's main train station or Florence coach station to make the most of your day. Head straight to the **Moser Glassworks and Museum** (p170) for a fascinating tour. Then bus it to the centre and head into the spa for lunch at **Tusculum** (p172).

Afternoon

In the afternoon, buy a spa cup from a streetside kiosk and sample the gurgling hot mineral springs as you go. If it's cold, warm up at the 73°C geyser that splutters into a glass copula. Make a lightning visit to the **Diana lookout tower** (p173) before buying that souvenir bottle of Becherovka and catching the last train or coach back to the capital.

Seasonal Highlights

The region enjoys very distinct seasons and has the food and festivals to fit each one. Don't assume summer is the best time to come – the snowy winters lend a new dimension to this destination.

JANUARY
Snow blankets the mountains and forests, the skiing season hits top gear and cosy taverns light their wood burners. Most castles are closed but museums can get you out of the cold for a bit.

MAY
The biggest bash of the year takes place in Mariánské Lázně: the grand opening of the spa season. The town fills with visitors and the highlight is a free concert at the colonnade by a Czech or Slovak superstar.

JUNE
One of the biggest medieval parties in central Europe takes place in Český Krumlov – the Five-Petalled Rose Festival (p192) – which sees the entire centre turned into a medieval pageant with processions, jousting and jesters.

A Two-Day Break

Day One
For overnighters from the capital, the first stop should be **Plzeň** (p184), Bohemia's second city and its industrial epicentre. Here you can combine a visit to the **Pilsner Urquell Brewery** (p184) with some light sightseeing in the historical centre, or you can spend the day experimenting at **Techmania**. (It's a squeeze to do both in a single day.)

Day Two
On day two it's an hour by train to swish little **Mariánské Lázně** (p178) to explore the spa area with its colonnades, churches, 40 refreshingly cold mineral water springs, British royal connections and soothing green backdrop of the **Slavkovský Forest** (p182). From the town you might just be able to squeeze in a short hike before making a lightning trip to **Bečov Castle** (p182) or **Loket Castle** (p175).

Take a Week Out

In a week you can explore the entire region and fit in a hike or two.

Spend the first day in **Karlovy Vary** (p170) enjoying the architecture and thermal springs.

Via a stop-off at **Loket Castle** (p175), perched dramatically above the Ohře River, you'll easily make it for lunch in the tranquil spa town of **Mariánské Lázně** (p178) on day two.

Day three brings you to **Plzeň** (p184) for the Pilsner Urquell Brewery tour and a stroll around the centre.

With a car you can detour to **Domažlice** (p189) on day four before hitting **Český Krumlov** (p190) and dinner by the Vltava River.

Spend day six exploring Krumlov further or hiking the surroundings.

Day seven delivers you to the easy-going city of **České Budějovice** (p195) and **Hluboká Castle** (p196).

THE GUIDE

SOUTH & WEST BOHEMIA

JULY
July is all about the Karlovy Vary International Film Festival (p172), one of the biggest events on the Czech calendar. The films shown are top-notch, tickets easily available and at least one Hollywood star shows up each year.

AUGUST
The Chod Festival in Domažlice, the Český Krumlov International Music Festival and the Mariánské Lázně Chopin Festival all take place in the heat of August. Also the best time to scavenge for blueberries in the forests.

SEPTEMBER
This is arguably the best month to travel when the weather is still good, the crowds have thinned in Český Krumlov and everything is still open. Observe real Czech life as towns reawaken after summer.

DECEMBER
The first snow falls in subalpine areas, and the region's best Christmas markets take place on Plzeň's main square and on the courtyard of Loket Castle. Czechs can be seen buying live carp on town squares.

Karlovy Vary

THERMAL SPAS | EXCLUSIVE GLASS | GRAND ARCHITECTURE

Karlovy Vary (Carlsbad, KV), or simply 'Vary' to Czechs, perhaps more than any other town in Central Europe best captures the lost glamour and elegance of 19th-century spa culture. The promenades, colonnades and most of all the grand neoclassical buildings dazzle the eye. In the resort's heyday, royals like Russia's Peter the Great and members of the Habsburg monarchy mixed here with the greatest thinkers, writers and composers of their time. Four decades of communism drew a grey curtain across proceedings but, since the 1990s, restoration here has been quicker than anywhere else outside Prague.

These days, visitors come mainly to admire the architecture and to stroll the impressive colonnades, sipping on the health-restoring sulphurous waters from spouted ceramic drinking cups. Away from the cure, the town has many other attractions and is a good base for hiking into the surrounding forested hills. It's also the jumping-off point for trips into the largely undiscovered Krušné Mountains.

GETTING AROUND

Karlovy Vary has two train stations, Dolní (Lower) and Horní (Upper). Trains from Prague pull in at the Upper station, those from Mariánské Lázně at the Lower station. Bus 1 runs to the spa from the Upper station, while the Lower station is within walking distance of the Tržnice, the central city bus interchange. Buses 2 and 13 go to the spa. Coaches from Prague arrive at the Lower station. The spa bulges away from the town proper along the Teplá Valley, but the whole thing is walkable. There's a large paid car park at the Lower station.

☑ TOP TIP

There are many springs in Karlovy Vary and you might be tempted to sample them all. However, be aware that the hot sulphurous water tastes pretty bad and too much of it may see you seeking a WC before long.

Watch the Glassblowers at Work

Visiting the Moser Glassworks

The most interesting reason to leave the spa area is to visit the **Moser Glassworks and Museum** (moser.com; adult/family 350/750Kč) around 4km to the west. Take bus 2 from the theatre.

The Moser company opened its first workshop in Karlovy Vary in 1857, and by 1873 had established a large glassworks and become the official supplier to the imperial court of Franz Josef I. He obviously put in a good word with his English friend, King Edward VII, as Moser also became the official supplier of glass to British royalty in 1907. Throughout the 20th century, this exquisite glassware was used by governments and heads of state and remains one of the world's most exclusive brands for wealthy clients in the know.

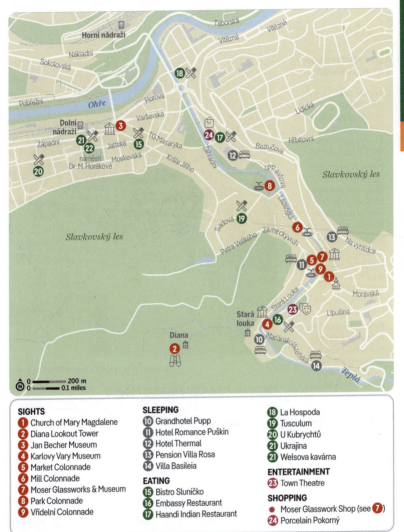

SIGHTS
1. Church of Mary Magdalene
2. Diana Lookout Tower
3. Jan Becher Museum
4. Karlovy Vary Museum
5. Market Colonnade
6. Mill Colonnade
7. Moser Glassworks & Museum
8. Park Colonnade
9. Vřídelní Colonnade

SLEEPING
10. Grandhotel Pupp
11. Hotel Romance Puškin
12. Hotel Thermal
13. Pension Villa Rosa
14. Villa Basileia

EATING
15. Bistro Sluníčko
16. Embassy Restaurant
17. Haandi Indian Restaurant
18. La Hospoda
19. Tusculum
20. U Kubrychtů
21. Ukrajina
21. Welsova kavárna

ENTERTAINMENT
23. Town Theatre

SHOPPING
● Moser Glasswork Shop (see 7)
24. Porcelain Pokorný

A visit to the glassworks is one of the most memorable things you might do outside Prague. Guided tours begin with a description of the glassmaking process before you are shown into the workshop. Here you can watch the glassblowers taking molten glass out of the furnaces and blowing it into all manner of receptacles using wooden moulds; you are allowed close enough to feel heat radiating from the orange-glowing glass.

After the glassworks, the museum traces the history of production in thousands of pieces of priceless glass. After that, head to the shop – prices will come as a shock. A single delicate wine glass will set you back around €100; a vase, thousands.

SOUVENIRS FROM KARLOVY VARY

Becherovka: This strong-tasting herbal liquor, made to a secret recipe, is available at every bar and grocery store.

Moser Glass: Visit the **Moser factory shop or Hotel Pupp** (p173) store for an eternal reminder of your trip.

Spa cups: Among the most popular Bohemian souvenirs are these curiously shaped cups, available from spa kiosks.

Porcelain: Head to **Porcelain Pokorný** (nábřeží J. Palacha 924/6) for a wide choice of locally produced wares.

Spa wafers: Typical Czech-spa toothrotters available at stalls in the spa zone.

Petrified roses: Roses left in the spring water accumulate mineral residue, essentially turning to stone; buy one from kiosks in the Vřídelní Colonnade.

Karlovy Vary International Film Festival

Experience Cinematic Magic

Eastern Europe's biggest film festival

The **Karlovy Vary International Film Festival** (*kviff.com*) in July is the region's biggest annual event, featuring around 200 films over eight days. Tickets are relatively easy to get, and there's a hip array of concurrent events. As the most important film event in Eastern Europe, it always features the year's top films and attracts the odd Hollywood star. It's somewhat behind the pace of the likes of Cannes, Venice and Berlin, but is well worth the trip from Prague. Most of the red-carpet action takes place in and around the Hotel Thermal but film screenings are spread around town. Winners take home exquisite art-deco figurines made by Moser; see one at the **Moser Glassworks and Museum** (p170).

EATING IN KARLOVY VARY: BEST FOR A SPECIAL MEAL

La Hospoda: Upscale take on a traditional Czech pub, serving staples as well as delicacies like baked goose and roast boar. *11am-10pm* €€

Ukrajina: Serves the huge, local Ukrainian refugee community, offering filling fare from their war-torn home country. *11am-10pm* €€

Tusculum: The best lunch or dinner option in town, Tusculum features organic, locally sourced ingredients. Lots of vegetarian options. *noon-10pm* €€

Embassy Restaurant: The restaurant of the Embassy Hotel plates up top-notch Czech standards for Munich prices. *noon-10pm* €€€

Hitting the KV Highs
Towering views of the town

For the best views of Karlovy Vary, hit the **Diana Tower** high above the town, reached by funicular railway from behind the Pupp. The tower is free to climb and affords memorable views across the spa and the surrounding forested hills. There's a restaurant and cafe here, and other attractions, including a worthwhile Butterfly House *(papilonia.cz)*.

Four Blasts from the Past
Seek out some of KV's illustrious history

If you're spa-ed out and looking for a break from all the salty mineral water, the town's museums and architecture will keep you occupied for a day.

Start at the **Karlovy Vary Museum** *(kvmuz.cz)*, for exhibits on the town's development as a spa resort. A few steps further along Nová Louka is the town's beautiful **theatre**, with original decorations by the Klimt brothers. Some 300m further is KV's main place of worship, the imposing **Church of Mary Magdalene**. It dates from the 1730s and is the work of baroque master Kilian Dientzenhofer, the architect of St Nicholas Church (p63) in Prague.

From the church, amble towards the Hotel Thermal, then continue to the **Jan Becher Museum** *(becherovka.com)* and learn all about Becherova, the alcoholic phenomenon still made in KV. The tour ends with a tasting session. Na zdraví!

Peek Inside Czechia's Top Hotel
Splash out at the Grandhotel Pupp

Arguably the country's most illustrious hotel, the sumptuous **Pupp** *(pupp.cz)* covers nearly the whole of the spa's southern end and oozes old-world glamour. Though established in the 18th century, the current 1907 building is the work of prolific Viennese architects Fellner and Helmer, the duo behind theatre buildings across the former Habsburg empire.

The hotel featured in the James Bond film *Casino Royale* and inspired Wes Anderson's *Grand Budapest Hotel*, which was also filmed there. These days it's a budget-blower, but worth the splurge for one of the period-style rooms. Even if you're not staying here, peek inside; the restaurants are very good, and the historic atmosphere perfect.

TWO TREATS FROM VARY

Apart from health-restoring mineral water, there are two less wholesome products that every Czech instantly associates with Karlovy Vary. The first is **Becherovka**, a herb digestif made to a recipe only known to two employees. It was created by the Becher family in the early 19th century, with the distillery located in today's Jan Becher Museum. It's an acquired taste, though one that former Czech president Miloš Zeman certainly did acquire. Beton is a cocktail of Becherovka, tonic and lemon.

It was Mariánské Lázně that gave the world the **spa wafer**, but many types are now made in KV. Traditional fillings are hazelnut, vanilla and chocolate, but some wafer presses now turn out all manner of flavours, from chilli to honey, ginger to plum.

 EATING IN KARLOVY VARY: BEST CHEAP SPOTS

Bistro Sluníčko: In the town proper, this bright and basic, cheap self-service canteen is great for a quick lunch. *8am-3.30pm Mon-Fri €*

Welsova kavárna: When it comes to hidden gems here, this 1920s coffee house/deli deep within a polyclinic on náměstí Milady Horákové tops the bill. *8am-4pm Mon-Fri €*

U Kubrychtů: Pleasant Czech pub restaurant in Moskevská Street with 130Kč lunch specials. *11am-10pm €*

Haandi Indian Restaurant: Few can walk past this highly visible Indian near the Thermal without being tempted by the cheap lunch mains and buffet. *11am-10pm €*

STROLLING THE COLONNADES

This gentle stroll takes you from one end of the spa zone to the other, following the River Teplá all the way.

START	END	LENGTH
Hotel Thermal	Grandhotel Pupp	1.6km, 2 hrs

As a first-timer, buy a *lázeňský pohárek* (a traditional porcelain drinking cup) and hit the colonnades and their mineral springs. Your stroll begins at the northern end of the spa area, whose entry is marked by the landmark communist-era ❶ **Hotel Thermal** built in the brutalist style. Inside, you'll find Saunia (saunia. cz), with the famous outdoor thermal pool with views across the town. Unmissable.

Cross the river south and on the other side of a small park is the first of the colonnades, the cast-iron ❷ **Park Colonnade** (Sadová kolonáda). This is your first chance to sample the waters. Continue for 300m along the River Teplá to the biggest and most impressive colonnade, the neo-Renaissance ❸ **Mill Colonnade** (Mlýnská kolonáda), with five different springs. Now head up Lázeňská to the impressive ❹ **Market Colonnade** (Tržní kolonáda); one of its two springs, the pramen Karla IV (Charles IV Spring), is the spa's oldest.

Just beyond the Market Colonnade stands the ❺ **Vřídelní Colonnade**, housed in a hulking 1970s brutalist building that was once dedicated to cosmonaut Yuri Gagarin. The tallest glass copula houses central Europe's only geyser. Here the waters are at their hottest. The street Stará Louka continues south for more splendour. At the end of the stroll stands the magnificent ❻ **Grandhotel Pupp** (p173), the resort's choicest hotel and the favoured haunt of well-heeled visitors.

The **Mill Colonnade** was built in 1881 and is the work of Josef Zítek, who designed Prague's National Theatre.

The thermal pool at the **Hotel Thermal** has a temperature of 38°C and can be enjoyed year round, even in the snow.

Above the **Vřídelní Colonnade** rises the Church of Mary Magdalene, a Baroque masterpiece by Kilian Dientzenhofer.

Beyond Karlovy Vary

Mountains riddled with mines, fairy-tale castles, radioactive spas and lots of opportunities to enjoy the great outdoors – that's the Karlovy Vary region.

In summer you can grow palm trees outdoors in fairly low-altitude Karlovy Vary, but north of the town rise the cold, mysterious and almost tourist-free Krušné Mountains (known as the Erzgebirge on the German side of the nearby border), culminating at Mt Klínovec. The last Czech mountain range to be 'discovered', this is a harsh but magical place to hike and cross-country ski. Another attraction here are the UNESCO-listed mines and the town of Jáchymov, which often leaves visitors in baffled wonderment. Also lost among the forested peaks is spectacular Loket castle, one of Czechia's finest. The third point of the West Bohemian Spa Triangle is the prim little town of Františkovy Lázně, a worthwhile half-day trip.

Places
Loket p175
Jáchymov p176
Františkovy Lázně p176

GETTING AROUND

Loket is served by fairly regular bus from Karlovy Vary, as is Jáchymov. For other places in the Krušné Mountains you'll need a car.

To get to Františkovy Lázně, take the train to Cheb and change. Some trains from Prague terminate there, too.

One interesting way of getting to Loket is via the Ohře cycle path *(cykloohre.cz)*, a picturesque 284km route from the source of the River Ohře in Bavaria to its confluence with the Labe (Elbe) in Litoměřice, via Karlovy Vary and Loket.

Loket
TIME FROM KARLOVY VARY: **17 MINS**

A scramble around Loket Castle

The town of Loket, a cluster of houses in pinks, greens and blues huddled around a fairy-tale castle, stands at a loop in the Ohře River. The loop is so extreme it almost makes an island (*loket* means 'elbow' in Czech, a reference to the river bend). 'JW Goethe's favourite town' (as tourism brochures describe it) is so pretty, if you saw it in a film you'd think it was a painted backdrop.

Loket's German name is Elbogen (also meaning 'elbow'), and it's been famous by that name since 1815 for the manufacture of porcelain, as have neighbouring towns Horní Slavkov (Schlackenwald) and Chodov (Chodan).

Impressive **Loket Castle** *(hradloket.cz; adult/child 175/140Kč)* was built on the site of a Romanesque fort, of which only the tall square tower and fragments of a rotunda and palace remain. Its present late-Gothic look dates from the 14th century and makes it one of the most visually striking piles, both inside and from down by the river where you'll get the best shots. You are free to wander the castle; exhibitions include Gothic murals, a gruesome tableaux of torture instruments, and two rooms full of locally produced ceramics.

The nearly impregnable castle played an important role in Bohemian history. Young Wenceslas, the future Holy Roman Emperor Charles IV, was imprisoned here as a child around the

UNESCO SPAS & MINES

Until recently, the Karlovy Vary region did not have a single UNESCO-listed site. But in the space of two years, a whopping eight were added. In 2019 UNESCO recognised the significance of the mining industry in the Krušné Mountains, bringing five mines and mining-related sites under its wing. In 2021 the long-awaited decision was made to add Mariánské Lázně (p178), Karlovy Vary (p170) and Františkovy Lázně (p176), the so-called West Bohemian Spa Triangle, to the World Cultural Heritage list, along with eight other spa towns across Europe, in a joint nomination. The COVID-19 pandemic put a slight dampener on celebrations, but these UNESCO listings could make an important contribution to tourism in what is the country's poorest region.

year 1320. He apparently enjoyed visiting the castle, though, later in life. From 1788 until 1947, the castle was used (and abused) as a local prison.

Jáchymov

TIME FROM KARLOVY VARY: **50 MINS**

Discover the fascinating town of Jáchymov

Defining the border between Saxony and Bohemia, the Krušné Mountains extend across the north of the country in a thousand forested peaks; it's paradise for hikers, berry pickers, mushroomers, cross-country skiers and those looking to escape the 21st century. The hiking possibilities are endless with hundreds of kilometres of marked trails. Of the countless places of interest across the range, the town of **Jáchymov** is particularly intriguing. In the 16th century, the silver mines here led to the foundation of a mint (now the town museum) that produced coins called Talers (from the town's German name, Joachims*tal*). This word would become 'dollar'. Also found in these hills is uranium, the same that Marie Curie used to isolate the element radium and which political prisoners extracted at great personal cost in the 1950s for shipment to the USSR. The town's third wow factor is Europe's only radioactive spa, with clients bathing in mildly radioactive water (perfectly safe) at the **Radium Palace** *(axxoshotels.com)* spa complex.

Nearby is **Mt Klínovec** (1244m), the highest peak in the Krušné Range, boasting its premier **ski resort** as well as a **bike park** with four thrilling downhill routes of varying levels of difficulty.

Františkovy Lázně

TIME FROM KARLOVY VARY: **30 MINS**

The third point of the spa triangle and its water park

The region's third spa town is Františkovy Lázně, a much more sedate affair than Karlovy Vary and Mariánské Lázně. It's a place of well-tended parks with statues and springs, the centre so perfectly renovated it hardly feels like Czechia at all. The town was listed by UNESCO in 2021 along with its bigger cousins.

The big draw for families is the excellent **Aquaforum** *(aquaforum-frantiskovylazne.cz; adult/family 320/690Kč)* water park. Part of a spa hotel, this is a great bad-weather option for the kids, and a place to soothe muscles after skiing or hiking. The location is adjacent to the Františkovy Lázně-Aquaforum train stop, making it an easy trip by public transport.

DRINKING IN THE KRUŠNÉ MOUNTAINS: BEST FOR BEER

Ryžovna: The lonely Ryžovna Brewery, 25km north of KV, produces three types of beer; the restaurant is a welcome place to eat. *11am-7pm Tue-Sun*

Červený Vlk: In Boží Dar, the Red Wolf brews five different beers served in a 21st-century dining area. *11am-10pm daily*

Krušnohor: Based in Tisová near Kraslice, Krušnohor brews the Krušné Mountain's best beers, which occasionally pop up elsewhere in Czechia. *10am-noon & 1-5pm Mon-Sat*

Hvězda: On the main square in Cheb, the superb Hvězda restaurant is the home of the Skaut microbrewery. *11am-10pm daily*

HIKE THE KRUŠNÉ MOUNTAINS

This fairly easy circuit takes you from Jáchymov's historical square to the highest parts of the Krušné Mountains and down again.

START	END	LENGTH
Jáchymov	Jáchymov	19km

We start in Jáchymov, outside the new ① **tourist information office**. From there, look for a yellow marked trail heading up the opposite side of the valley.

The climb gives ever more dramatic views down on Jáchymov, but these are soon obscured by thick forest. The first stop after 6km is detour to ② **Hadí Hora** (Snake Mountain), a boulder field viewpoint high above a valley. Opposite is Klínovec, the highest peak in the Krušné Mountains, which has a ski resort in winter and a bike park in summer.

Another 3km through the fir trees delivers you to ③ **Boží Dar** and lunch at the Červený Vlk microbrewery (p176). Quaint Boží Dar is the main skiing and hiking resort in the Krušné Mountains and has plenty of old Sudeten architecture. The border with Saxony is nearby. If you don't have the legs to go on, buses run back down to Jáchymov from here.

From the town, take the green marked nature trail called ④ **Božídarské rašeliniště** – the Boží Dar peat bogs. The boardwalk bounces over the bogs to the southwest of the town where many rare species grow.

After 1.7km a red marked trail leaves the road. Return to Jáchymov via a combination of trails, passing near a couple of ⑤ **UNESCO-listed mines**. The descent into Jáchymov is vista-rich.

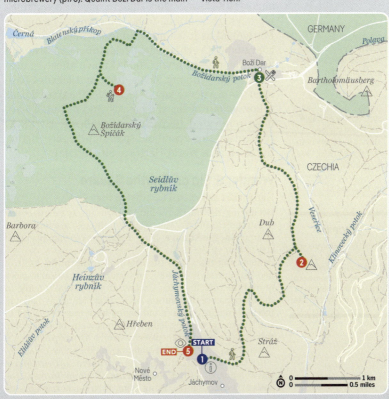

Mariánské Lázně

ROYAL CONNECTIONS | SPA ARCHITECTURE | MINERAL SPRINGS

GETTING AROUND

Mariánské Lázně is divided into two parts, the spa and the suburb of Úšovice where most local people live. Most visitors stay in the spa area where the vast majority of beds are. However, the bus and train stations are located 2.5km to the south – take trolleybus 5 or 7. The spa is easily walkable. If you find yourself staying in a short-term rental in Úšovice, the neighbourhood is served by trolleybuses 3 and 7.

☑ TOP TIP

Parking is a pain in the spa, so make sure your hotel has a spot ready for you before you arrive. The town has a central car park but it is a long way from the spa area.

Just over two centuries ago, enterprising monks from Teplá Monastery decided to make a little extra cash by building a spa in a swampy, inhospitable valley amid the dense Slavkovský Forest. What started out as a few timber guesthouses around a muddy hole quickly turned into one of Europe's most fashionable spa towns, attracting the great and good (and not so good) of the 19th and early 20th centuries. Returned almost to its former glory since the days of communist workers' recreation, today Mariánské Lázně (or Marienbad as it is known in German and English) is arguably Czechia's most relaxing, attractive and user-friendly spa town, and is known affectionately as Mariánky among locals. Its grand facades have been given a new coat of *kaisergelb* (the typical dark yellow colour of the spa houses) and its hotels have been renovated to Western standards. UNESCO recognised this grand old spa's significance, listing the town as a World Heritage Site in 2021.

Wander & Sip on Goethe Square

Mariánské Lázně's UNESCO-listed site

Occupying the northern end of town, the spa zone is one of Europe's grandest. Most places of interest are positioned around **Goethe Square**, named after the German poet who stayed here in the 1820s.

Anchoring the spa is the cast-iron **Colonnade**, built in neo-baroque style in 1889, an instantly recognisable piece of architecture for most Czechs. It was actually made at the other end of the country (in Blansko, Moravia), taken to pieces, brought by train and bolted back together again in situ. Its gently curving length reminds many of a Victorian train station. It's a lovely place to stroll with a cup of mineral water, a spa wafer (a filled wafer biscuit) or an ice cream.

In a neoclassical pavillion of its own at the northern end of the Colonnade is the **Cross Spring** *(Křížový pramen)*, the spa's first water source. Bring along a spa cup or buy a plastic

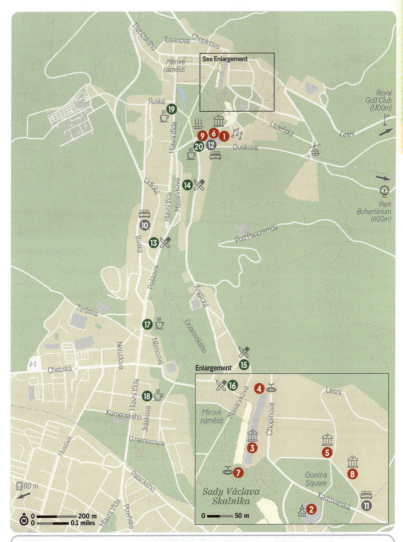

SIGHTS
1. Casino concert hall
2. Church of the Assumption of the Virgin Mary
3. Colonnade
4. Cross Spring
5. Municipal Museum
6. Royal Cabin
7. Singing Fountain
8. Weimar Hotel

ACTIVITIES
9. Ensana Health Spa Resort Nové Lázně

SLEEPING
10. Falkensteiner's
11. Hotel Hvězda
12. Hotel Nové Lázně

EATING
13. Bio Vegetka

14. Česká Hospůdka
15. Swisshouse
16. U Zlaté Koule

DRINKING & NIGHTLIFE
17. 18g
18. Café Pohoda
19. Modrá cukrárna
20. Vídeňská kavárna

WHY I LOVE MARIÁNSKÉ LÁZNĚ

Marc Di Duca, Lonely Planet author

I'll come clean – Mariánky is my home town and for me there is no better place to live. Strolling through the spa on a crisp winter morning, the *kaisergelb* facades contrasting with the freshly fallen snow – it's like living in a fairy tale.

The air is some of the cleanest in Europe, the architecture some of its most evocative. And that water! There are 40 mineral-rich springs in town, with another 60 rising in the forests around.

For trail runners, the hills and forests that cup the town are the ideal training ground. And when not enjoying the outdoors, a top-notch concert at the Casino for a couple of hundred crowns is a delightfully olde-worlde experience.

All in all, if Edward VII liked it here, that's good enough for me.

Park Boheminium

beaker to taste the water of the Cross Spring and two others that are piped here.

At the southern end is the famous 1980s **Singing Fountain**: 240 water jets that perform every two hours between May and October to popular tracks and classical pieces. Come after dark to watch the show with added lights.

From the fountain, head uphill to sloping Goethe Square, dominated by the **Church of the Assumption of St Mary**. To your left is a chain of interconnected hotels belonging to the **Ensana Resort**, the main spa treatment provider. The five-star **Hotel Nové Lázně** is the town's top hotel. In the top left-hand corner of the square is the excellent **Municipal Museum** *(muzeum-ml.cz; adult/child 90/50Kč)*, one of the oldest surviving buildings where Goethe stayed during his last visit to Mariánské Lázně in 1823. The exhibitions examine everything from spa procedures to Goethe, and from the traditions of the Sudeten Germans to local geology.

Tour Czechia in Miniature
See the country in an hour

One of the most popular attractions in the whole Carlsbad Region is **Park Boheminium** *(boheminium.cz; adult/child 190/140Kč)*, high above the spa in a location called Krakonoš.

EATING IN MARIÁNSKÉ LÁZNĚ: OUR PICKS

Česká Hospůdka: A cosy and popular Czech pub-style restaurant with a wood fire and excellent, inventive local cooking. *11am-10pm* €

Bio Vegetka: This long-established shop and cafe is the only dedicated source of vegetarian/vegan sustenance far and wide. *7am-5pm Mon-Fri* €

U Zlaté koule: Five-star class combines with cosy informality and a game-rich menu at this spa favourite. *11am-10pm* €€

Swisshouse: Light Czech and international dishes, the best food in ML, served at this intimate wellness hotel in the spa park. Phone ahead. *Hours vary* €€

The idea was to create the most significant pieces of architectural heritage in the country in miniature, enabling visitors to tour Czechia in an hour or so. It has taken two decades to create the 75 models on show in the park. These include very impressive and detailed replicas of well-known places such as Karlštejn Castle, Ještěd Tower and Český Krumlov Castle, as well as lots of lesser-known locations such as Lužná Train Station (where Czech Railways has its main museum), Písek Stone Bridge (the oldest bridge in the country) and Prague's Břevnov Monastery. There are also ponies to ride and a cafe, making it a great place to bring children.

Discover ML's British Royal Connections

Edward VII in Mariánské Lázně

The most illustrious visitor ever to take the waters at Mariánské Lázně was Edward VII, King of England. The most powerful man of the era, the son of Queen Victoria – who was related to almost every head of state in Europe – came here a total of nine times as Prince of Wales and king. Pretty young Mizzi the hatmaker of Hlavní Street may have been his main focus of interest at first, but later he described Mariánské Lázně as the most beautiful place he had visited.

The biggest event that ever took place in the town was the meeting between Edward VII and Emperor Franz Joseph of Austria in 1904 at the Kursaal, now the **Casino concert hall** (zso.cz) adjoining the Nové Lázně Hotel. Home to the West Bohemian Symphony Orchestra, it's well worth asking the receptionists if you can take a look inside as it's one of the grandest venues outside Prague. A performance here costs a couple of hundred crowns and takes you back to the days of Old Austria. In the Nové Lázně is the **Royal Cabin**, a spa room built specially for Edward VII.

Edward stayed at the **Weimar Hotel**, now a five-star ruin that dominates the top fringe of Goethe Square. It is slated for renovation costing around a billion crowns. The new name of the luxury hotel will be the King Edward.

Apart from leaving behind lots of gunned-down deer, many an empty dinner plate and one sad Sudeten hatmaker, the king bequeathed the town one of its main draws – the **Royal Golf Club** (golfml.cz). Once the only golf club in Europe to be bestowed with the title 'royal', this is a tricky course set almost 800m above sea level.

FILMS & FORESTS

Zuzana Stejskalová is a local cultural manager, UNESCO site manager, and founder of the international Marienbad Film Festival (marienbadfilmfestival.com).

The Marienbad Film Festival focuses on experimental cinematography and audiovisual essays and takes place in mid-June during the enchanting 'firefly' season.

The festival offers a unique opportunity to immerse yourself in the atmosphere of Alain Resnais' film *Last Year at Marienbad*, inspired by the town's charm, through its site-specific projections. You can explore the Alain Resnais Hall in the former Lesní mlýn hotel and engage in conversation with the owner, an expert on historic structures and architecture.

Mariánské Lázně is ideal during the hot summer months, enabling you to relax amidst the therapeutic forests. Don't forget to seek out Svodidla, a contemporary megalithic structure there.

 DRINKING IN MARIÁNSKÉ LÁZNĚ: COFFEE SPOTS

| **Vídeňská kavárna:** Elegant Viennese coffeehouse at the Nové Lázně with polite service and desserts made on the premises. *9am-6pm* | **Modrá cukrárna:** ML's oldest cafe on Hlavní with a traditional cake and coffee section and a more expensive modern cafe. *9am-6pm* | **Café Pohoda:** In Kamenný dvůr, this gem of a coffee spot south of the spa has great coffee and cakes and a thoroughly untouristy ambience. *9am-7pm Mon-Fri, noon-6pm Sat & Sun* | **18g:** Currently the best-quality espressos and americanos in Mariánky, right on the main drag through town. *9am-6pm Tue-Sun* |

Beyond Mariánské Lázně

If you enjoy wild natural beauty, romantic castles, uninhabited landscapes and winter nights by log fires, you'll love the area around Mariánské Lázně.

Places

Slavkovský Forest p182
Chodová Planá p183

GETTING AROUND

Bečov and Teplá are on a very scenic rail line running between ML and KV and Teplá can be reached by bus. Other places in the Slavkovský Forest have limited transport links and you will need your own transport.

The Mariánské Lázně microregion is all about the forest, getting out into nature and feeling the earth under your feet. To the north is the huge Slavkovský Forest, and to the south and west the Bohemian Forest, a virtually unpopulated protected landscape that extends south until it merges with the Šumava Mountains (p188). Characterful Bečov nad Teplou is the only town of size on the rail line and road between Mariánské Lázně and Karlovy Vary, its castle safekeeping one of the country's most precious objects. Kladská, just north of Mariánské Lázně, is a popular day trip, as is one of the country's most unusual breweries at Chodová Planá.

Slavkovský Forest

TIME FROM MARIÁNSKÉ LÁZNĚ TO KLADSKÁ: **11 MINS**

Hiking around beautiful Kladská

Extending between Mariánské Lázně and Karlovy Vary, the Slavkovský Forest is a largely untouristed, undiscovered 640 sq km of thick forest, cool-running streams, lonely trails and tiny underinhabited villages. The forest starts on the northern edge of the spa but it's an 8km hike or ride until you reach the first village, the beauty spot of **Kladská** with its Tyrolean chalets and protected peat bog. Do a circuit of the lake (1.5km), then retire to a local restaurant for some game and beer. From here, Czech Hiking Club marked trails and official cycling and cross-country skiing trails branch out in all directions.

Take a trip to Bečov nad Teplou's dramatic castle

The de facto capital of the Slavkovský Forest area is the gritty little town of **Bečov nad Teplou** (45 minutes from Mariánské Lázně by train), a railway junction in a sweeping forested valley with one stellar attraction – an impressive **castle** *(zamek-becov.cz; adult/child 240/70Kč)* and adjoining chateau clamped to the rock of a high promontory above the Teplá River. Though interesting in itself, the highlight of the

Bečov nad Teplou Castle

castle is the second most valuable object in all of the Czech lands: the dazzling **Reliquary of St Maurus**. Relocated before COVID-19 to a special wing, the golden casket containing the bones of St Maurus is illuminated before you as you are ushered into the dark room. Security is quite tight and no photography is allowed.

The rest of Bečov is worth an hour's exploration. Its high-perched square is lined with restaurants offering local trout, cosy pensions, antique shops and a few private museums. The train and road journey to Bečov is dramatic, ducking and weaving along the winding, thickly forested valley of the Teplá River. In 2019 the journey was rated as one of Europe's top 10 most scenic rail routes by British newspaper *The Guardian*.

Chodová Planá

TIME FROM MARIÁNSKÉ LÁZNĚ: **5 MINS**

Discover the Chodovar Brewery's mineral-infused beer

Some 10km south of Mariánské Lázně, the village of Chodová Planá would be just another bend in the road were it not for the presence of the **Chodovar Brewery** *(chodovar.cz)*. The family-owned brewery operates a beer spa as well as two restaurants, one of which is pretty unique in the Czech lands. Caves once used to store lager have been made into an impressive subterranean restaurant with 200 seats. To reach it, you pass through a free brewery museum with lots of copper piping and old beer mats and bottles. The region's biggest **beer festival** takes place in August in the grounds with hectolitres of the company's mineral-infused beer consumed and a Czech superstar up on the stage.

ST MAURUS & THE SECRET POLICE

A precious 13th-century reliquary made in Belgium was brought here by the last owners of Bečov castle, the Beauforts, Nazi collaborators who were expelled from Czechoslovakia in 1945. The last thing they did was hide the reliquary, never to return. In 1984 a mysterious US businessman and treasure hunter called Danny Douglas offered the Czechoslovak state US$250,000 to export a secret object (the hidden reliquary) but would not reveal what it was. Using snippets of info they gleaned (from an often intoxicated Douglas), the communist secret police (the StB) were able to locate the precious casket before Douglas could, and St Maurus remained at Bečov. It was certainly the brightest moment in the Czechoslovak StB's history.

EATING AROUND MARIÁNSKÉ LÁZNĚ: OUR PICKS

Pension Kladská: One of Czechia's top 100 restaurants with gourmet local fare. In Kladská. *Lunch & dinner* €€€

U Tetřeva: Meet the creatures of the surrounding forest – on a plate. Hunting-trophy-bedecked dining room with ceramic stove in winter. In Kladská. *11am-10pm* €€

Hradní Bašta: Warm and welcoming restaurant serving Czech classics at the gates of Bečov castle. *10am-9pm* €€

Restaurance Ve Skále: One of the country's most unusual spots serving Czech mainstays deep within a network of caves at the Chodovar Brewery. *11am-10pm* €€

Plzeň (Pilsen)

FAMED BREWERY | TECHNICAL HERITAGE | PERIOD ARCHITECTURE

Bohemia's second city Plzeň (Pilsen) is a grainy, industrial place with three stellar attractions that make it worth a trip from Prague or the spas to the north. The Pilsner Urquell Brewery and the Brewery Museum provide the most fascinating beer experience in the country, while Techmania is possibly Czechia's top kids attraction. The Great Synagogue is one of Europe's premier Jewish heritage sites, where size does matter. Otherwise the city has some light sightseeing possibilities around a pretty medieval square, as well as a few atmospheric pubs that pack out with students from the University of West Bohemia. But life in Plzeň is really all about heavy engineering, with the Škoda works occupying a massive area to the southwest of the centre, churning out trams and trains for export across Eurasia. So if you are weary of 21st-century hip, Plzeň is refreshingly lacking in it.

GETTING AROUND

The main train station (Plzeň hlavní nádraží) and the main bus station (Centrální autobusové nádraží, CAN) are located on two different sides of the historical centre, around 2.5km apart. You can walk from both to the central náměstí Republiky in 15 minutes or less.

The city has a comprehensive public transport network (PMDP, pmdp.cz) with trams and buses reaching every suburb. You can download the PMDP app onto your smartphone or buy tickets on board using your debit card.

Pilsen is the only city in the west where you can use Uber.

☑ TOP TIP

If you are heading to Techmania from Prague, stay on the train past the main train station and get off at Plzeň Jižní Předměstí, which is a short walk away.

Learn How Lager is Made
Plzeň's hop-infused heritage

The number one reason people come to Plzeň is to visit the famous **Pilsner Urquell Brewery** *(Prazdroj in Czech, prazdroj.cz; admission 380Kč)* where Pilsner lager was first cooked up in 1842. Arguably Czechia's best known and most copied beer, it was 'invented' when a Bavarian brewer named Groll, whose task it was to upgrade the slurry the locals were forced to drink, came up with a new way of brewing. The drink – pils lager – quickly spread to Prague's pubs and the world beyond. Entry to the brewery is by guided tour. Highlights include the old cellars (dress warmly) and a glass of unpasteurised nectar (tasting far better than the Urquell you get in pubs). Get beer merch at the brewery shop.

Across the Radbuza River is the **Brewery Museum** *(prazdrojvisit.cz; admission 150Kč)*, which offers an insight into how beer was made (and drunk) in the days before Pilsner Urquell. Highlights include a mock-up of a 19th-century pub,

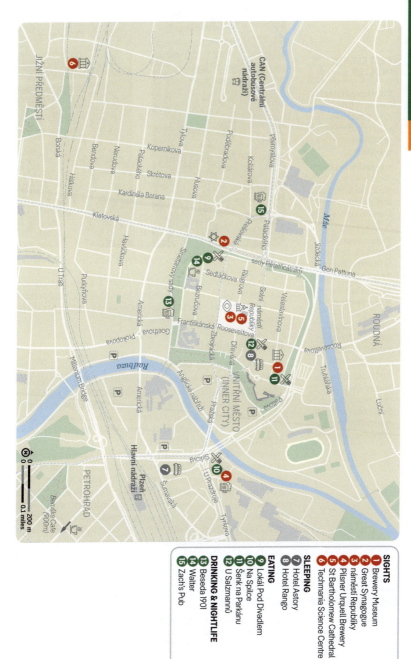

PLZEŇ (PILSEN)

SIGHTS
1. Brewery Museum
2. Great Synagogue
3. náměstí Republiky
4. Pilsner Urquell Brewery
5. St Bartholomew Cathedral
6. Techmania Science Centre

SLEEPING
7. Hotel Astory
8. Hotel Rango

EATING
9. Lokál Pod Divadlem
10. Na Spilce
11. Šenk na Parkánu
12. U Salzmannů

DRINKING & NIGHTLIFE
13. Beseda 1901
14. Walter
15. Zach's Pub

BEST EVENTS IN PLZEŇ

Christmas Markets: Prague or Dresden it ain't, but fewer visitors and lower prices mean that's a good thing!

Liberation Festival: 'Thanks America!', cry the locals in May as they celebrate the US liberation of their city in 1945.

Pilsner Fest: The city's beer festival is held at the brewery in early October.

Riegrovka Live Music Festival: Throughout the summer, central Riegrova street echoes to dozens of live music events.

TUTO Jídlo: Food festival over the first weekend in September featuring top-quality Czech and international cuisine.

Techmania

a huge, wooden beer tankard from Siberia, and a collection of beer mats. All have English captions and there's good printed English text. It's by far the best beer-related museum in Central Europe.

Get Technical!

The west's top kids attraction

Techmania *(techmania.cz; adult/child/family 240/240/ 1040Kč)* is arguably the best way to entertain the kids in the entire country – it's even worth a day trip from Prague. If you arrive in the morning, you can almost guarantee you'll be dragging your reluctant-to-leave offspring out of the door at closing time eight hours later.

Based in one of Škoda's huge former heavy-engineering workshops, kids are free to roam all day, trying out myriad experiments as they go. The concept fits in with Komenský's idea that learning should be fun. Some experiments change every six months or so but many are permanent fixtures. Sit back and relax as your little ones mess about with magnets, splash around in the water world, become TV news presenters in front of a green screen, see if they can outrun a cheetah, and build towers out of thousands of wooden blocks. There are also

 DRINKING IN PLZEŇ: BEST SPOTS

Beseda 1901: Multitasking art-nouveau restaurant/exhibition/pub space with a long tradition and almost gourmet takes on Czech cuisine. *8.30am-10pm Mon-Sat, to 8pm Sun*

Walter: Chic, minimalist coffee spot with excellent bean-based drinks and a breakfast and brunch menu. *7.30am-1pm Mon-Fri, from 9am Sat & Sun*

Zach's Pub: Cool student pub with live music most nights and its own beers. *1pm-late Mon-Fri, from 5pm Sat & Sun*

Beruška: Typical Czech *cukrárna* offering cakes, open sandwiches, coffee and alcoholic drinks for normal Czech prices. Take tram 2 to Radnice Slovany. *7am-6pm Mon-Sat*

excellent science demonstrations, a 3D planetarium and full-sized historic trains manufactured at the Škoda engineering works. All great fun for sponge-like minds.

Czech artist David Černý's epic Entropa installation is mounted on a giant wall in the main exhibition room. It's a not-so-subtle critique of the EU and originally hung in Brussels during the Czech presidency of the EU in 2009. Presciently, in view of Britain's decision to leave the EU, the artist represented the UK with an empty space.

Marvel at Pilsen's Great Synagogue
Admire a reminder of Bohemia's Jewish past

The main throughfare through Pilsen is the thundering sady Pětatřicátníků, where you cannot fail to notice the **Great Synagogue** *(zoplzen.cz; adult/child 120Kč/free)*: the city's finest slab of architecture, the second-largest Jewish place of worship in Europe and the third-largest in the world. It dates from the 1880s and was built in neo-Romanesque style with double onion domes and a huge star of David window in the front facade. There were some 2000 Jews in Pilsen at the time – not a huge number – but during WWII their synagogue was used as a store and thus escaped destruction (unlike a similar synagogue in Mariánské Lázně). After WWII the Jewish population fell to just a handful of returnees from concentration camps and by the 1970s the communists had closed the Great Synagogue. It was reopened in the 1990s, and visitors can now view the intricately decorated main prayer space with its columns and beautifully painted ceilings.

Wandering Republic Square
Gaze up at the country's tallest church

Pilsen's main square is **náměstí Republiky** *(Republic Square)*, the medieval market square that anchors the grid of streets that made up the original city. For a city that prides itself on heavy industry, the square is a surprise, its house fronts sporting elaborate facades and traditional, almost South Bohemian bell gables. The dominant feature on the square is the originally Gothic **St Bartholomew Cathedral** *(bip.cz/cs/katedrala-sv-bartolomeje)*, which has the tallest spire in the country, at 103m. Take the 301 steps to the top for panoramas across the city and beyond. The streets around Republic Square are a joy to explore, packed with cafes, shops, churches, museums and parks.

THANKS, AMERICA!

At the end of WWII, the US and Red Army divided Bohemia in two, with the liberating forces stopping at a line between Karlovy Vary and České Budějovice. That meant West Bohemia was liberated from the Nazis by the US, not the USSR. Throughout the communist era this was a problematic event – the communists even claimed Soviet troops in US uniforms freed Pilsen.

After the Velvet Revolution it became possible to talk freely about how WWII ended in this part of Europe. Pilsen goes further than that, organising its May **Slavnosti Svobody** (Liberation Festival) with an ever decreasing number of US soldiers who were here in 1945 as guests of honour. The *General Patton* and *Díky, Ameriko! (Thanks America!)* monuments are permanent reminders of the US Army's greatest moment in Bohemia.

EATING IN PLZEŇ: OUR PICKS

Lokál pod Divadlem: The Plzeň branch of a popular pub-restaurant serving Czech standards and good beer. *11am-11.30pm* €

Na Spilce: The pub-restaurant at the Pilsner Urquell Brewery is a great place to end the day in Plzeň. *11am-10pm* €€

U Salzmannů: Plzeň's oldest tavern with a proud tradition of serving well-chilled Urquell and belly-filling Bohemian cuisine. *11am-11pm* €€

Šenk na Parkánu: At the Brewery Museum, the beer at this typically Czech pub-restaurant is tops, but so is the traditional food. *11am-late* €€

Beyond Plzeň (Pilsen)

The Plzeň Region is a diverse area of gently wooded hills, pretty baroque towns and the rounded peaks of the Šumava.

Places
Šumava Mountains p188
Domažlice p189
Švihov p189

GETTING AROUND

Domažlice is easy to reach from Prague and Plzeň, but other places in this section are best explored by car. Bus is an option for getting round in the Šumava but for Švihov Castle, the train from Plzeň is best.

Plzeň is the de facto capital of a large region that extends up into the mountains that form the border in the south and west with Bavaria and Austria. Apart from the frontier-defining peaks of the Šumava and Bohemian Forest, this is an area known for its baroque architecture and Bohemian folk traditions. The Šumava is one of the best places in the country for light hiking and skiing, though it can be crowded with Prague day-trippers in summer. Pretty Domažlice is a truly beautiful place with lots of small-town life in the streets and a big dose of folk action. Little-visited Švihov Castle gives an insight into one of the Czechs' biggest Christmas traditions.

Šumava Mountains   TIME FROM PLZEŇ: 4½ HOURS

Shared between the Plzeň and South Bohemian regions, the mysterious Šumava mountain range – sometimes called the Green Roof of Europe – is a magnet for backcountry hikers, skiers of all types, holidaying Czech families and nature lovers. The hills, rising to over 1300m along the border, are carpeted in thick forest, much of which is a national park and firmly out of bounds. Hiking trails, maintained by the Czech Hiking Club (Klub českých turistů, KČT), will lead you to alpine lakes, high peaks, waterfalls, peat bogs, fast-flowing rivers and areas of virgin forest. KČT hiking maps 64 to 67 cover the region in superb detail.

Climbing Mt Plechý, the Šumava's highest peak

At 1378m, **Mt Plechý** is the highest peak in the Šumava Mountains, but is a fairly easy climb with superb views across two countries. Without a car, you'll need to get to remote Nová Pec train station (from Plzeň change in České Budějovice). From there, take a series of blue and green trails up to the ridge at Rakouská cesta. There, turn right and follow the ridge to the top of Mt Plechý. The peak is marked with a cross with Czech and German inscriptions. From the top, drop down on a yellow trail to incredibly picturesque Plešné

Lake. From there another yellow and then green trail takes you to the free campsite *(npsumava.cz/navstivte-sumavu/nouzova-nocoviste)* where, if you have a tent, you can legally wild-camp. With no tent, you'll have to have accommodation in Nová Pec. The whole route is around 20km long.

Domažlice

TIME FROM PLZEŇ: **1 HOUR**

A duo of museums

The town has two superb museums – the **Chodsko Museum** *(muzeum-chodska.com; adult/concession 80/50Kč)* has exhibitions on local traditions of the Chods, once an independent Slavic tribe that guarded the border with Bavaria, and other aspects of the region. Engaging temporary exhibitions often examine local customs and borderland culture and history. An interesting feature of the museum is that it is housed in Domažlice's castle right in the centre of town.

At the eastern end of the main square, the **Jindřich Jindřich Museum** *(muzeum-chodska.com; adult/concession 80/50Kč)* focuses firmly on the ethnography of the Chodsko Region, with exhibitions utilising the collection of 9000 objects put together by local ethnographer Jindřich Jindřich. There are interesting sections on the Chod dialect and folklore today. The latter arrives in town in style during the annual **Chod Festival** in August, a riot of traditional food, folk costumes and bagpipe and brass-band music.

Peace Square

One of Bohemia's most impressive medieval squares is **náměstí Míru** *(Peace Square),* a very wide, cobbled street with Gothic arcading topped with colourful baroque gables. Beyond the arches lurk tiny shops, some having changed little since communist days. It's a lovely place to wander, grab a coffee and soak up the small-town atmosphere.

Švihov

TIME FROM PLZEŇ: **40 MINS**

Meet Cinderella at this romantic castle

One of the stars of the Czech classic film *Three Nuts for Cinderella*, **Švihov Castle** *(hrad-svihov.cz; adult/child 220/70Kč)* 35km south of Plzeň attracts tens of thousands of Czechs a year, but few foreigners. They are drawn to what was essentially the backdrop to most of the film, with a special trail to shooting locations, cardboard cutouts of scenes and a special exhibition on the 1973 movie. So it may be a good idea to watch the slightly surreal film (think medieval Bohemia with 1970s costumes) before you get here!

Though not a major Bohemian castle, there is a bit more to Švihov than just its communist-era cinematographic links. The interiors are bedecked in precious frescoes and more often than not Gothic vaulting leaps overhead. The Dance Hall (Taneční sál) with its intricate cassette ceiling is probably the most impressive interior.

THREE NUTS FOR CINDERELLA

Any guesses which Czech film is the most watched abroad? A New Wave film from the 1960s perhaps? Or Oscar-winning *Kolya* from the mid 1990s?

Nope, it's the Czechoslovak-DDR co-production of Cinderella, in Czech called **Three Nuts for Cinderella** *(Tři oříšky pro Popelku).* So how did an obscure 1970s fairy tale become the Czechs' most successful movie?

This was no ordinary film – the cast were half East German, half Czech, including superstars Libuše Šafránková and Pavel Trávníček. Karel Gott, the biggest singing superstar of them all, looked after the lyrics to the score. The atmospherically snowy backdrop means it is shown every Christmas in many European countries (there's a cult around the film in Norway). Domestically it is aired every 24 December.

Český Krumlov

MEDIEVAL MARVEL | COLOSSAL CASTLE | SCHIELE CONNECTION

GETTING AROUND

Český Krumlov can only really be explored on foot. The only time you might need the town's buses is if your hotel is out of town. A car might be useful for day trips but is not at all essential.

If arriving by train, the station is to the north of the old centre, around a 20-minute walk. Buses pull in a ten-minute walk from the central náměstí Svornosti.

In case you think cycling round Český Krumlov might save your legs, the hills, cobbles and crowds will soon change your mind.

☑ TOP TIP

Sadly, the special beauty of Český Krumlov is no longer the secret it once was, and from April to October overtourism is the word that comes to mind. This is one destination where it pays to visit in the off season.

Wrapped around a tight bend in the River Vltava deep in Bohemia's south, Český Krumlov is a gem in every sense of the word. It's like a Prague in miniature – a UNESCO World Heritage Site with a huge castle complex, an old town, Renaissance and baroque architecture, and hordes of tourists milling through the streets – but all on a smaller scale. You can walk from one end of town to the other in 20 minutes. There are plenty of lively bars and riverside picnic spots and in summer it's a popular hang-out for backpackers. In winter, when the crowds are gone and the castle is blanketed in snow, it's a truly fairy-tale place.

Before the COVID-19 pandemic struck, Český Krumlov had become synonymous with overtourism. The crowds are still yet to return to those levels but when they do, it's easy to escape onto the river or to hike the surrounding hills.

Explore Krumlov's XXL castle

A tour of Czechia's second largest castle

Český Krumlov's striking Renaissance **castle** (*zamek-ceskykrumlov.cz; adult/child 300/90Kč*), occupying a promontory high above the town, began life in the 13th century. It acquired its present appearance in the 16th to 18th centuries under the stewardship of the noble Rožmberk and Schwarzenberg families. This is the second largest castle complex in the country – Prague Castle is the biggest in the world and locals joke that Krumlov is only a bathroom smaller! There are over 360 rooms in the castle, and tours examine only a fraction. The interiors are accessible by guided tour only, though you can stroll the grounds unsupervised.

The guided tours run only from April to October and there are three routes offered: Tour 1 (one hour) takes in the opulent Renaissance and baroque interiors; Tour 2 (one hour) visits the Schwarzenberg portrait galleries and their 19th-century apartments. Tour 3 (40 minutes, 10am to 3pm Tuesday to Sunday May to October) explores the chateau's nearly perfectly

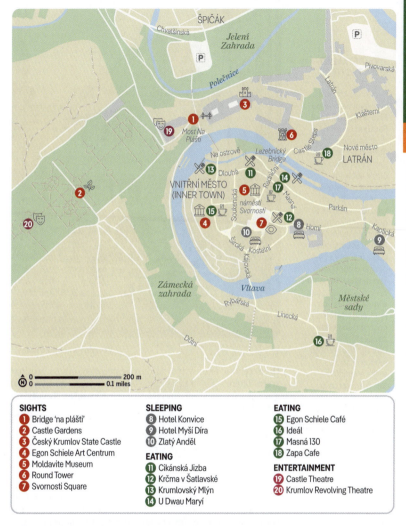

SIGHTS
1. Bridge 'na plášti'
2. Castle Gardens
3. Český Krumlov State Castle
4. Egon Schiele Art Centrum
5. Moldavite Museum
6. Round Tower
7. Svornosti Square

SLEEPING
8. Hotel Konvice
9. Hotel Myší Díra
10. Zlatý Anděl

EATING
11. Cikánská Jizba
12. Krčma v Šatlavské
13. Krumlovský Mlýn
14. U Dwau Maryí
15. Egon Schiele Café
16. Ideál
17. Masná 130
18. Zapa Cafe

ENTERTAINMENT
19. Castle Theatre
20. Krumlov Revolving Theatre

preserved baroque theatre. Be aware that it would take all day to do all three tours. No 1 is the standard tour, with knowledgeable guides not only leading tourists around the period interiors, but filling in a lot of background on the noble families that built and rebuilt the castle, the White Lady who appears here now and again and the alchemists who once worked for its residents.

Even if you don't take the tour, part of the fun here is getting lost in the passages, arcading and gangways on the south side, which lead to the **bridge 'na plášti'** (*Cloak Bridge*) – an amazing Renaissance structure rising incredibly high above the gorge. Other highlights include the beautifully painted **Round Tower** dominating the scene and the castle's **baroque**

FIVE-PETALLED ROSE FESTIVAL

Bohemia's biggest medieval bash is the **Five-Petalled Rose Festival** (slavnostipetilisteruze.cz), a three-day Renaissance party that takes place each June. The entire historical centre is roped off (you need a ticket to get in even if you are just sightseeing) and myriad events take place in every street, park and courtyard. The biggest day is the Saturday, which sees a huge procession featuring many a silly costume somehow squeeze its way through the crooked medieval streets. In the evening the focus is Svornosti Square where there are swordfights, puppeteers, medieval music and tons of food and drink. In other places there are demonstrations of horsemanship, archery, folk music, street theatre and more food. It's definitely a spectacle that makes for a special trip.

Krumlov's cobbled lanes

theatre, one of only two in Europe preserved in its original state. There's also a large museum and a huge set of formal **gardens** where you'll find the famous **Krumlov Revolving Theatre**.

Lose Yourself in Český Krumlov's Old Cobbled Lanes

Svornosti Square and around

The main focus of visitor interest in Český Krumlov is the Inner Town (Vnitřní město), which rises on what is essentially an island created by a tight loop in the Vltava River. Pass through the narrow streets packed with tiny shops and cafes to reach **Svornosti Square**, a small, painfully pretty piazza where there's always something going on – this is the focus of the Five-Petalled Rose Festival and the venue for the town's Advent markets. The town hall rests on six Gothic arches on the square's northeast flank, one of them providing shelter for the tourist office. There are also a few hotels and restaurants occupying prime spots. Radiating out from Svornosti are cobbled lanes, alleyways and streets that are sheer travel joy to explore.

Learn about Schiele's Time in Krumlov
Experience the Egon Schiele Art Centre

Housed in the enormous former brewery in Široká Street, the excellent, private **Egon Schiele Art Centrum** *(esac.cz; adult/concession 250/180Kč)* houses a small retrospective of the celebrated and controversial Viennese painter and tells the story of his relationship to Český Krumlov. The upper floors are dedicated to his life and copies of his works – he produced 3000 drawings and 330 oils by the time he died of Spanish flu at the age of 28.

Downstairs, the institution's main activity is organising world-class contemporary art exhibitions by artists from across the globe. The XXL gallery is ideal for displaying works that would not fit in spaces of ordinary dimensions.

Next to the gallery is a popular shop where you can source all of your Schiele merch.

Unearth Bohemia's Unique Semi-Precious Stones
Krumlov's intriguing Moldavite Museum

Český Krumlov has many a touristy museum aimed at the milling daytrippers that have very little to do with the town or Czech culture (torture, film legends). But one museum you should give an hour of your time to is the **Moldavite Museum** *(vltaviny.cz; admission 129Kč)*. Known as Vltavín in Czech, Moldavite is a semi-precious stone found in various spots across West and South Bohemia, but nowhere else on earth. It was formed when a meteorite hit Western Bavaria, showering what is now the Czech lands with chunks of a green, molten glass-like substance.

The museum starts with an informative, 12-minute film on how Moldavite was formed and continues with lots of beautifully illuminated examples unearthed over the ages. Moldavite formed filigree-like stones which look amazing uncut in jewellery. When polished, the green they shine is like nothing else. At the museum shop you can buy a certified piece, and next door there is a jewellery shop. Needless to say, many Czech women own pieces of moldavite jewellery, a stone often combined with the other semi-precious nugget found in Bohemia, garnet.

SCHIELE IN ČESKÝ KRUMLOV

The Austrian expressionist painter Egon Schiele's (1890–1918) connection to Český Krumlov comes through his mother, Marie Soukupová, who was born here. Schiele himself lived in Krumlov in 1911, spending most of his time here painting his Dead Towns pictures, a far cry from the explicit nudes for which he is famous. However, things did not go well when he returned to those naked female forms – he raised the ire of the townsfolk by hiring underage girls as nude models and was eventually chased out of town.

 EATING IN ČESKÝ KRUMLOV

Krumlovský Mlýn: This huge, heavy-beamed tavern right on the tourist trail serves Bohemian staples and has seating next to the Vltava. *11am-10pm* €€

Krčma v Šatlavské: Slightly upmarket medieval cellar with meat-heavy menu. Reservations essential. *11am-midnight* €€

U Dwau Maryí: Old Bohemian recipes washed down with mead and ale at this tavern where time has stood still. *11am-10pm* €€

Cikánská Jizba: Raucous, tightly packed pub-restaurant that's been around forever. Nightly gypsy music. *5pm-midnight Mon-Sat* €€

OVERTOURISM IN ČESKÝ KRUMLOV

Until the early 1990s, few had heard of this pretty town in Bohemia's south. If you had visited in those days, you would have found few foreign tourists, just locals dwelling among soot-cracked medieval facades. Things began to change in 1992, when Krumlov was one of the first places in the country to be declared a World Heritage Site by UNESCO, kicking off a tourist onslaught that culminated in 2018 when 412,000 overnight stays were recorded and millions of tourists, many from Asia, brought the town to a daily standstill. Since COVID-19 (a period when many Czechs rediscovered Krumlov), numbers have not yet reached 2018 levels and the town has a slightly calmer, more thoughtful ambience.

Canoeing, River Vltava

Take to the River!

Rafting and canoeing on the Vltava

One of the most popular activities in Český Krumlov away from the medieval madness is to get wet on the Vltava. Looking down from the castle ramparts on a sunny day you'll see countless locals and tourists rafting and kayaking the river (well, attempting to). There are several agencies that can get you kitted out. Try **Maleček** *(malecek.cz)*, which rents out boats for between 30 minutes if you just want a taster to several days for Czech-style river expeditions. A good option is their Zlatá Koruna trip, taking you from Krumlov to the famous monastery on the Vltava in three to four hours. The guys from the agency then pick you up and bring you back to Krumlov.

DRINKING IN ČESKÝ KRUMLOV: COFFEE SPOTS

Masná 130: This cool little espresso bar brews the strongest shots in town and has a couple of people-watching tables out on Masná. *9am-6pm Wed-Sat, to 4pm Sun*

Egon Schiele Café: Characterful old cafe under vaulting opposite the ticket office at the Schiele Art Centrum. *11am-6pm Tue-Sun*

Zapa Cafe: Great spot on the main tourist route for a coffee or ice cream. *8am-8pm Mon-Fri, 10am-7pm Sat & Sun*

Ideál: This tiny roastery and cafe south of the old centre offers the freshest brews in town and some very tasty cakes. *9.30am-7pm*

Beyond Český Krumlov

Discover a UNESCO-listed village, the Czech Stonehenge, the regional capital and a neo-Gothic castle near Krumlov.

Beyond the crowds of Český Krumlov's Inner Town, the bucolic region of South Bohemia attracts few foreign tourists but boasts a fascinatingly eclectic range of sights to see. The capital of the south is České Budějovice, home to the original Budweiser beer and one of the country's most neatly renovated centres. Just outside the city to the north is Hluboká, Bohemia's finest neo-Gothic castle. More architecture awaits in Holašovice, an entire village listed by UNESCO for its examples of the rare folk baroque style. Outside the village lurks a mysterious stone circle, often dubbed the Stonehenge of South Bohemia. With a car, you could in theory see all of these places in a single day trip.

Places
České Budějovice p195
Hluboká nad Vltavou p196
Holašovice p196

GETTING AROUND

Buses run two to three times an hour between České Budějovice and Český Krumlov, completing the journey in 30 minutes. Many buses and trains run to Hluboká. Within České Budějovice you are unlikely to need the town's public transport – the medieval centre can be explored on foot. Reaching Holašovice without a car would be time-consuming, but Hluboká can be reached from České Budějovice by bus and train.

České Budějovice  TIME FROM ČESKÝ KRUMLOV: **30 MINS**

Tick off the highlights in the capital of the South

The place to start in České Budějovice to get your bearings is **náměstí Přemysla Otakara II**, the square named after the city's founding monarch. It's the biggest town square in the country, with attractive arcaded buildings grouped around the 1727 **Samson's Fountain** (*Samsonova kašna*). And when they say square they mean it – its exactly 133m on all four sides. Among the architectural treats around the edge is the 1555 Renaissance **town hall** (*Radnice*), which received a baroque facelift in 1731. The figures on the balustrade – Justice, Wisdom, Courage and Prudence – are matched by an exotic quartet of bronze gargoyles. Just off the square to the northeast is the Gothic-Renaissance **Black Tower** (*Černá věž*). It's 72m tall and was built in 1553. Climb its 225 steps (yep, we counted them) for fine views. The tower's two bells – Marta (1723) and Budvar (1995; a gift from the brewery) – are rung daily at noon. Beside the tower is the **Cathedral of St Nicholas** (*Katedrála sv Mikuláše*), built as a church in the 13th century, rebuilt in 1649, then made a cathedral in 1784.

One of the highlights of a trip to České Budějovice is seeing where original Budweiser beer was born, at the **Budweiser Budvar Brewery** (*budejovickybudvar.cz; adult/concession 250/180Kč*). The tour highlights modern production methods, with the reward being a glass of Budvar in the brewery's chilly cellars. The brewery is 2km north of the main square.

BOHEMIA'S LONGEST RIVER

That river flowing through České Budějovice...well, that's the Vltava, the same watercourse under those rafts in Český Krumlov and home to the swans you can feed from Prague's Charles Bridge. For the Czechs, the Vltava isn't a river, but *the* river, the longest in the country at a whopping 430km. (How does it all fit?) It rises in a boggy valley 6km south of the Šumava town of Kvilda. By the time it is swallowed by the Labe (Elbe) at Mělník, it has drained all of south and west Bohemia and swelled to a major, navigable waterway. The greatest cultural opus to celebrate the Vltava is Bedřich Smetana's *Vltava* symphony, part of his *Má vlast* (My Homeland) cycle, which traces the river from source to demise in an emotional orchestral masterpiece.

Finally, if you're travelling during the ice-hockey season (September to March) catch the home team ČEZ Motor České Budějovice in action at **Budvar Arena**, a short walk south of the square across the river. Tickets can be bought at the arena on game days.

Hluboká nad Vltavou

TIME FROM ČESKÝ KRUMLOV: **40 MINS**

Tour Bohemia's most famous neo-Gothic pile

One of the most celebrated chateaux in the country, **Hluboká Castle** *(zamek-hluboka.cz; adult/child 280/80Kč)* draws day visitors from as far as Prague as well as people on half-day trips from Budějovice and Krumlov. It was originally built by Přemyslid rulers in the 13th century and the building changed ownership several times until it was acquired by the Schwarzenbergs in the 17th century. They gave the castle its English Tudor makeover, modelled on Britain's Windsor Castle, in 1871. Entry is by guided tour only and there are five routes to choose from; most visitors choose tour 1, which lasts about an hour. Buy tickets on the day.

Housed in a former riding school next to Hluboká Chateau, the exhibition of the South Bohemian **Aleš Gallery** *(ajg.cz; adult/concession 225/180Kč)* mixes modern and historical art concepts, highlighting Czech religious art from the 14th to 16th centuries as well as 17th-century Dutch masters.

Holašovice

TIME FROM ČESKÝ KRUMLOV: **35 MINS**

Folk-baroque architecture and Bohemia's Stonehenge

The tiny village of **Holašovice** would just be another bus stop with a pub were it not for an architectural composition, the type of which you won't see anywhere else. Listed by UNESCO, this is a unique collection of folk-baroque bell gables ringing a pretty **village green**. Almost all of the houses are ordinary dwellings – only one is a small museum with exhibits on country life in the south. It's a pretty place to wander and admire the folksy decoration on some of the houses and the huge stucco gables rising into South Bohemia's sunny skies.

On the southeast edge of the village is a prehistoric **stone ring**, one of the most impressive in the country and sometimes dubbed the South Bohemian Stonehenge. The owners of the land are in the process of hailing other standing stones here to create a kind of prehistoric open-air museum.

 EATING BEYOND ČESKÝ KRUMLOV: OUR PICKS

Holašovická hospoda: One of a few places to refuel in Holašovice, this pub serves Czech staples and cold beer to tour groups and passing cyclists. *10am-midnight Fri-Sun* €

Naše farma: This restaurant in Budějovice has dishes made from local produce grown on organic farms in the region. *11am-10pm Tue-Sat* €€

Masné Krámy: Czech food and cold Budvar beer in a České Budějovice institution. *11am-11pm Mon-Fri* €€

U Tří Sedláků: The traditional Czech food here – think rabbit, venison, dumplings – is among the best in Bedějovice. *11am-11pm Mon-Sat* €€

Places We Love to Stay

€ Budget €€ Midrange €€€ Top End

Karlovy Vary p170

Villa Basileia €€ Long-established guesthouse by the river Teplá with very cosy rooms and a restaurant within walking distance of the city's sights.

Hotel Romance Puškin €€ Superb spa area location, very comfortable rooms and a cooked breakfast.

Pension Villa Rosa €€ Perched high above the river, the family-run Villa Rosa combines traditionally furnished rooms with a spectacular location.

Grandhotel Pupp (p173) **€€€** Book early for this central European gem with five-star service and a guestbook that reads like a Forbes list.

Loket p175

Penzion Ve Skále €€ Built into the rock of the canyon through which the River Ohře passes, this intimate Loket guesthouse has superb views of the castle.

Jáchymov p176

Zelený Dům €€ Take a trip to the past in this typical mountain lodge right in the centre of Boží Dar with its hunting trophies, warm and welcoming restaurant and olde-worlde rooms.

Radium Palace (p176) **€€€** Bathe in mildly radioactive water at this luxurious spa hotel in Jáchymov.

Mariánské Lázně p178

Hotel Hvězda €€ A grandly facaded spa hotel with a brightly lit interior, view-rich rooms, a huge pool and a full spa service.

Falkensteiner €€€ Five-star Austrian-owned hotel near the Russian church with a spa, a good restaurant and spick-and-span facilities.

Nové Lázně (p180) **€€€** One of the country's top hotels, with luxurious rooms, a full spa service and one of the best restaurants in West Bohemia.

Kladská p182

Lovecký zámeček Kladská €€ Sleep at a hunting lodge with serene views over the peat bog at Kladská near Mariánské Lázně – a true hidden gem of a hotel. Offline and cash only.

Bečov nad Teplou p182

Hradní Bašta €€ Stay right at the gates of Bečov Castle at this cosy guesthouse with clean, modern rooms and the town's best resto-pub downstairs.

Plzen (Pilsen) p184

Hotel Astory € The most convenient hotel for the main train station and the Prazdroj Brewery with clean and well-kept rooms from the 21st century.

Hotel Rango €€ Pilsen's most character-packed boutique hotel, with sumptuous rooms, a great restaurant and a convenient location.

Šumava Mountains p188

Nouzová nocoviště Šumava € There are seven official wild campsites in the Šumava range, which line up just below the ridge path.

Domažlice p189

Zlatá včela €€ On the main square in Domažlice, the Golden Bee has grand rooms for a three-star hotel, olde-worlde communal areas and a great resto-bar downstairs.

Český Krumlov p190

Myší Díra €€ This hotel has a superb location overlooking the river, and bright, spacious rooms with lots of blonde wood and quirky handmade furniture.

Hotel Konvice €€ An attractive, old-fashioned hotel with romantic rooms and period furnishings. Many rooms have impressive old wood-beamed ceilings.

Zlatý Anděl €€ The Golden Angel occupies an enviable position right on Svornosti Square and has a mix of rooms, from frumpy to clean-cut business.

České Budějovice p195

Cuba Bar & Hostel € Smart, modern and clean hostel with dorms and private rooms that put you right in the centre of Budějovice.

U Tří hrušek €€ This cleverly adapted historic building on a peaceful street in Budějovice offers smart, stylish and good-value rooms of many different cuts.

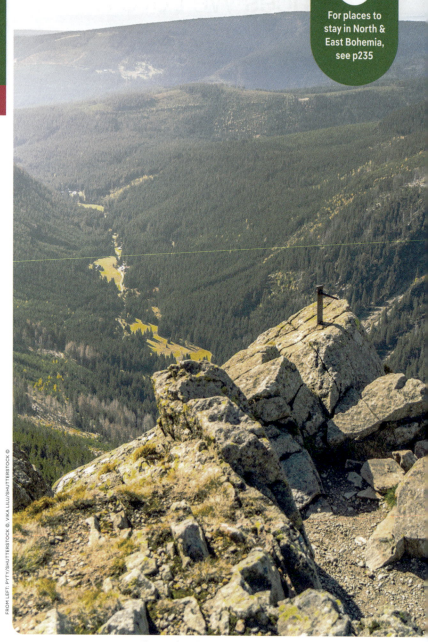

Above: Krkonoše Mountains (p208); Right: Sedlec Ossuary (p219)

Researched by Marc Di Duca

North & East Bohemia

SANDSTONE ROCKS AND BONE CHURCHES

Northeast of Prague rise mountain ranges punctuated by weird-and-wonderful rock formations – ideal hiking country. Human-made structures include fairy-tale castles and one rather spooky church.

Though joined at the hip, Bohemia's north and east differ from one another quite significantly, the northern border areas all rugged mountain ranges (including the country's highest peak Sněžka in the Krkonoše range) and outdoor adventure, while east of Prague extend the low, fertile plains along the Elbe River (Labe in Czech), an area peppered with the cultural heritage of the Czech heartlands.

If you are towing tots along to Bohemia, Liberec is arguably the country's most entertaining city, with attractions galore, including iQLANDIA science centre, which will stimulate developing minds all day long. They'll even enjoy the cable-car ride up to the Ještěd Tower (though perhaps not the uphill slog of a hike). If hiking boots are weighing down your luggage, set them free on the thrilling trails of the Czech Switzerland National Park or other less-frequented paths through the Elbe Sandstone Rocks. This is some of the most memorable hiking in the whole country.

A very popular day trip from Prague, Kutná Hora is best known for its ossuary (or 'bone church', as many dub it). However, the town was once the silver capital of Europe, and the local mint and mines are the real story here. Little Litomyšl in the far east of Bohemia and pretty Pardubice are all about grand Renaissance architecture, some of the best north of the Alps.

THE MAIN AREAS

LIBEREC	**CZECH SWITZERLAND**	**KUTNÁ HORA**	**LITOMYŠL**	**PARDUBICE**
Top city for kids.	National park made just for hiking.	Macabre bone church and silver-mining heritage.	Renaissance gem of the east.	Gingerbread capital of Bohemia.
p204	p211	p219	p225	p231

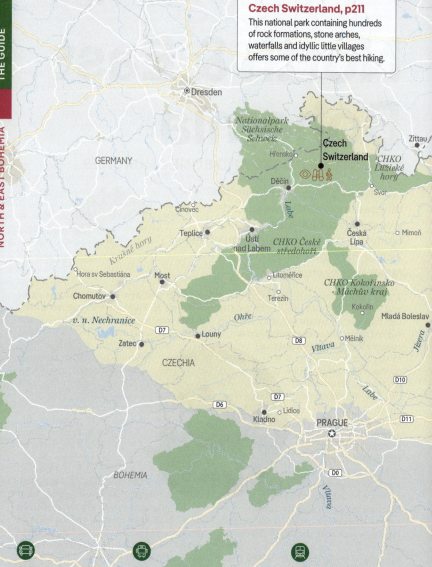

Czech Switzerland, p211
This national park containing hundreds of rock formations, stone arches, waterfalls and idyllic little villages offers some of the country's best hiking.

CAR
The D10 motorway runs from Prague almost all the way to Liberec and is the main access route for the far north. Take the D8 to reach Děčín, the D11 east towards Kutná Hora and Litomyšl.

BUS
Bus is best to Litomyšl, and the train is better for other cities. Local buses are good for reaching trailheads but are timetabled to ferry schoolchildren and workers from rural areas to the towns in the morning and back again in the afternoon.

TRAIN
Liberec, Děčín and Kutná Hora are all well-served by train from Prague. However, hardly any places in the mountains have rail service – there you'll have to rely on local buses.

Find Your Way

This part of the country is well-served by public transport, with buses taking over where the trains can't reach. However, having a car is a big advantage in the more remote mountainous areas.

Liberec, p204
Fun is the name of the game in this regional capital, with several entertaining attractions in the city centre and Ještěd Tower looming above.

Pardubice, p231
Small-town East Bohemia comes in the form of this sweet-scented city, where the architecture resembles the gingerbread for which Pardubice is renowned.

Kutná Hora, p219
When you've seen the famous church decorated with human bones, head into the centre to discover the town's silver-mining heritage.

Litomyšl, p225
This Renaissance spectacle features one of the country's most exquisite chateaux and a longstanding classical music tradition.

Plan Your Time

The north and east can be tackled in a variety of ways, depending on your travel circumstances and how much time you have.

Pravčická Brána (p213)

Hiking Day Trip from Prague

Fancy some hiking but only have one day spare to escape the capital? The **Czech Switzerland** (p211) is close enough to Prague for a one-day trek and you can be back in time for dinner. You might want to approach a tour company that runs hiking trips, but a DIY excursion is easy enough to arrange.

An early train from Prague (change to bus in Děčín) can see you on the main red trail in **Mezní Louka** (p213) by 11am. That gives you the rest of the day to take in the **Pravčická Brána** (p213) and/or the **gorges on the Kamenice River** (p214).

Take a picnic lunch to save you time. The last connection back from Hřensko is just after 7pm.

Seasonal Highlights

Anytime is a good time to head to the Czech mountains. Arriving in low season in Kutná Hora and Litomyšl gives a different perspective.

JANUARY

The **skiing season** gets into gear in the Krkonoše – book early if you plan to stay during the winter-sports frenzy. Liberec also has skiing – if there's snow, that is.

FEBRUARY

Clip on cross-country skis to join the **Jizerská 50**, a 50km skiing race in the Jizerské Mountains. Or just watch. Many schools head to the mountains as the ski season peaks.

JUNE

The best time for classical-music fans, who can head to the Litomyšl for the **Smetana's Litomyšl** festival (p229), held annually in honour of Bedřich Smetana, the Czechs' favourite composer who was born here.

Czech Mountain Odyssey

The **Stezka Českem** (Czechia Trail) is a nationwide initiative that has created a hiking trail around the entire circumference of the country, mostly piecing together existing Czech Hiking Club marked routes.

One of the most challenging sections is the northern stretch between the **Labské Pískovce** (p218) protected area and the eastern reaches of the **Krkonoše** (p208), a distance of around 200km. This route starts in Tisá and ends in Žacléř, taking 10 days to three weeks, and including the **Czech Switzerland** (p211), the **mountains** around Liberec and the high-rise **Krkonoše Mountains** (p208).

The Stezka Českem is currently one of the most talked-about challenges among the Czech outdoor community and has been the subject of a whole Czech TV series and several books.

Long Weekend

For those seeking culture and history, the towns of **Kutná Hora** (p219) and **Litomyšl** (p225) form the ideal double act for a weekend away from the capital.

Head first to Kutná Hora, some 75km east of Prague, where a full day is enough to explore the **Sedlec Ossuary** (p219), the town's rich silver-mining heritage and the **Cathedral of St Barbara** (p221), the finest church outside the capital.

On Sunday morning it's a 90km drive, or two-hour train journey east to **Litomyšl** (p225), where you can enjoy lunch at a local restaurant, before joining a tour of the **chateau** (p228) and stroll on the fairy-tale main square. Prague is then an easy two-hour evening trip away by train or along the fast D11 motorway.

JULY
The last weekend of July sees Liberec's **Benátská!** festival, a musical extravaganza featuring big names on the Czech pop/rock scene, plus a handful of big acts from abroad. Suzi Quatro headlined the 2024 edition.

AUGUST
Mushrooming is a national sport across Czechia, but nowhere more so than in the cool air of the mountains. August is the first month you might spot basket-wielding Czechs scouring the forests.

OCTOBER
Arguably the best time to hit the Czech Switzerland trails, as autumn gets into its full, multihued swing. The first snow appears on the highest peaks, such as **Sněžka** (p208), the highest of them all.

DECEMBER
Every Sunday throughout Advent, Litomyšl holds an atmospheric **Christmas market** in and around the chateau. On the evening of 5 December you'll spot St Nicholas, as well as a demon and an angel giving out gifts to kids.

Liberec

KIDS' ATTRACTIONS | OUTDOOR ADVENTURE | SPACE-AGE ARCHITECTURE

GETTING AROUND

Buses leave regularly from Prague's Florenc and Černý Most stations and pull in at the main bus station next to the train station in the city centre.

Once in Liberec, the city has four tramlines (a fifth actually runs to the neighbouring town of Jablonec) and myriad bus routes. One very useful tram is the No 3 that runs between the zoo in the northeast and the cable car for Ještěd in the southwest suburb of Horní Hanychov via the city centre. Several trams (Nos 2, 3, 5 and 11) trundle from the train station to the centre.

☑ TOP TIP

If you plan to use Liberec's trams and buses, download the DPMLJ app, which allows you to buy tickets and look up connections on your smartphone.

Two decades ago, few foreign visitors ever found their way to this northern city, but how things have changed! The capital of the Liberec Region, a city of over 100,000, now has several good reasons for getting on the train from Prague. Though the city itself could never be described as the country's most fetching, it makes a great base for exploring a region of mountains, castles and glass workshops, as well as its own few big-name sights. The iQLANDIA science centre is only rivalled by Pilsen's Techmania if you find yourself in Bohemia with children. However, the city's main attraction rises high above even the tallest communist block – the 1970s, space-age Ještěd TV tower is one of the country's most instantly recognisable structures and essential viewing if in the region.

Get Hands-On at iQLANDIA

The north's top kiddie attraction

The engaging **iQLANDIA** (*iqlandia.cz; adult/child 350/235Kč*) is a great day out for children and adults alike, even those with little interest in science. iQLANDIA is packed with experiments, demonstrations, exhibitions and fascinating facts, all totally hands-on and commendably kid-proof. Stealth learning has never been such fun!

The centre has six levels, the top five linked by a spiralling walkway. The ground floor is all about water. Kids are encouraged to splash around in specially designed water features, inside and out, and program the interactive fountain that dominates the central atrium. One level up, the spiral brings you to the Elements, where you can learn about the weather and experience a hurricane. The next floor up exhibits the human body and the senses – experience what it's like to be blind and test your strength and stamina. The most popular floor is the next level, where things get technical – see a car cut in half, ride a Mars rover simulator and test your braking skills in an interactive driving game. Here also is the Planetarium (additional ticket required). The top-floor roof terrace has several musical instruments for children to bash and hammer.

NORTH & EAST BOHEMIA LIBEREC

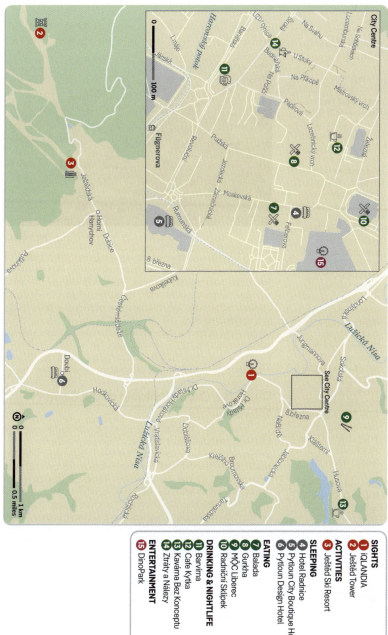

SIGHTS
1. IQLANDIA
2. Ještěd Tower

ACTIVITIES
3. Ještěd Ski Resort

SLEEPING
4. Hotel Radnice
5. Pytloun City Boutique Hotel
6. Pytloun Design Hotel

EATING
7. Balada
8. Gurkha
9. MŮC Liberec
10. Radniční Sklípek

DRINKING & NIGHTLIFE
11. Barvírna
12. Cafe Kytka
13. Kavárna Bez Konceptu
14. Ztráty a Nálezy

ENTERTAINMENT
15. DinoPark

205

FERDINAND PORSCHE

Though usually described as 'Austrian born', Ferdinand Porsche (1875–1951) actually saw first light in the Liberec suburb of Vratislavice nad Nisou (then part of the Austrian Empire), where he lived until he was 18. Having studied electronics (a revolutionary subject at the time) at Liberec college, Porsche launched his career in the automotive industry, inventing and building the first fully electric cars and hybrid models in the early 20th century, though he's most famous for designing the Volkswagen Beetle and establishing the Wolfsburg Volkswagen factory. Porsche remains controversial for his WWII activities when he served in the SS, though that didn't stop him and his son establishing the Porsche car brand in 1947.

Mt Ještěd

Below the ground floor is a fascinating, very much hands-off exhibition of obsolete technology, most of it chunky, nostalgia-inducing, communist-era junk. Kids will wonder at 1980s landline telephones and typewriters, while older Czechs walk around exclaiming 'we still have one of those' at some of the less antiquated stuff.

The canteen serves cheap lunch, or bring a picnic, as there are no readmissions (you can pop out to the car if need be). Get there early, as you are certain to be dragging any accompanying children out of the door come closing time.

Climb the Czech Building of the Century
Ascend Mt Ještěd

That odd thing pointing into the sky to the southwest near Liberec is **Mt Ještěd**, a 1012m-tall peak topped with a 1970s TV tower that *Thunderbirds* or a James Bond villain would be proud of. Czech architect Karel Hubáček won the coveted Perret Prize in 1969 for the design of this 100m-tall pinnacle that rises from a 33m-wide circular base containing a restaurant and hotel. In 2000 it was declared 'Czech building of the 20th century'. It's the region's top sight and well worth the effort to reach it, if only for the stupendous views on all sides (it's said you can see Prague 100km away when visibility is good). The tower, bristling with telecommunications aerials and disks, is

EATING IN LIBEREC: OUR PICKS

Radniční Sklípek: Cheap, filling Czech food and Svijany beer in atmospheric cellars beneath the town hall. *11am-11pm Mon-Sat, noon-4pm Sun* €€

MỌC Liberec: This local chain of Vietnamese venues serves the best Asian food in the north. *11am-10pm* €

Balada: Long-established, central restaurant serving traditionally Czech dumpling-and-meat combos. *10.30am-11pm Mon-Fri, from noon Sat* €€

Gurkha: Head here for the cheapest all-you-can-eat Nepali-Indian lunch buffet in town. *11am-10pm Mon-Sat* €

a real timepiece, the whole building a retro experience taking visitors back to 1970s Czechoslovakia. The bistro is relatively inexpensive, the hotel usually hopelessly booked up.

Getting up to the Ještěd Tower is half the fun and there are several ways to reach the top. The easiest and most boring is to drive there and park in the car park next to the tower. However, even on quieter days this fills quickly and space is tight, so if you drive, leave the car at the Výpřež car park and either walk up the road (2.8km) or through the forest (1.7km), which is steep and rough in places. Most people take the cable car, which leaves from near the end of tram line No 3. In winter this serves skiers visiting Ještěd's slopes. An accident in 2022 brought the service to a halt, but a brand-new cable car is planned. Obviously the most strenuous but rewarding way to summit is on foot – take the blue marked hiking trail from the tram terminus. The 3.4km-long walk is uphill and rough underfoot all the way.

When you're up at the tower, marked Czech Hiking Club trails shoot off in every direction. A good, 4.5km leg-stretcher to **Červený kámen** *(Red Stone)* will lead you to a high-perched picnic table with views looking back up at the tower, a shot most other tourists won't get. There are countless rock formations in the wider area to aim your boots at. One of the most photogenic is the **Kamenná vrata** *(Stone Gate)*, where there's a slit in a huge rock that you can pass through.

Mt Ještěd also has a **ski resort** *(skijested.cz)*, with lifts starting at Horní Hanychov. However, this is one of the lowest situated slopes in the country and often now has to rely on artificial snow.

Explore the Crystal Valley
More than 60 glass-themed attractions

Liberec is by far the best base for exploring the so-called **Crystal Valley** *(crystalvalley.cz)*, a loose association of glass-themed attractions (the largest on earth) that stretch across the north of Bohemia, from Kamenický Šenov in the west to Harrachov in the east. At over 60 sites across the region you can watch glass being blown, twisted, cut and polished by master craftspeople, sometimes one-person operations. There are also glass museums to visit, students to chat with, jewellery to admire and countless glass souvenirs to buy. At smaller workshops and studios it is best to call ahead so they know you are coming – few are open at the weekend. See the website for a comprehensive list of places to visit.

WHY I LOVE LIBEREC

Marc Di Duca, Lonely Planet author

As a father of two, I love that Liberec has more to do for families than any other regional capital. You could keep the kids entertained here for many days on end, with iQLANDIA and the Babylon Centre the obvious attractions, but with the **DinoPark** also in the mix.

And then there's Ještěd, a surefire hit with kiddies who will enjoy the ride up and the fixed telescopes at the top, which they can use to find your hotel back in Liberec far below. Older children also enjoy the easily created circuit hikes around Ještěd and clambering around the area's rock formations; and if your kids, like mine, are confident on skis, the ski slope is one of Bohemia's more low-key, family-friendly centres.

 DRINKING IN LIBEREC: OUR PICKS

Cafe Kytka: Plant-filled cafe offering a peacefully verdant haven in which to enjoy a coffee and cake break. *9am-7pm*

Kavárna Bez Konceptu: A cool, studenty place in town for a morning-after breakfast, brunch or just a coffee. *8am-8pm*

Ztráty a Nálezy: Very cosy tavern in the backstreets of Liberec serving local beer. *11am-10pm Mon-Fri*

Barvírna: Best craft beer in town and Liberec's finest burger menu. *4-10pm Mon-Fri, from noon Sat & Sun*

Beyond Liberec

Beyond Liberec in almost every direction you'll discover places of exquisite natural beauty, many off the tourist trail.

Places
Krkonoše Mountains p208
Mladá Boleslav p209
Český Ráj p209

GETTING AROUND

Although having your own car in this mountainous region will save you a lot of time and hassle, the Krkonoše resorts and the Český ráj area are well-served by public transport. A change of bus/train to bus is needed to reach the Krkonoše from Liberec. Turnov is the jumping-off point for the Český ráj, with buses making the trip regularly throughout the day from Liberec. Mladá Boleslav is very well connected to both Prague and Liberec by road and public transport.

If you're into hiking, biking and skiing, then the wider area around Liberec is one of the best places in the entire country to lace up or click on. To the south is the Český ráj (literally Czech Paradise) which, as the name suggests, is one of the most alluring parts of Bohemia. However, the real treat is in the east, where the highest peaks in the country – the Krkonoše mountains – draw all kinds of adrenalin-sports enthusiasts. This is where you'll find Sněžka, the highest mountain in the country with the biggest ski resorts. When you've had your fill of slogging up and down mountains, a change of gear awaits at the Škoda Museum in Mladá Boleslav.

Krkonoše Mountains TIME FROM LIBEREC: **2 HRS**

A short drive from Liberec, the **Krkonoše mountains** (sometimes called the Giant Mountains in English) form the country's most frequented national park (especially during the winter-sports season). These peaks rise up against the Polish border, their slopes and deep-cut valleys swathed in spruce forests. Most Czechs associate the area with skiing – the main ski centres are **Špindlerův Mlýn**, **Harrachov** and **Pec pod Sněžkou** – the last in the list sits in the shadow of Mt Sněžka, the country's highest peak at 1602m.

Climbing Sněžka – the Czechs' highest peak

Before you pull on those boots, it has to be said that most people actually don't climb **Mt Sněžka** – they take the cable car! In fact, they have to take two: one from the lower station at Úpské údolí, the second a shorter service from Růžová hora.

But if you fancy ascending to the country's highest point in the old-fashioned way, there are several ways to hike to the top of Sněžka, a fairly easy climb whichever way you go. The most direct and shortest route is along a blue trail directly north out of Pec along Obří důl. However, this is tarmac for the first 3km before the path climbs steeply. For a better outdoor experience, take the red marked trail, then the green west to Výrovka, then red and blue routes to the top via Luční bouda – 10.5km in total. You can then descend via the blue trail (or take the cable car). Another option is to follow a green trail to Růžohorky, then the yellow path that runs underneath the cable car.

Despite the relatively modest altitudes of these mountains, it's usually windy and cold year-round at the higher elevations. Even in summer, mountain fog creates a hypothermia risk. Open-toed shoes at 1600m are not a good idea. Don't go up without the appropriate gear.

Hiking the Krkonoše

Once up on Sněžka, you can follow the red-marked ridge path east or west, then descend whenever you've had enough. A good day out on the trails involves taking the cable car to the top of Sněžka, then hiking along the blue marked trail to Špindlerův Mlýn (12.5km) along the beautiful valley of the White Elbe River. Buses run from Špindlerův Mlýn back to Pec very regularly. Another route to Špindlerův Mlýn is to stay on the ridge heading east (mostly on the Polish side of the ridge, with amazing views) as far as Špindlerova Bouda, where a bus leaves for Špindlerova Bouda three times a day. Head down into Špindlerův Mlýn on foot along a yellow trail for more buses back to Pec.

The shoulder seasons (April–May and September–October) are the best times to hike here. Summer sees crowds on Sněžka, and in winter the trails can be under 2m of snow.

Mladá Boleslav   TIME FROM LIBEREC: 1 HR

Automotive history at the Škoda Museum

The Czechs' once maligned, now widely respected, Škoda cars are mostly bolted and welded together in the affluent town of Mladá Boleslav, less than an hour northeast of Prague. The story of one of Europe's oldest carmakers is related at the **Škoda Museum** (museum.skoda-auto.cz; adult/child 100/50Kč), the republic's best automotive history experience. Housed in a former production facility from the early days of the company, the museum has 350 exhibits, mostly cars but also bikes and motorcycles that launched the company in the late 19th century. Organised chronologically, the exhibitions take you on a ride from the bone-rattlers of the pre-WWI period to the swish and curvaceous First Republic limousines, the spartan models of the communist period, the boxy Favorit of the 1990s to the Škodovky we see today on Czech roads. There's a large section dedicated to electric cars of the past and present and, in stark contrast, a section on barn finds and renovation. There are scary 1990s police cars, Škoda rally specials from the 1980s and much more besides. The museum shop can provide all the Škoda merch you might ever want to own, and the **Václav** (p210) restaurant is a great place to end the day.

Český Ráj   TIME FROM LIBEREC: 30 MINS

Spectacular landscapes dotted with the ruins of audaciously located castles make this maze of sandstone 'rock towns' and basalt volcanic fingers a fairy-tale place to explore, especially on foot. Walking trails weave through the bizarre protected

THE MYTHICAL KRAKONOŠ

It won't be long before you see an image of Krakonoš, a legendary figure deeply associated with the Krkonoše mountains. He is known as the guardian of the range, normally depicted as a wise, powerful old man with a long beard. Krakonoš is believed to control the forces of nature, often helping the good-hearted while punishing those with bad intentions. His character embodies both justice and mischief, as he sometimes plays tricks on travellers to test their virtues. In Czech culture, he represents the spirit of the wilderness and is often featured in stories, plays, and fairy tales. Embodying the need to protect the alpine environment, Krakonoš is an enduring symbol of the Krkonoše region's mystical allure.

Trosky Castle

ŠKODA & THE TWO VÁCLAVS

The Škoda car company is one of Europe's oldest. It all started with Václav Laurin and Václav Klement who began to make bicycles in 1895 and motorised bikes three years later.

In 1905 the two Václavs took things to the next level and produced their first car, which can be seen in the Škoda Museum in Mladá Boleslav. Laurin & Klement cars were exported across the globe before WWI, but in 1925 the company found itself in trouble and had to look for a strategic partner. In stepped the Škoda heavy engineering works in Pilsen. Since that time the cars have been known as Škoda and the badge became the winged arrow we know today.

landscape, as the **Czech Paradise** ascends gently to morph into the foothills of the Krkonoše mountains. During the Czech National Revival (České národní obrození), poets, sculptors and painters were inspired by the compelling panoramas, and today the collages of weirdly shaped sandstone and basalt attract hikers and climbers.

A hike through the Czech Paradise

The best route through the Czech Paradise is the red trail that runs the length of the northern section of the protected area. Starting near the train station in Turnov, the trail heads through the area to **Trosky Castle**, one of the most distinctive sights in North Bohemia, with its two ruined towers rising high above a plain. En route you pass countless rock formations, rocky viewpoints, Valdštejn Castle, Hruboskalské 'rock town' and Hrubá Skála Castle. The whole route is 15km and at the end you can take a bus back to Turnov: a great day out.

 EATING BEYOND LIBEREC: OUR PICKS

Václav: The sleek, white-hued restaurant at the Škoda Museum in Mladá Boleslav has excellent beer goulash and even saffron risotto. *9am-5pm* €

U Koubusu: Just 500m off the main red trail through the Czech Paradise area near Turnov. Refuel before/after a hike. *3-10pm Fri, from noon Sat, noon-8pm Sun* €€

Luční bouda: Highest restaurant in the land is part of the mountain chalet 3.5km west of Sněžka. Buffet popular with hikers. *10am-10pm Mon-Sat, to 5pm Sun* €€

Bouda pod Sněžkou: Join Krakonoš himself at this traditional alpine tavern on the blue trail up/down from Sněžka for filling mountain fare. *8am-8pm* €€

Czech Switzerland

ROCK FORMATIONS | TOP HIKING | MAGICAL VIEWS

Almost at the northernmost point of the country, the Czech Switzerland *(České Švýcarsko)* is a real treat for anyone looking to hike while in Bohemia. Declared a national park in 2000, this is an area of gargantuan stone towers, cliffs, rock fingers, arches and caves that often rise horizontally from the trails and surrounding forests. These natural features provide astonishing views across the landscape, making every hike a rather stop-start but memorable affair!

Most visitors head straight for the Pravčická Brána *(Pravčická Gate),* Europe's largest natural stone arch, but there are countless other less-frequented places of equally dramatic natural beauty further along the trails.

In the long, very dry summer of 2022 the Czech Switzerland suffered one of the biggest forest fires the country has ever witnessed, with firefighters drafted in from across the country to extinguish the flames. Huge swathes of woodland were affected – some damage will still be visible when you visit.

Discover the German Side of the National Park
Nationalpark Sächsische Schweiz

The rock revelry doesn't stop at the border with Saxony – the smaller Saxon Switzerland (Sächsische Schweiz in German) mirrors the Czech Switzerland and has some equally good hiking and awe-inspiring natural features.

Coach parties almost always lay siege to the **Bastei**, a huge rock formation rising almost 200m above the River Elbe, accessed by bridges and walkways. The organised, quite commercial nature of this part of the park is in stark contrast to the wilder Czech side. However, the rest of the park has fantastic hiking, with countless trails, rock formations, waterfalls and gorges that you could spend weeks traversing. Unfortunately, few trails on the Czech side link with those in the German park.

One human-made attraction – **Königstein Fortress** – lies around 15km from the Czech border. This is said to be the

GETTING AROUND

Regular trains run from Prague's main train station to Děčín, where you can change onto buses to Hřensko, Mezní Louka and Jetřichovice. To reach the Pravčická Brána from Hřensko you need to get 2.7km up the road to where the red trail veers off to the left and leaves the road. You can walk, time things to go by bus or grab a taxi in Hřensko. If driving, note that you cannot park on the road heading to Pravčická Brána. Leave the car in Hřensko and walk. There's paid parking in Jetřichovice.

☑ TOP TIP

A full day on the trails is feasible as a trip from Prague (1½ hours south). Several Prague-based tour companies run trips to the national park. However, staying overnight enables you to go further than the day-tripper experience.

CZECH SWITZERLAND NORTH & EAST BOHEMIA

CZECH SWITZERLAND

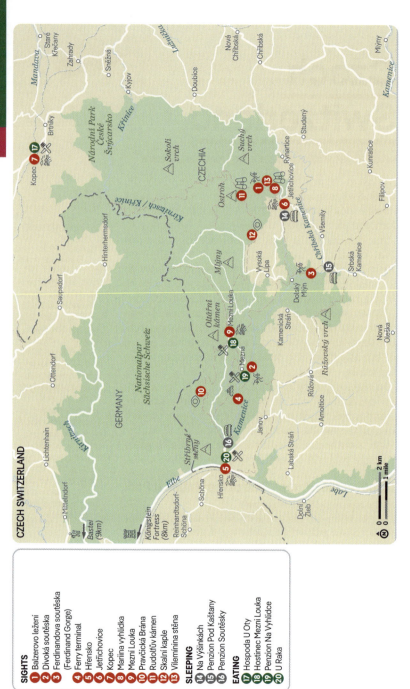

SIGHTS
1. Balzerovo ležení
2. Divoká soutěska
3. Ferdinandova soutěska (Ferdinand Gorge)
4. Ferry terminal
5. Hřensko
6. Jetřichovice
7. Kopec
8. Mariina vyhlídka
9. Mezní Louka
10. Pravčická Brána
11. Rudolfův kámen
12. Skalní kaple
13. Vilemínina stěna

SLEEPING
14. Na Vyšinkách
15. Penzion Pod Kaštany
16. Penzion Soutěsky

EATING
17. Hospoda U Oty
18. Hostinec Mezní Louka
19. Penzion Na Vyhlídce
20. U Raka

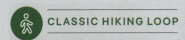

CLASSIC HIKING LOOP

This is the classic Czech Switzerland hike that takes in the best-known sights in the national park.

START	END	LENGTH
Hřensko	Hřensko	16km; 6 hours

From ① **Hřensko** village, where the River Elbe flows into Saxony, head to the trailhead 2.7km east. Follow the red marked trail along the road or take a taxi.

The trail starts properly at Tři prameny, from where it's a 2km climb to the ② **Pravčická Brána**, a mammoth, natural rock arch under which sits a restaurant and refreshments kiosk. It's the symbol of the region and one of the country's most impressive sights.

From the arch, the red trail bucks and weaves between stone pinnacles and rock formations with imaginative names like Fortress (Pevnost), Chinese Wall (Čínská zeď) and Cone (Homole), until you reach the hamlet of ③ **Mezní Louka** 4.8km later.

Between November and March, you have to take the green trail through Mezná, then a yellow path back to Tři prameny. From April to October you can take the blue trail and a short stretch of road to ④ **Divoká soutěska** for one of the most unusual hiking experiences in Czechia.

The Kamenice River cannot be hiked all the way, with two very narrow gorges (Divoká soutěska and Edmundova soutěska) blocking the path. Instead, small ferry boats carry hikers along the river. From the last ferry berth, it's a 2.5km amble back into Hřensko along a yellow marked trail.

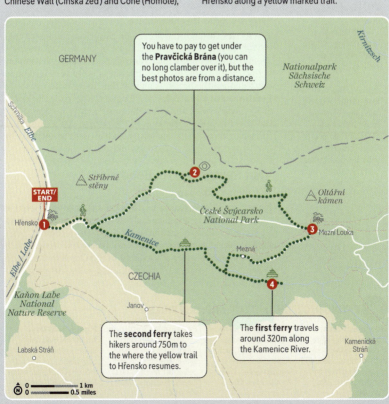

CZECH HIKING CLUB TRAILS

Czechia has the densest and best organised system of hiking trails in the world, a fact you will certainly appreciate when rambling through the Czech Switzerland.

The entire national network of over 44,000km is overseen by the **Czech Hiking Club** (Klub českých turistů; KČT), which sends out an army of volunteers on a rolling basis equipped with paintpots and brushes.

Trails are marked in four colours – red, blue, green and yellow; any others you see are local markers. Red trails are long-distance paths. The same system is used to a large extent in Slovakia, the Carpathian Mountains in Ukraine, and some parts of Croatia. See the club's website *(kct.cz)* to learn more about this remarkable organisation.

River Kamenice

largest fortress in Europe, sitting atop a massive rock bluff high above the River Elbe.

The offline map app mapy.cz will guide you along the paths on both the Czech and Saxon sides of the border. Alternatively, the Kompass *Elbsandsteingebirge* map does a good job, too.

Seek Out Less-Visited Gorges

Ferry along the River Kamenice

The ferries through the gorges on the River Kamenice take visitors through two short sections of the River Kamenice. From Divoká soutěska the river continues to squeeze through high cliffs. Most of this stretch is out of bounds so that boats don't disturb the precious habitat, but there is access to the **Ferdinandova soutěska** *(Ferdinand Gorge)* from the bridge at Královský smrk and from the south from the campsite at the U Ferdinanda Campsite. In the spring and autumn you can have this gorge to yourself, though no path runs the entire length and you may have to wade through the water.

Visit Switzerland in Bohemia

The village of Kopec

Kopec, a village in the far north of the national park, looks as though it has been picked up and transported from Switzerland, its timber houses scattered around pretty meadows. It's a 16.5km hike along a blue marked trail through the wonderfully picturesque but under-visited east of the Czech Switzerland. When you get there, a restaurant and a campsite await.

 EATING IN CZECH SWITZERLAND: OUR PICKS

Hostinec Mezní Louka: In the village of Mezní Louka, popular pub-restaurant serving big meaty platters and filling desserts. *11am-10pm* €€

U Raka: In a traditional stone-based house in Hřensko, enjoy Czech staples at chunky wooden tables. *11am-9pm Thu-Sun* €€

Penzion Na Vyhlídce: Cosy restaurant within Na Vyhlídce guesthouse with interesting wall and ceiling art, and a menu of Czech standards. *10am-10pm* €€

Hospoda U Oty: Traditional mountain tavern in Kopec – a very cosy place to end a hike in the national park. *noon-11pm Fri, 11am-10pm Sat, 11am-8pm Sun* €

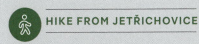

HIKE FROM JETŘICHOVICE

This loop is one of the most dramatic hikes in the country, with dramatic views from the top of rock towers.

START	END	LENGTH
Jetřichovice	Jetřichovice	8km; 3 hours

This 8km circuit starts from ❶ **Jetřichovice village**, where buses from Děčín and Hřensko pull in and you can park the car. Jetřichovice is a popular place and has several restaurants and a couple of shops for hiking supplies.

Taking the red trail north out of the village, it's a 1km climb to the first stop, ❷ **Mariina vyhlídka** (Marie's Viewpoint), a carved timber pergola perched high atop a rock tower and reached by stone and metal steps. Views of the surrounding mountain-scape are stupendous.

Passing ❸ **Balzerovo ležení**, a huge overhang protecting carved benches and a firepit, it's then less than 1km to your next photo op, the ❹ **Vilemínina stěna** (Vilemína's Wall), where a sidepath leads to a viewing point.

The red path twists through tall formations to ❺ **Rudolfův kámen** (Rudolf's Rock). At the top is another hut reached by more precariously narrow paths, ladders and steps. The view from the top, arguably the best in the national park, makes the slightly challenging climb worth the effort.

The going is easier after Rudolf's Rock, another 2.8km taking you to ❻ **Skalní kaple** (Rock Chapel), a tiny shrine cut from a boulder. There you part company with the red trail and switch to blue, which leads you back down to Jetřichovice.

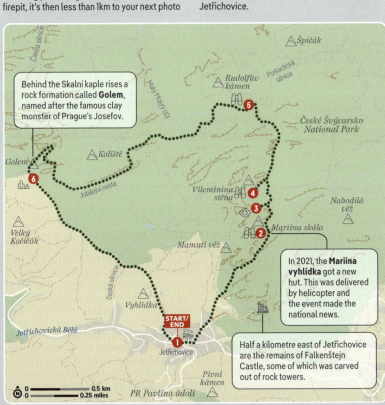

Beyond Czech Switzerland

The Czech Switzerland National Park is only the most precious kernel in a vast area of rock formations.

Places
Děčín p216

GETTING AROUND

There are regular train connections between Děčín and Prague. In Děčín, change onto buses for all destinations across the region. To reach Tisá, a change in Libouchec is required (or walk from there) and it is far easier to make the trip by car. A great way to reach Hřensko from Děčín is to take the cruise boat. Děčín has a small bus network but you are unlikely to need it.

To the north and west of the Czech Switzerland the rock formations continue to thrust their towers and cliffs into the crisp, pine-scented air. The main body of the Labské Pískovce (Elbe Sandstone Rocks) Protected Area lies to the west of the Elbe and the city of Děčín, a worthwhile city stop if only to visit the castle and stock up on hiking supplies. Far less visited than the Czech Switzerland National Park, the Labské Pískovce reserve is a superb place to escape the day-tripping crowds and tour groups, with some parts no less idyllic than the more celebrated national park. For a different perspective on the area, take a mini river cruise along the Elbe to Hřensko.

Děčín
TIME FROM CZECH SWITZERLAND: **27 MINS**

Town wedged among the rocks

The largest town in the area (just 12km by road from Hřensko), Děčín is a workaday sort of place, sitting astride the wide Elbe as it hurries the combined waters of Bohemia towards the border. You may find yourself here with time to spare when changing on public transport, but the town is also an offbeat kind of place, where you can best observe everyday life in Bohemia without tourist crowds.

The town has a few attractions worthy of your time. Top draw is **Děčín Chateau** (*zamekdecin.cz; adult/concession 140/100Kč*) which towers high above the Elbe. It was in the ownership of the Thun-Hohensteins until 1932, and they transformed the complex over the centuries from a Renaissance chateau to a neoclassical residence. Tours explore the grand interiors. Interestingly, the chateau was used as a military barracks during the Cold War – including by Soviet troops from 1968 until 1991, who left it in a sorry state.

Opposite the chateau looms the **Paštýrská stěna** (*Shepherd's Wall*), a sandstone cliff with wonderful views from the top. Up here you'll also find **Děčín Zoo** (*zoodecin.cz; adult/child 150/100Kč*), where animals are kept in large enclosures and are well cared for; a restaurant; and the beginning of a marked trail into the Labské Pískovce.

Hřensko

Cruising the Elbe on the slow boat to Hřensko

The Elbe is navigable all the way between Prague and Dresden and, away from the trails, one of the best ways to spend a day or longer in these parts is to take a cruise along the river. The small boats are operated by **Labská Plavební** (*labskaplavebni.cz*) and run between Děčín and Dresden (Drážďany in Czech) via Hřensko, Bad Schandau, Königstein and Pillnitz.

If you don't have the time to go all the way to Dresden, just a mini-cruise to **Hřensko** is a great way to combine a boat trip with a bit of hiking. Boarding takes place just below the castle in Děčín and the journey takes 50 minutes.

The wide, sluggish river, swollen with every drop of water that enters every stream and river across the whole of Bohemia, passes along the picturesque Elbe Valley, lined with high sandstone cliffs and pretty pastel houses. There's a bar on board if you've not had breakfast or are hungry after a hike. There's only one stop on the way to Hřensko at Dolní Žleb, from where hiking trails head across the border to access interesting rock towers in Saxony.

Departure is usually in the morning, returning in the afternoon, giving you ample time to make it up to the Pravčická Brána at the very least.

REAL-LIFE NARNIA

The 2005 Disney film *The Chronicles of Narnia* was partly shot in a part of the Labské Pískovce called the **Tiské stěny** (Tisá cliffs; p218) near the village of Tisá. Director Andrew Adamson chose Tisá as the backdrop thanks to its fairy-tale atmosphere: as close to Narnia as any place could probably get. Another local feature also appears in the film – the Pravčická Brána in the Czech Switzerland National Park. *Narnia* is just one of countless blockbuster movies to be shot on location in Bohemia, which attracts filmmakers for its authentic backdrops and low costs. To see where other famous films have been shot, check out prague.org/movie-locations-in-prague-czech-republic, though the list is a lot longer than that featured there.

 EATING IN DĚČÍN: OUR PICKS

Coffee & Books: Sandwiches, cakes, books, cosy atmosphere – what more could you wish for? *7am-7pm Mon-Fri, 8am-6pm Sat & Sun* €

Arrigo: Surprisingly flash Italian job for these parts, with excellent Czech dishes, too. *7.30am-10pm* €€

Prostor: Cool hangout that moved some years ago from Prague, with smooth coffees and light meals. *8am-6.30pm, Mon-Fri, 11am-5pm Sat* €

Pivovarská Restaurace Kapitán: In an old brewery converted into a shopping centre, brewpub with its own dark lager and Czech staples. *8am-6.30pm, Mon-Fri, 11am-5pm Sat* €€

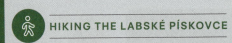

HIKING THE LABSKÉ PÍSKOVCE

This easy hike takes you through the Labské Pískovce protected area, with rock towers and views galore.

START	END	LENGTH
Tisá	Děčín	18km; 4 hours

Waking up in Děčín, your first task is to get the bus to ❶ **Tisá** (change in Libouchec or walk from there). It's better to go to the end of the trail and walk back, due to bus timings, and there are many early morning connections.

The ❷ **Tiské stěny** rock formations are the most magical in North Bohemia, though you have to buy a ticket to see them. Sandy pathways wriggle and squeeze their way between towers of weathered sandstone, and steps climb to unprotected vantage points. Due to their appearance in the film *The Chronicles of Narnia*, the rocks are a popular weekend destination for Prague folk.

Just 2km north of the Tiské stěny rise more huge sandstone towers, the ❸ **Nebeská říše** *(free)*. Hundreds more lurk in the forest to the north, with unmarked paths running between them.

A 6km hike on green then red trails brings you to the top of ❹ **Mt Děčínský Sněžník** (723m), where there is a viewing tower; an old stone-built affair providing views into the Czech Switzerland and over Saxony. A sidepath here runs to ❺ **Drážďanská vyhlídka**, from where you can see as far as Dresden in Saxony on a good day.

It's an easy 9km downhill back into Děčín passing more rock towers, the zoo and the ❻ **Pastýřská stěna viewing tower** en route.

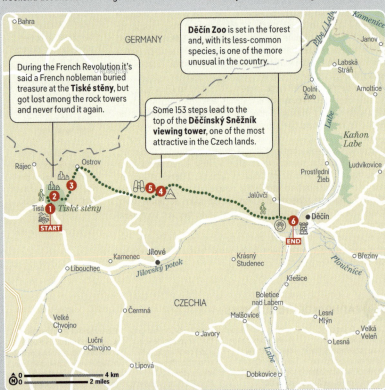

Kutná Hora

SILVER HERITAGE | UNESCO-LISTED SITES | BONE CHURCH

Enriched by the silver ore that once veined the surrounding hills, the medieval city of Kutná Hora became the seat of Wenceslas II's royal mint in 1308, producing silver *groschen* that were then the hard currency of Central Europe – a kind of medieval forerunner to the euro. Boom-time Kutná Hora rivalled Prague in importance, but by the 16th century the mines began to run dry, and the town's demise was hastened by the Thirty Years' War and a devastating fire in 1770.

KH became a UNESCO World Heritage Site in 1996, luring visitors with a smorgasbord of historic sights. One of those sights is the reason most make the short journey from Prague – the Sedlec Ossuary, known to most day-trippers as the 'Bone Church'. Surely the eeriest spectacle in the land, this chapel is decorated with thousands of stacked and arranged human bones.

Czechia's Most Ghoulish Spectacle

Discover Sedlec Ossuary

When the Schwarzenbergs purchased Sedlec monastery (2.5km northeast of the town centre) in 1870 they allowed local woodcarver František Rint to get creative with the bones in the crypt (the remains of an estimated 40,000 people), resulting in **Sedlec Ossuary**, a remarkable 'bone church' (*Kostnice; sedlec.info; adult/child 220/80Kč*). The skeletons found their way into the church when the surrounding cemetery was reduced in size. The human remains here are mostly plague victims and those who perished in the Hussite wars. Garlands of skulls and femurs are strung from the vaulted ceiling, while in the centre dangles a vast chandelier containing one of each bone in the human body.

Four giant pyramids of stacked bones squat in the corner chapels, and crosses, chalices and monstrances of bone adorn the altar. There's even a Schwarzenberg coat-of-arms made from bones, and Rint signed his name in bones at the foot of

GETTING AROUND

Hourly buses leave Prague's Háje station. There are direct trains from Prague's main train station to Kutná Hora-hlavní nádraží about every two hours.

The 'Bone Church' is in the suburb of Sedlec. City buses run half-hourly between the main train station and the bus station 700m north of the main square. Alight at the Kostnice stop for the Sedlec Ossuary. Local trains usually meet expresses at the main station for the short run to Kutná Hora Město. Otherwise, from the main train station it's a 20-minute walk to the Ossuary (1.3km) but a 3.4km hike to the centre.

☑ TOP TIP

Even most Czechs wouldn't know that Kutná Hora produces its own wine. The town's winery is in the Convent of St Ursula in Jiřího z Poděbrad Street and a bottle or two make for a very unusual souvenir.

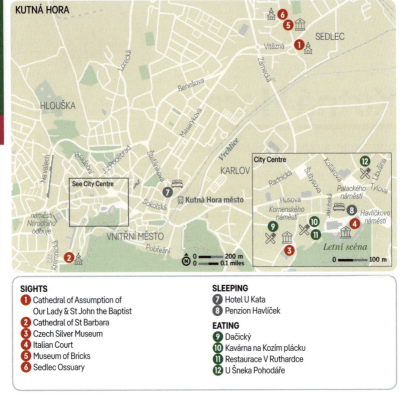

SIGHTS
1. Cathedral of Assumption of Our Lady & St John the Baptist
2. Cathedral of St Barbara
3. Czech Silver Museum
4. Italian Court
5. Museum of Bricks
6. Sedlec Ossuary

SLEEPING
7. Hotel U Kata
8. Penzion Havlíček

EATING
9. Dačický
10. Kavárna na Kozím plácku
11. Restaurace V Ruthardce
12. U Šneka Pohodáře

the stairs. It's all very ghoulish and most cannot quite believe their eyes when they see the place, but it's actually not the only one in the country.

Disappointingly, photography is not officially permitted in the ossuary.

Tour the Czech Silver Museum

Learn about KH's silver-lined heyday

Originally part of the town's fortifications, the Hrádek (Little Castle) was rebuilt in the 15th century as the residence of Jan Smíšek, administrator of the royal mines, who grew rich from silver mined illegally under the building. It now houses the **Czech Silver Museum** (*cms-kh.cz; adult/concession 90/60Kč*). There are two guided tours; the second includes a visit down an ancient silver mine. **Tour 1** (one hour) leads through the main part of the museum where the exhibits examine the mines that made Kutná Hora wealthy, including a huge wooden device once used to lift huge loads from the 200m-deep shafts. **Tour 2** (1½ hours) allows you to don a miner's helmet and explore 500m of medieval mineshafts beneath the town.

Cathedral of St Barbara

Gaze Up at the Miners' Cathedral
Cathedral of St Barbara

Kutná Hora's greatest monument is the Gothic **Cathedral of St Barbara** (*chramsvatebarbory.cz*). Rivalling Prague's St Vitus in size and magnificence, its soaring nave culminates in elegant, six-petalled ribbed vaulting, and the ambulatory chapels preserve original 15th-century frescoes, some of them showing miners at work. Take a walk around the outside of the church; the terrace at the eastern end enjoys the finest view in town.

There are five guided tours you can take of the building. The general tour relates the history of how it was built and points out the most significant features. Other tours head up onto the roof and examine the church's huge organ.

If you want to attend a service here, it takes place only once a week on Tuesdays at 6pm.

Visit the Former Royal Mint
Take a tour of the historic Italian Court

The **Italian Court** (*pskh.cz; adult/concession 120/90Kč*), aka the former Royal Mint, gets its name from the master artisans from Florence brought in by Wenceslas II to kick-start the business. They began stamping silver coins – the famous Prague *groschen,* the currency in 14th-century Europe – here in 1300. This remained the royal Bohemian mint until 1727, and the original treasury rooms hold an exhibit on coins and minting. The tour then continues to the Royal Audience Hall, with its murals depicting the election of Vladislav Jagiellon as Czech king and the Chapel of Sts Wenceslas and Vladislav decorated in bright art-nouveau style. In the giftshop a machine strikes copies of the famous silver coin (though not made of silver).

FIVE CENTURIES IN THE MAKING

It took over 500 years to complete Kutná Hora's cathedral of St Barbara. Construction began in 1380 under Jan Parléř, son of Petr Parléř, Charles IV's favoured architect. The Hussite Wars soon intervened and work was interrupted, but between 1489 until his death in 1506 another star architect, Matěj Rejsek (of Prague's Prašná brána fame), added the cathedral's impressive vaulting, and another architectural superstar, Benedikt Ried (of Old Royal Palace at Prague Castle fame), finished off the naves after that. But when the silver ran out, construction work was abandoned completely in 1558, and for over three centuries nothing much happened. It was only in the late 19th century that the cathedral was completed in neo-Gothic style.

Cathedral of Assumption of Our Lady & St John the Baptist

BRICK OBSESSION

Miloš Křeček is the owner of the largest collection of Lego sets in the world, the vast majority of which are on display at the five-branch Brick Museum (Prague, Kutná Hora, Poděbrady, Špindlerův Mlýn and Hatě u Znojma). As of autumn 2024, Mr Křeček had assembled almost 7000 sets, which gained him a place in the Guinness Book of Records. He received his first set as a five-year-old and never looked back. As wedding presents he and his wife exchanged rare Lego pieces and they often would hunt the flea markets of Denmark for obscure bricks. In 2010 he got the idea to show off his collection to the public, and the Museum of Bricks (actually in no way affiliated to the Lego company) was born.

Admire a Gothic-Baroque Basilica
KH's other UNESCO-listed site

Several sites in Kutná Hora are listed by UNESCO, but Sedlec also gets in on the act. Opposite the Sedlec Ossuary, the **Cathedral of Assumption of Our Lady & St John the Baptist** is a basilica rebuilt in the 18th century in the rare Gothic-baroque style by none other than the architect Jan Blažej Santini-Aichel. Another of his creations – the Church of St Nepomuk on the Green Mountain near Žďár nad Sázavou, 80km east – is also a UNESCO site. From the outside, you can see Santini's hand, the curves and unusual forms so out of character for the times he worked in. Inside, the main nave is a much more classical affair, following a 19th-century makeover.

See the Bone Church – in Lego
Marvel at the Museum of Bricks

The largest Lego collection in the world, the **Museum of Bricks** *(museumofbricks.cz; adult/child 270/170Kč)* sports thousands of Lego sets spread out over five museums; and one branch is in Kutná Hora, right next to the Ossuary in Sedlec. Over 200 sq metres you can see more than 1000 models, but the highlights are a Lego replica of the Bone Church containing 50,000 pieces, and the Cathedral of St Barbara.

 EATING IN KUTNÁ HORA: OUR PICKS

Restaurace V Ruthardce: Old Bohemian tavern with heavy Czech favourites and views of the St Barbara Cathedral. *11am-11pm* €€

Dačický: Old Bohemian, wood-panelled beerhall with lager and dumplings galore. *11am-8pm* €€

U Šneka Pohodáře: Enjoy a pizza and a Bernard beer at the 'Easy-going Snail'. *11am-10pm* €

Kavárna na Kozím plácku: Cute cafe with big timber beams and mismatched 1950s furniture. *9am-7pm* €

Beyond Kutná Hora

The tranquil Sázava River, a tributary of the Vltava, flows from Žďár nad Sázavou to the southern outskirts of Prague.

As it gathers strength before it is consumed by the mighty Vltava to the south of Prague, the idyllic River Sázava cuts a deep valley, hemmed by ancient, rounded hills and thick forests. Popular among Czechs for lazy summer rafting and canoe trips, the Sázava flows through many pretty provincial towns (most overlooked by visitors on their way elsewhere) and lends its name to many. Of the many sights along its length, Český Šternberk Castle is the most dramatic, a huge fortress towering over the village and river. The Church of St Nepomuk on the Green Mountain just outside Žďár nad Sázavou is a UNESCO-listed church in a style few would think possible for the times in which it was built.

Places
Český Šternberk p223
Žďár nad Sázavou p224

GETTING AROUND

The main railway line from Prague to Moravia follows the River Sázava religiously all the way to Žďár nad Sázavou, making places along the valley easily accessible by train. A branch line leaves the mainline at Zruč nad Sázavou and heads north to Kutná Hora.

Český Šternberk   TIME FROM KUTNÁ HORA: **50 MINS**

Tour a mighty fortress high above the river

Some 40km southwest of Kutná Hora, **Český Šternberk** (*hradceskysternberk.cz; adult/child 300/200kč*) is one of the oldest castles in the country and still in the ownership of the Šternberg family who established it in 1241. This Gothic pile towers over the slow-moving waters of the River Sázava, and were it nearer Prague it would be a major attraction in the Czech lands. Inside, the early baroque alterations were enhanced in the 20th century when central heating and electricity were installed. For visitors there is just one guided tour that takes in 15 rooms on the 2nd floor. Highlights include the Knights Hall with its baroque stucco decoration and the study of the current owner's grandfather, Jiří Šternberg. Interestingly, when the castle was nationalised by the communists in 1949, Jiří Šternberg was allowed to stay on as castle warden until his death in 1965 – unheard of anywhere else in the country. The castle was returned to his son Zdeněk Šternberg in the restitution process of the early 1990s.

After the tour, follow the red/blue marked hiking trail for 250m to find the **South Tower**. This looks like a ship's hull from one side and was designed to protect the castle from attack. In addition to the interiors, the views of and from the castle are commendably photogenic, its hulk rising over a picturesque bend in the river.

SANTINI-AICHEL – MASTER OF THE GOTHIC BAROQUE

A Prague-born architect of Italian descent, Jan Blažej Santini-Aichel (1677–1723) was a maverick who simply did things differently.

The churches and chateaux to which he applied his blend of Gothic and Baroque packed with symbolism differ completely from what his contemporaries were designing, and were highly unusual for the 17th century. This has earned two of his works (the Cathedral of Assumption of Our Lady & St John the Baptist in Kutná Hora, and the Church of St Nepomuk on the Green Mountain in Žďár) a UNESCO listing. Other Santini-Aichel creations you might want to seek out are the Cistercian Monastery in Plasy (near Pilsen) and Karlova Koruna Chateau in Chlumec nad Cidlinou.

Church of St Nepomuk on the Green Mountain

Žďár nad Sázavou
TIME FROM KUTNÁ HORA: 1½ HRS

Climb to Žďár's Five-Star Attraction

The UNESCO-listed **Church of St Nepomuk on the Green Mountain** (zelena-hora.cz) is the reason the vast majority of visitors alight at the unpretentiously gritty town of Žďár nad Sázavou. Around 4km north of the train station, Santini-Aichel's zany Gothic-baroque church rises atop a hill and is built in the shape of a five-pointed star surrounded by a decagonal cloister. Five stars are said to have appeared over the spot where St John of Nepomuk was cast into the Vltava in Prague by Václav IV for refusing to divulge the confessional secrets of the queen. The church is full of symbolism in the shape of stars, multiples of five, and tongues, another symbol of St John of Nepomuk. For the time, the design was a daring and outrageous architectural statement.

 EATING BEYOND KUTNÁ HORA: OUR PICKS

Pod Hradem: Nearest the castle in Český Šternberk, slightly overly modern pub-restaurant with menu of purely Czech standards. 11am-9pm Wed-Sun €€

Penzion v parku: Next to the train station in Český Šternberk, hotel built to accommodate the first tourists still has a convenient restaurant. 10am-10pm €€

Poppet: In Žďár nad Sázavou, traditional-looking restaurant with surprisingly imaginative Czech and international dishes. 10.30am-10pm Mon-Sat, to 3pm Sun €€€

Süssův hostinec: In central Žďár nad Sázavou, not much has changed at this 19th-century tavern in the last four decades. Filling, simple Czech food. 10am-late €

Litomyšl

UNESCO-LISTED CHATEAU | CLASSICAL MUSIC | PRETTY SQUARE

A strong contender for the title of East Bohemia's prettiest town, little Litomyšl lies 50km southeast of the regional capital Pardubice. The main reason to come here is for the country's most eye-catching and best-preserved renaissance chateau, one of the finest north of the Alps. Listed by UNESCO in 1999, it has been in the ownership of the Czech state since the end of WWII.

Litomyšl is also the birthplace of one of the Czechs' most beloved composers, Bedřich Smetana (1824–84), who was actually born at the chateau brewery and lived there until he was six. The Smetana's Litomyšl classical-music festival is one of the highpoints of the highbrow Czech cultural calendar. Throw in one of the country's prettiest Gothic-baroque-Renaissance squares, a couple of rewarding art galleries and some sugary baroque religious heritage, and you have some very good reasons to head to this corner of Bohemia.

Savouring Litomyšl's Food Festival
Celebrating the nation's most famous cook

Magdalena Dobromila Rettigová (who died in the town in 1845) is still the nation's go-to cook – her cookbook is used in Czech kitchens to this day, and Litomyšl even named its May food festival (Gastronomické slavnosti M D Rettigové, *gastroslavnosti.cz*) after her. Overshadowed somewhat by the famous Smetana music festival (p229), this foodie fest is tasty fun and provides a chance to try dishes from all over Bohemia and Moravia.

Portmoneum
Wonderfully weird

In stark contrast to the restrained Renaissance splendour on display across town, to the southeast of the chateau, in a fairly non-descript bungalow on a quiet residential street,

GETTING AROUND

If you don't have a car, getting to Litomyšl can be a mini adventure. From Prague, a change is always necessary, whether you come by bus or train. Major express trains heading to all points east stop in Česká Třebová, from where there are buses to Litomyšl. Other buses leave from Svitavy, Choceň, Pradubice and Hradec Králové.

In town, the only way to explore is to walk. The compact historical centre, where you will find both the square and the chateau, can be crossed in minutes on foot. The train station is just to the north of the square; buses pull in south of the square.

☑ TOP TIP

Litomyšl has a particularly well-run tourist information office *(ticlitomysl.cz)* located on the main Smetanovo Square. The website and staff are a font of information on sights and what's going on in town.

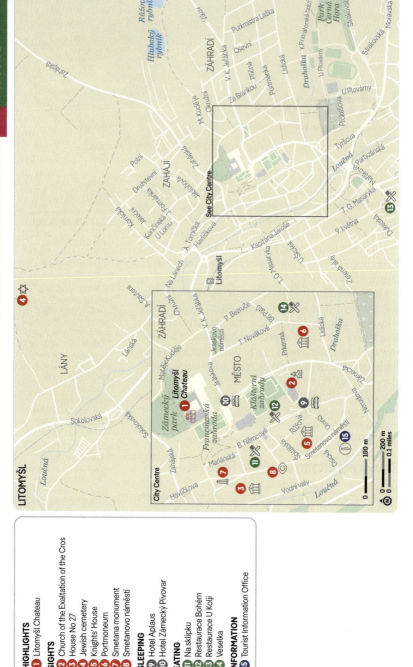

Smetanovo náměstí (Smetanovo Square)

stands the wondrous **Portmoneum** *(portmoneum.cz)* where the walls, ceilings and furniture are covered in the hyper-real paintings of idiosyncratic Josef Váchal (1884–1969).
Váchal completed the paintings from 1920 to 1924 for the house owner, Josef Portman, and the proto-psychedelic images blend Christian iconography and Hindu inscriptions with a deliciously ghoulish bent. It's wonderfully weird like some forgotten album cover from an obscure 1970s rock band.

Váchal is a slightly forgotten Czech artist who excelled in many disciplines, from painting to woodcarving, poetry to graphic art. He was a Renaissance man, a suitable accolade in this town.

Explore Litomyšl's Lost Jewish Past
Echoes of a once thriving community

Litomyšl once had a small but vibrant Jewish community with members dispersed through the town and not confined to a ghetto. Some fragments of their culture remain today, most notably the **Jewish cemetery** 2km north of the centre. The scattered, Hebrew-inscribed tombstones rise crooked among mature trees, a thought-provoking sight.

The tourist information centre on Smetanovo náměstí organises guided Jewish-themed tours.

 EATING IN LITOMYŠL: OUR PICKS

| **Na sklípku:** Lively, very characterful resto-pub does imaginative takes on Czech staples in an ancient vaulted building. *11am-10pm Mon-Sat, 3-9pm Sun* €€ | **Restaurace Bohém:** In the Hotel Aplaus (p235) and next to the Church of the Exaltation, Bohém has the classiest menu in Litomyšl. *11am-11pm* €€ | **Restaurace U Kolji:** A clean, Scandi-style interior and light cuisine makes this a good lunch option. *11am-10pm, to 5pm Sun* €€ | **Veselka:** Litomyšl's best traditional pub has chequered tablecloths, cold beer and a menu of tasty, filling Czech food. *11am-10pm* € |

TOP EXPERIENCE

Litomyšl Chateau

Northeast of Smetanovo Square stands Litomyšl's spectacular *zámek* (chateau), the country's finest Renaissance Palace. It was commissioned by the Pernštejn family in the 16th century and left virtually untouched, at least on the outside, since those times. The *zámek* also wrote a significant chapter in Czech cultural history when one Bedřich Smetana was born at the chateau brewery in 1824.

DON'T MISS

- Sgraffito 'envelope' decoration
- Chateau theatre
- Great Dining Room
- Trompe-l'oeil decoration
- Smetana Birthplace Exhibition
- Monastery Gardens
- Empire bedroom

Sgraffito & Loggia

Before you even enter the courtyard, the exterior of the Litomyšl's chateau is well-known among the architecturally aware for two features. The first and more notable is the sgraffito 'envelope' (*psaníčko* in Czech) decoration on the facade. There are a whopping 8000 'envelopes' and it's claimed that no two motifs within them are repeated across the entirety of the huge building, a feat of virtuosity indeed. The second unusual feature is the triple-tier loggia of the courtyard, quite unique in the Czech lands.

Practicalities
Scan this QR code for prices and opening hours.

The Basic Tour

Entry is by guided tour only and there are two tours to choose from. The main route takes you through the grand rooms used by the Valdštejns in the early 19th century, part of the chateau that underwent extensive renovation in 2021. This includes the **Great Dining Room** with its amazing trompe-l'oeil decoration by Dominik Dvořák, a local artist who spent his entire life decorating various parts of the chateau. The chandeliers here are not old – they were left behind after Miloš Forman filmed *Amadeus* here in 1984. The **Empire bedroom**, the **games room** and the pièce de résistance at Litomyšl chateau, the rare Baroque Theatre (see below), are other definite highlights.

Thurn-Taxis Tour

A second tour explores the wing occupied by the Thurn-Taxis family, the last owners of the chateau who were forced to leave in 1945. The rooms have a more 'lived in', practical feel and are fascinating to explore. Interestingly, the Thurn-Taxis family had a monopoly on the imperial Austrian postal and transport system in the 19th century, and from their surname we get the word 'taxi'.

Baroque Theatre

The most valuable space at the chateau is the incredibly well-preserved, private family theatre dating from 1797, which still sports most of its original features. The decoration of the theatre is the work of Josef Platzer who also adorned the Estates Theatre in Prague and Vienna's court theatre. It is one of only three theatres to have survived from that period in the Czech lands. As they are largely made of wood, most of the others went up in flames at some point.

Smetana Birthplace Exhibition

The Czechs' most celebrated composer, Bedřich Smetana (1824–84) was born in the former castle brewery in the grounds of the chateau, and the building now houses the Smetana Birthplace Exhibition (Rodný Byt Bedřicha Smetany), a modest museum examining the composer's early childhood in Litomyšl. It's part of the Litomyšl Regional Museum (as is the **Portmoneum**).

Monastery Garden & Havel Square

After the tour, be sure to visit the **Monastery Gardens** on the southwest side of the chateau lying between two churches, a good spot for a picnic or just a stroll in the sun. The small space to the south is **Václav Havel Square**, surprisingly one of only a handful of public areas in the entire country named after the Czechs' most famous president. His widow usually blocks the naming of streets and squares after her late husband.

SMETANA'S LITOMYŠL

The 19th-century composer Bedřich Smetana is by far Litomyšl's most illustrious son, and the town knows how to celebrate the fact. The **Smetana's Litomyšl** classical-music festival is the second-oldest such event in the country (first held in 1946) and takes place annually in the last two weeks of June. Venues include the chateau itself, the town's churches and the chateau riding school.

TOP TIPS

- Always check the chateau website (see above) before you plan a visit to make sure there isn't an event that halts tours.

- Buy tickets online from the chateau website to save time.

- No dogs or any other pets are allowed in the gardens or in the chateau.

- Tours still run, even during the Smetana's Litomyšl classical music festival.

- Litomyšl Chateau doesn't entirely shut up shop over winter – see the website for details of tours between November and March.

- Before visiting, seek out the film *Amadeus* (1984) directed by Miloš Forman, featuring scenes shot at the chateau.

A STROLL THROUGH HISTORY

Discover layer on layer of Czech history and culture as you explore Litomyšl's 'other' attractions.

START	END	LENGTH
Chateau	Portmoneum	1.3km; 1 hour

A few steps along the alleyways west of the chateau bring you to ❶ **Smetanovo náměstí**, the town's main square, a slender procession of burghers' houses with baroque and neo-classical facades, most of them resting on Gothic arcading. The oldest and most impressive house on the square is the ❷ **Knights' House** (dům u Rytířů), dating from the 1540s. Today it houses Litomyšl's municipal gallery.

At the northern end of the square rises the ❸ **Smetana monument**, which was erected in 1924 to mark a century since the composer's birth. The ❹ **House No 27**, near the Smetana statue, is where the most famous Czech female writer, Božena Němcová, lived between 1839 and 1840 and where she gave birth to her son Karel.

At the southern end of the square, double back up Smilkovského Street to the ❺ **Church of the Exaltation of the Cross** (kostel Povýšení sv Kříže), which is an impressive wedge of baroque. Fully restored, it features a huge organ inside, and it's one of the venues for the Smetana's Litomyšl Festival.

In a nondescript bungalow 200m east of the square on a quiet residential street (ul. Novákové) stands the wondrous ❻ **Portmoneum** (portmoneum.cz), where the walls, ceilings and furniture are covered in the hyperreal paintings of idiosyncratic Josef Váchal (1884–1969).

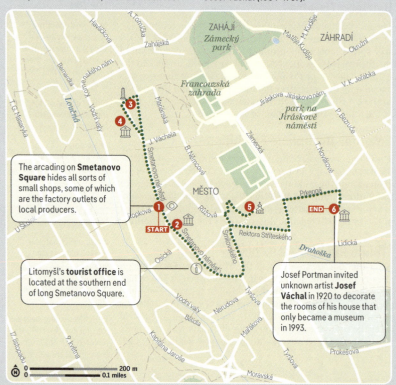

The arcading on **Smetanovo Square** hides all sorts of small shops, some of which are the factory outlets of local producers.

Litomyšl's **tourist office** is located at the southern end of long Smetanovo Square.

Josef Portman invited unknown artist **Josef Váchal** in 1920 to decorate the rooms of his house that only became a museum in 1993.

Pardubice

RENAISSANCE CHATEAU | CHARMING SQUARES | SMALLTOWN VIBE

A little-known regional capital around 100km to the east of Prague, cute little Pardubice is normally ignored by foreign tourists. But that's all the more reason to head to this intimate city of 90,000. Apart from observing everyday life on its cobbled streets, the star attraction is its Renaissance chateau, but aimless wandering of the pretty, generally tourist-free squares and lanes can be a magical experience, especially after too much Prague.

Apart from Pardubice's attractions, there are two other reasons foreigners find themselves here. One of the country's top concert venues is here, and with Prague often fully booked for years ahead, some big acts are choosing to perform in regional capitals (Scorpions, Alice Cooper and Seal have packed out the Enteria Arena). The second reason is similar but involves airlines – Smartwings and Ryanair use Pardubice airport for cheap flights, and as the schedule at Prague Airport fills up again after COVID-19, Pardubice will take up the slack.

Tour a Renaissance Palace

Pardubice Chateau

A typical example of a Gothic fortress transformed into a Renaissance palace, Pardubice's **chateau** originally dates from the 13th century. Seeking a bit more comfort than a draughty medieval castle could provide, the Lords of Pernštejn rebuilt it in the 15th and 16th centuries into their Renaissance residence, blending the structure's Gothic foundations with Italian architectural influences, such as sgraffito decoration of the 'envelope' type (as at **Litomyšl Chateau**, p228).

GETTING AROUND

Like most small Czech towns and cities, Pardubice is best tackled on foot. However, you will need to use the city's buses to get from the main train station to the historical centre. Take bus Nos 6, 8 or 9 to **náměstí Republiky** at the heart of the Old Town.

☑ TOP TIP

The country's biggest horserace, the **Velká Pardubická** (Great Pardubice Steeplechase) is a major national event and the only time most Czechs have a bet on anything. It's held in mid-October at the racecourse to the southeast, next to the airport.

PARDUBICE

SIGHTS
1. Automatic Mills
2. Church of John the Baptist
3. Green Gate (Zelená Brána)
4. Museum of East Bohemia
5. Pardubice Chateau
6. Pernštýnské náměstí
7. Theatre of East Bohemia (Východočeské Divadlo)

SLEEPING
8. Hotel 100
9. U Zlatého Anděla

EATING
10. Mléčné Lahůdky
11. Nejen Dvorek
12. Plzeňka
13.4. Tady&Teď

SHOPPING
14. Machoňova Pasáž

Today, Pardubice Castle is the main branch of the **Museum of East Bohemia** (*vcm.cz; adult/concession 220/110Kč*). You can take a tour of the Renaissance halls with their shockingly colourful frescoes; peruse the temporary exhibitions that are mostly on a local theme, put together from the three quarters of a million items held in the permanent collections here; or explore the atomic bomb shelter under the chateau, built in the 1950s for the communist elite.

At the end of your visit there's a decent cafe in a vaulted space and a good museum shop.

A WANDER THROUGH PARDUBICE'S ARCHITECTURAL PAST

Take this easy route through Pardubice's Old Town, an architectural feast with everything from Gothic to art-deco on the menu.

START	END	LENGTH
Church of John the Baptist	Chateau	2km; 1 hour

Start at the diminutive ❶ **Church of John the Baptist**, a 16th-century cemetery church that once had an ossuary opposite. The cemetery is long gone but this step-gabled Gothic chapel still marks the entrance to the Old Town.

Head for 400m along Třídy Míru (Peace Avenue) – on the right is the ❷ **Machoňova Pasáž**, a First Republic shopping arcade still with all its original art-deco elements in place. There are also plenty of little shops occupying the original 1930s units.

Another 200m brings you to náměstí Republiky, the main bus stop for the Old Town. The architectural highlight here is the ❸ **Theatre of East Bohemia** (Východočeské Divadlo), one of the finest art-nouveau buildings in the country.

From the square, head through the tall ❹ **Green Gate** (Zelená Brána) to access ❺ **Pernštýnské náměstí**, Pardubice's grand, centrepiece piazza. It is ringed with tall Renaissance townhouses with high-flying gables in every pastel hue. Compact and perfectly renovated, it's one of Bohemia's most intimate and character-full town squares. It's also home to Pardubice's rather grand town hall.

From the eastern end of the square, head up Perštýnská and Zámecká, passing cafes and souvenir shops as you go, to the bridge that crosses the moat surrounding the ❻ **chateau** (p231) which houses the Museum of East Bohemia.

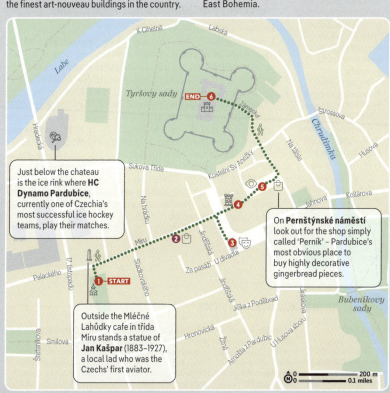

PARDUBICE GINGERBREAD

Ask any Czech what their first association with Pardubice is, and the answer will most certainly be gingerbread.

Actually gingerbread is a bad translation of the Czech *perník*, as this sweet bread contains no ginger, with honey and pepper lending it a spicy flavour. *Perník* has been baked here since the 16th century and there's nothing more traditional than an intricately decorated gingerbread heart, bell or horseshoe. Some of the designs are incredibly elaborate and take hours to complete.

The castle hosts the annual Slavnosti perníku (Gingerbread Celebrations) in mid-May (inexplicably on a Wednesday!) but the gingerbread can be bought year-round.

It makes a great souvenir, as the honey and pepper guarantee it never really goes off, just hard.

Automatic Mills

Discover Pardubice's Automatic Mills
Multipurpose cultural complex

Reopened in 2019, the so-called **Automatic Mills** (*Automatické mlýny, automatickemlyny.eu*) were originally built in 1910 by the Winternitz brothers who brought in the most famous architect of the day, Josef Gočár (of House at the Black Madonna in Prague fame) to design the building opposite the chateau. The red-brick, Renaissance-style structure mimics other much older buildings in town, and few would guess this was in fact a mill. In 2016, work began on this national monument to create a multipurpose space for some of the town's cultural institutions. It is now home to the Regional Gočár Gallery, the Pardubice Municipal Gallery (GAMPA), the Sféra Education Centre and a branch of the Pardubice tourist information centre. However, renovation work is ongoing, with more institutions and dining venues set to move in by 2026.

 EATING IN PARDUBICE: OUR PICKS

Tady&Teď: Wonderfully period cafe styled in the 1930s fashion, like the shopping arcade it calls home. *7.30am-10pm Mon-Sat* €

Plzeňka: Typical Urquell-branded tavern serving Pilsen beer and very traditional meat-dumpling combos. *11am-10pm* €€

Mléčné Lahůdky: Huge survivor from the socialist republic, selling Czech cakes, pastries, open sandwiches and drinks. *6am-6pm Mon-Fri* €

Nejen Dvorek: Enjoy well-crafted dishes (Czech and un-Czech) against a backdrop of plants and earthy furniture at this courtyard restaurant. *11am-10pm* €€

Places We Love to Stay

€ Budget €€ Midrange €€€ Top End

Liberec p204

Hotel Radnice € Traditional, slightly old-fashioned but super-central hotel within walking distance of the sights that won't break the budget.

Pytloun Design Hotel € Best price-to-quality ratio in town, with renovated rooms and a superb breakfast. Self-check-in, 3.5km south of the centre and lots of parking.

Pytloun City Boutique Hotel €€ Fresh and central, this luxurious four-star number behind a dramatically curving facade is part of the local Pytloun hotel empire.

Krkonoše p208

Labská Bouda € Controversial mega-project jutting out into thin alpine air at 1340m. Rooms are basic communist-era affairs with improvements here and there.

Martinova Bouda € Pretty high-perched chalet named after Czech tennis player Martina Navratilova who spent some of her childhood here. The restaurant here is particularly warm and cosy when the snow falls outside.

Luční Bouda €€ The Krkonoše's oldest ridge chalet and one of Europe's largest, with surprisingly luxurious private rooms, a basic sleeping bag area and a big buffet restaurant.

Czech Switzerland p211

Penzion Soutěsky € Wonderfully restored, six-room timber guesthouse at the end of the gorge in Hřensko.

Penzion Pod Kaštany € Basic guesthouse in Srbská Kamenice with a trek-launching breakfast and warm, cosy rooms.

Na Výšinkách €€ This comfortable, eight-room Jetřichovice farmhouse pension is run with love and care by the family who own it. The tiny pub serves Rakovník beer, the country's best.

Grand Hotel Hradec €€€ Right in the centre of Pec pod Sněžkou, this luxury Minecraft-esque hotel is the antidote to the region's scuffed mountain huts. Parking, a restaurant, a wellness centre and uniformed staff are just some of what you'll find here.

Děčín p216

Hostel Děčín Na Skřivánce € Basic hostel with some shared facilities, a decent breakfast, basic dorms, a kitchen and helpful staff.

Česká Koruna €€ The 43 standard rooms here put you right at the heart of town. Decor comes in various layers of post-communist style.

Pension Via Ferrata €€ This hotel at the foot of the Pastýřská stěna has crisp, film-themed rooms, lovely castle and Elbe views, self-check-in and an American dining venue.

Kutná Hora p219

Penzion Havlíček € This historic house, just across the street from the Italian Court, sports a stylish cafe and five converted bedrooms.

Hotel U Kata € The name of this good-value family-run hotel translates as the 'Executioner' but the excellent facilities and friendly staff here mean you won't lose your head.

Litomyšl p225

Hotel Zámecký Pivovar €€ Stay in the building where composer Bedřich Smetana was born up at the castle in Litomyšl. Rooms are understatedly basic.

Hotel Aplaus €€ Put your hands together for the high standards of this very well-appointed hotel just off the main square. The 21 doubles are beautifully decorated and there's a cafe and restaurant on-site.

Pardubice p231

U Zlatého Anděla €€ Stay as near to the chateau as possible at this historical guesthouse perched on the approach lane to the chateau bridge.

Hotel 100 €€ Just behind Pernštýské náměstí, this small, understated mini-hotel occupies an ancient building just below the chateau.

Researched by Becki Enright

Moravia & Silesia

SPLENDOUR, FOLKLORE AND VINEYARD-COVERED HILLS

Heritage cities, festive locals and viniculture traditions, Moravia is the mellow to Bohemia's bustle.

Venture into Czechia's easternmost province, Moravia, for a rurally resplendent flip on its western counterpart, Bohemia. Here, tradition and folklore take centre stage, dedication to vineyards surpasses breweries, and big-hitter sights fill tiny towns, chronicling the former dynasties of medieval Moravia to the Habsburg Empire.

At its core, though geographically south, is the provincial capital Brno – Moravia's gateway and trendsetting student city carves a somewhat rebellious, artistic path in creating a new identity overground while showing off its historic cache beneath. Olomouc, Moravia's first capital and former Habsburg stronghold, conceals its baroque beauty – the prettiest city in the region is surprisingly overlooked.

Contrastingly, Northern Ostrava platforms Silesia's industrial past, turning mines and ironworks into culture locales.

Beyond the urban appeal, Moravia's scattering of UNESCO sites, chateaux and ancient citadels – the archbishop bastion Kroměříž, Renaissance monument Telč, the Jewish Quarter of Třebíč and the former aristocratic stomping grounds of the Lednice–Valtice Cultural Landscape – are its microcosm masterpieces. And while peaks hug Moravia on the borders with Poland and Slovakia, the southern quilt of winemaking hills from Znojmo to Mikulov, woven into protected parks like Pálava and Podyjí, is where it sparkles.

Moravia may seem off-radar, but its deep-rooted celebration of tradition and its historical repository are anything but hidden; if you have days to spare, come and see Czechia's other side.

THE MAIN AREAS

BRNO	**MIKULOV**	**ZNOJMO**	**OLOMOUC**	**OSTRAVA**
Underground, overground in Moravia's lively capital.	Castle-topped town and winemaking centre.	Wineland historical hilltop hamlet.	Czechia's hidden beauty in the east.	Turning mining sites into cultural hubs.
p242	p255	p262	p265	p269

For places to stay in Moravia & Silesia, see p273

Left: Třebíč (p251); Above: Lednice Chateau (p259)

Find Your Way

Moravia's regional bus and train networks cover all major hubs; the most direct routes are often from Brno. Ditch the car unless you plan to visit outlying destinations. Plan your route with the IDOS Czech public transport app.

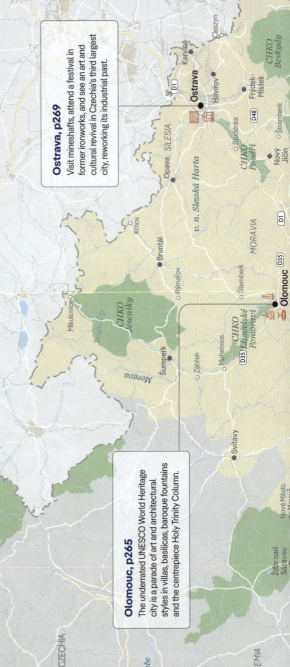

Ostrava, p269
Visit mineshafts, attend a festival in former ironworks, and see an art and cultural revival in Czechia's third largest city, reworking its industrial past.

Olomouc, p265
The underrated UNESCO World Heritage city is a parade of art and architectural styles in villas, basilicas, baroque fountains and the centrepiece Holy Trinity Column.

MORAVIA & SILESIA

Brno, p242
In Czechia's second city, find a modernist architectural hub, a labyrinth of historical sites, playful art and an energetic pace driven by the student population.

Mikulov, p255
Hike through Pálava's forests, bike vineyard village hills, and sample local vintages in the bars and taverns of this castle-topped town, Czechia's winemaking centre.

Znojmo, p262
Stomp old royal ground in the slope-top castle and Romanesque mural-decorated Rotunda, tour the underground city, and hike to the vineyard viewpoints of Podyjí National Park.

TRAIN
Moravia's main train lines pass through Břeclav and Brno, connecting Prague and Vienna. From Brno, fast trains go to Olomouc and Ostrava. Břeclav links to Mikulov. Regional S8 connects Znojmo, Mikulov and Valtice; other lines serve smaller towns like Slavkov u Brna.

CAR
The D1 motorway runs through Moravia, linking Prague with Brno, Olomouc and Ostrava. A car is advantageous for reaching southern vineyard villages and the mountain regions on the borders of Poland and Slovakia; otherwise, intercity public transport works well.

BUS
The Moravian bus network is the best way to get around. Brno connects to Mikulov and Znojmo in the south and Olomouc and Ostrava in the north; the bus to Zlín stops at Kroměříž. The Munich-bound FlixBus stops at Třebíč and Telč.

Plan Your Time

Moravia's compactness of sites and connected transport network are well-geared for city-hopping or day-tripping. Start in the cool capital, Brno, but venture beyond for vino-fuelled, UNESCO and culture-brimming cities.

Telč (p254)

A Moravian Weekender

With two days for a taster of Moravia, combine the capital with a lesser-known city or a day in the wine area. Start Saturday in **Brno** (p242) with an early subterranean tour of the **Labyrinth under the Vegetable Market** (p244). Cross the city's quirky sculpture-marked squares, visit Europe's second-largest ossuary at the Church of St James, pre-book an afternoon tour of UNESCO-listed functionalist Villa Tugendhat or enjoy the views from Špilberk Castle.

On Sunday, trip to **Olomouc** (p265) for its baroque architecture bundle, including six fountains and the UNESCO-listed Trinity Column, alongside its socialist realism astronomical clock and emerging street art.

Or head to nature-bound **Mikulov** (p255) to bike tour vineyards or join the day-trippers combining a historic centre walk around with feasts in wine cellars.

Seasonal Highlights

The eastern region knows how to celebrate. Moravia hosts some of the country's biggest and best cultural fiestas, with an events calendar full of folk, food and music festivals.

MARCH/APRIL
Head to **Rožnov pod Radhoštěm** Wallachian open-air museum to see the Moravian folk spectacle Easter Monday ritual of symbolically whipping women and girls with willows to keep them healthy and beautiful.

MAY
Folk festivals spring up in late May with Vlčnov's ceremonial procession **Ride of the Kings** (Jízda králů) and in late June with the International Folklore Festival in Strážnice, home of the National Institute of Folk Culture.

JULY
The Dolní Vítkovice former ironworks site transforms into the stages of the multi-genre mega-gig, **Colours of Ostrava** – one of Central Europe's biggest and best music festivals.

Five-Day Southern Wine Trip

Swap cities for the rock-top castle towns and national parks of South Moravia's winelands.

In **Mikulov** (p255), tour the former **Dietrichstein Castle and family tomb**, visit the Jewish sites and **historic houses** (p255) and trek up Holy Hill for sunset.

Spend another day hiking through **Pálava National Park** (p261), biking around vineyards or joining a tour of the local wineries.

With two days in **Znojmo** (p262), spend one on a castle and Rotunda of St Catherine visit, climb the Wolf Tower and tour the **underground tunnel** (p262). Next, trail a city slope walk or trek to hilltop vineyards, like Šobes in Podyjí National Park.

On the last day, wander the corridors of the Liechtenstein noble residence of **Valtice Castle** (p259), also home to the Wine Salon of Czechia.

Moravia Mapped in Seven Days

An entire week gives you enough time to cover the best of the eastern province.

South Moravia's capital, **Brno** (p242), is the natural starting point, where you can extend your city saunter with more sub-ground sites like the atmospheric Water Tanks or browse the contemporary art ensemble at the **Museum of Applied Arts** (p247).

With more time for day jaunts, get adventurous in the **Moravian Karst caverns** (p249), head to historical sites like the **Austerlitz battlefield** (p252), marvel at the functionalist city of **Zlín** (p250), or heritage-hop the UNESCO trio of **Třebíč** (p251), **Telč** (p254) and **Kroměříž** (p252).

Next, head south for a wine tour, basing yourself in **Mikulov** (p255) or Znojmo for Pálava and Podyjí National Park bikes, hikes and tastings before moving north to picture-perfect **Olomouc** (p265) and unconventional, post-industrial **Ostrava** (p269).

AUGUST

Telč might be tiny, but its band stage, beer-tent streets and courtyards are acoustically alight with Czech folk music during the two-week **Prázdniny v Telči** music festival.

SEPTEMBER

Join the historical celebrations and performances on streets and musical stages at Znojmo's **Znojemské historické vinobraní** and the **Pálavské vinobraní** in Mikulov – two of the biggest and best wine festivals in Czechia.

NOVEMBER

Considered one of the best opera festivals in the world, **Janáčkovo Brno** shines a nearly month-long spotlight on classical music and the work of Czech composer legend Leoš Janáček.

DECEMBER

Brno goes big on **Advent**, with stall-packed squares, a giant nativity scene and festive installations. Olomouc's casual yuletide setup fills the Upper and Lower Squares and includes an open-air ice rink.

Brno

MEDIEVAL SITES | UNDERGROUND ATTRACTIONS | ART & ARCHITECTURE

GETTING AROUND

Brno's main train station, on the southeast side of the centre, is connected via direct trains to Prague, Vienna, Budapest and Bratislava.

Long-distance and international buses like FlixBus and RegioJet pull into a small bus station opposite Grandhotel Brno, and regional buses leave from ÚAN Zvonařka. While Brno has a walkable city centre encased by the Ring 1 road, its public transport network runs through it and beyond to the Ring 2 fringes for sites like Villa Tugendhat.

The international Brno–Turany Airport (BRQ) has some budget flights from London and European cities.

☑ TOP TIP

Use Brno as your main base. As the provincial capital of Moravia, it's the most well-connected hub, with extensive public transport options for easy excursions to surrounding towns and cities in under two hours.

Prague may take centre stage, but Brno isn't trying to compete. Not many Czech cities get as authentic as this, far from the tourist throngs. Brno's vibrancy comes from the university students and start-ups filling the city with youthful energy and creative enterprise. It shreds its nod to the Habsburg era 'suburb of Vienna' nickname in its playful reinvention, which includes quirky sculptures and tongue-in-cheek statues and pays tribute to its industrial boom in the protection of its functionalist architectural icons like Villa Tugendhat. Below ground, history is burrowed in medieval labyrinths and subterranean cellars, crypts and water chambers. In a region known for wine, Brno flips the script with a thriving beer scene and is an epicurean feast packing more cool cafes, bistros and bars than you can cram on a first visit. Sure, Brno is not as pretty as Prague, but is it the hip capital of Czechia? Absolutely.

Old Town Vistas & Viewpoint Climbs
Historical Brno highs

Entrance to the medieval **Old Town Hall** *(Stará radnice)* includes the 13th-century vaulted treasury and 16th-century judicial-themed, fresco-daubed hall, but climb the 173 wooden stairs through the clocktower to the 63m-high renaissance pavilion *(gotobrno.cz; adult/child 90/50Kč)*. The panorama across Brno takes in the city spires and pastel facades and, as it is bang in the middle of Brno's landmarks, it also has the best views of the hilltop icons, Špilberk Castle (p246) and the **Cathedral of Sts Peter and Paul**.

It's a steep stroll up **Špilberk Park** to reach the city's highest point for far-reaching views from the castle walls and angle switch on the gothic cathedral. Want a 360-degree bird's-eye vista? Climb the castle's **lookout tower** *(spilberk.cz; 120/50Kč)*.

The **cathedral's tower balconies** *(katedrala-petrov.cz; 60/40Kč)* give unrivalled southern views towards the Pálava hills or you can admire the view from a lower point in the neighbouring **Denis Gardens**, connected via a stone walkway.

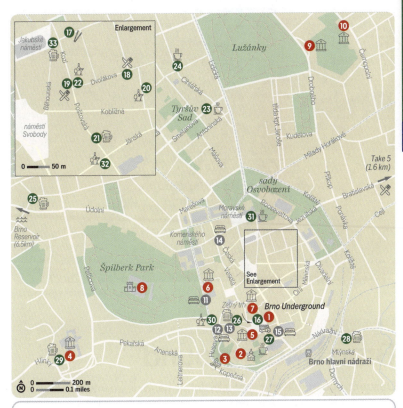

HIGHLIGHT
1 Brno Underground

SIGHTS
- 10-Z Bunker (see 1)
- Bunker Denis (see 1)
- Capuchin Crypt (see 1)
2 Cathedral of Sts Peter & Paul
- Cellar under the New Town Hall (see 1)
3 Denis Gardens
- Labyrinth under the Vegetable Market (see 1)
4 Mendel Museum
5 Moravian Museum
6 Museum of Applied Arts
7 Old Town Hall
- Ossuary at St James (see 1)
8 Špilberk Castle
9 Villa Löw-Beer
10 Villa Tugendhat
- Water Tanks (see 1)

SLEEPING
11 10-Z Bunker
12 Barceló Brno Palace
13 Enjoy Downtown Boutique Apartments
14 Hotel Avion
15 Masarykova N°30

EATING
16 Bucheck
17 Cà Phê Cô
18 Eggo Truck Brno
19 Lokál U Caipla

DRINKING & NIGHTLIFE
20 4pokoje
21 Axiom
22 Bar, Který Neexistuje
23 Kafe Fridrich
24 Kimono
25 Lucky Bastard Beerhouse
26 Malt Worm
27 Monogram Espresso Bar
28 Schrott
29 Starobrno Brewery
30 Super Panda Circus
31 Typika
32 Vinotéka U Tri Knižat
33 Výčep Na stojáka

Ossuary at the Church of St James

TOP EXPERIENCE

Brno Underground

Descend into medieval cellar labyrinths, head down into bone-stacked burial chambers and Capuchin crypts, stand in the historical water tank cathedrals and tour the once-classified wartime bunker hideouts. Get beneath the surface of squares, streets and hills, and you'll find another city entirely. If you do only one thing in Brno, go underground.

Subterranean Medieval Maze

The Vegetable Market has been a firm fixture in Brno since the 13th century. But, as the city grew around it, so did a subterranean counterpart, which remained unknown until modern reconstruction uncovered a multilevel, kilometre-long maze of chambers and passageways. Walk 212 steps below ground to tour the cellars of old city merchants and alchemists on a one-hour walk through the **Labyrinth under the Vegetable Market** (*Labyrint pod Zelným trhem*).

> **DID YOU KNOW?**
>
> Aside from the illusionary aesthetics of the Water Tanks, their superb acoustics have turned the site into a new concert and performance venue.

Practicalities
Scan this QR code for prices and opening hours.

The **Cellar under the New Town Hall** (*Sklep pod Novou radnicí*) is less of a tunnel exploration and more of an interactive and multimedia exhibit of Brno's history and legends through the ages, located in the former coin-making Mint Master's Cellar (Mincmistrovský sklep).

Historic City Cisterns

Brno recently opened its pillar-vaulted, cathedral-like **Water Tanks** (*Vodojemy Žlutý kopec*) as a showcase of the architectural ingenuity in Brno's 19th-century water supply history. The self-guided tour with a downloadable audio guide takes you through three historic structures: the first brick tank from 1874, with its vaulted floors and seemingly infinite chambers; the 1894 brick tank with a simplified arched design; and the 1917 tank, whose vaulted ceiling and 87 concrete pillars create an atmospheric sound-echoing chamber. Špilberk Castle's water tank exhibit, on the other hand, is used to present a collection of stone sculptures and engravings.

Czechia's Colossal Catacombs

It's a sombre walk through the floor-to-ceiling, delicately displayed bone-stacked burial shaft of the **Ossuary at the Church of St James** (Kostnice u sv Jakuba) – the resting place of 50,000 people who perished in the Thirty Years' War and the plagues. This vault, the second-largest ossuary in Europe after the Paris Catacombs, was discovered in 2001 during work on the square, and the bones were rearranged in an act of remembrance.

Mummified Capuchin Monks

For over 100 years, until 1784, Friars of the Christian Capuchin Order were buried in the **Capuchin Crypt** (*Kapucínská hrobka*) below the Church of the Discovery of the Holy Cross on Capuchin Square. It's a macabre close encounter, but a respectful display of the bodies of the monks given a simple burial here, naturally mummified because of the monastery's ventilation system. Benefactors of the order were also entombed here, many in open caskets.

Brno's Nuclear Bunkers

A 1959 communist-era construction turning a former Nazi civil defence shelter into a Cold War nuclear fallout bunker to protect the city's political elite, **10-Z** was luckily never used for its intended purpose. It remained a classified secret until 1993 and only opened to the public in 2016. A self-guided tour through the artefact-packed original operational rooms and living spaces for around 500 people can be eerie, especially if devoid of visitors; tours are only in Czech.

Bunker Denis (*Kryt Denis pod Petrovem*) is a second nuclear shelter, a 1km track of rock-carved corridors burrowed under Petrov Cathedral hill, with a capacity of up to 2500 people. Currently, limited Sunday-only tours are only in Czech; no English audio or paper guides are available.

WINE CELLARS TODAY

Not all cellars are obsolete. While not as deeply subterranean, Brno still has step-down wine cellars serving samples of the vinos from South Moravia. Beneath a tucked-away courtyard in the city centre, **Vinotéka U Tri Knižat** is the historic cellar pick. Try wines by the glass from 25Kč per 100ml and take away your favourites the traditional way – straight from the barrel or box in plastic bottles.

TOP TIPS

● Opening hours vary, with many underground sites closed on Monday.

● Book ahead for English tours of the Labyrinth under the Vegetable Market; spaces fill quickly.

● Pack an extra layer for the drop in temperature a few metres below ground. Sturdy footwear is advised, especially for some slippery surfaces in the Water Tanks.

● Save 10% on tickets if visiting two underground sites in one day, or 25% on three, or consider the city attraction BRNOPAS if visiting more, alongside other Brno attractions.

BEER CULTURE IN A WINE LAND

Moravia is wine country, but Brno is hop-loving at its heart. Nothing is quite going to knock Pilsner Urquell off the foam-topped *pivo* pedestal, but if you want to try Brno's local brew, head to the **Starobrno Brewery** *(Pivovarská Starobrno).*

From sours to stouts, **Lucky Bastard Beerhouse** is the local crafter to visit. **Axiom** has a bar in the city, tapping the latest from its microbrewery in nearby Prostějov. Choose from special and microbrewery beers on tap at **Výčep Na stojáka**; *'na stojàka'* means stand up, which here is typically outside, sipping to DJ beats on St James' Square. **Malt Worm** is a top-rated craft tap bar with courtyard seating.

Wander the Halls of Špilberk Castle
The exhibit packed fortress

The mid-13th-century fortification of **Špilberk Castle** *(spilberk.cz; adult/child 160/95Kč)* turned 18th-century notorious Habsburg lockup is today a museum complex. Top exhibitions include the **Prison of Nations** with the dungeon and torture exhibits; the eight-part, artefact-packed **Brno on Špilberk** timeline from medieval stronghold to the Capital of Moravia; and a preserved 18th-century **Baroque Pharmacy**. Other rooms are chock full of artworks from Austrian Moravia to the modern day.

UNESCO-Listed Villa Tugendhat
Czechia's functionalist architecture masterpiece

Brno was no exception to the 1920s interwar period boom in modern architecture, with **Villa Tugendhat** being its greatest example of functionalist design. This simple, purist-style living space, created by German architect Ludwig Mies van der Rohe, was completed in 1930 for the Jewish industrialist family Greta and Fritz Tugendhat, though they had to flee eight years later. Restored in 2012, it's the only modern architecture listing among the Czech Republic's 17 UNESCO World Heritage Sites, and was where the Czechoslovakia separation agreement was signed in 1993. Entry is by a 60- or 90-minute guided **tour** *(tugendhat.eu; adult/child 400/250Kč)*, ideally booked at least a month or two in advance. However, free garden access is without reservation, linking to the art-nouveau **Villa Löw-Beer** that belonged to Greta's parents.

Boating Brno's Lake
The castle on the water

A city escape northwest of the city, locals head for the paddleboarding beaches and bathing lawns around the **Brno Reservoir** – an expanse of water that spills from the Brno Dam between the two tributaries of the Svratka River. Between April and October, steamers criss-cross the reservoir from the Bystrc pier *(buy tickets on board, 170Kč return)* and cruise upstream on the narrow stretch of Svratka to **Veveří Castle** *(Hrad Veveří; hrad-veveri.cz; courtyard admission 60Kč;*

 EATING IN BRNO: OUR PICKS

Eggo Truck Brno: Punk rock tunes with your mimosa or coffee-fuelled breakfast or brunch at this uber-cool bistro. *9am-1pm Mon, 8am-2pm Tue-Sat, 9am-1pm Sun* €

Bucheck: Teeming food truck tucked off the side of the Vegetable Market (Zelný trh) serving banging pulled pork burgers. *11.30am until sold out, Tue-Sun* €

Cà Phê Cô: Of all the Vietnamese restaurants in Brno, this trendy joint has the tastiest street-food-style *pho*, rolls, rice and *banh mi*. *11am-10pm Mon-Sun* €€

Lokál U Caipla: Traditional Czech eats from goulash soup to grilled meats, served with a perfectly poured beer. *11am-midnight Mon-Thu, to 1am Fri & Sat, to 1pm Sun* €€

tours in Czech only) – a forested, rock-topped stone castle and one of Moravia's oldest, from the late 12th-century. One of the largest castle grounds in the country, it's worth the wander of the courtyards of this historic hunting lodge of Moravian Margraves.

Palaeolithic Musing in the Moravian Museum
Home of Moravia's Venus

The **Moravian Museum**'s *(mzm.cz; adult/child 220/130Kč)* repository of 6 million natural history, archaeology and ethnography artefacts housed in the reconstructed 1616 Dietrichstein Palace is the country's second-largest museum and Moravia's oldest. Collections span the Palaeolithic era to the Middle Ages and, despite the lack of English text, it's worth visiting for the museum's prized exhibit: the 30,000-year-old *Venus of Dolní Věstonice* – the oldest ceramic figurine in the world, found during an excavation in a South Moravian village in 1925.

In the Discovery Footsteps of Mendel
Brno's genetic science origins

In the mid-19th century, Augustinian monk Gregor Mendel began experimenting with pea plant breeding in a monastic garden in a suburb of Brno; humble observations that unknowingly founded genetic science. Only after his death was Mendel revered as the 'Father of Genetics' for his discovery. The **Mendel Museum** *(mendelmuseum.muni.cz; adult/child 130/100Kč)*, an institution of the Masaryk University, is in the precinct of the abbey where the monk lived and details his life's work and the story of his revolutionary findings through audiovisual exhibits and personal objects.

Brno's Progressive Art
Czech contemporary design

From the giant cloud canopy artwork looming over its terrace, head inside the **Museum of Applied Arts**' *(moravska-galerie.cz; free entry, except temporary third-floor exhibitions)*, two-floor collection that covers industrial design to fashion runways, with striking interior art displays and a robotic cafe.

BRNO'S BEST COFFEE

Adam Neubauer, three-time Barista of the Year from Brno's top coffee shop, Monogram Espresso Bar *(monogram espressobar.cz)*, shares his favourite spots.

Take 5: To feel like a local, head to this place in the eastern Židenice neighbourhood. Great coffee, excellent pastries and friendly owners behind the bar.

Kafe Fridrich: Head north of the centre for this cosy cafe. They serve tasty coffee and incredible vegan sweet treats – possibly the best banana bread in the city.

Typika: Brno's newly opened hangout has a coffee garden in the courtyard of the Moravian Gallery. Spacious and comfortable, you might end up staying a few hours.

Kimono: This small, hip espresso bar has a stylish, wood-panelled interior and serves top brew classics and speciality coffees.

DRINKING IN BRNO: BEST BARS

Super Panda Circus: Find the door behind the circus curtain, ring the buzzer and indulge in this experimental cocktail world. *7pm-2am Mon & Tue, 6pm-2am Wed-Sat*

4pokoje: This neon-lit, exposed brick hipster hangout becomes a buzzing bar after its daytime bistro persona. *5pm-1am Mon & Tue, to 3am Wed, to 4am Thu-Sat*

Bar, Který Neexistuje: The 'bar that doesn't exist' is the city's trendy, decked cocktail bar. *5pm-2am Sun-Tue, to 2.30am Wed-Thu, to 3.30am Fri & Sat*

Schrott: Brewery and bar with courtyard garden in an old industrial building with unique upcycled scrap decor. *3pm-1am Mon-Sat, 3pm-midnight Sun*

STROLL THROUGH BRNO'S ALTERNATIVE ART & ARCHITECTURE

Find Brno's aesthetic quirks and humorous, legend-steeped statues and sculptures on this city centre walking tour.

START	END	LENGTH
Vegetable Market	Malinovsky Square	2km; 45 minutes

Starting in the ❶ **Vegetable Market**, spot the Mozart statue with an adult face on a child's body outside Reduta Theatre, where he played in 1767. Head north onto Radnická to the ❷ **Old Town Hall**, whose gothic portal by sculptor Anton Pilgram has a bent pinnacle, rumoured to be a metaphorical middle finger for unpaid work. Inside, walk beneath the suspended Brno Dragon. Continue on to Mečová, right onto Starobrněnská, and another right to the sculpture-marked courtyard of the contemporary ❸ **G99 Gallery**. On Dominikánská take a left onto ❹ **Dominican Square** for its giant pipes water feature.

Turn right onto Zámečnická to ❺ **Freedom Square** and the controversial black stone Brno astronomical clock and geometric Omega Palace shopping centre. Head towards Česká Street. At number 20, find the ❻ **Hotel Avion** functionalist monument by Czech Architect Bohuslav Fuchs and one of Europe's narrowest hotels.

Continue right onto Solniční to ❼ **Moravian Square** for the *Statue of Courage*, depicting Margrave Jobst of Moravia on a leggy horse. Walk underneath it and look up for a humorous perspective. Opposite, the *Statue of Justice* portrays a man balancing the heavy block of society.

Continue south to Rašínova, left onto Freedom Square, then Kobližná to ❽ **Malinovsky Square**. Here, a lightbulb sculpture honours Thomas Edison, who lit up Mahen Theatre opposite – Europe's first with electrical lighting.

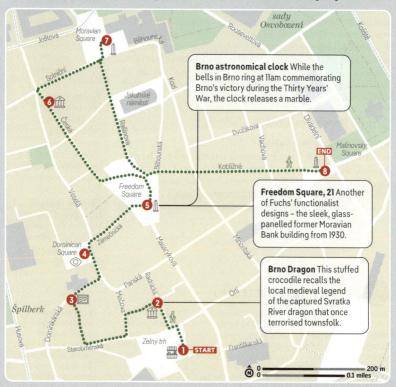

Brno astronomical clock While the bells in Brno ring at 11am commemorating Brno's victory during the Thirty Years' War, the clock releases a marble.

Freedom Square, 21 Another of Fuchs' functionalist designs – the sleek, glass-panelled former Moravian Bank building from 1930.

Brno Dragon This stuffed crocodile recalls the local medieval legend of the captured Svratka River dragon that once terrorised townsfolk.

Beyond Brno

With Brno as your base, switch up trips between hinterland caves and historic battlefields, functionalist sites and UNESCO cities.

The wine towns can wait; day trips from the provincial capital are all about the varied landscapes, monuments and heritage sites that pocket the region. Step into the limestone hulk valleys and caves of the Moravian Karst, visit the Napoleonic Wars battleground of Austerlitz, see the unique functionalist architecture of Baťa shoe enterprise in Zlín, or wander throught the preserved buildings of the UNESCO-listed Jewish Quarter of Třebíč, the Moravian Renaissance centre of Telč, and the art-packed chateau and baroque gardens of Kroměříž. If you thought there wasn't much to do between the swathes of the southern vineyards and the big cities, prepare to be surprised by the area around Brno.

Places
Moravian Karst Protected Landscape Area p249
Zlín p250
Třebíč p251
Slavkov u Brna p252
Kroměříž p252
Telč p254

Moravian Karst Protected Landscape Area   TIME FROM BRNO: 40 MINS 🚆 & 🚌
Moravia's ancient caverns

One of Europe's most extensive cave systems lies north of Brno. The 100-sq-km **Moravian Karst** *(Moravský kras; caves.cz)* is a forested canyon limestone labyrinth of 1100 grottos, sandwiched with millions-of-years-old, water-fissure-formed stalagmites and stalactites and filled with sinkholes and subterranean rivers.

The caving centre is Skalní Mlýn. Book Punkva Caves tours at the tourist information office; tickets quickly sell out, so advanced online bookings are recommended. The Katherine Caves are 10 minutes on foot; buy tickets on-site without reservation. It's a 30-minute walk or a ticketed eco-train ride between the two systems. The caves are closed in January, February and December; the main visiting season is between June and September, when buses between Blansko and Skalní Mlýn are more frequent, and the caves open for longer. Signposted hiking trails from Skalní Mlýn connect them all.

The **Punkva (Punkevní) Caves and Macocha Abyss tour** *(adult/child 320/160Kč)* tracks 1km through the narrow limestone hollows of Czechia's longest cave system, leading to the bottom of the 138m collapsed chamber of the Macocha Abyss. It ends with a boat trip on the subterranean Punkva River passage via the Masaryk Dome. After one hour in the

GETTING AROUND

Brno's public transport connections are the most convenient for day trips. For the Moravian Karst, take the S2 train to Blansko and pick up bus 226, which loops to and from the Skalní Mlýn cave centre. The S6 train and Bus 106 go to Slavkov u Brna for Slavkov Castle; Bus 48 goes directly to the Cairn of Peace for the Austerlitz battleground site. Take bus 955 to Zlín and Kroměříž, and FlixBus direct to Třebíč and Telč.

Sloup-šošůvka Cave

THE DARKER CAVE

Výpustek Cave once shared the natural geological beauty of its gargantuan grotto neighbours but was permanently altered by zealous human activity.

In the early 20th century, phosphorus-rich clay was mined, damaging the cave's structure and stalactites. The Czechoslovak Army took it over in 1938, blasting tunnels and walls for the creation of a military depot.

The Germans caused further destruction with concrete fillers when they converted it into an arms factory during WWII (and later tried to blow it all up). After the war, the Czechoslovak Army repurposed it as a Cold War nuclear fallout shelter, which you can visit today.

However, sections allegedly mapped by earlier explorers remain undiscovered.

7°C deep, ride the **cable car** to the rock ridge **Macocha Abyss viewing platforms** *(140/100Kč return)*.

The **Katherine Caves** *(Kateřinská; 140/80Kč)* tour is a 40-minute wander through the enormous Main Dome, the unique stalagmite-stacked Bamboo Forest and the crushed-rock Dome of Chaos. When it comes to illusionary rock formations, this cave's famed stalagmite Witch is impressive.

Have time to venture further? The **Balcarka Cave** *(150/80Kč)* conceals humongous galleries; the Foch's Dome is one of the largest in the Moravian Karst. **Sloup-šošůvka Cave** *(170/90Kč)* has sinkhole drops viewed from a bridge; the Nagel Abyss is the deepest at 80m. Adrenaline junkies can opt for the active clamber and crawl tour into the cave's greater depths.

Zlín

TIME FROM BRNO: **1½ HRS**

Baťa's experimental industrial town

In the early 20th century, the small town of Zlín became an interwar functionalist architecture icon, pioneered by global shoe empire entrepreneur, Tomáš Baťa. Uniform redbrick factory buildings, offices, housing, stores and community spaces were designed for an efficient work-life environment.

EATING IN ZLÍN: OUR PICKS

jedním tahem: This espresso bar is as hipster as Zlín gets, with breakfast, vegan snacks, homemade desserts and a speciality coffee menu. *8am-7pm Mon-Fri, 9am-7pm Sat & Sun* €

Comic Cone Food Truck: Colourful food truck, serving sandwiches, smash burgers and tacos. Located on Kvítková 611, 10 minutes from Park Komenského. *11am-1pm & 4pm-6pm Thu-Fri, 11am-1pm Sat* €

Bistrotéka Valachy: Food store, bakery and bistro with breakfast, lunch and seasonal speciality menus in the Zlín Department Store. *7am-10pm Mon-Fri, 8am-9pm Sat, 9am-8pm Sun* €€

La Villa: 1941 villa of Baťa's director turned fine-dining restaurant under the current owner. With lunch, evening, tasting and degustation menus. *hours vary; closed Sun & Mon* €€€

The Baťa factory closed in the 1990s; new enterprises and museums occupy Zlín's industrial monuments today.

Baťa's Skyscraper 21 *(muzeum-zlin.cz)* was commissioned by Tomáš' brother and successor, Jan Antonín Baťa, and completed in 1939. Ride the original elevator A to the 16th-floor terrace for views of the town and emblematic box brick houses. The 8th floor, when open, has kept its original design. The 2nd floor features a unique lift office that Jan Antonín Baťa never used, fleeing the country before the building's completion. View this architectural feat in the exhibition room; you can only ride it with advanced reservations *(1000Kč)*.

Inside **Building 14|15 Baťa Institute** *(14-15.cz; adult/child 149Kč/69)* is the permanent exhibition: The Baťa Principle: Fantasy Today, Tomorrow Reality. The brimming floor and shoe museum is an encyclopaedic walk through the Baťa company's history; visitors receive a clock card to punch at each station, echoing the factory legacy.

The functionalist glass-clad **Baťa Memorial** (Památník Tomáše Bati; *(pamatnikbata.eu; 149Kč/99)* was built in 1933 to commemorate Tomáš Baťa, who tragically died in a plane crash; its atrium features a suspended replica of the plane.

Třebíč

TIME FROM BRNO: 1 HR

Wander a World Heritage Jewish Quarter

Třebíč hit the traveller's radar in 2003 when UNESCO inscribed its Jewish Quarter and medieval basilica on the World Heritage List in testament to the former coexistence of two cultures. The **Jewish Quarter** evolved after Třebíč estate owner Jan Josef Wallenstein ordered the separation of Jewish and Christian communities in 1723. The historic ghetto is interconnected by narrow streets and house passages; the alley through the building at 16–18 Leopolda Pokorného Street is a good example. Dedicate half a day to this area; signage highlights the most significant of the 123 surviving buildings, useful for a self-guided walk-through.

The Renaissance **Rear Synagogue**, dating from 1669, is the most hallowed, with preserved baroque paintings and a model of the ghetto as it was in 1850 after its abolition. Tours include entry to the **Jewish Museum** in the neighbouring **Seligmann Bauer House** *(visittrebic.eu; admission 80Kč; tours 210Kč)*. Some 350m up Hrádek Hill is the 17th-century **Jewish Cemetery** – one of the largest in the country with 3000 headstones and 11,000 graves, the oldest dating to 1631.

SHOEMAKER OF THE WORLD

You'll find a Baťa shoe shop in nearly every major Czech town and city. A small family business founded in 1894 by Tomáš Baťa in Zlín started with Wallachian slipper production and turned to military footwear for the Austro-Hungarian army.

By the 1920s, Baťa became an industrial powerhouse, producing affordable footwear and controlling half of the Czech market. By the 1930s, with factories in more than 30 countries and stores in over 80, annual production hit 35 million pairs.

After WWII, the company was nationalised and renamed Svit, while the Baťa family members who had left the country rebuilt the brand abroad.

Today, Baťa has headquarters in Toronto, Canada, and remains globally influential, with founder Tomáš Baťa's grandson Thomas G. Bata continuing the 130-year-old Moravian legacy.

EATING & DRINKING IN TŘEBÍČ: OUR PICKS

Obývák bistro a káva: Healthy, hearty breakfast and lunch and specialty coffee in this colourful, trendy bistro cafe. *7am-5pm Mon, to 6pm Tue-Fri, 8.30am-1pm Sun* €

Café Art Trebic: Rustic cafe in the Jewish Quarter. Outdoor seats fill quickly. *1pm-10pm Mon-Thu, 1pm-1am Fri, 11am-1am Sat, 11am-10pm Sun* €

St Procopius' Parish Café: Cosy cafe perfect for a fresh lemonade and homemade cake stop before the St Procopius Basilica tour. *10am-5pm Mon-Fri, to 6pm Sat-Sun* €

JAK JINAK: Craft beers on tap and a barbecue menu in this courtyard-set gastropub off Charles Square. *11am-10pm Mon-Thu, to midnight Fri & Sat, to 3pm Sun* €

COMMEMORATING AUSTERLITZ

The Annual Commemoration of the Battle of Austerlitz is a multiday event held around the battle's anniversary. It is not a celebration of warfare but a way of fostering understanding and reflection on one of Europe's most decisive confrontations that divided the continent. The re-enactment of the Battle of the Three Emperors brings the historical event to life, with participants from over a dozen countries performing troop parades and military manoeuvres in live displays, including period costumes, horses and cannon fire. This tribute culminates in the solemn 'act of piety' remembrance event at the Cairn of Peace monument, paying homage to the fallen soldiers.

On the descent, stop at **Fotopoint Hrádek** for the best vistas of the 13th-century Town Tower and Třebíč's other UNESCO site – the hill-topping **St Procopius Basilica** *(200/170Kč; tours in Czech with English text)*, built upon the foundations of a Benedictine Monastery. The Romanesque-Gothic basilica is only accessible by guided tour, including a visit to the preserved crypt from 1230.

Slavkov u Brna

TIME FROM BRNO: **25 MINS**

The battleground of Austerlitz

On 2 December 1805, Slavkov (Austerlitz) became the stage for one of the most decisive battles of the Napoleonic Wars. In the Battle of the Three Emperors, Napoleon defeated the combined forces of Austrian emperor Ferdinand I and Russian Tsar Alexander I.

On Prace hill (Pracký kopec), 10km west of Slavkov u Brna town, the **Cairn of Peace** *(Mohyla míru; mohylamiru. muzeumbrnenska.cz; adult/child 125Kč/65; multilanguage audio)* memorial and chapel honours the fallen. The on-site **museum**, with a four-room multimedia virtual battle presentation, is a poignant reminder of the battleground area on which the monument stands.

After his victory, Napoleon transferred his headquarters to **Slavkov Chateau** *(zamek-slavkov.cz; 180Kč/150)*; you can tour the castle's western wing, including the Historical Hall where the armistice with Austria was signed. Without a car, you'll need to Uber between town and the Cairn of Peace.

Kroměříž

TIME FROM BRNO: **40 MINS**

UNESCO-listed castle and gardens

The former summer residence of the archbishops of Olomouc, compact Kroměříž crams majesty into its UNESCO World Heritage Site chateau and garden complex. The **Archbishop's Chateau** *(Arcibiskupský zámek; zamek-kromeriz.cz; adult/child 300Kč/200; Czech tours, English text)* is unmissable with its guidepost 84m-high tower next to the arcaded **Great Square** *(Velké náměstí)* – a Přemyslid, Gothic, then Renaissance palace destroyed in the Thirty Years' War and reborn a baroque masterpiece under Prince-Bishop Karl II von Liechtenstein-Kastelkorn between 1664 and 1695.

The **Via Residentia tour** through the first-floor princely parlours includes the lavishly rococo **Assembly Hall** *(Sněmovního sálu)* – the meeting place for the 1848 Austrian

 EATING & DRINKING IN KROMĚŘÍŽ: OUR PICKS

Velo Café: Hip cafe with coffee, wine and homemade light bites in a 17th-century house on Velké náměstí. *hours vary* €

Černý Orel: Microbrewery with award-winning lagers and restaurant with Czech classics in a 16th-century house. *11am-11pm Mon-Thu, to 1am Fri, to midnight Sat, to 10pm Sun* €€

Nováková zahrada: Speciality coffee and cake in a modern cafe with garden courtyard on cobblestoned Ztracená leading to the chateau. *9am-6pm Mon-Fri, 1pm-6pm Sat* €

Octárna: Upscale dining with courtyard in former Franciscan monastery serving classic-contemporary. *9am-10pm Mon-Fri, 11am-10pm Sat, 11am-6pm Sun* €€

Flower Garden, Archbishop's Chateau

Constitutional Assembly and backdrop in Miloš Forman's 1984 Oscar-winning film *Amadeus*. The tour also includes access to the 40m-high tower viewpoint. On the self-guided **Via Magnifica tour** *(300Kč/200; audio guide)* of the second most valuable art gallery in Czechia, muse on 15th and 16th-century Gothic and Renaissance paintings from Central Europe, Germany and the Netherlands, and marvel at Italian, Flemish and Dutch works from the 17th century, including works by Cranach, Brueghel and the prized *Flaying of Marsyas* by Venetian master Titian. More collections abound in the 60,000-volume Old Library, the Chapel of St. Sebastian, Bishop's Mint Coin and Music Cabinet.

A palatial 19th-century English-style **Chateau Garden** *(Podzámecká zahrada)* spreads behind the chateau to the Morava River; it's open year-round and free to visit. A 15-minute walk west is the gigantic, geometric **Flower Garden** *(Květná zahrada; kvetnazahrada-kromeriz.cz; 180Kč/50)*, showcasing European garden art of the 17th century, best viewed from the terrace of its 244m-long colonnade. The garden's central rotunda houses a Foucault Pendulum device demonstrating Earth's rotation.

Kroměříž artist Max Švabinský

Browse six halls of painter and graphic artist Max Švabinský's works on the 1st floor of the **Kroměříž Museum** *(muzeum-km.cz; adult/child 50Kč/30 per exhibit)*. The 2nd floor charts Kroměříž's history from 1848-1948, and the cellar houses medieval archaeological finds. Švabinský's mosaic lunettes (arched murals) at the Franciscan monastery (now Hotel

A TEMPORARY HABSBURG CAPITAL

Kroměříž temporarily became a Habsburg political centre between 1848 and 1849, when revolutionary unrest was sweeping the Austrian Empire.

Because of the instability in Vienna, the town was chosen as the meeting place for the Austrian Constitutional Assembly. On 22 November 1848, the grand hall of the **Archbishop's Château** (p252) hosted the sessions of 383 delegates from all Austrian nations to deliberate the political crisis and restoration of order.

On 2 December, at the Archbishop's Palace in Olomouc, Habsburg ruler Emperor Ferdinand I abdicated, and his 18-year-old nephew, Franz Joseph I, became emperor. Franz Joseph later dissolved the Assembly on 7 March 1849, rejecting the proposed reforms as too liberal and making his own proclamation.

Octárna) were initially intended for Prague's National Theatre.

Telč

TIME FROM BRNO: 1¾ HRS

Time-hop in a World Heritage historic centre

A day trip to tiny Telč on the Bohemian–Moravian border is a Renaissance time-stop from the 16th century when the lords of Hradec transformed the town – an undertaking that earned Telč early UNESCO recognition in 1992, alongside Prague and Český Krumlov.

Masterpiece **Zacharias of Hradec Square** *(náměstí Zachariáše z Hradce)* is the visual core of the town – a belt of pastel-painted Renaissance and baroque burgher houses with arcades and gable toppers, filled with elaborate fountains and a Marian column.

On one side of the square is **Telč Chateau** *(Státní zámek Telč; zamek-telc.cz; adult/child 240/70Kč; tours in Czech, English text),* a Gothic castle transformed by Italian-influenced lord Zachariáš z Hradce into a Renaissance palace. The impressive interiors, untouched by later owners, are accessible only by guided tour. **Route I: Renaissance Halls** *(50 minutes)* passes through sgraffito rooms, ornamental chambers and the Golden Hall with its gilded waffle ceiling. **Route II: Suite of the Last Owners** *(40 minutes, 160/50Kč)* explores the living quarters and chateau library of the Podstatský-Liechtenstein family, the last residents from 1760 to 1945.

Telč's centre is bookended by climbable towers and hemmed by old defensive gates and ponds. The Renaissance **Upper Gate** *(Horní brána)* leads to the **Ulický lake**, while the **Lower Gate** *(Dolní brána)* opens to **Štěpnický lake**. The 13th-century **Tower of the Holy Spirit** *(věž sv. Ducha)*, the town's oldest surviving monument, has 49m high square-side views, while the 60m **tower of the Church of St James** *(kostel sv Jakuba)* offers the best lookout (after a steep stair clamber) over the town and surrounding countryside.

Below, 150m of medieval **Telč Underground** *(Telčské podzemí; jihlavskepodzemi.cz; 100/50Kč; book at tourist information office)* corridors hold a multimedia history display; tours run Friday-Monday. The tour is only in Czech and focuses on film set remnants.

TELČ'S BEST RENAISSANCE & BAROQUE HOUSES

The most prominent and prized houses on Zacharias of Hradec Sq include:

No 10: The Town Hall is the square's largest building, with a Renaissance battlement design, cornice topper and vaulted entrance.

No 15: The green house with a unique oriel bay window displays a characteristic Renaissance biblical sgraffito.

No 48: Given a baroque facade in the 18th century with a minimalist single scroll style volute gable.

No 59: Pretty-in-pink, this house is considered the most typical of the baroque style, including pillar columns.

No 61: Has a detailed Renaissance facade rich in monochrome sgraffito, said to be by the same artist who decorated the chateau.

EATING & DRINKING IN TELČ: OUR PICKS

Bistro Café Friends: Popular all-day bistro has wholesome breakfast, brunch and dinner options, or wine, coffee and dessert. *9am-6pm Sun, Wed & Thu, 9am-9pm Fri & Sat* €

Cukrárna-Kavárna Haas: Grab coffee and a sweet treat at the university campus cafe and patisserie with a hidden courtyard behind the main square. *9am-5pm* €

Olikova bouda: Laid-back cafe shack and garden next to Štěpnický lake, serving coffee, beer, wine and sandwiches. *2pm-10pm* €

Švejk Restaurant Telč: Traditional pub next to the castle, with Czech classics and Pilsner and Gambrinus beers on tap. *11am-10pm Mon-Thu, 11am-11pm Fri & Sat, 11am-10pm Sun* €€

Mikulov

RENAISSANCE ARCHITECTURE | WINE TASTING | JEWISH HERITAGE

Synonymous as the home of winemaking, surrounded by limestone hills and verdant grapevine folds, Mikulov is arguably the most beautiful town to visit for a sun-ripened sip of South Moravia. Visible from afar, its centrepiece chateau peaks from the rocky outcrop, a former fortress turned noble home of the Dietrichstein family and beacon to the beautiful old town centre they ruled at its foot.

Mikulov was also once the most important centre of Jewish life and culture in Moravia; today's preserved Jewish Quarter includes a revived baroque synagogue, the renovated houses of influential rabbis and a cemetery with centuries-old tombstones. Leaving Mikulov brings you to landscapes as glorious as the old town's confines. Set out on a hike through the lofty rock, ruin-poked, prehistoric paths of the Pálava Protected Landscape Area, or bike to vineyards and village wine cellars. Quintessentially, Mikulov is typically admired, drink in hand, from the perimeter of its beautiful main square.

Gateway to Splendour & Scenery
Mikulov's historic centre

Visitors naturally converge on **Náměstí** *(square),* Mikulov's historic core and centre of town life. Below the chateau entrance sits an enclosure of preserved 17th-century Renaissance townhouses, including the standout **Knights House** *(U Rytířů)* with monochrome biblical sgraffito panels, the baroque Holy Trinity sculpture and a Pomona goddess of abundance statue fountain from the early 18th century. Often, the square fills with the stalls of local wineries offering tastings, and the square-side cafes create a lively alfresco fringe.

The most prominent landmark is the **Dietrichstein Tomb** *(Dietrichštejnská hrobka; mikulov.cz; adult/child 120/80Kč),* the noble family crypt built upon the ruins of St Anne's Church. The two-tower, baroque facade is the design of Austrian master Johann Bernhard Fischer von Erlach of Schönbrunn Palace

GETTING AROUND

Getting to Mikulov by train typically involves a change at Břeclav for the S8 train that connects Mikulov to Znojmo. Bus 105 departs regularly on a daily schedule from Brno's ÚAN Zvonařka Station. Both journeys take around 75 minutes. The town is compact enough to explore on foot, and its sloping roads are not too exhausting; getting up to the peak of Holy Hill requires a little stamina. If you want to head out into the Pálava hills, lace up your hiking boots, hire a bicycle in town or join an organised wine tour.

☑ TOP TIP

Those planning to tour Mikulov's main historic sites, note that the Castle museums, Dietrichstein Tomb and Synagogue are only open from March/April to November. Check *rmm.cz* for up-to-date opening hours.

MIKULOV

SIGHTS
1. Church of St Wenceslas
2. Dietrichstein Tomb
3. Goat Hill
4. Holy Hill
5. Jewish Cemetery
6. Knights House
7. Mikulov Chateau
8. Mikve Jewish Bath
9. Upper Synagogue

SLEEPING
10. Hotel Desatero
11. Hotel Tanzberg
12. Hotel Templ
13. Stajnhaus

EATING
14. KUK Bistro
15. MOJI café
16. Pivnice Golem
17. Šilová Winery

DRINKING & NIGHTLIFE
18. (Ne) Vinná Kavána
19. Olivea Wine Mikulov
20. Vinotéka Mikulov
21. Zahrádka U Zajíce

fame. Entrance is by 40-minute tour only, including a stair climb to the rooftop before visiting the ground floor chapel arcade rooms displaying 45 tombs of the Dietrichstein family, dating from 1617 to 1852.

Step into Mikulov's Stronghold
The hilltop noble monument

From an 11th-century timbered fort to a medieval Liechtenstein stronghold two centuries later, the Renaissance transformation of **Mikulov Chateau** (*rmm.cz; adult/child 180/90Kč*) came from the aristocratic Dietrichstein family rule from 1575 until 1945. Much of it was burned down by German forces; the opulent interiors and surviving objects are from intensive post-war restoration.

Accessible only by guided **tour** (*120/60Kč*), **From Gothic to Empire** is a romp through significant castle rooms like the frescoed Hall of Ancestors and the Dietrichstein portrait gallery. Entrance to the original 18th-century 11,000-book-stuffed Castle Library, fortunately left unscathed in the fire of 1945, or the Castle Dungeon with Europe's largest wine barrel from 1643, require separate tickets. Exhibitions on the Romans and Germans in the region or the history of Mikulov's viticulture in the **Wine across the Centuries** exhibition (*120/60Kč*) are self-guided tours for historical deep dives; it's also free to stroll through the Italian baroque Chateau Garden.

Jewish Quarter Monuments
Historic Husova Street and around

Husova Street is the historic artery of Mikulov's former Jewish Quarter; around 90 of the original 317 buildings are protected cultural monuments denoted by gold plaques. The main-feature **Upper Synagogue** (*Horní synagoga*) is the only surviving synagogue in Czechia of the 'Polish' style with a baroque quad-domed ceiling and four-post pillar. Built in 1550, it has undergone several reconstructions, with the work in 2014 restoring it to its pre-1938 appearance. Its small exhibition, 'Rabbi Löw and Jewish Education in Moravia', is an informative starting point (*50/25Kč; Czech exhibit, English handout*). Nearby U Staré brány street leads to the ruins of a late 18th-century **Mikve Jewish Bath**, a stone cellar with stairs descending to a ritual purification pool.

More than 4000 symbolically carved tombstones decorate the 2-hectare **Jewish Cemetery** (*Židovský hřbitov*) on

SOUTH MORAVIA'S VITICULTURE

Roman legionnaires, who drank wine for good health, planted the first vineyards in the Moravian region nearly 2000 years ago.

During the Middle Ages, winemaking ramped up for sacramental use during the spread of Christianity in the Great Moravian Empire and later became a booming aristocratic trade.

Today, the Moravian wine region, stretching south from Brno to the Austrian and Slovak borders across Znojmo, Mikulov, Velké Pavlovice and Slovácko, packs 96% of Czechia's vineyards across 182 winemaking estates in 30 villages. The limestone terroir of the Pavlovské hills, warmer temperatures and slow grape ripening produces full-bodied, high-mineral and aromatic white wines, including Pálava, Ryzlink vlašský (Welschriesling), Veltlínské zelené (Grüner Veltliner) and Müller Thurgau.

 EATING IN MIKULOV: BEST SPOTS

MOJI café: Trendy joint with a breakfast menu, specialty coffee, organic wines, and homemade baked treats. *8.30am-6pm Sun-Fri, 9am-6pm Sat* €

Pivnice Golem: Ambient beer hall of Hotel Tanzberg with grill menu and perfect Pilsner, Radegast and Gambrinus pours. *2pm-midnight Mon-Fri, from noon Sat, noon-11pm Sun* €

KUK Bistro: Chic bakery bistro in front of St Wenceslas Church, with breakfast menu, pastries, Italian coffee, ciabatta bread, soups and platters. *8am-10pm* €

Šílová Winery: Upscale restaurant in a contemporary winery using local ingredients, with a seasonal menu with wine pairings. Reservation required. *Noon-10pm* €€

MIKULOV'S JEWISH LEGACY

Mikulov was not just the Austro-Hungarian Empire princely territory of the Liechtenstein and Dietrichstein families; from the 16th century under the Dietrichsteins, it became a refuge for Moravian Jews after their expulsion from Lower Austria and Vienna.

Mikulov's importance grew when it became the seat of the Moravian Chief Rabbi for some 300 years, who built renowned *yeshivas* (religious schools) and published significant religious commentaries; the first Chief Regional Rabbi of Moravia and creator of the Jewish folklore Golem tale, Rabbi Judah Loew ben Bezalel, lived for 20 years in the house that's now Hotel Tanzberg. Though the population was devastated during WWII, today's residents try to preserve Moravia's Jewish legacy

Holy Hill

neighbouring Kozí Hill. The oldest remaining gravestone dates to 1605, and Rabbis Peak is the designated resting place of Moravian Chief Rabbis. Visitors enter through the 1898-built Ceremonial Hall, which features an introductory exhibit on Jewish burial rites.

Sacred Trails & Viewpoints
Mikulov from up high

The **Holy Hill** *(Svatý kopeček)* limestone mound rises 363m over Mikulov – an ancient pagan ritual site turned Catholic pilgrimage route in the 17th century. The 40-minute walk on the blue trail from Svobody Street follows the winding **Way of the Cross** studded with 14 tiny chapels. It leads to the Chapel of St Sebastian, the bell tower and the Chapel of the Holy Sepulchre – the sacred summit with a spectacular panorama of Mikulov.

Climb the 135 stairs of the Renaissance tower of the 16th-century **Church of St Wenceslas** *(kostelnivez.cz; 50/30Kč)* for the best close-up sweep over Moravia's main square, Holy Hill and the chateau from its sixth-floor arcade. Climb **Goat Hill** and the two-storey ruins of the rock-top former defence **Goat Tower** *(Kozí Hrádek; 30/20Kč)* and look out over Mikulov as protectors of the town did in the 15th-century when it was first constructed. It's only open when the flag is flying.

 DRINKING IN MIKULOV: BEST FOR WINE

Zahrádka U Zajíce:	**Vinotéka Mikulov:**	**Olivea Wine Mikulov:**	**(Ne) Vinná Kavána:**
Courtyard bar and cellar off Náměstí with wines from local producers. The liveliest evening hangout. *5pm-midnight Wed & Thu, to 1am Fri & Sat*	Wine shop with the region's best winemakers, plus Enoteca wine-dispenser machines for the best tastings. *9am-7pm Sun-Thu, to 10pm Fri & Sat*	Pocket-sized cellar wine bar and shop on a quaint street. Order the tasting set and snacks for the perfect local vino introduction. *10am-10pm*	The rustic decked (No) Wine Café is stacked with vino and is Náměstí's all-day degustation station with tasty snacks. *9am-10pm*

Beyond Mikulov

Interwoven with sunny, south-facing vineyards, historic wineries and noble castles, South Moravia is a reserve of ancient wine traditions.

The heartland of the South Moravian region stretches along the border with Austria, unfurling a countryside of rolling limestone hills skirted with autumn ripening vines, royal showpiece complexes and protected nature reserves stowing ancient ruins. North of Mikulov, hike through the Pálava Protected Landscape Area on trails through steppe, rare flora and 13th-century castle ruins. East of town, the UNESCO-listed Lednice-Valtice Cultural Landscape is a staggering noble spread of majestic châteaux, landscaped gardens and grand cellars. Tour the neo-Gothic architecture of Lednice Castle or the baroque Valtice Castle, which is also home to Czechia's National Wine Centre and the largest cache of the year's prized wines to sample. Here's where you'll find the antidote to city-hopping.

Places
Lednice-Valtice Cultural Landscape p259
Mikulov Wine Trail p260
Pálava Protected Landscape Area p261
Archeopark Pavlov p261

Lednice-Valtice Cultural Landscape

TIME FROM MIKULOV: **15-30 MINS**

UNESCO World Heritage estate

The UNESCO-protected Lednice-Valtice Cultural Landscape preserves a 283-sq-km area fashioned by the House of Liechtenstein over seven centuries into a monumental two-castle royal estate. It remained in their ownership until post-WWII confiscation in 1945.

The mighty **Lednice Chateau** (*zamek-lednice.com; adult/child 300/90Kč*) evolved from a Renaissance manor to a baroque palace before its English neo-Gothic makeover, with showpiece interiors and gardens adorned with noble architectural flexes, including a 60m-high lakeside Turkish minaret and a mock medieval castle. Entry is via guided tour. The ground-floor **Representative Rooms tour** includes the illustrious library and Turquoise Social Hall with its oak spiral staircase; the 1st-floor **Princely Apartments tour** explores the Liechtenstein private chambers. Other tours cover the children's room, greenhouse and minaret halls.

Valtice Chateau (*zamek-valtice.cz; 260Kč/80*) was the Liechtenstein ruling seat. Elevated from the small town at

GETTING AROUND

The S8 train links Mikulov with Valtice in 10 minutes; from Brno, link to the S8 via a change in Břeclav. If visiting Valtice and Lednice on the same day, bus 555 connects the two towns, or it's a one-hour walk between them on the joining park alley. From Mikulov, bus 585 goes to Valtice, bus 570 to Pavlov and Lednice, and bus 540 connects to Dolní Věstonice.

A WALK IN NATURE

Pick up a Palava Visitor Map *(návštěvnická mapa)* from the Mikulov Tourist Information Centre on Náměstí 1. It highlights the red trail connecting Mikulov to Dolní Věstonice and marks the ruins, monuments and mega hills. For offline navigation, download the route planner *mapy.cz* app.

Cars and bikes are prohibited on this trail; going off the marked paths is prohibited by law.

Pack your sturdy, super-grip hiking boots; this half-day hike through a nature reserve includes some rock scrambling to the hilltop castle ruins.

A smartphone translation app will come in handy; information boards detailing the history of the area, archaeological finds, and the rare flora and fauna are only in Czech.

its foot, the former 11th-century castle's medieval foundations were remodelled into a baroque chateau. The grounds and gardens are free to enter, but guided tours get you entry to the main rooms. The **Grand Representation tour** shows the rooms where the most esteemed stayed, including Emperor Franz Joseph I; the Princely Apartment tour visits the quarters of Franz I of Liechtenstein. You can also tour the frescoed Baroque Chapel and Theatre.

A nod to the Liechtenstein winemaking tradition, Valtice's cellared **Wine Salon of the Czech Republic** *(vinarske centrum.cz/en/salon-vin; 649Kč; 150Kč per 30 minutes over duration)* is a stock of Czechia's best-judged vino from the National Wine Centre's annual competition. Pay for a 120-minute entry and work through the country's top 100 rated wines. You'll be armed with a plate of bread for palate neutralising and a basket to carry the bottles to buy. One bottle of each wine is always open, with accompanying detailed presentation boards.

Mikulov Wine Trail
TIME FROM MIKULOV: **8HR LOOP**
Wineland highlights by bike

Biking while inebriated is not a good idea, but if you want to explore the countryside and tour South Moravia's vineyards, criss-crossing it on two wheels will help you cover some ground.

The **Mikulov Wine Trail** runs 82km through vineyards, wine cellars and castle monuments on flat roads and mildly steep hills; the first half connects Mikulov to Lednice-Valtice. Pass the wine village of Sedlec at Nesyt lake, view Valtice from the elevated Rajstna Hill colonnade and continue from Valtice through the lake village of Hlohovec to Lednice. Loop back to Mikulov via the Dyje River forest path before passing through Pavlov, Dolní Věstonice, the nearly 150 cellars that dot Brod nad Dyjí and the Novosedly vineyards with old press houses.

Opt to cycle segments of the trail in either direction. If taking the train back from Valtice, note that available bike space on regional trains is limited. Route advice and cycle maps for the Moravia Wine Region are freely available from Mikulov's Tourist Information Centre on Náměstí 1. You can hire road and e-bikes at **Mikolovna** on Česka street *(mikolovna.cz; adult/child 550Kč/450; price includes GPS route planner)*.

EATING & DRINKING IN LEDNICE-VALTICE: OUR PICKS

Chokolito: Valtice Castle's sweet shop has handmade pralines. Sample with a coffee, but you'll likely leave with a box. *10am-6pm* €

Hostina Valtice: Minimalist cafe with a courtyard serving speciality coffee and cold brew, homemade bagels and bakes. *9am-7pm* €

Pedro's Foodtruck: Lednice branch of the Mikulov outlet, with a daily menu of tasty burgers, hot dogs and street-food snacks. *11.30am-3pm* €

Pivovar Feldsberg: Valtice's only brewery. The modern gastropub has a hearty menu of soups, steaks, stews and schnitzels. *11am-10pm* €€

Pálava Protected Landscape Area

Pálava Protected Landscape Area
TIME FROM MIKULOV: **30 MINS**

Hike through a UNESCO Biosphere Reserve
Lace up your hiking boots, pack a handy map from the tourist information centre *(https://en.mapy.cz/s/rejoratupu)*, and get into the **Pálava Protected Landscape Area** and UNESCO Biosphere Reserve on a half-day trail that passes white limestone plateaus, centuries-old castle ruins, soft sloping vineyards and the famed Pálava hills.

Pick up the red trail in the village of Dolní Věstonice, north of Mikulov, where a steady climb through the vines rewards with **Děvín** – the highest of the Pálava hills at 550m, upon which **Děvičky Castle** *(Dívčí hrady; deviky.cz; adult/child 50/30Kč)* rises steeply. Head to this 13th-century ruin and wander through what remains of its brick wall slabs, the windows of which overlook the patchwork green archaeological bed of Dolní Věstonice and Pavlov villages on the Nové Mlýny reservoir.

The trail continues to the rock-peaking **Orphan Castle** *(Sirotčí hrádrek)* ruins – the remains of the 13th-century residence of the Wehingen family – and passes **Tabulová Nature Reserve's Table Mountain** *(Tabulová hora)*, a flat limestone plateau where rare Ethiopian sage grows. Pass the geological cave area of **Turold** before reaching the centre of Mikulov, where a glass of the Pálava vineyard vintage awaits.

Archeopark Pavlov
TIME FROM MIKULOV: **30 MINS**

Ice-age excavation exploration
Burrowed underground like a giant excavation pit, the **Archeopark Pavlov** *(archeoparkpavlov.cz; 150/80Kč)* details, through skeletal remains, artefacts and multimedia exhibits, the life of the mammoth-hunting, ice-age Homo sapiens who lived on the Pálava ridge 30,000 years ago. The *Venus of Dolní Věstonice* was discovered here in 1925; a copy of the ceramic figurine is in the exhibition, and the original is in the Moravian Museum in Brno.

SOUTH MORAVIA'S WINE REVIVAL

Andrea Kotašková, recognised Czech wine expert and owner of the travel agency, Wine Travel in Czech (*winetravelinczech.com*).

Czech viticulture was decimated during the communist regime. Since the Velvet Revolution, the industry has undergone a modern revival, with many Moravian winemakers pushing in new directions with quality products.

Sonberk was the first modern winery – built in 2008 to the design of leading Czech architect Josef Pleskot. Try their Rieslings and international award-winning Pálava, a white varietal developed in Moravia in 1953.

Gurdau Winery, more contemporary hobbit village than traditional wine cellar, produces pure, balanced Rieslings and Grüner Veltliners on the slopes above Kurdějov village.

Family-run **Obelisk** continues the Lichtenstein winemaking tradition and has revived Sylvaner, the original grape grown in this region.

Znojmo

HISTORIC MONUMENTS | UNDERGROUND ATTRACTIONS | NATIONAL PARK

GETTING AROUND

Znojmo is linked to Mikulov on the S8 train route; change in Břeclav if coming from Prague or Brno. Znojmo also has excellent connections to Vienna, with a 90-minute train connecting to the northern Wien Floridsdorf Bahnhof station. Bus 818 goes to the Louka Monastery and the village of Hnanice for the hike to Šobes vineyard, and bus 809 goes to Popice. Znojmo's compact historic centre is accessible on foot.

☑ TOP TIP

A near-border town between Prague and Vienna, Znojmo is a great stopover and introduction to South Moravia if travelling between Czechia and Austria. Not as expensive as Mikulov, it's also an excellent base for exploring the wine region.

Znojmo, the once-fortified Přemyslid dynasty stronghold near the Austrian border, rises upon a steep, rocky slope above a forested river valley. Its historical core preserves medieval fortifications, noble streetscapes and the castle ground's Romanesque Rotunda of St Catherine with precious frescoes. Beneath it all is one of Czechia's largest underground labyrinths, a refuge from besieging enemies and the cellars of early wine production. Venture down Znojmo's zigzagging slopes for views of the castle and into Podyjí National Park on the town fringes; Czechia's smallest national park has half a dozen hiking routes to viewpoints and vineyards, like the oldest vineyard of Šobes. Back in town, sample the work of the local winemakers in a baroque monastery or modern *vinotéka*. Znojmo is more than a place to rush through; stay longer than a day and savour the unexpected from this westernmost wine region of South Moravia.

Znojmo Historic Centre
Labyrinths, fortifications and medieval monuments

Znojmo's dominant landmark has towered 80m above the town since the 15th century. The Gothic **Town Hall Tower** (*Městská radnice*) spikes between **Masaryk Square** (*Masarykovo náměstí*) with its burgher houses and **Upper Square** (*Horní náměstí*) with its knot of lanes. The former guard tower is now a 60m-high observation deck, closed at the time of writing for extensive renovations. The **Wolf Tower** (*Vlkova Tower*) is the largest remaining fortification from 1448; a 22m-high gallery overlooks the preserved lower gate fortification system and **Powder Tower**.

The **Znojmo Underground** (*znojemskabeseda.cz; adult/child 130/80Kč*) is among Europe's largest medieval braid of passageways, covering 27km over four levels. The one-hour

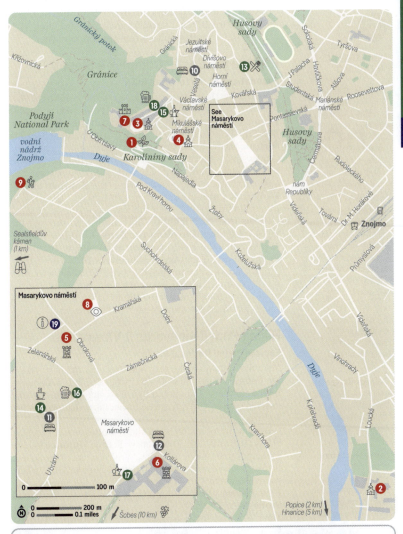

SIGHTS
1. Carolina Gardens
2. Louka monastery
3. Rotunda of Our Lady & St Catherine
4. St Nicholas Church
5. Town Hall Tower
6. Wolf Tower
7. Znojmo Castle
8. Znojmo Underground

ACTIVITIES
9. Podyjí National Park

SLEEPING
10. Hotel Lahofer
11. Stará Pekárna
12. TGM Hotel Residence

EATING
13. Půlnapůl

DRINKING & NIGHTLIFE
14. Balance Coffee & Wine
15. Enotéka
16. Pivnice U šneka
17. Wine Bar Chatka
18. Znojemský městský pivovar

INFORMATION
19. Tourist Information Centre

WINE TASTING IN ZNOJMO

Wine Bar Chatka: Vinařství Nešetřil is the only wine made in the town. Sample 12 Georgian clay-pot-, steel-tank- and barrel-fermented wines while touring the underground cellars *(390Kč)*.

Enotéka: Sample from 120 wines in the tasting hall with pre-paid card self-service machines – the largest selection in Czechia *(deposit 150Kč)*.

Wolf Tower: Climb the viewing tower and try eight by-the-glass samples of VOC Znojmo–certified wineries on the ground floor *(from 15Kč)*.

Balance Coffee & Wine: All-day brunch cafe with a wine list showcasing local small producers *(from 50Kč)*.

Louka Monastery: Visit the 12th-century monastery cellars and winemaking museum; taste Znovín Znojmo wines in the visitor centre bar *(from 13Kč)*.

Classic track guides visitors through cellars, wells and siege hideouts. Three adrenaline tracks are more demanding, with ladders, water wading and squeeze-through corridors.

Explore the Castle Complex & Slopes
Foundations of the fortified town

Znojmo Castle *(muzeumznojmo.cz; adult/child 100/70Kč)* was South Moravia's mightiest 11th-century border stronghold, home to the Premyslids and the Habsburgs. By 1721, the lords of Deblín razed it to build a baroque chateau; the burghers turned the courtyard into a brewery. Guided tours visit the frescoed Entrance Hall and Deblin Chapel, and gilded chambers with period furniture. The only surviving medieval structure is the **Rotunda of Our Lady & St Catherine** *(150Kč)*, with frescoes depicting 19 Přemyslid princes and their biblical ancestry.

Tracks from **St Nicholas Church** descend through the vineyard-quilted **Carolina Gardens** *(Karolíniny sady)*. Tracks from the castle connect to Hradiště, the oldest Premyslid settlement on St Hippolytus Hill, with a 13th-century late Gothic church and impressive valley views. Pick up the signposted trail below the Vyhlídka na znojemský hrad observation platform on Přemyslovců street, a 1.6km route that takes 40 minutes each way *(maps.cz)*.

Hiking Podyjí Vineyards & Viewpoints
Explore Podyjí National Park

Moravia's only national park and Czechia's smallest, 63-sq-km **Podyjí** follows the Dyje River from Znojmo Castle to the hilltop chateau in Vranov nad Dyjí. It's a vineyard-covered and forested reserve with rare species including orchids, butterflies and woodpeckers.

A scenic introduction is the hike to **Šobes**, one of Czechia's oldest vineyards. The 50-minute walk from **Hnanice** follows the signposted trail outside Hotel Vinice, crossing the Šobésk Bridge *(Šobeská lávka)* before the steep climb to Šobes, where you can sample Znovín Znojmo wines at the summer hut. From **Popice**, hike the 90-minute loop trail to the **Sealsfield Stone** *(Sealsfieldův kámen)* for a view over the Dyje ravine. Maps of longer hikes are available at the **Znojmo Tourist Information Centre**.

EATING & DRINKING IN ZNOJMO: OUR PICKS

Půlnapůl: Stylish and delectable patisserie, coffee shop and bakery with a hidden garden courtyard amongst the old city walls. *Thu-Sun 9am-6pm €*

Pivnice U šneka: Wood-panelled pub serving Czech craft beers and pickled, grilled and *šneka* (snail) snacks. *Mon-Thu 1pm-midnight, Fri & Sat 2pm-1am, Sun 2pm-10pm €*

Wine Bar Chatka: Beyond superb wines, Chatka's small menu uses only local ingredients, from pastry starters to veggie and fillet mains. *Tue-Sun 4pm-midnight €€*

Znojemský městský pivovar: Brewery on the castle grounds continuing the brewing tradition since 1720 with classic and craft beers and mod-trad Czech restaurant. *11am-11pm €€*

Olomouc

BAROQUE MONUMENTS | UNESCO HERITAGE | CREATIVE ART

Somehow, Olomouc has evaded discovery; Czechia's prettiest city outside Prague flies entirely under the radar. Once the seat of the Czech monarchy and Moravia's first capital before it moved to Brno, the town is plump with grandeur. Its well-preserved urban core is a municipal conservation area, protecting its main squares ringed with baroque buildings, fountains and the centrepiece UNESCO heritage monument, the Holy Trinity Column. Olomouc was a fortified city and Habsburg military centre until the end of the 19th century, and is now fringed by remnants of the medieval and crown fortresses. Its scattering of churches and cathedrals spotlight its Catholic importance as the Archbishopric of Olomouc. Today a city of 100,000 and home to Czechia's second oldest university, here embedded heritage blends with creativity in bistros and microbreweries, design stores and street art. Olomouc is Moravia's most majestic metropolis, with all the characteristics of a grand capital but without the crowds.

Squares, Fountains & UNESCO Monuments
Olomouc's historical centre

The star of Olomouc's main **Upper Square** *(Horní náměstí)*, is the 32m-high **Holy Trinity Column** *(Sloup Nejsvětější Trojice)*, an 18th-century devotional masterpiece carved by local artists with depictions of 18 saints, 12 light bearers, 12 apostles, and the Assumption of Mary and the Holy Trinity. It took 37 years to build; Empress Maria Teresa attended its 1745 consecration. The largest and tallest baroque sculpture in Europe, it was inscribed on the UNESCO World Heritage List in 2000. The column was undergoing major restoration during research, due for completion in 2026.

The gothic-towered, 15th-century **Town Hall** *(Radnice)* is known for its **Astronomical Clock**, renovated in the 1950s communist era in the style of socialist realism. The mosaic is topped by the folk tradition Ride of the Kings and worker murals at its base. Its moving procession of proletariat workers

GETTING AROUND

There are regular daily train services between Prague and Olomouc; express services connect the two cities in just over two hours; regional trains from Brno, mainly the R12 and R13, have hourly departures. Regional Arriva buses run from Brno; FlixBus also offers a service from Brno to Olomouc on a Vienna-Warsaw route. The pedestrianised historic centre wraps its trove of sites within the two main squares and the spread of townhouse-lined cobbled streets, although there is a great tram network, which is useful to get to the cathedral on the outskirts.

☑ TOP TIP

Climb the 75m-high **Town Hall Tower** (p265) or head up the 206 stairs to the 45.5m-high viewing terrace of **St Maurice Church Tower** (p267). Both grant the best views of Olomouc.

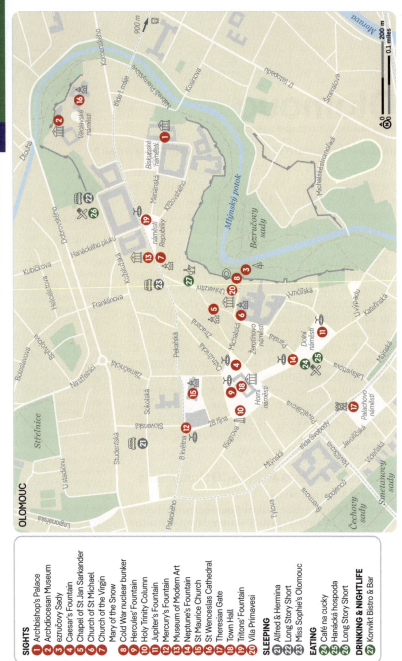

OLOMOUC MORAVIA & SILESIA

SIGHTS
1. Archbishop's Palace
2. Archdiocesan Museum
3. Bezručovy Sady
4. Caesar's Fountain
5. Chapel of St Jan Sarkander
6. Church of St Michael
7. Church of the Virgin Mary of the Snow
8. Cold War nuclear bunker
9. Hercules' Fountain
10. Holy Trinity Column
11. Jupiter's Fountain
12. Mercury's Fountain
13. Museum of Modern Art
14. Neptune's Fountain
15. St Maurice Church
16. St Wenceslas Cathedral
17. Theresian Gate
18. Town Hall
19. Tritons' Fountain
20. Vila Primavesi

SLEEPING
21. Alfred & Hermina
22. Long Story Short
23. Miss Sophie's Olomouc

EATING
24. Café na cucky
25. Hanácká hospoda
26. Long Story Short

DRINKING & NIGHTLIFE
27. Konvikt Bistro & Bar

Hercules' Fountain

can be seen at noon. South of the action, **Lower Square** (Dolní náměstí) is an alfresco space of cafes punctuated with the 1715 Marian Plague Column.

Around these landmarks are six mythological baroque fountains built between 1683 and 1735. On Upper Square: the **Hercules' Fountain** (Herkulova kašna) and **Caesar's Fountain** (Caesarova kašna), with **Mercury's Fountain** (Merkurova kašna) north of it. On Lower Square: **Neptune's Fountain** (Neptunova kašna) and **Jupiter's Fountain** (Jupiterova kašna). The Rome-inspired **Tritons' Fountain** (Tritonů kašna) is on the road to the cathedral.

Palaces, Cathedrals & Churches
Moravia's seat of bishops

The city's origins trace back to Ostrava Castle on **Wenceslas Square** (Václavské náměstí). Little remains of the medieval site where the Přemyslid dynasty ended with the assassination of King Wenceslas III in 1306. Some ruins are visible in the **Archdiocesan Museum**, packing 1000 years of Olomouc archdiocese culture into art collections and the Romanesque Bishop's Palace (muo.cz; adult/child from 80/50Kč).

The 100m-high **St Wenceslas Cathedral** (Katedrála sv Václava; katedralaolomouc.cz) is a 12th-century Romanesque basilica rebuilt in Gothic style, with a crypt entombing Olomouc bishops. To the south, the **Archbishop's Palace** (arcibiskupskypalac.cz; tours 180/120Kč) has been the Olomouc archbishopric's headquarters since 1685 and was where Franz Joseph I was declared Emperor of Austria in 1848.

The Olomouc archdiocese's significance is reflected in its mass of Roman Catholic churches. 15th-century Gothic **St Maurice** (Chrám sv Mořice) houses Central Europe's largest organ with 10,000 booming pipes. The tri-domed 17th-century **Church of St Michael** (Kostel sv Michala) glimmers with

OLOMOUC'S PRESTIGIOUS PUNGENT CHEESE

Love it or hate it, you haven't been to Olomouc until you've tasted its culinary speciality.

Olomoucké tvarůžky is a distinctive Czech delicacy, a matured cheese with a pungent aroma and piquant flavour. This tiny yellow dairy disk is a Haná region tradition dating back to the 15th century; it is considered Czechia's oldest cheese and an integral part of Moravian heritage.

You'll find it on menus around the city, served fresh, fried, spread and garnished.

The cheese is so important that it is celebrated annually at the Olomouc Cheese Festival in April: a mix of folk pageantry, chef presentations and musical revelry, with cheese and its best accompaniment, beer.

WHY I LOVE OLOMOUC

Becki Enright, Lonely Planet writer

There's Prague's showy magnificence and Brno's alternativeness, but what is it about Olomouc that makes it unmatched by any other Czech city? Its cobblestone core is a cultural evolution – you can walk through the riverside gardens below the old walls, have coffee in an old Jesuit commune, step inside baroque, Renaissance and art-nouveau houses, dine in part of the old fortress and admire modern murals.

I love Olomouc because it has nothing to prove; it's grand without being flashy.

---

neo-baroque interiors, while the 18th-century **Church of the Virgin Mary of the Snow** *(Kostel Panny Marie Sněžné)* pops with colourful stucco. The tiny **Chapel of St Jan Sarkander** *(Kaple sv Jana Sarkandra)* was built in 1909 upon the prison site where priest Jan Sarkander was tortured to death in 1620 for refusing to divulge confessions. His canonisation as Moravia's patron saint occurred in 1995 in Olomouc with Pope John Paul II. His remains lie in St Wenceslas Cathedral.

Medieval Walls & Crown Fortress Defences
The fortification of Olomouc

By 1655, following the Thirty Years' War, the walled medieval Moravian capital became a baroque fortress town; it was declared a Habsburg Crown Fortress by Empress Maria Teresa during the Prussian wars a century later, and became a military centre under Emperor Franz Joseph I. Trace the **Theresian Walls** in Bezručovy sady, a ribbon of gardens following the river around the Crown Fortress remnants. A time-warp entrance near Vila Primavesi leads downstairs through a fort tower next to a **Cold War nuclear bunker**. The preserved **Theresian Gate** *(Terezská brána)* stands in its original location on tř Svobody street; opposite, a wedge of redbrick fortifications hosts cafes, restaurants, and bars.

Street Art & Modern Art
Olomouc's contemporary coat

Olomouc's art-packed cultural monument is the Viennese art-nouveau **Vila Primavesi** *(vilaprimavesi.cz; 70Kč)*, built in 1906 by Viennese architects Franz von Krauss and Josef Tölk for Otto and Eugenie Primavesi and filled with Wiener Werkstätte decor by sculptor Anton Hanak and artist Gustav Klimt. Tour the restored ground-floor interiors; replicas of the Klimt paintings replace originals now displayed in international galleries.

Street art fills gaps in Olomouc's baroque building ensemble. The famed brick-wall painting of British king Edward VII with a selfie stick greets you near the train and bus stations on Denisova Street, opposite a muralled tunnel and next to the **Museum of Modern Art** *(muo.cz; adult/child 250Kč/150)*, with its ledge-hanging thief sculpture by Prague's David Černý. Smaller tongue-in-cheek murals of historical figures are dotted around Uhelná and Lafayettova streets; otherworldly sculptures guard Šemberova Street.

 EATING & DRINKING IN OLOMOUC: OUR PICKS

Hanácká hospoda: Modern-twist beer hall in an old Renaissance palace, with Czech classics and share platters. *Hours vary* €€	**Long Story Short:** From fortress bastion and military bakery to contemporary cuisine eatery, with small bites and veggie dishes. *8am-10pm Mon-Sun* €€	**Konvikt Bistro & Bar:** Trendy hangout in a former 17th-century Jesuit community house. Come here for the veggie-laden lunch menu. *8.30am-10pm Mon-Fri* €	**Café na cucky:** Breakfast and brunch in this arty lounge cafe, that's also a gallery and theatre space. *1pm-9pm Mon, 8am-9pm Tue-Sat, 9am-7pm Sun* €

Ostrava

REVIVED CITY | ARTS & CULTURE | MINING HERITAGE

Overlooked in the Poland-bordering, northern Moravian–Silesian region, Czechia's third-largest city, Ostrava, is the country's underdog. Unlike Prague's cultural prestige and Brno's textile boom, Ostrava was a coal-mining powerhouse. Its Dolní Vítkovice ironworks, built in 1828, supplied the Habsburg Empire's railroads and, during the communist era, was the 'steel heart of the republic'. When the last mine shut in 1994, Ostrava had to reinvent itself, overturning economic ruin by repurposing the relics of its industrial heritage into cultural spaces. The former ironworks hosts Colours of Ostrava, one of Europe's major music festivals; the abandoned Landek Park Mine is a shaft-set museum; and the still-smoking Ema slag heap, a beloved hiking spot. Though its centre's heritage buildings are sparse, Ostrava brims with top-notch gastronomy and cafe culture, ateliers and art galleries, adding to a decades-long revival in overturning the 'Black Ostrava' moniker and making the city a truly worthwhile visit.

Ostrava's Compact Heritage Core
History, heights and highlights

Ostrava is a modern city, but a little digging uncovers some earlier foundations. Stand in **Masaryk Square** (Masarykovo náměstí), framed by soft-hued facades, the old city hall and a 12m-high baroque column, and you're in an archetypal Czech city. Nearby, **St Wenceslas Church** (Kostel svatého Václava) stands its ancient ground amongst its block contemporaries as one of Ostrava's oldest buildings dating from 1297. Many of the city's relics are found in the square's **Ostrava Museum** (ostrmuz.cz; adult/child 70/50Kč), charting its history from the prehistoric to its medieval Amber Trail trade route foundations in 1297, empire industrial heritage and the fall of communism in 1989.

Though the medieval fortifications no longer exist, ruins of the **Silesian Ostrava Castle** (slezkoostravskyhrad.cz; 90/60Kč/) can be found on the banks across the Ostravice River.

GETTING AROUND

Ostrava is on the D1 motorway connecting to Prague but is easily reached by trains and buses. The town has two train stations: Hlavní nádraží (in the city centre) and Ostrava-Svinov (west of the centre). České dráhy railways has direct services to Ostrava from Prague, Olomouc and Brno; RegioJet connections end at Ostrava-Svinov. FlixBus connects to Ostrava on the Vienna-Warsaw service. Leoš Janáček International Airport is 25km from the city, reachable by the S4 train. The city centre is walkable, but its public transport network (DPO) is ideal for reaching surrounding areas.

✅ TOP TIP

Book ahead for accommodation in July, when over 40,000 music lovers fill Dolní Vítkovice for the four-day music festival, Colours of Ostrava.

SIGHTS
1. Bolt Tower
2. Dolní Vítkovice
3. Gallery of Fine Arts
4. Masaryk Square.
5. New City Hall Viewing Tower
6. Ostrava Museum
7. *Ostravská Madona*
8. PLATO Gallery of Contemporary Art
9. Silesian Ostrava Castle
10. St Wenceslas Church

ACTIVITIES
11. Mound Ema

SLEEPING
12. Imperial Hotel Ostrava
13. Kampus Palace

EATING
14. Hogo Fogo
15. La Petite Conversation

DRINKING & NIGHTLIFE
16. Cafe Club Dock
17. CØKAFE Centrum

ENTERTAINMENT
18. Antonín Dvořák Theatre
19. Janáček Philharmonic Ostrava

EATING & DRINKING IN OSTRAVA: OUR PICKS

Hogo Fogo: Chic bistro in a historic house with courtyard, serving a seasonal menu using local ingredients. Book ahead. *11.30am-10pm Mon-Fri* €€

La Petite Conversation: Homely Belgian spot serving international dishes, Belgian classics and a great wine selection. *8am-10pm Mon-Fri, 9am-3pm Sat* €€

CØKAFE Centrum: Speciality coffee shop with healthy, homemade small plates and sweet pastries and cakes. *7.30am-7pm Mon-Fri, 8.30am-7pm Sat & Sun* €

Cafe Club Dock: Casual and cool riverside cafe bistro by day and vibrant bar by evening. *hours vary* €

New City Hall Viewing Tower

The **New City Hall Viewing Tower** *(Statutární město Ostrava; vyhlidkovavez.cz; 80/40Kč)* is the cherry on Ostrava's reclaimed skyline. The highest town hall tower in Czechia at 85.6m, its observation deck offers panoramic views of the city from 73m, including the Dolní Vítkovice ironworks, the Beskydy and Jeseníky mountain ranges and, on a clear day, neighbouring Poland.

Visit Former Mines & Slag Heaps
Transformation of mining relics

Exploring sunken mine shafts and collieries is an unusual activity, but these industrial relics now serve as profound educational spaces and national cultural monuments in Ostrava. For those who lost their jobs in the closures, they've also become a source of income, with former miners and rescuers leading the tours with first-hand stories.

Head north of the centre to Petřkovice for the **Mining Museum in Landek Park** *(landekpark.cz; adult/child 280/210Kč)*. Czechia's largest mining museum inconspicuously sits in the middle of a recreational area ringed with walking trails, sports courts and camping areas. This is the only place in Ostrava where you can head down into the sooty shafts of the former Anselm mine, descending in the original mining cage lift to tour 250m of coal mine tunnels. A little further out in the eastern district of Michálkovice is the colossal **Michal Mine complex** *(dul-michal.cz; 150Kč/60)*. A look at the operational buildings above a filled-in shaft gives a stark stop-in-time snapshot of the mine's final day of operation on 2 June 1994. The 'Miner's Journey to Work' tour takes visitors through the abandoned dress and wash areas, electrical engine and compressor rooms, tracks and pit lifts, and the miners' canteen, all preserved as they were left..

It's worth the clamber up **Mound Ema** *(Halda Ema)*, a 315m-tall slag heap still smouldering from underground combustion. Despite its smoking, sulphuric fumes, the affectionately dubbed Ostrava Volcano is a prime viewpoint over the city, especially at sunset. The hike begins across the Miloš Sýkora Bridge and follows a yellow trail to the top.

MODEL SOCIALIST CITY

The industrial districts of Vítkovice and Mariánské are a redbrick mix of complexes and workers' cottages, but not western **Poruba**.

Its grandiose socialist realism architecture, a style of the 1950s communist era, was intended to create a new city that glorified the mining industry and communist community ideals. Gargantuan apartment blocks line park-backed broad boulevards and miner statues front imposing facades.

Its main artery, Hlavní Třída (formerly Lenin Avenue), features a showpiece crescent residential complex with an ornamental hammer and sickle and labour family upon the triumphal arch.

A protected historical monument, modern Poruba thrives as a residential hotspot, the youthful home of the VŠB-Technical University of Ostrava and the space for trendy hangouts and enterprises.

BEST OF THE ARTS IN OSTRAVA

Gallery of Fine Arts *(gvuo.cz)*: The largest and oldest art gallery in Ostrava houses over 23,000 masterpieces, including a version of Klimt's *Judith*.

Plato Gallery of Contemporary Art *(plato-ostrava.cz)*: Striking modern art gallery in a repurposed former 19th-century slaughterhouse.

City Street Art: Ostrava's iconic mural is the *Ostravská Madona* portrait by Nils Westergard near the Imperial Hotel.

Antonín Dvořák Theatre *(ndm.cz)*: The region's oldest theatre (established 1919) presents around 500 opera, ballet, drama and musical performances annually.

Janáček Philharmonic Ostrava *(jfo.cz)*: Home of the Ostrava Orchestra with world-class composers performing works by Czech masters like Leoš Janáček.

Dolní Vitkovice

Mining Cultural Revival
Ostrava's iconic cultural complex

Dolní Vitkovice *(Dolní oblast Vítkovice or DOV)*, the poster child of industrial heritage reimagining, is Ostrava's symbolic landmark. The copper ironworks site with soaring smokestacks, gigantic blast furnaces, bulbous tanks and jumbo pipelines was a coal-mining and iron-forging behemoth from 1828 to 1998. From afar, it's hard to tell that the former industrial site is more artistic epicentre than a post-apocalyptic-looking relic. A climbing wall towers on a former mining pit; Svet Techniky Museum brings science to life in an old hangar; performances fill the concert hall in a former gas collector; and the workers' quarters are now a cabaret hall and cinema.

Dolní Vitkovice's standout landmark is the glass-clad, flame-mimicking **Bolt Tower** atop Blast Furnace No 1, paying homage to the roaring fires that fuelled the ironworks below and named in honour of Olympian Usain Bolt, who inaugurated the site in 2015. At 78m, it's the city's highest point, offering vistas of Ostrava from its observation deck. Take a guided tour of the Blast Furnace Circuit *(dolnivitkovice.cz; adult/child 280Kč/210Kč)* or skip straight to the Bolt Cafe *(300Kč; advance reservation only)* for an iron-clad, sky-high experience.

In July, the site transforms into more than 20 stages for the **Colours of Ostrava** music festival *(colours.cz)* – an international platform showcasing world-greats and homegrown talent alongside theatre performances, art exhibits, and workshops. Ranked among Europe's top music festivals, few can match this unique and alternative backdrop.

Places We Love to Stay

€ Budget   €€ Midrange   €€€ Top End

Brno   p242

10-Z Bunker € An extraordinary stay in the former nuclear fallout shelter, forgoing comforts for a more authentic experience, even if just for one night.

Hotel Avion €€ Reconstructed functionalist-style hotel designed by Czech architect, Bohuslav Fuchs. A National Cultural Monument with colour block rooms and a design museum.

Enjoy Downtown Boutique Apartments €€ Five stylish, modern studio rooms in the historic centre from the Goodnite Brno accommodation group.

Masarykova N°30 €€ Beautifully furnished modern apartment rooms close to the train station and next to the best coffee shop in town.

Barceló Brno Palace €€€ Prestigious building from the 1850s turned luxury hotel with 199 rooms, courtyard lobby bar and fine dining restaurant.

Kroměříž   p252

Hotel U Zlatého Kohouta €€ A meld of classical hotel and budget modern hostel, with main-square-view roof terrace, wellness spa and wine bar.

Hotel La Fresca €€ Stylish hotel, renovated with period features and furniture. The house restaurant with show kitchen serves mod-traditional Czech cuisine.

Hotel Octárna €€ Tranquil hotel on the premises of the former Franciscan monastery with classic-elegant decor and courtyard restaurant. Features the Max Švabinský mosaic lunettes.

Telč   p254

Pension Telč No. 20 €€ Homely stay in a rustic, family run 6-room guesthouse in a 15th century burgher house on Zacharias of Hradec Sq.

Hotel Celerin €€ Twelve modern-classic rooms in a square-side hotel with a garden. Popular hangout because of the on-site patisserie.

Mikulov   p255

Hotel Tanzberg €€ Seventeen-bedroom hotel and restaurant in 16th-century Jewish Quarter with on-site pub Golem.

Hotel Desatero €€ Ten rooms, from doubles to suites, in a renovated historic house, with slick design touches by Czech architect and industrial designer, Přemysl Kokeš.

Hotel Templ €€ Beautifully reconstructed, period-feature hotel with restaurant of Slovak chef, Marcel Ihnačák. Neighbour of Desatero.

Stajnhaus €€ Five chic-minimalist rooms in a renovated Renaissance-baroque house with on-site wine cellar.

Znojmo   p262

TGM Hotel Residence € Spacious, bright, minimalist design rooms in historically restored courtyard house on the old town's Masaryk Square.

Hotel Lahofer €€ City hotel of the Znojmo region Lahofer Winery with 32 modern rooms in a 13th-century building; breakfast included.

Stará Pekárna €€ Elegant revival of a former bakery building keeping vaulted ceilings, beams, stone floors and other original features.

Olomouc   p265

Miss Sophie's Olomouc €€ Restored 14th-century listed monument building with eight boutique-antique rooms. The in-house cafe serves a local coffee roast and homemade food.

Long Story Short €€ Sophisticated hostel with dorms and private rooms. The cafe, bistro and bakery nod to the site's former use as a military bakery.

Alfred & Hermina €€ Recently restored 500-year-old house with 11 cool hotel rooms and breakfast-brunch café.

Ostrava   p269

Kampus Palace € Youthful accommodation option with common room, mixing student dorms, hotel rooms and apartments.

Imperial Hotel €€ Ostrava's first hotel (from 1904) revived with a classic-contemporary renovation, in the heart of the city centre.

Hotel city.city €€ Modern, minimalist hotel on the city's northern fringes, close to the main train station.

TOOLKIT

The chapters in this section cover the most important topics you'll need to know about Czechia. They're full of nuts-and-bolts information and valuable insights to help you understand and navigate Czechia and get the most out of your trip.

Arriving
p276

Money
p277

Getting Around
p278

Accommodation
p280

Family Travel
p281

LGBTIQ+ Travellers
p282

Health & Safe Travel
p283

Food, Drink & Nightlife
p284

Responsible Travel
p286

Accessible Travel
p288

Nuts & Bolts
p289

Language
p290

Český Krumlov (p190)
O. KALACHEVA/SHUTTERSTOCK ©

Arriving

Prague is the obvious gateway for anyone arriving in Czechia. Václav Havel Airport is by far the country's largest and is located 15km by road from the city centre. There are two terminals – Terminal 1 is for flights originating outside the Schengen zone, while Terminal 2 handles flights to/from all other destinations.

Visas
EU nationals don't require a visa for any length of stay. Travellers from UK, Canada, New Zealand, US and Australia can stay for up to 90 days in any six-month period without a visa.

SIM Cards
Cards for unlocked phones can be purchased from a Vodafone vending machine in Terminal 2. EU phones work in Czechia as they do at home.

Wi-Fi
Free Wi-Fi is available at both terminals and is fairly reliable, if slow. Elsewhere in Czechia, Wi-Fi access is better than in some Western European countries.

Cash
It's good to have a little cash when heading into the city centre, and there are ordinary ATMs belonging to Czech banks (not fee-charging Euronet) at both terminals issuing Czech crowns.

Travel to Prague from airport

AIRPORT EXPRESS (BUS) — 30mins 100Kč

UBER — 30mins 570Kč

TROLLEY/ BUS/ METRO — 30mins 40Kč

UBER FROM PRAGUE AIRPORT

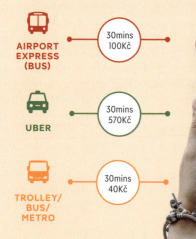

The only ride service permitted to operate from Prague Airport is Uber Airport – no other taxis are available. To book a ride, use the app as you would anywhere or there are special terminals at arrivals. Another option is to book through the taxi desk, also at arrivals. Allowing Uber to operate the service has rid the airport of a problem that had plagued it since the end of communism: crooked taxi drivers who would charge astronomical amounts for the relatively short ride into the city. You are strongly advised to use Uber when returning to the airport.

Money

CURRENCY: CZECH CROWN/KORUNA ČESKÁ (KČ)

Card Payments

COVID-19 pushed the vast majority of businesses to take on card-payment systems, though it was quite widespread before. All large hotels, shops and restaurants take cards, as do Prague's public-transport ticket machines and post offices. However, you may find small shops and cafes where cash is still the only option.

Tipping

Tipping is not really expected in Czechia. Adding 10% to the bill as a gratuity will be met with a dumbfounded (or overjoyed) reaction. Here, people round up the bill to the nearest 100Kč. It's common practice but not necessarily anticipated. Never reward huffy service with tips.

Euros

Increasingly it is possible to pay with euros in Czechia, though you should never count on it. Even some supermarkets take euros – the exchange rate will be slightly lower than at a bank and your change will come in Czech crowns. US dollars or UK pounds are not accepted.

HOW MUCH FOR A...

Ticket for the National Museum
300Kč

Canoe hire per day
300Kč

Cinema ticket
200Kč

Public toilet
20Kč

HOW TO... Save on Currency

Never change your local currency into crowns before arriving in Czechia. Exchange rates are lousy in Western Europe, never mind the rest of the world. Withdraw money from ATMs once in Czechia. Never use freestanding Euronet ATMs that charge a fortune, and when asked by machines about conversion, always choose your own bank/ without conversion. Change any unspent crowns back into your local currency before you get to the airport.

LOCAL TIP

Never change money on the street in Prague. Unsuspecting tourists have been handed Bulgarian Lei and worthless Belorussian roubles instead of Czech crowns. Always use banks or, if you must, exchange offices.

ROUNDING UP & DOWN

Price tags in shops don't always correspond with the price you actually pay at the till. This is because the crown is divided into 100 hallers (haléř), which do not physically exist. (These worthless coins were phased out two decades ago.) However, prices are still quoted in hallers but rounded up or down at the checkout.

Something priced 9.90Kč actually costs 10Kč. An item costing 8.40Kč is 8Kč. Two items that together cost 17.70Kč will come to 18Kč. These days, prices in hallers only seem to appear in supermarkets.

Getting Around

Prague has one of the best public-transport systems in the world. The rest of the country has excellent links, mostly by bus and train. Motorways are a work in progress.

TRAVEL COSTS

Train Ticket Prague–Brno
360Kč

Petrol
About 35Kč/L

Bus Ticket Prague–Karlovy Vary
180Kč

10-Day Motorway e-sticker
290Kč

Hiring a Car

Cars can be hired at Prague Airport. Be aware that car-hire points in the regions are not so common. Vehicles are usually of a good EU standard. All cars and vans come with the motorway toll prepaid.

Czech Motorways

Czech motorways are new but all too often unfinished. There is a charge for using them, which is paid online at edalnice.cz. Never pay through any other site, as they are scams. You can also pay the toll at service stations and at any post office.

Train

Czechia has one of the densest rail networks in the world, with trains running to surprisingly small villages and along mountain valleys. Big cities are linked by express trains, though journey times can be slow. České dráhy is the national rail company, but some services are run by others.

Bus

Buses go where the trains don't, usually linking district and regional capitals to outlying villages and small towns. Express coaches operate from Prague to major population centres. Buses are often cheaper than trains and are sometimes the faster option.

DRIVING ESSENTIALS

Drive on the right

Speed limit is 50km/h in urban areas, 90km/h on secondary roads, 130km/h on motorways

.00

Blood alcohol limit is 0g/L

CITY TRANSPORT

Every town with a population of over around 10,000 people has some kind of city transport, usually buses, but often trams and trolleybuses. These are cheap to use and run regularly throughout the day, though rarely at night, except in very big cities (Prague, Pilsen, Brno).

Tip

The website idos.idnes.cz is a one-stop shop for all transport timetables and information across the country.

OTHER MODES OF TRANSPORT

Apart from the buses, trains and trams mentioned here, your other modes of transport could include cable car and boat. The former climb mountains, such as Sněžka and Ještěd, taking skiers in winter and hikers in summer. Boats ply some lakes and reservoirs as ferries, and the navigable Vltava and Elbe (Labe) as cruise liners. Only Prague has a metro system. There are no scheduled domestic flights within Czechia.

Prague Transport Tickets

When you buy a paper ticket, you must validate it in the yellow machines at the entrance to metro stations and on buses/trams/trolleybuses. If using the Lítačka app, you have to activate the ticket. Failing to do so will mean a fine if you are caught.

Prague Ticket Costs

Tickets for Prague's buses, trams, metro and trolleybuses are timed with 30-minute (30Kč) and 90-minute (40Kč) validity. If you are planning on making more than three or four journeys in one 24-hour period, a 120Kč day ticket is better. There also exists a 72-hour pass for 330Kč.

Czech Roads

Away from the unfinished motorway system, other roads are a mixed bag, with anything between decent, European-standard tarmac and potholed communist-era asphalt rumbling beneath your wheels. Road markings can be brand new or completely worn out.

Czech Drivers

Czech road users tend to be more aggressive and erratic than you may be used to. The biggest hazards are dangerous overtaking and tailgating, a real Czech speciality, especially if you drive around the speed limits, which are generally ignored. Supermarket car parks are a minefield for foreign drivers, as older Czech motorists may stick to the rule of giving way to any traffic coming from the right while younger drivers don't!

Road Hazards

Czech roads are generally safe but there are some specific hazards you should be aware of before aiming that hire car out of Prague Airport. Road surfaces tend to be fairly decent but post-winter potholes are still an issue. Animals on the roads, especially in forested and mountain areas are probably the biggest danger – deer and wild boar often dart across roads. Also in forested regions there can be branches and other tree debris on the tarmac, especially after wind and rain. Between November and March, the country is usually blanketed in snow and roads can ice up. Beware a condition Czechs call 'bílá tma' – literally 'white darkness' – basically whiteout, which can be particularly disorienting.

ROAD DISTANCE CHART (KM)

	Brno	Český Krumlov	Karlovy Vary	Mikulov	Ostrava	Plzeň	Prague
Brno	–	238	341	51	170	298	208
Český Krumlov	238	–	250	213	405	154	171
Karlovy Vary	341	250	–	377	505	82	130
Mikulov	51	213	377	–	216	334	247
Ostrava	170	405	505	216	–	464	372
Plzeň	298	154	82	334	464	–	97
Prague	208	171	130	247	372	97	–

Accommodation

Haughty Habsburg Hotels

Prague, the spa towns and the odd large city have some very special historical hotels with olde-worlde, five-star traditions going back to the days of the Austrian Empire. The Pupp (pictured right) in Karlovy Vary is the country's most illustrious hotel, but the Nové Lázně in Mariánské Lázně and the Paříž in Prague are not far behind.

Be My Guest

The humble *penzión* (guesthouse) can be anything from a family-run B&B to a small hotel. These often have breakfast rooms, if not a small restaurant. Some larger hotels have co-opted the word to sound homely, but in general pensions have more character and are smaller than hotels. Often, they are the best choice of accommodation in large towns.

Bunking Down

A hostel here can offer anything from a bunk bed in a room of 12 to a double room with shower, the common factor being that you pay by the bed (if you want a double to yourself, you have to pay for two beds). Outside Prague and Český Krumlov there aren't a lot of backpacker-style hostels.

Sleep High

In the Krkonoše Mountains and some other ranges, mountain chalets – more often than not housing a decent restaurant – are some of the most characteristic places to stay in the country. Accommodation ranges from three-star rooms to space on a floor for your camping mat. Book well ahead for July and August.

HOW MUCH FOR A NIGHT IN A…

Hostel
450Kč

Penzión (Double Room)
1700Kč

Campsite pitch
400Kč

Under the Stars

Campsites are normally fields with basic facilities, tents pitched randomly in a big open field in the centre, and cabins arranged around the edge. Most have some food service. The Czech climate means most camping grounds are open from May to October only, though there are exceptions. Wild camping is kind of tolerated, but avoid making fires.

SHORT-TERM RENTALS

Booking websites such as Airbnb and Booking.com are very much part of the Prague over-tourism problem. Whole streets in the city centre have been bought up for short-term rentals, turning blocks into ghost towns and playing havoc with municipal planning. Noisy guests and lampposts bristling with key safes have led to crusading locals lobbying the city council to have these services either banned or heavily taxed. It's all got rather nasty so, if possible, try to avoid booking through these websites – reserve direct with a hotel or guesthouse instead.

Family Travel

Czechia is a relatively family-friendly destination and you should have few issues travelling with children. Locals are often sympathetic to families with kids and, outside Prague, may even go out of their way to assist. Children's facilities are often excellent and baby products widely available, though probably more expensive than back home.

Sights

The maximum age for child discounts on admission fees varies from 12 to 18; children under six often get in for free. An ever-increasing number of museums have interactive elements in their exhibitions as well as hands-on displays. However, it has to be highlighted that many sights lag way behind Western Europe when it comes to making things interesting for kids.

Facilities

Rough pavements, nonexistent changing facilities, missing lifts and lack of highchairs in restaurants are just some of the issues you may encounter. That said, playgrounds are usually new and of a high standard, a kids' corner can be found in even cheap accommodation, and Czechs are generally very accommodating to families. Some hiking routes have been made pram- and wheelchair-friendly.

Eating Out

Many (though definitely not most) restaurants offer a dětský jídelníček (children's menu) – usually fried cheese or a chicken schnitzel, served with chips. Highchairs and kids cutlery are quite rare. Typical cafe bakeries – called *cukrárny* – are great places for kids.

Getting Around

All children up to the age of 18 receive a discount of 50% on all public transport. To receive this discount, all children should have photo ID with them. Under-15-year-olds pay nothing on Prague's public transport.

CHILD-FRIENDLY PICKS

iQLANDIA
Hands-on science centre that probably just pips Plzeň's Techmania as Czechia's top for tots.

Techmania Science Centre
The west's most kid-centric attraction, with a huge workshop's worth of science-based experiments, hands-on exhibits, fascinating displays and interactive attractions; in Plzeň.

Prague Zoo
Czechia's best zoo is a must for Prague-bound little ones.

National Technical Museum
Just about the country's best classic museum for children, with countless bits of old tech and yesteryear vehicles.

GET 'EM OUTDOORS

A trip to Czechia is a wonderful opportunity to get those kids off their devices and breathing fresh air. Hitting a trail, scavenging for berries, having a snowball fight on a mountainside or splashing around in a lake – this country has options galore for family fun days out in the open. Take a cable-car ride up a peak and hike down, hunt mushrooms in the forest, have a pine-cone battle, get your kids skiing lessons, spot deer in a remote valley or just find the nearest playground – the possibilities are truly endless.

LGBTIQ+ Travellers

For a former communist country, the Czechs are surprisingly tolerant of same-sex relationships. Prague is the most open-minded city. The industrial areas of north Bohemia and north Moravia have the most conservative views, but rarely will openly gay couples experience negative reaction anywhere. Same-sex registered partnerships have been possible since 2006. Gay marriage is likely to become reality in coming years.

Prague Pride

Mid-August sees the biggest openly gay event take place in the capital – Prague Pride (praguepride.cz). Attracting members of the LGBTIQ+ community from across the world, this bash has taken place annually since 2010. The main stages are at Letná, across the river from the Old Town, but there is also a procession on Wenceslas Square. In a city that is surprisingly tolerant of homosexuality, Prague Pride is all about celebration and colourful costumes rather than demonstration. Many nongay Praguers and tourists attend simply for the great street-party atmosphere.

STUD

STUD (stud.cz) is one of the biggest NGOs promoting gay rights in the Czech Lands. The group has been active in lobbying the government and in assisting the gay community with all kinds of issues since 1996. This group of friends holds events in the country, including the popular Queerball and Mezipatra. They also operate an online library of 500 publications on a gay theme.

Queer Ball

An extravaganza held since 2012, Queer Ball (queerball.cz) takes place in September in Prague and Brno and it is exactly what the name suggests. Each year the organisers give the event a theme, with participants turning up in fancy dress accordingly.

BRNO PRIDE

Not to be outdone, Brno now has its very own pride procession. Brno Pride (brnopride.cz) has existed in some form or other for almost two decades (with some breaks) but in 2024 the first Pride Week culminated in a full-blown procession through the Moravian capital.

Czech Railway Ad

Illustrating just how nonjudgemental the Czechs are about homosexuality, in the summer of 2022, Czech Railways ran a national ad featuring an openly lesbian couple; unthinkable a couple of decades ago. Scan the QR code to view the YouTube video.

RESOURCES

Three good online sources of information include **Travel Gay Europe** (travelgay.com), **Prague Gay Travel Guide** (patroc.com/gay/prague) and **Prague Pride** (praguepride.cz). The first two maintain up-to-date lists of the best bars and clubs, the last in the list is more about events. **Prague City Tourism** (prague.eu) maintains a list of gay- and lesbian-friendly hotels and pensions.

Health & Safe Travel

INSURANCE

Insurance is not compulsory to travel to Czechia but it's good to have in the event that things don't go to plan. Consider a policy that covers flight cancellation and medical care. Alternatively, or additionally, EU travellers can apply for the European Health Insurance Card (EHIC) that covers emergency medical treatment free of charge.

Ticks

The most dangerous creature in the forest? Wolves or crazed wild boars? No, the tiniest of them all – the tick. These guys can carry two diseases – tick-borne encephalitis and Lyme disease. The latter can be treated with antibiotics, the former is rarer but can only be avoided by prior vaccination. Use repellents and cover up.

Mountain Safety

The Czech mountain-rescue service are called out on a daily basis throughout the year to save people who have set out on hikes without sufficient knowledge of the terrain they will be walking or the right equipment. Google the conditions you might encounter and dress accordingly, carry emergency food and water, and tell someone where you are going.

SOLO TRAVEL

Czechia is one of the safest places in the world – women travelling solo are unlikely to encounter hassles.

OUTDOOR TOURIST SIGNS

Hiking
Pěší značení

Cross-Country Skiing
Lyžařské značení

Cycling
Cykloznačení

Forest Fires

Climate change seems to be making Czech forests more prone to summer blazes. These occasionally happen after prolonged dry and very hot periods. If a fire breaks out in your location, then evacuate immediately. These are far more destructive events than most can imagine, and highly dangerous to human life.

TWELFTH FOR SAFETY

Welcome to one of the safest places on earth! The Global Peace Index 2024 rated Czechia as the 12th-safest country on earth, and when you consider that the vast majority of misdemeanours are committed in Prague, it leaves the rest of the country with one of the lowest crime rates in the world.

Food, Drink & Nightlife

When to Eat

Snídaně (breakfast, 7am–9am) At home, a quick slice of bread with something; in hotels, a lavish German-style spread.

Svačina (mid-morning snack, 10am) By mid-morning Czechs are peckish for pastries, sandwiches and coffee.

Oběd (lunch, 11.30am–2pm) Main meal of the day, often three courses. Most restaurants offer cheap set menus.

Večeře (dinner, 6pm–8pm) Modest affair involving light dishes.

Where to Eat

Restaurace (restaurant) This can be anything from a Michelin-starred spot to a grotty station pub.

Hospoda (pub) Those from English-speaking countries will be surprised to find sitting room only in Czech pubs, places to drink beer and eat simple dishes.

Cukrárna (cafe bakery) These typically Czech cafes have largely disappeared from Prague's centre, but every self-respecting town has a couple, serving cakes, strudel, coffee and even wine.

Jídelna (canteen) Cheap, quick, often stand-up affairs.

MENU DECODER

Jídelní lístek: It's good to know how to say 'menu' in Czech, just in case it's not brought to your table automatically. These are often leatherette-bound, multipage works of culinary literature, often amusingly/badly translated into umpteen unnecessary languages (Finnish, Korean!).

...dle denní nabídky: This phrase basically means '...of the day' and is often useful at lunchtime if you want soup.

Přílohy Side dishes. At the end of every menu is a list of side dishes. Listed main courses very often don't include a side, which costs extra.

Perlivá/neperlivá voda Sparkling/still water. It's not enough to simply ask for water in the Czech lands. You must specify sparkling or still. Never ask for tap water – Czechs simply do not drink it.

HOW TO... Eat Out in Czechia

The etiquette around eating out probably differs from your home country, so here's how to do it. First of all, be aware that waiting staff in Prague (nowadays often not Czech themselves) are used to foreign quirks and aren't too finicky about following the rigid norms of acceptable Czech behaviour, but beyond the end of Prague's metro lines things are different. Menus in the capital are always in English, but don't count on this anywhere else. Attracting the waiter's attention isn't usually the ordeal it once was, but clicking fingers and waving is a real no-no. Drink orders are taken first, then orders for food when the drinks arrive. Mains often don't come with sides, which must be ordered separately. Since COVID-19, paying by card has become absolutely normal, though you may be asked to go to the bar to do so. Round up the bill to the nearest 100Kč.

HOW MUCH FOR A...

Espresso
70Kč

Beer
60Kč

Weekday Lunch Menu
100–200Kč

Restaurant Main Course
150–250Kč

Bottled Water
20Kč

Glass of Wine
50–80Kč

Slice of Gateau
40–60Kč

Open Sandwich (Chlebíček)
30Kč

HOW TO... Survive a Czech Pub

So you've chosen a pub and entered the building. Already the locals are staring in your direction suspiciously. So, what should you do in order to avoid more disapproving looks from the regulars? Pub etiquette is an important part of the whole beer-imbibing process. Firstly, don't barge in and start rearranging chairs – if you want to share a table or take a spare seat, first ask *je tu volno?* (is this free?). It's normal practice in crowded Czech pubs to share tables with strangers.

Take a beermat from the rack, put it in front of you, and wait for the staff to come to you; waving for service is guaranteed to get you ignored. When the waiter approaches, just raise your thumb for one beer, thumb and index finger for two etc – it's automatically assumed that you're here for the beer. Waiters sometimes still keep track of your order by marking a slip of paper that stays on your table; don't write on it or lose it.

When the level of beer in your glass falls to within an inch of the bottom, an eagle-eyed waiter will be on their way with another. If you don't want any more, place a beermat on top of your glass. To pay, just say *zaplatím* (I'll pay). The marks on your slip of paper are added up, and you pay the bill.

Beer Champions

The Czechs have by far the largest per capita beer consumption in the world at 128L per person per year? Lager-loving Germany is 4th with 99L, and boozy Britain drinks half what the Czechs do (70L).

GOING OUT

In Prague, a daily and nightly onslaught of classical music, ballet, opera, theatre, rock, jazz, musicals, exhibition openings and festivals keeps locals and tourists entertained.

Classical music is of international standard, while large venues in Prague are often on the tour schedule of some of the world's biggest pop and rock stars. One strange phenomenon is catching a show by forgotten 1970s or 1980s US or UK stars, still touring unbeknown to all but diehard fans. (Jethro Tull played Loket Amphitheatre in 2024.)

Opera is another big draw (homegrown, plus Mozart) though theatre and musicals (the latter often recycled Broadway and West End shows) are in Czech only.

Clubbing is big in Prague and perhaps Pilsen, Brno and Ostrava – the rest of the country is quieter in the evenings. A night out in small towns usually involves a meal in a restaurant, a theatre performance or a visit to the cinema. The spas are pretty much dead in the evenings, elderly spa guests tucked up in bed by 8pm.

There's a small gay scene in Prague, centred around the Vinohrady neighbourhood.

Recently, Czech pubs have been falling in number for a whole host of reasons (mainly financial) but on Friday and Saturday nights they are still places to head for a truly local experience. Sports bars are great places to go to when the Czechs are playing ice hockey, less so these days when there's football on TV.

Responsible Travel

Climate Change & Travel

It's impossible to ignore the impact we have when travelling; Lonely Planet urges all travellers to engage with their travel carbon footprint, which will mainly come from air travel. While there often isn't an alternative, travellers can look to minimise the number of flights they take, opt for newer aircrafts and use cleaner ground transport, such as trains. One proposed solution—purchasing carbon offsets—unfortunately does not cancel out the impact of individual flights. While most destinations will depend on air travel for the foreseeable future, for now, pursuing ground-based travel where possible is the best course of action.

The **UN Carbon Offset Calculator** shows how flying impacts a household's emissions

The **ICAO's carbon emissions calculator** allows visitors to analyse the CO2 generated by point-to-point journeys

Recycle

In the EU, the Czechs are second behind Germany when it comes to recycling. Help them in their admirable efforts by throwing all rubbish into special bins that can be found on every street corner.

Beware Greenwash

Some tourist businesses, especially in Prague, are particularly guilty of bigging up their green credentials. Some visitors might like to check any claims made about sustainability and environmental friendliness before handing over their money.

Take a look at Prague Tourism's **Enjoy Respect** campaign, which highlights how the city would like visitors to behave when holidaying in the capital. There's everything from church etiquette to where to park your scooter.

Prague has one of the world's best public-transport systems – so use it! You may be used to jumping in an Uber back home, but metro and trams are cheaper and quicker.

TAKE IT WITH YOU

If you see plastic bottles or anything else that doesn't belong in pristine natural surroundings, take it out with you and bin it (put it in a recycling bin in the next village).

HIKING ETIQUETTE

Hiking has seen a huge increase in popularity but beauty spots littered with tissue paper, nappies, wet wipes and worse puts some off. Make sure you take everything home with you from an outdoor adventure.

Souvenirs
Avoid the mass-produced souvenir shops of Prague and the spas, those selling Russian dolls, cannabis lollipops and fake communist paraphernalia. Source local items instead from shops such as Botanicus and Manufaktura.

Ukrainian Refugees
No one knows exactly how many Ukrainians there are in Czechia, but this country has done more than most to help its wartorn neighbour. Any initiatives you notice helping Ukrainian refugees are likely to be worthwhile supporting.

Forest Food
When eating out, choose Czech venison, duck and wild boar over internationally imported pork and beef. The former live freely as wild animals, the latter can be artificially fattened and/or pumped with hormones or antibiotics.

Over-tourism
Prague's over-tourism problem is starting to make a full comeback. Try to avoid Airbnb ghettos, Uber instead of trams, scam exchange offices, Balkan *trdelník* (chimney cake) sellers, Thai massage, British stag groups.

Go Meat-Free
Meat production is one of the most environmentally unfriendly activities of all. Czechs may love their schnitzels and goulash, but perhaps you might want to choose at least one meat-free meal a day.

In summer, avoid all open flames in the countryside, especially in tinder-dry forests.

Prague's farmers markets are a superb alternative to the big international supermarket chains.

High Sustainability Ranking
The Global Sustainability Index ranks Czechia a surprisingly high 12th place worldwide. This seems rather odd for a country whose sustainability and green policies lag behind those of most Western European countries.

RESOURCES

uklidmecesko.cz
In early April the Czechs clean up their country.

mzp.cz
Czech Ministry for the Environment.

kct.cz
Czech Hiking Club often organises forest clean-ups etc.

FROM LEFT: SAROJ KHUENDEE/SHUTTERSTOCK ©, SERGII FIGURNYI/SHUTTERSTOCK ©, KOJIN/SHUTTERSTOCK ©

Accessible Travel

Sadly, progress is slow when it comes to making Czechia accessible to all. Challenges remain and often accessibility is a low priority, despite legal requirements.

Steps

For visitors with any sort of mobility or sight issues, steps are the biggest problem everywhere in Eastern Europe. Lifts are becoming more common, but don't count on them, even in Prague.

Airport

Prague airport has a full assistance service for those with mobility or sight issues. See prg.aero/en/persons-reduced-mobility-and-orientation for full details. There are 20 contact points around the airport from which passengers with disabilities can call for assistance.

Accommodation

Choose your accommodation carefully, as very few have fully accessible facilities. Only the most expensive (and/or recently built) hotels have fully barrier-free rooms. Out in the sticks this is virtually unheard of.

MINES, VIEWING TOWERS & CASTLES

Making some visitor attractions accessible to all is simply beyond the abilities of even the most determined engineers. Mines, viewing towers with 200 steps and crumbing medieval fortresses probably aren't accessible in any country.

Travel in Prague

The official public-transport website lists all of the metro stations that can be used by visitors with a disability. See https://www.dpp.cz/cestovani/bezbarierove-cestovani/metro. The vast majority of stations now have lifts.

Senior Discounts

All people over 65, Czech or not, are eligible to 50% off public-transport fares across the country. Drivers and ticket sellers should offer you the saving automatically. Carry your passport as proof of age.

RESOURCES

Prague Wheelchair Users (presbariery.cz) Works to promote barrier-free architecture and improve the lives of people with disabilities. Consult the website for resources.

Czech Blind United (sons.cz) Represents the vision-impaired; provides information but no services.

VozejkMap (vozejkmap.cz) Provides maps of accessible places for people with mobility issues.

Kudyznudy (kudyznudy.cz) The official domestic-tourism website, in Czech; it lists many places open to visitors with disabilities.

WOMEN TRAVELLERS

Czech men are generally very respectful of women and you should have no problem in their company. Marauding international visitors on stag trips are a different matter. Avoid these guys if you can.

Czech society remains largely intolerant of foreign cultures, especially when it comes to people of different skin colour to them and Muslim visitors. Prague is the least problematic Czech city, but some locals' reactions to foreigners in smaller towns can be shocking.

Nuts & Bolts

OPENING HOURS

Banks 8am–5pm Monday to Friday

Bars Noon–2am

Cafes 8am–5pm

Clubs 11pm–4am Thursday to Saturday

Restaurants 11am–10pm

Supermarkets 7am–10pm

Shops 9am–5pm Monday to Friday, 9am–1pm Saturday

Toilets

Public toilets are difficult to find, especially outside Prague. Where you do find them, they are never free, most charging between 10Kč and 20Kč.

Weights & Measures

Czechia uses the metric system. Decimals are indicated by commas, thousands by points.

Water

Throughout Czechia, tap water is safe to drink and of very good quality.

GOOD TO KNOW

Time zone
CET/UTC +1 in winter,
CEST/ UTC +2 in summer

Country calling code
+42

Emergency number
112

Population
10.7 million

Electricity
Type E; 230V/50Hz

PUBLIC HOLIDAYS

There are 12 public holidays in Czechia. Some businesses and nonessential services may be closed on these days.

New Year's Day
1 January

Easter Monday
March/April

Labour Day
1 May

Liberation Day
8 May

Sts Cyril & Methodius Day
5 July

Jan Hus Day
6 July

Czech Statehood Day
28 September

Republic Day
28 October

Struggle for Freedom & Democracy Day
17 November

Christmas Eve
24 December

Christmas Day
25 December

St Stephen's Day
26 December

Language

Czech people generally have a good command of English, with German and Russian also widely spoken. Outside Prague the use of English is reduced, so a few key words and phrases will take you far. Let's get started.

Basics

Hello. Ahoj. *uh·hoy*
Goodbye. Na shledanou. *nuh·skhle·duh·noh*
Excuse me. Promiňte. *pro·min'·ten*
Sorry. Promiňte. *pro·min'·te*
Please. Prosím. *pro·seem*
Thank you. Děkuji. *dye·ku·yi*
Yes./No. Ano./Ne. *uh·no/ne*
How are you? Jak se máte? *yuhk se ma·te*
Fine. And you? Dobře. A vy? *dob·rzhe a vi*
What's your name? Jak se jmenujete? *yuhk se yme·nu·ye·te*
My name is ... Jmenuji se ... *yme·nu·yi se ...*
Do you speak English? Mluvíte anglicky? *mlu·vee·te uhn·glits·ki*
I don't understand. Nerozumím. *ne·ro·zu·meem*
One moment, please. Počkejte chvíli. *poch·key·te khvee·li*

Directions

Where's the (market)? Kde je (trh)? *gde ye (trh)*
What's the address? Jaká je adresa? *yuh·ka ye uh·dre·suh*
Can you show me (on the map)? Můžete mi to *moo·zhe·te mi to* ukázat (na mapě)? *moo·zhe·te mi to u·ka·zuht (nuh muh·pye)*

Signs

Vjezd Entrance
Východ Exit
Otevřeno Open
Zavřeno Closed
Zákazáno Prohibited
Toalety/WC Toilets
Páni/Muži Men
Dámy/Ženy Women

Time

What time is it? Kolik je hodin? *ko·lik ye ho·dyin*
It's (10) o'clock. Je (deset) hodin. *ye (de·set) ho·dyin*
Half past 10. Půl jedenácté. *pool ye·de·nats·tair* (lit: half eleven)
yesterday včera *fche·ruh*
today dnes *dnes*
tomorrow zítra *zee·truh*

Emergencies

Help! Pomoc! *po·mots*
Go away! Běžte pryč! *byezh·te prichl'm ill*
Call ...! Zavolejte ...! *zuh·vo·ley·te ...*
    a doctor lékaře *lair·kuh·rzhe*
    the police policii *po·li·tsi·yi*

Eating & Drinking

What would you recommend?
Co byste doporučil/doporučila (m/f)
tso bis·te do·po·ru·chil/do·po·ru·chi·luh
I'll have ... Dám si ... *dam si ...*
Cheers! Na zdraví! *nuh zdruh·vee*
That was delicious! To bylo lahodné!
to bi·lo luh·hod·nair
bill účet *oo·chet*
menu jídelníček *yee·del·nyee·chek*

NUMBERS

0 nula *nu·luh*
1 jeden *ye·den*
2 dva *dvuh*
3 tři *trzhi*
4 čtyři *chti·rzhi*
5 pět *pyet*
6 šest *shest*
7 sedm *se·dm*
8 osm *o·sm*
9 devět *de·vyet*
10 deset *de·set*

GOOD TO KNOW

Before Czechs start eating, they say Dobrou chuť! do·broh khut' (Bon appétit!), and before having a drink they toast with *Na zdraví! nuh zdruh·vee* (Cheers!). When making a toast, always look into the other person's eyes.

Word stress in Czech is easy – it's always on the first syllable of the word. Stress is marked with italics in the coloured pronunciation guides here.

Czech (Čeština *chesh·tyi·nuh*) belongs to the western branch of the Slavic language family, with Slovak and Polish as its closest relatives. It has approximately 12 million speakers.

Even though it sounds much like the English 'no', remember that the Czech word **ano** *uh·no* is actually the affirmative – 'yes'.

Czech Placenames

If you're having trouble with placenames and the locals don't understand you, practice your pronunciation. Here's a list of placenames you'll probably need while making your way around the Czechia – in particular, remember to say Praha *pruh·huh*, not 'Prague', when admiring the Golden City!

Brno *br·no*
České Budějovice *ches·kair bu·dye·yo·vi·tse*
Český Krumlov *ches·kee krum·lof*
Děčín *dye·cheen*
Hradec Králové *hruh·dets kra·lo·vair*
Karlovy Vary *kuhr·lo·vi vuh·ri*
Kutná Hora *kut·na ho·ruh*
Mělník *myel·neek*
Olomouc *o·lo·mohts*
Plzeň *pl·zen'*
Třebíč *trzhe·beech*
Telč *telch*

WHO SPEAKS CZECH?

Czech (Čeština *chesh·tyi·nuh*) belongs to the western branch of the Slavic language family, with Slovak and Polish as its closest relatives. It has approximately 12 million speakers.

Around **12 million** people speak Czech as a native language

Czech is a minority language in countries such as Poland, Serbia and Ukraine

THE PRAGUE & CZECHIA
STORYBOOK

Our writers delve deep into different aspects of Czech life

A History of Czechia in 15 Places
For more than a thousand years Czechia hs stood at the heart of European affairs.

Mark Baker

p294

Meet the Czechs
Under that blunt exterior, Czechs are friendly, generous people with a great sense of humour.

Iva Roze Skochová

p298

Architecture: The Battle over Communist Buildings
Decades after the fall of communism, Czech society remains divided on its architectural legacy.

Mark Baker

p300

Czech Humour: A Penchant for the Absurd
Czechs have a wonderfully irreverent sense of humour that infuses every aspect of day-to-day life.

Mark Baker

p304

Sport: Natural-Born Athletes
Sport plays a central role in Czech culture to an extent that visitors may find surprising

Mark Baker

p308

Czech Spa Culture
Why is Czechia such a special place when it comes to medical and wellness spas?

Mark Di Duca

p312

Industrial Relic Revival
There is a cultural resurgence in Czechia's post-mining landscapes

Becki Enright

p314

Statue of the Fighting Giant, Prague Castle (p56)

A HISTORY OF CZECHIA IN
15 PLACES

For more than a thousand years Bohemia and Moravia have stood at the heart of European affairs – both in good times and bad. Over the centuries, Prague has served at various times as Europe's leading city, while the territory of modern-day Czechia has found itself, reluctantly, at the middle of the continent's most destructive wars. By Mark Baker

THE HISTORY OF Prague and Czechia starts with the dramatic rise of Great Moravia and the Bohemian Kingdom around the turn of the first millennium and then, moving forward, reads like a ride on a roller-coaster. For much of the 14th century, under Emperor Charles IV, Prague served as the seat of the Holy Roman Empire – in effect, the capital of Europe as it existed at that time.

A century later, much of Bohemia and Moravia were laid to waste by the religious strife of the Hussite wars. The pattern repeated itself in the 16th century, when, under Emperor Rudolf II, Prague found itself as the capital of the sprawling Habsburg Empire.

And then came the wanton devastation across Europe of the Thirty Years' War, which began in 1618. Fast forward a couple of centuries and, in 1918, independent Czechoslovakia rose from the ashes of the old Austro-Hungarian Empire.

Just two decades later, the young country was tragically occupied by Nazi Germany. The horrors of WWII were followed by four decades of Soviet domination as part of the communist Eastern bloc. The peaceful anti-communist Velvet Revolution of 1989 allowed Czechia to start an optimistic new chapter as a parliamentary democracy and member of the European Union.

1. Dolní Věstonice
PALEOLITHIC PIECE OF ART

Incredibly, archaeological digs around this tiny village in Southern Moravia have revealed evidence of one of the oldest human settlements ever discovered. A small grouping of mammoth hunters apparently lived here more than 25,000 years ago, during the Upper Palaeolithic period of the Stone Age.

The early inhabitants left an eye-popping abundance of ancient artwork, including the famed *Venus of Dolní Věstonice,* a startling ceramic figurine of a nude woman, with large breasts and wide hips.

For more on Dolní Věstonice, see page 247.

2. Vyšehrad, Prague
FAIRY-TALE BEGINNING

Fittingly for a city that embraces so much mystery, the origins of Prague are shrouded in a fairy tale. Princess Libuše, the daughter of early ruler Krok, is said to have stood on a high hill one day in the 8th century and foretold of a glorious city that would one day become Prague. Legend has it this hill may have been Vyšehrad, an abandoned fortress on a scenic outcropping south of Prague Castle (across the river), though there's sadly scant archaeological evidence to support the story.

For more on Vyšehrad, see page 148.

3. Brno
MORAVIA'S HISTORIC MOMENT

Moravia often plays second fiddle to larger Bohemia, but Czechia's eastern province was the seat of one of the earliest and most powerful empires of the early Middle Ages. The Great Moravian Empire, in the 8th and 9th centuries, stretched far beyond Moravia's current borders. Brno, along with Znojmo and Olomouc, was one of the early capitals. Attesting to the importance of Great Moravia, the early, celebrated missionaries Cyril and Methodius travelled here in 863 CE to spread both the Christian liturgy and their Glagolitic script, the oldest known Slavic alphabet.

For more on Brno, see page 242.

4. Old Town Square, Prague
MARKETPLACE FOR CENTRAL EUROPE

Prague's Old Town Square has stood at the centre of the capital's commercial and urban activity since around the 10th century. Historically, the square benefitted from the city's position along major medieval trading routes across Europe, and the proceeds earned here over the generations helped to fund the magnificent buildings you see around the square and throughout the historic core. These days, Staromák – the square's nickname – is lined by some of Prague's most important buildings and remains at the heart of city life.

For more on Old Town Square, see page 81.

5. Charles Bridge, Prague
A 14TH-CENTURY SHOWPIECE

When construction of Prague's Charles Bridge began in 1357, the span was widely viewed as one of the engineering marvels of the known world. The starkly beautiful Gothic bridge, connecting the banks of the Vltava River, was seen as a fitting landmark for what was, under the rule of Holy Roman Emperor Charles IV, Europe's most important city. The baroque statues, which complete the bridge's aesthetic appeal, were not part of the original design, but added only a few centuries later.

For more on Charles Bridge, see page 68.

6. Kutná Hora
SOURCE OF SILVER WEALTH

The small, medieval town of Kutná Hora, east of Prague, incredibly once rivalled the capital in terms of wealth and importance. Enriched by the silver ore that ran through the surrounding hills, the town became the seat of the royal mint as early as the 14th century. The mines and mints here produced the silver groschen that circulated widely throughout Central Europe. Kutná Hora's ride ended by the 17th century, when the mines ran dry, though this silver legacy can be still seen in the surviving impressive churches and buildings.

For more on Kutná Hora, see page 219.

7. Prague Castle
SITE OF A TRAGIC DEFENESTRATION

Stately Prague Castle has been the heart of Czechia's storied history for more than 1000 years, though perhaps the castle's high point came at the turn of the 16th and 17th centuries, under the rule of Holy Roman Emperor Rudolf II. Rudolf's leadership brought widespread prosperity to Bohemia but failed to resolve bitter

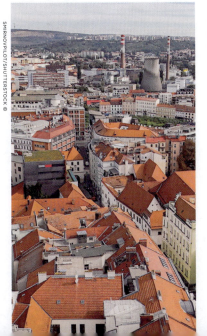

Brno (p242)

disputes at the time between Protestants and Catholics. In 1618, two Catholic governors were pushed from one of the castle's high windows by Protestants. The 'defenestration' precipitated a brutal war across Europe that would last three decades.

For more on Prague Castle, see page 56.

8. Josefov, Prague
JEWISH 'GOLDEN AGE'
Jews have lived in the territory of modern Czechia for centuries. Through the ages, Jewish settlements here have endured periods of hardship and persecution interspersed with decades of relative peace and prosperity. The 16th century is often considered to be a golden age for Prague's Jews, and the historic splendour of this time can still be seen in the surviving buildings of the city's former Jewish ghetto, Josefov, adjacent to the Old Town. Tour the synagogues and Old Jewish Cemetery to appreciate the community's size and influence in this period.

For more on Josefov, see page 252.

9. Slavkov u Brna
A SLAUGHTER OF EMPIRES
Slavkov (better known abroad as Austerlitz) and its surrounds, near Brno, were almost as significant in the Napoleonic Wars of the 19th century as the feared Frenchman himself. As the setting for the pivotal Battle of the Three Emperors, in 1805, it was here that Napoleon defeated the combined (and superior) forces of Austrian emperor Ferdinand I and Russian tsar Alexander I. The battle was later vividly described by Russian writer Leo Tolstoy in his *War and Peace*.

For more on Slavkov u Brna, see page 252.

10. Olomouc
FRANZ JOSEPH ASSUMES THE THRONE
Unlike much of the rest of Bohemia and Moravia, the stately college town of Olomouc served as a bastion of support for the ruling Habsburg family of the Austrian Empire for centuries. During the revolution of 1848, when the emerging middle classes across the empire revolted against their rulers, the Habsburgs fled here for their personal safety. Austrian emperor Franz Joseph I was even crowned at Olomouc's Archbishop's Palace that year at the tender age of 18.

For more on Olomouc, see page 265.

11. Wenceslas Square, Prague
BIRTH OF CZECHOSLOVAKIA
The cataclysm of WWI splintered the old Austro-Hungarian Empire into several smaller, independent states. These included a newly minted Czechoslovakia that brought together for the first time the Czech lands (the western provinces of Bohemia and Moravia) and Slovakia to the east. From near the top of Prague's Wenceslas Square, Czech historian Alois Jirásek read aloud the declaration of independence to cheering throngs on 28 October 1918. Though Czechoslovakia, as an entity, no longer exists, the date is still celebrated as a national holiday.

For more on Wenceslas Square, see page 100.

Slavkov u Brna (p252)

Terezín Fortress (p161)

12. Terezín
HOLOCAUST FORTRESS

Terezín (also known as Theresienstadt) began life in the 18th century as a garrison for Austrian soldiers. During WWII, occupying Nazi Germany transformed the fortress town into a concentration camp and weigh station for tens of thousands of Jewish prisoners who would later be sent off to be murdered at Auschwitz and other extermination camps. Around 35,000 men, women and children died here of hunger, disease or suicide before they could be transported. The town has been preserved much as it was during the war.

For more on Terezín, see page 161.

13. Plzeň
LIBERATED BY THE US ARMY

At the start of WWII, Bohemia and Moravia were occupied by Nazi Germany (Slovakia became an independent Nazi-puppet) and remained under German domination until the final days of the conflict, in May 1945. Much of Czechoslovakia was liberated by the Soviet Red Army. The exception was the extreme western part of the country, around Plzeň, which was freed by units of the US Army, led by General George S Patton. The people of Plzeň have never forgotten and celebrate the liberation with a festival in early May.

For more on Plzeň, see page 184.

14. Národní Třída, Prague
PEOPLE, POWER, REVOLUTION

Communist governments in Central and Eastern Europe fell like dominoes during the historic year of 1989, but none of the people-power revolutions that year captured the world's imagination quite like Czechoslovakia's peaceful Velvet Revolution. The demonstrations started on 17 November, when security forces violently put down a student protest on central Národní třída, one of the capital's main boulevards. Within six weeks, the communist government had been deposed and playwright-dissident Václav Havel installed as the country's first post-communist president.

For more on Národní třída, see page 95.

15. Villa Tugendhat, Brno
DISSOLUTION OF CZECHOSLOVAKIA

Brno had a reputation in the 1920s as a centre for modern architecture, and the finest example can be seen in this family villa, designed by modern master Mies van der Rohe for Greta and Fritz Tugendhat in 1930. In 1992, as Czechoslovakia was heading toward a 'velvet' divorce, Czech prime minister Václav Klaus and his Slovak counterpart, Vladimir Mečiar, chose the Tugendhat's shady garden as the venue to hammer out the final details of the breakup. Entry to the villa (and garden) is by guided tour, booked in advance.

For more on Villa Tugendhat, see page 246.

MEET THE CZECHS

Expect to be treated with suspicion, even distrust. But under that tough, blunt exterior, Czechs are friendly, generous people with a great sense of humour. Disclaimer: it does take a lot of time and beer to get there. Iva Roze Skochová introduces her people.

AN ITALIAN FRIEND recently returned from his first trip to Prague and he was perplexed. 'The city is incredibly beautiful. But why are the people so…grim?' he asked. To be fair, grim is one of the gentler verdicts I hear about my people.

Usually, it's 'rude' or 'miserable', or at the very least 'blunt'. And they have a point. Czechia consistently ranks low in surveys like 'the friendliest countries' or 'the most empathetic people in the world'. Many have tried, and failed, to import optimism and positive thinking into this region since communism crumbled in 1989. It's proven far more difficult than importing democracy and capitalism. Don't even try. Instead, try to find some amusement in the gloom. Yes, the beer helps.

When you switch into the 'glass half empty' mode, beware – you might even enjoy it. Before you know it, you might be sitting in a local pub drinking your fifth plzeň, or Pilsner Urquell, with Honza or Jiří, commiserating about the tram being three minutes late.

If there's one quality that Czechs truly value, it's being on time. Annoyingly so. If you invite people over at 8pm, be ready for some to show up at 7.45, while other guests might be stressing out because they are running a few minutes late. Probably because of the tram. The country happens to have an excellent public transport system, which, of course, doesn't stop the locals from complaining about it.

Complaining is a national sport, an ancient craft passed from generation to generation as a way to bond with thy neighbour. Bragging about how much you love your job or how talented your kids are is often met with an eye roll.

Smiles and light-hearted pleasantries don't come easily to the Czechs, so you might be fooled into thinking etiquette isn't important at all. And you might be wrong. It's surprisingly important here to have 'good manners'.

This can mean any-thing from taking your shoes off in someone's home and handling your cutlery properly to accepting copious amounts of unsolicited advice and predictions of calamity (your new business venture is naive and bound to fail) while offering up your seat to the elderly or pregnant.

Granted, the last thing you need after a long day dealing with grumpy people is an eager teenager courteously springing up from his seat because they cast you as 'old enough to need to sit'. But hey, at least the tram arrived on time, am I right?

> **RELIGION**
>
> Czechia is one of the least religious countries in the world and getting more so with each new generation. Young Czech people are the least religious in Europe: 91% of 16- to 29-year-olds say they have no religion.

NEW-FOUND FREEDOMS

I grew up in the highlands in the middle of what used to be Czechoslovakia, sheltered from just about everything deemed dangerous: high winds, high fashion, Western music and most forms of freedom.

I was 12 years old when communism ended and that's when everything changed. Our history books at school were hastily replaced with updated ones. It wasn't mandatory to learn Russian anymore. Our Russian teachers became English teachers overnight, although they were just a couple chapters ahead of us. Most of us didn't know what to do with all this newfound freedom but we were hungry to travel and see new places. Especially places that had high winds and high fashion. I was 17 the first time I saw an ocean. Coming from a sheltered, landlocked place, this was a life-changing experience. I was hooked. Out of all the freedoms out there, the freedom to see an ocean is still my favourite.

1970s Communist-style building, Prague (p48)
IOANNIS7/SHUTTERSTOCK ©

ARCHITECTURE: THE BATTLE OVER COMMUNIST BUILDINGS

Prague and Czechia are filled with impressive historic architecture, but opinions get heated over whether communist-era buildings are worth preserving. By Mark Baker

A HIGHLIGHT OF any trip to Czechia is the chance to get up close and personal with some exquisitely preserved examples of European architecture through the ages. A trip here is not unlike attending a university seminar on historic architecture – but with the chance to drink beer in the classroom as well.

Thanks to the fact that much of the country was spared significant war damage over the centuries, visitors are treated to a nearly unbroken line of architectural development. The earliest surviving buildings – from the Romanesque period around the turn of the first millennium – seamlessly give way to the grand 13th- and 14th-century Gothic structures of Prague, like Prague Castle or the Old Town Hall. Later centuries brought the symmetrical, Italian-influenced Renaissance and lavish, hypnotic baroque favoured by the Catholic Church and Habsburg monarchy. Czechia is also brimming with examples of revivalist 'neo' styles – such as 'neo-Renaissance' and 'Neoclassical' – that were all the rage in the 19th century. Fans of sumptuous, early-20th-century art nouveau need look no further than Prague's Municipal House to get their fix. Cities like Brno and Zlín were hotbeds of 1920s' functionalism and early-Modern. Brno's ground-breaking Villa Tugendhat predated by decades the massively popular 'mid-century modern' style that wouldn't come to the rest of the world until the 1950s and '60s.

Czechs certainly understand the value of historic architecture and the necessity of preserving old buildings. That is, however, until you get to the legacy of buildings designed and built during the communist period from the late 1940s through the 1980s. That's where the consensus on preserving the past starts to fray and opinions on aesthetics start to get heated.

More than three decades since the fall of communism, Czech society remains deeply divided on the architectural legacy of communism. Some people want to fix up and preserve the buildings for practical reasons and as a reminder of the country's recent history; others want to rip everything down and pretend communism never happened.

Máj department store

What is Communist Architecture?

The earliest examples of communist-era architecture, from the late 1940s and 1950s, were built in the style of Socialist-Realism and imported directly from the Soviet Union.

Socialist-Realist buildings tend to be grossly oversized and marked with mosaics and decorations that uphold the ideological line at the time of glorifying workers and peasants. One of the best-known Socialist-Realist buildings in Prague is the 1956 Hotel International in the district of Dejvice, with its soaring towers, mosaics and impressive interiors.

Olomouc's unique Socialist-Realist astronomical clock, built on the face of the town hall in 1955, provides a marked contrast to Prague's much-older astronomical clock. Instead of a parade of figurines from the Middle Ages, as in Prague, Olomouc's clock features a surprisingly modern display of industrial workers and tradesmen.

In the 1970s, Czech architects started to look more toward international trends and crafted their own brand of communist-era 'brutalism' – and this is the style Czechs most closely associate with communism. Brutalism takes its name from the French term for raw concrete *(béton brut)* and was extremely popular around the world (Boston's City Hall and London's Barbican Centre are good examples). Czech brutalism is similar to its international cousins in that the buildings typically reject decorative elements and instead highlight less aesthetically pleasing aspects, such as the construction materials used to build it (often raw concrete or steel) or details like exposed pipes and ducts. The conceptual idea behind brutalism was to reveal the buildings' innards in order to make them more transparent. In reality, brutalist buildings are hard to love. Britain's King Charles III (then as Prince Charles) once famously called one these buildings 'a monstrous carbuncle'.

Czechia is filled with excellent examples of brutalism. In Prague alone, both the prominent Kotva and Máj (located at the corner of Národní and Spálená streets) department stores are pure 1970s brutalism. Máj is said (charitably) to be modelled on Paris's Centre Pompidou. The former Hotel Intercontinental in Prague's Old Town is another brutalist gem (or eyesore). Hotel Thermal in Karlovy Vary – host venue for the city's international film festival – might well be the country's best-known brutalist building.

War over Memory

Like urban warfare, the battles over whether to preserve these buildings are often fought house-to-house.

In 2019, the Kotva department store finally gained protected status from the Czech Ministry of Culture, ensuring it cannot be knocked down.

In 2024, the Máj department store reopened as a combined shopping and amusement centre, called 'Máj Národní' (complete with two fighter planes comically sporting butterfly wings – the work of artist David Černý – affixed to the building's exterior). Máj's repurposing (not to mention those butterflies) would have shocked the building's original communist-era architects.

Czechia's cultural officials say they take several factors into consideration when deciding whether to grant a building protected status. These include things like how important the structure was at the time it was built and how effectively it articulates a particular style.

The real battle, though, seems to have little to do with the quality of the buildings themselves, but rather the continual tug-of-war concerning the legacy of communism itself. Some three decades after it ended, a significant proportion of Czech society continues to see nothing redeeming about an authoritarian system that controlled their lives and limited their freedoms. For them, the buildings are constant reminders of a corrupt and immoral system. Local architects designing today, they say, would be better off adopting the best of contemporary styles or turning the clock back to the last great Czech architectural iteration: functionalism from the 1920s.

On the other side, preservationists point out that fashions invariably change over time, and what one generation considers to be hideous can be viewed by later generations as something beautiful (or at least interesting). After all, the baroque statues on Charles Bridge were also once considered eyesores – the work of overzealous Catholic overlords despoiling a dignified Gothic bridge. These days, of course, it's exactly that tension between Gothic and baroque that gives the bridge its unique energy and beauty.

'THE REAL BATTLE SEEMS TO HAVE LITTLE TO DO WITH THE QUALITY OF THE BUILDINGS THEMSELVES, BUT RATHER THE CONTINUAL TUG-OF-WAR UNDERWAY CONCERNING THE LEGACY OF COMMUNISM ITSELF.'

Hotel International (p132), Prague
PETR PE/SHUTTERSTOCK ©

CZECH HUMOUR: A PENCHANT FOR THE ABSURD

While it might not immediately jump off the page, Czechs have a unique and wonderfully irreverent sense of humour that infuses every aspect of day-to-day life. By Mark Baker

CZECH HUMOUR IS hard to describe in a few words without resorting to generalisations, but the local wit has much in common with British humour – think Monty Python – in that it's dry, dark and drawn to absurdity. There's rarely any room for pathos, hypocrisy or overt sentimentality.

It's no coincidence that old British TV series, such as *Monty Python's Flying Circus*, remain wildly popular with local audiences. Sir Michael Palin, one of the members of the original Monty Python troupe, even once famously repaid the compliment, remarking that Czechia, among nations, may have the world's greatest sense of humour. Speaking to British television in 2019, shortly after being knighted for service to culture, Palin said Czechs simply 'have a feeling that everything is up for laughter'. He said many countries have a 'laughter ceiling', meaning that some sensitive subjects remain off-limits. 'But not in the Czech Republic'.

This local appreciation of the absurd was on full display a few years ago in a TV poll where Czechs were asked to name the 'greatest' Czech person who'd ever lived. Instead of selecting one of several deserving figures, such as Emperor Charles IV, Jan Hus, Tomáš Masaryk or Václav Havel, viewers instead overwhelmingly went with a fictional, comical everyman named Jára Cimrman, created in the 1960s for a popular radio comedy. Carrying the farce a step further, Cimrman was later disqualified for the honour, because he had never actually 'lived'.

Lampooning the Empire

It's not clear just when and how Czechs developed this penchant for irreverence. Certainly, early historical figures like Charles IV or the ever-stern Jan Hus weren't exactly famous for their great sense of humour. Czech wit really came about during the late 19th and early 20th centuries, when the emerging nation found itself trapped within an ageing Austro-Hungarian Empire. The Habsburg monarchy, already widely seen as a holdover from the Middle Ages, was rife with the kind of empty symbolism,

STORYBOOK

hypocrisy and stale tradition that was ripe for lampooning.

In his 1921 comic classic, *The Good Soldier Švejk,* Czech author Jaroslav Hašek took full aim at the absurdities of life under the empire with his epic tale of a Czech 'Forrest Gump' figure who manages to ride out the horrors of WWI through sheer stupidity (or perhaps through intelligence masquerading as stupidity?). While not many Czechs identify with the dopey Švejk – the novel's central character – they certainly recognise the dire (and ludicrous) situation the nation found itself in during that war, when Czechs were called on to defend to death an archaic empire built largely on bombast. Hašek appeared to be saying that idiocy was the only rational response to the situation.

Right from the book's first sentence, readers know they're in for a comic ride. It begins with an immortal line spoken by Švejk's cleaner, Mrs Muller. She remarks: 'And so they've killed our Ferdinand'. Here, she's referring to the tragic assassination in Sarajevo in 1914 of the Austrian archduke Franz Ferdinand and his wife that sparked World War I and would drag the Czechs into war. Švejk responds with his characteristic cluelessness. He apparently has no idea which Ferdinand she might talking about: 'Which Ferdinand, Mrs Muller? I know of two. One is a messenger at Prusa's, the chemist's, who once drank a bottle of hair oil there by mistake. And the other is Ferdinand Kokoška, who collects dog manure. Neither of them is any loss'.

Humour as a Tonic

Dark humour was a necessary and healthy reaction to the difficult years of the Nazi occupation during WWII and of Soviet-imposed communism after the war. In the first decade of communism, during the 1950s, most of the jokes aimed at the system were forced underground and shared only between close friends and family members.

In one of his early books, fittingly titled *The Joke,* from 1967, Czech author Milan Kundera writes of what could happen when a private joke went public. In the book, the main character, a young man named Ludvik, feels rejected by his girlfriend, a devoted communist. In a fit of pique, he sends her a postcard emblazoned with a tongue-in-cheek reference to Marx and, in the process, ends up changing his life forever. Echoing Marx's famous line that 'Religion is the opiate of the people', Ludvik writes jokingly that 'Optimism is the opiate of mankind! A healthy spirit stinks of stupidity! Long live Trotsky!' Things proceed poorly from there.

A brief political thaw and easing of censorship in the mid-1960s allowed, once again, for a fuller, public display of Czech humour. Film directors from the period, like Miloš Forman and Jiří Menzel, skilfully tiptoed around existing restrictions and crafted masterpieces like *The Fireman's Ball* (Hoří, má panenko), *Loves of a Blonde* (Lásky jedné plavovlásky) and *Closely Watched Trains* (Ostře sledované vlaky), which went on to win major prizes around the world.

These films drew on classic, bawdy elements of Czech humour, the slapstick and appreciation of the absurd, while also telling stories that moved the heart and gently took the ruling communists to task. Forman's *Loves of a Blonde,* for example, takes place in a bleak factory town where lonely women work dull, endless shifts as shoemakers. The factory director decides to try to improve morale by inviting over a group of soldiers from a nearby base for a party. Things don't go according to plan. The soldiers are older and homelier than expected (many are married). In a classic comic scene from the film, one of the soldiers is so eager to rip off his wedding ring, that he pulls a bit too hard. The ring then rolls all the way across the dance floor and up to the shoes of one of the young women waiting to dance

Joking under Duress

Czechs' innate sense of comic creativity helped them immeasurably to cope with their darkest moment in modern history: the Soviet-led Warsaw Pact invasion of August 1968. The Kremlin had ordered tanks and troops over the border to put down a series of political and economic reforms that the Russians deemed too liberal. With the Czechoslovak Army confined to barracks, the general population did what they could to thwart the invaders. They painted over street signs and changed road-markers in order to confuse the Soviet tank drivers.

The period of 'normalisation' that followed the invasion put an end to the manic creativity of the 1960s, but elements of classic Czech humour thrived in the 1970s and '80s, and films from this period remain popular today. While directly criticising the Soviet Union was off-limits, film directors instead poked fun at social conventions of life within Czechoslovakia. One classic from the period, *Run, Waiter, Run! (Vrchní, prchni!)*, starring comedic icons Josef Abrhám and Zdeněk Svěrák, follows a frustrated bookstore manager (Abrhám) who concocts a crazy scheme to earn money by masquerading as a pay waiter and pocket-ing people's tabs in restaurants. Needless to say the deception lands him in hot water – most famously in a scene where Svěrák's character recognises him on the street and Abrhám comically modifies his voice to evade detection. The conceit is so ridiculous (a fundamental element of local humour that endures to this day), that it's laugh-out-loud funny.

Wit & Wisdom of David Černý

Something of this signature Czech cheekiness – sharpened to make larger political or cultural points – can be seen around Prague today in the various installations of local artist David Černý. Černý gained fame in the years after the 1989 Velvet Revolution for painting over a sombre Soviet WWII war memorial in Prague – an old Russian tank – in a shocking shade of pink. With this thin coating of paint, Černý covered over generations of Soviet-era myth-making and machismo surrounding the war. Some people, naturally, complained the act was irreverent and sought to punish the artist, but most people simply, instinctively, laughed it off. The tank was suddenly transformed into a monument to Soviet hypocrisy.

Highlighting the absurdities of life under communism was a common early theme of Černý's, such as with his big bronze sculpture, *Quo Vadis*, which stands today in the garden of the German embassy in Malá Strana (sadly off limits to the public). The work depicts an old East German car, a Trabant, standing on four legs. It recalls the dramatic days of late 1989, when thousands of East Germans fled in their cars to Prague on their way to new lives in West Germany. Here, the artist mocks the old regime and calls out the obvious irony of people bolting communism in their own decrepit, communist-made vehicles.

Černý can be just as tough on Czech heroes and Czech history. One of his most beloved works, *Horse (Kůň)*, hangs from a ceiling in the Lucerna shopping passage, just off Wenceslas Square, for all to see. In this piece, he's placed one of the country's patron saints, St Wenceslas, ludicrously seated astride an obviously dead horse (complete with tongue hanging out). Another classic Černý work, *Streams (Proudy)*, in Malá Strana, depicts two men standing and urinating into a basin shaped like the Czech Republic. It's shockingly anatomically correct.

> 'THE [MOVIE'S] CONCEIT IS SO RIDICULOUS (A FUNDAMENTAL ELEMENT OF LOCAL HUMOUR THAT ENDURES TO THIS DAY), THAT IT'S LAUGH-OUT-LOUD FUNNY.'

SPORT:
NATURAL-BORN ATHLETES

Czechs are not just inveterate sportspeople, but sport itself plays a central role in Czech culture to an extent that visitors may find surprising. By Mark Baker

CZECHS APPEAR TO be natural-born athletes. Starting from a very young age, children, through organised school trips, are introduced to activities like hiking and skiing. By the time a child has reached their early teens, they may have already started to specialise in a particular sport like gymnastics, tennis, volleyball, football (soccer) or, especially, ice hockey. High school students who show promise in any of these sports are invariably promoted to play in the various developmental leagues, supported by the biggest sports clubs and national associations.

This strong emphasis on sport and athletic achievement has its roots in the Czech national revival of the 19th century and widespread efforts across society at the time to support and build an independent Czech (as opposed to Austrian) identity within the ruling Austro-Hungarian Empire. Bohemia's leading sporting association from that time, Sokol, was founded in 1862 with the twin aims of promoting the benefits of physical activity and fostering a budding Czech national identity through athletic prowess and achievement.

After the country won its independence in 1918, Czechoslovak officials poured significant resources into the national Olympic team as a way of raising the young country's profile on the global stage. During the communist period, the authorities turned once again to sport – this time to a series of mass spectacles of synchronised gymnastics – known as Spartakiads – as a way of legitimising their rule and promoting national cohesiveness. These Spartakiads were held at five-year intervals, from 1955 to 1985, at Prague's massive Strahov Stadium (just west of the top station of the Petřín funicular railway). They were phenomenally popular (or at least well-attended); the Spartakiad in 1960, for example, involved 750,000 participants and was witnessed by more than 2 million spectators.

After the fall of communism in 1989, the Spartakiads were eventually abandoned (and Strahov Stadium has since fallen into ruin), but sport remains central to the country's heart and identity. For proof, one need look no further than the way the country's streets and pubs empty out whenever Czechia or individual Czech athletes compete in an important international competition, like the Olympic Games, Wimbledon, the World Ice Hockey Championships or the FIFA World Cup. The entire country remains glued to the TV, and national pride invariably rises or falls according to the result.

My Heart Belongs to Hockey

Czechs play and excel at many different sports, including cycling, kayaking, skiing, tennis, football and speed-skating (Martina Sáblíková is one of the best speed-skaters in Olympic history), but the nation's heart belongs to ice hockey. It's not entirely clear how Czechs settled on hockey as their national sport, but the experience of guiding a puck along a frozen pond in winter is universal for local kids – mostly boys but an increasing number of girls – growing up in a cold climate.

Czechoslovakia (and later Czechia) translated this love of hockey into genuine global success on the rink. Since the debut of the annual World Hockey Championships in 1920, the Czechoslovak and Czech men's teams have won gold around a dozen times – most recently in 2024 – and taken home more than 40 medals. The Czech women's team hasn't enjoyed quite the same level of success, but they have won bronze medals at two recent Ice Hockey World Championships (2022, 2023) and looks to have a bright future.

Czechia's successes are no doubt rooted in the competitive nature of the junior leagues all the way up to the country's premier league, the Extraliga, where perennial powers like HC Sparta Praha and HC Kometa Brno often battle it out for the top spot. Czech players are staples on the rosters of many teams in the North American National Hockey League (NHL). Past greats – still household names – include Jaromír Jágr (b 1972), who won the Stanley Cup with Pittsburgh in 1991 and '92. Dominik Hašek (b 1965), the 'Dominator', was once regarded as the world's best goaltender after winning a Stanley Cup with the Detroit Red Wings in 2001.

Ice hockey plays such an important role in the country's psyche that it's indelibly linked to the most important political and historical moments. At the 1969 World Ice Hockey Championships in Sweden, the Czechoslovak men's team stunningly defeated the Soviet Union twice. The final victory, 4-3 on 28 March 1969, set off delirious riots on Prague's Wenceslas Square and all around the country. The championship came just seven months after the Soviet-led Warsaw Pact invaded Czechoslovakia to crush the country's budding political and economic reforms; emotions on both sides were running hot.

At the 1998 Winter Olympic Games in Nagano, Japan, the Czech men's team repeated that feat, beating the rival Russian Federation by a score of 1-0 to win the gold medal. The country erupted with joy and, once again, Wenceslas Square was flooded with revellers. Ecstatic fans climbed atop Myslbek's famous statue of St Wenceslas at the upper end of the square.

Masters of Tennis

If Czechs have a second-favourite sport, it would probably be tennis. Nearly every park or field of green has a court nearby. Promising players are typically identified at a young age and steered into highly competitive local and regional tournaments as a launchpad for the international game.

Similar to hockey, Czechs have converted their love of the sport into phenomenal success on the world stage. Indeed, two of the all-time greatest players, Ivan Lendl (b 1960) and Martina Navrátilová (b 1956), honed their craft here before moving on to global dominance. Lendl commanded the men's circuit for much of the 1980s, winning a total of 11 Grand Slam titles and participating in some 19 finals matches (a record only broken in recent years by Roger Federer). Navrátilová's feats are, if anything, even more impressive. In the late 1970s and throughout the 1980s, she won some 18 Grand Slam singles titles, including a whopping nine victories at Wimbledon, the last coming in 1990. At one point she won six Grand Slam singles titles in a row.

Czechs, particularly female players, continue to perform well in international matches. Two national players currently rank among the world's top players. Barbora Krejčíková took first at Wimbledon in 2024, carrying on what by now has become an annual Czech tradition on grass – countrywoman Markéta Vondroušová won the same tournament just a year earlier 2023.

Planning an Active Holiday

Visitors to the country are warmly encouraged to share in Czechs' love of sport. Thousands of kilometres of marked hiking and cycling paths crisscross Bohemia and Moravia and invite endless exploration.

Local's fondness for skiing has resulted in the country having several decent resorts, including at Špindlerův Mlýn in North Bohemia – arguably the best of the resorts. In terms of other participation sports, there are always tennis, golf and beach volleyball. Visitors can also try their hand (or foot) at nohejbal, a uniquely Czech fusion of football and tennis that was first played here in the 1920s.

Czechia is also an excellent destination for spectator sports. The professional ice hockey season runs from September to April and the quality of play is high. The top-league Extraliga's 14 teams are spread out among big cities throughout the country, including Prague, Brno, Olomouc, Karlovy Vary, České Budějovice and Plzeň. Tickets are affordable and often easy to snag mid-season (ticket availability tends to dry up during playoff time).

Attending a football match is also a fun way to spend time and gain insight into the local culture. Czechs' fondness for their national team waxes and wanes in step with how the team performs. The golden age for the men's team arguably came in the late 1990s and early 2000s. In 1996, the Czechs made it to the finals of the UEFA Euro tournament, before losing 2-1 to Germany in a nail-biter at Wembley Stadium. A few years later, in 2004, the national team went on a historic run and nearly won it all before being knocked out in the semi-finals by eventual champs, Greece. These days, the men's team hovers somewhere in the middle tier of world rankings and doesn't garner nearly the attention it used to. The Czech women's team has improved in recent years but, at the time of writing, has not yet qualified for a major international tournament.

Despite the ups and downs of the national squad, Czechia's leading professional football league, the Chance Liga (First League), is highly competitive. In recent years, the 16-team league has been dominated by Prague's own AC Sparta Praha, though the capital's second team, SK Slavia Praha, and FC Viktoria Plzeň usually make a credible showing. The season runs from August to May. As with ice hockey, tickets are affordable and easy to get mid-season.

Of course, football is played at all levels all around the country. Often the best matches – and the best evenings out – are spent in smaller stadiums, holding a beer and cheering on the local heroes.

'ICE HOCKEY PLAYS SUCH AN IMPORTANT ROLE IN THE COUNTRY'S PSYCHE THAT IT'S INDELIBLY LINKED TO THE MOST IMPORTANT POLITICAL AND HISTORICAL MOMENTS.'

VITALII VITLEO/SHUTTERSTOCK ©

Colonnade, Mariánské Lázně (p178)
PETERI/SHUTTERSTOCK ©

CZECH SPA CULTURE

Why is Czechia such a special place when it comes to medical and wellness spas? By Marc Di Duca

IN 2021, THREE spas in West Bohemia – Karlovy Vary, Mariánské Lázně and Františkovy Lázně – were added to UNESCO's list of World Cultural Heritage Sites. This acknowledged the Czechs' position as a European spa superpower. But just what is 'spa culture'?

Why So Many Spas?

At the last count, there were officially 30 spa towns in Czechia, from big, brash Karlovy Vary to tiny Mšené-lázně, northwest of Prague. But why does this small country have so many? It's all to do with geology – mineralised water rises in many parts of Bohemia and Moravia where volcanic activity millions of years ago pushed minerals close to the earth's surface. Water is the basic ingredient at every spa, as well as mineralised mud and the natural CO_2 gas that rises with the water. One ingredient that has nothing to do with mineral-rich H_2O is the air – some spa towns, such as Lázně Kynžvart, are so-called climatic spas, where doctors can prescribe exercise in the pristine air as a procedure.

The all-important water differs immensely from town to town, sometimes from spring to spring within a single town. Karlovy Vary has its sulphurous hot jets, Mariánské Lázně has sweet, gaseous springs, while in Luhačovice mineral-rich *aqua mineralis* gurgles gently to the surface.

Mariánské Lázně has some springs that are over 90% gas. This is used for various treatments, such as gas baths, wraps and even scary-sounding gas injections.

Medical vs Wellness

Many foreigners from countries without a spa tradition often become confused about what they might experience at a Czech spa. Those anticipating hot-stone massages and chocolate wraps amid scented candles and soothing oriental music may be shocked to encounter busy white-coated staff, daunting syringes and weirdly vibrating electronic devices. Most spas in Czechia are medical spas that often treat locals for a whole medical dictionary of ailments. Wellness is seen as a completely separate product at Czech spas, some of which do offer a wide range of relaxing experiences. Many procedures, such as mineral baths, overlap between the two. The spas also usually offer sessions that have little to do with either, such as physiotherapy, diet advice and even Nordic Walking classes.

The Spa Day

Things kick off early, typically around 6.30am when the first baths are filled and the first masseurs oil up their palms. This early start has a reason – spa procedures typically lower blood pressure, meaning many spa guests are napping by mid-afternoon.

Throughout the morning, spa-goers are bathed and wrapped, dunked and jabbed, pummelled and rubbed until they've worked up a big appetite for lunch. Some users have prescribed diets, others make full use of the buffet, including the dessert trolley.

Some guests still undergo procedures after lunch but by around 3pm it's all over.

Most medical staff are on their way home by then, leaving guests to stroll in the ubiquitous spa park, take part in activities, such as city tours or lectures, and generally take it easy. Dinner involves another full-on buffet, after which many spas have some kind of cultural programme, such as a lobby bar band, dancing or other entertainment. Then it's early to bed for the 6.30 start next day.

Spa doctors recommend two to four weeks for the spa life to have an effect on most ailments. A month, with a minimum of four procedures a day, equates to a total of 120 treatments!

Illustrious Visitors

The golden days of the Central European spas were definitely the late 19th century and the early decades of the 20th century, when anyone who was anyone came to take the waters in some of the most fashionable and grand places on the continent. Edward VII, the British king, visited Mariánské Lázně a total of nine times; Kafka spent a miserable few days there; and even Mark Twain published his experiences in the town in a London magazine in an article called 'The Tramp Abroad Again'. Goethe took the cure in Karlovy Vary a whopping 13 times, Peter the Great turned up there in 1711 and 1712, Sisi (aka Empress Elizabeth of Austria) also sipped the scalding waters, and many a Hollywood star has crumpled pillows in KV during the international film festival (which, incidentally, originated in Mariánské Lázně).

Most other spas have similarly glitzy guestbooks, though during the communist decades the spas were largely reserved for worker recreation.

Spa on Prescription

Most outsiders are astounded to learn that Czechs can be prescribed a two-week stay at a spa by a doctor, essentially for free as part of their health-insurance plan. This often includes three meals a day, use of all facilities, such as swimming pools and gyms, and four or five procedures a day. Normally Czechs have to pay a supplement to avoid being billeted with a complete stranger in one room, but that is usually it. The spas have similar agreements with health-insurance companies in some other countries, such as Germany, and states in the Middle East.

Issues Facing Czech Spas

All the spas in Bohemia and Moravia underwent renovation in the post-communist period, most bringing standards back up to their pre-WWII level. The industry witnessed a boom after the millennium, with Russians and Germans flocking to the relatively inexpensive but newly renovated spa hotels. However, despite UNESCO listings, the spas have had a rough ride of late. The COVID-19 pandemic hit hard and, before the damage had been fully assessed, the Russian clientele evaporated following the Kremlin's invasion of Ukraine. The spas are now in the process of looking for new markets, most vigorously in the Middle East.

Colours of Ostrava music festival (p272)
BECKI ENRIGHT/LONELY PLANET ©

INDUSTRIAL RELIC REVIVAL

Colourful, music-pumping festivals and a striking cultural resurgence can be found in Czechia's post-mining landscapes. By Becki Enright

THE SOUND OF revelry reverberates through the protruding industrial steelwork skeleton of Dolní Vítkovice, a collection of jutting smokestacks, gasometers and furnaces wedged with lawn lounges, beach bars and jumbo pipe-lined pathways. It's hard to imagine that this site was a smoking, smouldering coalmine and iron-forging behemoth between 1828 and 1998. Today, the grind and grime of metallurgy are replaced by an 18-stage rhapsody of folk and gypsy jazz, Balkan beats and blues, pop, rock and megastar headliners when it transforms into the Colours of Ostrava music festival every July.

Czechia's heritage is a visual array spanning medieval strongholds to grand Empire cities, with architectural masterpieces from the Gothic, Renaissance and baroque to the art nouveau and modernist, alongside a natural assembly of mountains and caves, lakes and gorges, vineyards and forests, bio reserves and national parks. But its unexpected side is its long and embedded mining history as a European industrial powerhouse, which has also shaped its landscape.

Mining in the western Ore Mountain region began as early as the 12th century, becoming a European hub of silver extraction. The town of Jáchymov rose to prominence in the 16th century, minting the silver 'thaler' coin currency on which countries worldwide modelled theirs, including the first US dollar. History took a darker turn here with the discovery of uranium ore, and communist Czechoslovakia supplying the Soviet Union during the Cold War arms race after WWII, using political prisoners as forced labourers. The Red Tower of Death in the nearby town of Dolní Žďár is a former forced-labour-camp uranium-sorting house; today, it is a National Cultural Monument honouring those who suffered there.

The discovery of black coal in the northeastern Moravian-Silesian city of Ostrava in 1763 propelled the city into an Austro-Hungarian Empire bulwark; by 1828, the Dolní Vítkovice ironworks were pumping out the materials for the bourgeoning railroad network, all while a slate-mining industry boom in the region was producing the core roofing material for Empire construction. Communism once again kept the pedal on, and Ostrava became a workers' 'city of coal and iron' and the 'steel heart of the republic'.

Slate mines became water-filled abandoned quarries, and the last mine closed in Ostrava in 1994, leaving a scarred

landscape of empty mineshafts, slag heaps, abandoned plants and towns in economic crisis. Czechia's former industrial regions underwent a striking metamorphosis, from mines to cultural monuments, turning industrial relics into unique experiences and attractions for visitors, who can also explore the postindustrial reinvented towns, cities and landscapes.

Ostrava is a testament to resilience and reinvention. Dolní Vítkovice is a museum and performance hub outside its festival. Anselm Mine, the oldest in Czechia, is now the largest mining museum within the city's nature-reclaimed Landek Park. Michal Mine, a former coalmine turned left-as-it-was museum, offers an immersive experience into the life of a miner, many of whom now work as guides.

The Slate Landscape Geopark in the Nízký Jeseník mountains is a green valley area, with walking trails through forests with flooded slate-mine quarries and foliage poking silver-slate mounds. Visitors can learn how slate was mined in the former mill turned Muzeum břidlice (Slate Museum) in Budišov nad Budišovkou or tour 400m of underground shale tunnels of the Flaschar Mine Museum in Odry, leading to a mammoth slate deposit chamber.

Bastions of resilience and legacy heritage sites, Czechia's industrial regions visually strike in a way that goes against the grain of mainstream tourism highlights, instead pushing visitors to explore the relics of mining town communities that would otherwise have been left behind. In the music-thumping grounds of Dolní Vítkovice, where even world-famous artists announce their arrival in Ostrava with initial confusion, you certainly won't forget where you've been.

INDEX

A

accessible travel 288
accommodation 280
activities 40-5, 311
Antonín Dvořák Theatre 272
Archbishop's Palace 267
Archdiocesan Museum 267
architecture 8-9, 16, 57, 101, 103, 132, 300-3, 314-15
Army Museum 111
art galleries & museums
  Automatic Mills 234
  Bishop's Palace 267
  Bold Gallery 131
  Center for Contemporary Arts Prague 131
  Chemistry Gallery 131
  City Street Art 272
  DOX Centre for Contemporary Art 123
  Egon Schiele Art Centrum 193
  Futura Gallery 144
  Gallery of Fine Arts 272
  House of the Black Madonna 87
  Kunsthalle 74
  Lapidárium 137
  MeetFactory 142
  Museum of Applied Arts 247
  Museum of Decorative Arts 77
  Museum of Modern Art 268
  Musoleum 142-3
  Plato Gallery of Contemporary Art 272
  Polansky Gallery 131
  Portmoneum 225-7
  Prague Castle Picture Gallery 57
  Schwarzenberg Palace 54
  Trade Fair Palace 126
  Trafo Gallery 131
Astronomical Clock (Prague) 52, 81, 82
Astronomical Clock (Olomouc) 265
Astronomical Tower 92
Automatic Mills 234

Map Pages **000**

B

Baroque Fortress 153
Basilica of St George 57-8
Basilica of Sts Peter & Paul 151
Bať'a, Tomáš 251
Battle of Austerlitz 252
Bečov Castle 169
Bečov nad Teplou 182-3
beer 17, 18-19, 285
Benešov 157
Bethlehem Chapel 89
Bishop's Palace 267
Bolt Tower 272
books 35
breweries
  Budweiser Budvar Brewery 195
  Chodovar Brewery 183
  Ossegg 119
  Pilsner Urquell Brewery 93, 169, 184
  Starobrno Brewery 246
  Staropramen Brewery 144-5
  Vinohradský Pivovar 119
Brewery Museum 184-6
bridges
  bridge *'na plášti'* 191
  Charles Bridge 24, 52, 53, 68-9
  HolKa pedestrian bridge 131
Brno 28, 31, 240, 241, 242-8, **243**
beyond Brno 249-54
drinking 247
food 246
itineraries 248
travel within 242
Brno Underground 244-5
Bubeneč & Dejvice 132-41, **134**
drinking 137, 139, 141
food 140
itineraries 136
budgeting 277, 278-9, 280, 285
Budweiser Budvar Brewery 195
Building 14|15 Bať'a Institute 251
bus travel 278-9
business hours 289

C

car travel 278-9
Carolina Gardens 264
castles 14-15
  Bečov Castle 169

Český Krumlov 190-2
Český Šternberk 223
Děvičky Castle 261
Hluboká Castle 169
Karlštejn Castle 25, 155
Křivoklát Castle 158
Loket Castle 169
Orphan Castle 261
Ostrava Castle 267
Prague Castle 24, 52, 53, 56-8
Silesian Ostrava Castle 269-70
Špilberk Castle 246
Švihov Castle 189
Trosky Castle 210
Veveří Castle 246-7
Znojmo Castle 264
Cathedral of Assumption of Our Lady & St John the Baptist 222
Cathedral of St Barbara 203, 221
caves 249-50
cemeteries
  Dietrichstein Tomb 255-6
  Jewish Cemetery (Litomyšl) 227
  Jewish Cemetery (Mikulov) 257-8
  Jewish Cemetery (Třebíč) 251
  New Jewish Cemetery 109
  Old Jewish Cemetery 90-1
  Olšany Cemetery 111-12
  Royal Mausoleum 60
  Vyšehrad Cemetery 53, 150
Černín Palace 62
Černý, David 73, 103, 142-3, 144, 304-7
České Budějovice 27, 195-6
Český Krumlov 27, 30, 169, 190-4, **191**
beyond Český Krumlov 195-6
drinking 194
food 193
travel within Český Krumlov 190
Český Ráj 209-10
Český Šternberk 223
Chapel of St Jan Sarkander 268
Chapel of St Wenceslas 60
Charles Bridge 24, 52, 53, 68-9
chateaux, *see* palaces & chateaux
Chodová Planá 183
Chodsko Museum 189
churches & cathedrals 10-11
  Basilica of St George 57-8

Basilica of Sts Peter & Paul 151
Bethlehem Chapel 89
Cathedral of Assumption of Our Lady & St John the Baptist 222
Cathedral of St Barbara 203, 221
Chapel of St Jan Sarkander 268
Chapel of St Wenceslas 60
Church of Mary Magdalene 173
Church of Our Lady Before Týn 52, 81, 82-3
Church of Saint Ludmila 120-1
Church of St James 85
Church of St Michael 267
Church of St Nepomuk on the Green Mountain 224
Church of St Nicholas 81, 84, 85
Church of Sts Cyril & Methodius 106
Church of St Wenceslas 258
Church of Sts Peter & Paul 159
Church of the Assumption of St Mary 180
Church of the Most Sacred Heart of Our Lord 118
Church of the Virgin Mary of the Snow 268
Rotunda of Our Lady & St Catherine 264
Rotunda of St Martin 148-9
Sedlec Ossuary 203, 219-20
St Bartholomew Cathedral 187
St Maurice 267
St Nicholas Church (Prague) 24, 63
St Nicholas Church (Znojmo) 264
St Vitus Cathedral 24, 53, 59-60
St Wenceslas Cathedral (Olomouc) 267
St Wenceslas Church (Ostrava) 269
Church of Mary Magdalene 173
Church of Our Lady Before Týn 52, 81, 82-3
Church of Saint Ludmila 120-1
Church of St James 85
Church of St Michael 267
Church of St Nicholas 81, 84, 85
Church of St Wenceslas 258

Church of Sts Cyril & Methodius 106
Church of Sts Peter & Paul 159
Church of the Assumption of St Mary 180
Church of the Most Sacred Heart of Our Lord 118
Church of the Virgin Mary of the Snow 268
Clam-Gallas Palace 93
climate change 286
clothes 34
Colonnade 178
Colours of Ostrava 33, 240, 269, 272
Communism 12, 71, 84, 103, 300-3
Convent of St Agnes 52, 80
convents & monasteries
 Convent of St Agnes 52, 80
 Loreta 61, 71
 Strahov Monastery 61
costs 277, 278-9, 280, 285
credit cards 277
crypts, *see* cemeteries
Crystal Valley 207
currency 277
cycling 42, 44-5, 101, 283
Czech Museum of Music 70-1
Czech Silver Museum 220
Czech Switzerland 202-3, 211-15, **212**
 beyond Czech Switzerland 216-18
 food 214
 travel within 211
Czechia
 basics 34-5
 humour 304-7
 itineraries 30-1
 people 298-9, 304-7, 308-11
 travel to/from 276
 travel within 278-9

Dancing House 103
Děčín 216
Dejvice, Dancing House 103
Dejvice, *see* Bubeneč & Dejvice
Denis Gardens 242
Diana Tower 168, 173
DinoPark 207
disabilities, travellers with 288
Divoká Šárka Nature Park 139
Dolní Vitkovice 272
Domažlice 169, 189
DOX Centre for Contemporary Art 123
drinking 17, 18-19, 20, 37, 285, 289, *see also individual locations*
Dubček, Alexander 101
Dvořák Hall 77
Dvořák Museum 105

East Bohemia, *see* North & East Bohemia
Egon Schiele Art Centrum 193
electricity 289
emergencies 289
Estates Theatre 76, 85
etiquette 34, 286
events, *see* festivals & events

F

family travel 41, 281
 DinoPark 207
 House of Fun 95
 iQLANDIA 204-6
 Techmania 186-7
festivals & events 33, 37
 Brno Pride 282
 Burning of the Witches 33
 Český Krumlov International Music Festival 169
 Chod Festival 169, 189
 Colours of Ostrava 33, 240, 269, 272
 drinking festivals 37
 Five-Petalled Rose Festival 33, 168, 192
 food festivals 37
 Gastronomic Festival of MD Rettigová 37
 Karlovy Vary International Film Festival 33, 169, 172
 Liberation Festival 186
 Litomyšl food festival 225
 Marienbad Film Festival 181
 Mariánské Lázně Chopin Festival 169
 Masopust 33
 Pilsner Fest 186
 Prague Burgerfest 37
 Prague Festival of Micro-Brewers 37
 Prague Pride 282
 Prague Spring International Music Festival 33
 Riegrovka Live Music Festival 186
 St Martin's Day 37
 St Nicholas Day 33
 Three Kings' Day 33
 TUTO Jídlo 186
 Znojmo Wine Festival 37
films 35, 304-7
Five-Petalled Rose Festival 33, 168, 192
food 36-9, 284, *see also individual locations*
football (soccer) 122, 141
Forum Karlín 111
fountains
 Colonnade 178
 Olomouc 267
 Singing Fountain 180
Františkovy Lázně 176
Franz Kafka Museum 70
Futura Gallery 144

Gallery of Fine Arts 272
Gate of Infinity 127-9
Goat Tower 258
Goethe Square 178
Golden Gate 60
golf 181
Gothic Cellar 151
Gottwald, Klement 84
Grandhotel Pupp 173
Granovsky Palace 87
Great Synagogue 187
Gröbe Villa 120

Havel, Václav 12, 101
Havlíček Gardens 120
health 283
highlights 8-21
hiking 40-1, 44-5, 283, 287
 Czech Switzerland 202, 213, 214
 high-altitude trails 42
 Jetřichovice 215
 Krkonoše Mountains 208-9
 Krušné Mountains 177
 Labské Pískovce 218
 Mound Ema 271
 Mt Ještěd 206-7
 Pálava Protected Landscape Area 261
 Slavkovský Forest 182
 Stezka Českem 203
 Šumava Mountains 188-9
history
 Battle of Austerlitz 252
 Brno 295, 297
 communism 12, 71, 84, 103, 300-3
 Dolní Věstonice 294
 industry 314-15
 Kutná Hora 295
 Plzeň (Pilsen) 297
 Prague 294, 295, 296, 297
 Slavkov u Brna 296
 Terezín Fortress 297
 Velvet Revloution 12
 WWII 106
Hluboká Castle 169
Hluboká nad Vltavou 196
Holašovice 196
Holešovice 123-31, **124-5**
 drinking 129, 131
 food 127, 131
 itineraries 130
Holy Hill 258
Holy Trinity Column 265
House of Fun 95
House of the Black Madonna 87
Hradčany 53, 54-62, **55**
Hradčany Square 56
Hřensko 217
Hus, Jan 83, 89

ice hockey 131, 196, 308-11
Infant Jesus of Prague 71
iQLANDIA 204-6
itineraries, *see individual locations*

Jáchymov 30, 176
Jan Becher Museum 173
Janáček Philharmonic Ostrava 272
Jewish Cemetery 257-8
Jewish history 13, 296, 297
 Gate of Infinity 127-9
 Jubilee Synagogue 108
 Litomyšl 227
 Mikulov 258
 Prague Jewish Museum 90
 Terezín Fortress 25, 91, 161
 Třebíč 251-2
Jindřich Jindřich Museum 189
Jiřího z Poděbrad Square 119
John Lennon Peace Wall 73
Jubilee Synagogue 108

Kafka, Franz 58, 70, 84, 109
Kampa Park 53, 72
Karel Zeman Museum 74
Karlín, *see* Žižkov & Karlín
Karlovy Vary 26, 30, 168, 169, 170-4, **171**
 beyond Karlovy Vary 175-7
 food 172, 173
 itineraries 174
 travel within 170
Karlovy Vary International Film Festival 33, 172
Karlovy Vary Museum 173
Karlštejn 25, 154-6, 157
Karlštejn Castle 25, 155
kayaking 194
Kinský Palace 81, 84
Kladská 182
Klaus Synagogue 91
Klementinum 92
Kokořín 160
Konopiště 157, 158
Kopec 214
Křivoklát 158
Krkonoše Mountains 203, 208-9
Kroměříž 28, 241, 252-4
Krušné Mountains 176-7
Kunsthalle 74
Kutná Hora 27, 31, 203, 219-22, **220**
 beyond Kutná Hora 223-4
 food 222, 224
 travel within 219

L

Labské Pískovce 203
language 35, 290-1
Lapidárium 137-8
Lednice-Valtice Cultural Landscape 259-60
Leopold Gate 151
Letná Beer Garden 129
Letná Gardens 127
LGBTIQ+ travellers 120, 282
Liberec 204-7, **205**
 beyond Liberec 208-10
 drinking 207
 food 206, 210
 travel within 204
libraries
 Klementinum 92
 Strahov Library 61
Lidice 156
Litomyšl 203, 225-30, **226**
 food 227
 itineraries 230, **230**
 travel within 225
Litomyšl Chateau 203, 228-9
Lobkowicz Palace 57, 58
Loket 169, 175-6
Loreta 61, 71
Lucerna Music Bar 107
Lucerna Palace 103

M

Maisel Synagogue 91
Malá Strana 63-75, **64-5**
 drinking 72, 73
 food 70-1
 itineraries 75, **75**
Malá Strana Bridge Tower 69
Mariánské Lázně 169, 178-81, **179**
 beyond Mariánské Lázně 182-3
 drinking 181
 food 180, 183
 travel within 178
Marienbad Film Festival 181
markets
 Dejvice Farmers Market 139
 Holešovice Market 131
 Manifesto Market 144
 Náplavka 107
 Plzeň (Christmas) 186
Masaryk Square 269
measurements 289
MeetFactory 142
Mělník 158-60
Memorial of Silence 129

Memorial to the Victims of Communism 71
Mendel Museum 247
Mikulov 29, 31, 240, 241, 255-8, **256**
 beyond Mikulov 259-61
 drinking 258
 food 257
 travel within 255
Mikulov Chateau 257
Mining Museum in Landek Park 271
Mirror Maze 67
Mladá Boleslav 209
mobile phones 276
money 276, 277
Moravian Museum 247
Moravia & Silesia 236-73, **238-9**, see also Brno, Mikulov, Olomouc, Ostrava, Znojmo
 accommodation 273
 festivals & events 240-1
 itineraries 28-9, 240-1
 navigation 238-9
 travel within 239
Moser Glassworks & Museum 168, 170-1
Mound Ema 271
Mt Ještěd 206-7
Mucha, Alfons 59, 102
Mucha Foundation Museum 102
Mucha Museum 102
Municipal House 85
Municipal Museum 180
Museum Kampa 72
Museum of Bricks
 Kutná Hora 222
 Prague 89
Museum of Communism 103
Museum of Decorative Arts 77
Museum of East Bohemia 232
Museum of Modern Art 268
Museum of Prague Ghosts & Legends 72-3
Museum of the Senses 95
music 35
Musoleum 142-3
museums, see also art galleries & museums

N

náměstí Republiky 187
National Film Museum 95
National Memorial to the Heroes of the Heydrich Terror 106
National Monument on Vítkov Hill 112
National Museum 25, 53, 98-9
national parks 40-1, 44-5
 Pálava Protected Landscape Area 31
National Theatre 53, 105, 107

New City Hall Viewing Tower 271
New Jewish Cemetery 109
New Town Hall 105
nightlife 17, 285
North & East Bohemia 199-235, **200-1**, see also Czech Switzerland, Kutná Hora, Liberec, Litomyšl, Pardubice
 accommodation 235
 festivals & events 202-3
 itineraries 26-7, 202-3
 navigation 200-1
 travel within 200
Nové Město 25, 95-108, **96-7**
 drinking 103, 106
 food 105
 itineraries 104, **104**
nuclear bunkers 101, 245, 268

O

off-beat experiences 21
Old Jewish Cemetery 90-1
Old Royal Palace 57
Old Town Bridge Tower 69
Old Town Hall 81, 82
Old Town Square 52, 81-4
Old Wastewater Treatment Plant 139
Olomouc 28, 31, 240, 265-8, **266**
 drinking 268
 food 267, 268
 travel within 265
Olšany Cemetery 111-12
opening hours 289
ossuaries, see churches & cathedrals
Ostrava 269-72, **270**
 drinking 270
 food 270
 travel within 269
Ostrava Castle 267
Ostrava Museum 269

P

Palác Akropolis 111
palaces & chateaux
 Archbishop's Chateau 252
 Černín Palace 62
 Clam-Gallas Palace 93
 Děčín Chateau 216
 Granovsky Palace 87
 Kinský Palace 81, 84
 Konopiště Château 157
 Lednice Chateau 259
 Litomyšl Chateau 203
 Lobkowicz Palace 57, 58
 Mělník Château 158-9
 Mikulov Chateau 257
 Old Royal Palace 57
 Pardubice Chateau 231-2
 Slavkov Chateau 252
 Šternberg Palace 61
 Telč Chateau 254
 Troja Chateau 133

Valtice Chateau 259-60
Villa Winternitz 146
Wallenstein Palace 74
Palach, Jan 100-1, 111
Pálava National Park 241
Pálava Protected Landscape Area 31, 261
Pardubice 231-4, **232**
 itineraries 233
 travel within 231
Pardubice Chateau 231-2
parks & gardens
 Archbishop's Chateau Garden 253
 Carolina Gardens 264
 Denis Gardens 242
 Gröbe Villa 120
 Havlíček Gardens 120
 Kampa Park 53, 72
 Letná Gardens 127
 Malá Strana 74
 Monastery Gardens 229
 Petřín 66
 Prague Botanical Gardens 137
 Rieger Gardens 115
 Royal Garden 53, 58
 Špilberk Park 242
 Stromovka Park 138
 Wallenstein Gardens 74
Petřín 66-7
Pilsner Urquell Brewery 93, 169, 184
Pinkas Synagogue 91
planning 34
Plato Gallery of Contemporary Art 272
plugs 289
Plzeň 26, 169, 184-7, **185**
 beyond Plzeň 188-9
 drinking 186
 food 187
 sights 184-6
 travel within 184
Podyjí National Park 264
Portmoneum 225-7
Powder Gate 87
Prague 26, 30, 48-163, , see also Holešovice, Hradčany, Malá Strana, Nové Město, Prague Castle (neighbourhood), Staré Město, Vinohrady & Vršovice
 accommodation 162-3
 basics 34-5
 beyond Prague 154-61
 itineraries 24-5, 52-3
 navigation 50-1
 travel to/from 276
 travel within 109, 115, 123, 132, 142, 148, 278-9
 travel within Prague 51, 54, 63, 76, 95
 walking tours 75, 86, 104, 121, 130, 136, 147, 152, **75, 86, 104, 121, 130, 136, 147, 152**

Prague Beer Museum 119
Prague Botanical Gardens 137
Prague Castle 24, 56-8
Prague Castle (neighbourhood) 52, 53, 54-62, **55**
  drinking 61
  food 62
Prague Jewish Museum 52, 90-1
Prague Zoo 140-1
Průhonice 156
public holidays 289

religion 298
resources 282, 287, 288
responsible travel 286-7
Rieger Gardens 115
Rotunda of Our Lady & St Catherine 264
Rotunda of St Martin 148
Round Tower 191
Royal Garden 53, 58
Royal Mausoleum 60
Rudolfinum 76-7, 85

Sächsische Schweiz National Park 211
safe travel 283
Schwarzenberg Palace 54
sculptures 73, 103, 142-3, 144
Sedlec Ossuary 219-20
Silesia, see Moravia & Silesia
Silesian Ostrava Castle 269-70
Singing Fountain 180
skiing 42, 43, 44-5, 207, 283
Slavkov u Brna 252
Slavkovský Forest 169, 182
Smetana Hall 85
Smíchov 142-7, **143**
  drinking 143, 147
  food 144
  itineraries 147
solo travel 283
South & West Bohemia 164-97, **166-7**, see also Český Krumlov, Karlovy Vary, Mariánské Lázně, Plzeň
  accommodation 197
  festivals & events 168-9
  itineraries 26-7
  navigation 167-8
  travel within 166
Spanish Synagogue 91
spas 312-13
Špilberk Castle 246
Špilberk Park 242
squares
  Goethe Square 178
  Hradčany Square 56
  Jiřího z Poděbrad Square 119

Masaryk Square 262, 269
Náměstí (Mikulov) 255
náměstí Míru 189
náměstí Republiky 187
Old Town Square (Prague) 52, 81-4
Svornosti Square 192
Upper Square (Olomouc) 265
Václav Havel Square 229
Wenceslas Square (Olomouc) 267
Wenceslas Square (Prague) 53, 100-1, 103
St Bartholomew Cathedral 187
St John of Nepomuk 60
St Maurice 267
St Nicholas Church (Prague) 24, 63
St Nicholas Church (Znojmo) 264
St Vitus Cathedral 24, 53, 59-60
St Wenceslas Cathedral (Olomouc) 267
St Wenceslas Church (Ostrava) 269
Staré Město 52, 76-94, **78-9, 88**
  drinking 85, 89, 93, 94, 108
  food 77, 85, 87
  itineraries 86, **86**
  travel within 76
Starobrno Brewery 246
Staropramen Brewery 144-5, 146
State Opera 107
Štefánik Observatory 67
Šternberg Palace 61
Story of Prague Castle 57
Strahov Library 61
Strahov Monastery 61
street art 76, 268, 272, see also sculptures
Stromovka Park 138
St Vitus Cathedral 24, 53, 59-60
St Wenceslas Cathedral (Olomouc) 267
St Wenceslas Church (Ostrava) 269
Šumava Mountains 188-9
sustainable tourism 194
Švihov 189
synagogues
  Great Synagogue 187
  Jubilee Synagogue 108
  Klaus Synagogue 91
  Maisel Synagogue 91
  Old-New Synagogue 91
  Pinkas Synagogue 91
  Rear Synagogue 251
  Spanish Synagogue 91
  Upper Synagogue 257

Techmania 186-7

Telč 29, 241, 254
tennis 310-11
Terezín Fortress 25, 91, 127-9, 160, 161
theatres & venues
  AghaRTA Jazz Centrum 89
  Antonín Dvořák Theatre 272
  Český Krumlov 192
  Chapeau Rouge 89
  Church of St James 85
  Church of St Nicholas 85
  Duplex 107
  Dvořák Hall 77
  Estates Theatre 76, 85
  Forum Karlín 111
  Industrial Palace 137
  Janáček Philharmonic Ostrava 272
  Jazz Dock 145
  Jazz Republic 89
  Karlovy Vary 173
  Kasárna Karlín 114
  Krumlov Revolving Theatre 192
  Lucerna Music Bar 107
  National Theatre 53, 105, 107
  Palác Akropolis 111
  Reduta Jazz Club 107
  Roxy 89
  Rudolfinum 76-7, 85
  Smetana Hall 85
  State Opera 107
  Švandovo Divadlo 145
  Vagon 89
  Výstaviště Exhibition Grounds 137
ticks 283
time zones 289
tipping 277
toilets 289
Trade Fair Palace 126
train station 278-9
travelling with children, see family travel
travel seasons 32-3
travel to from Czechia 276
Třebíč 241, 251-2
Troja Chateau 133
TV Tower 111
Týn Courtyard 87

Uber 276
Upper Square 265

V

vegan & vegetarian travellers 38
Velvet Revolution 12, 48, 101, 294, 297
Veveří Castle 246-7
viewpoints
  Bolt Tower 272
  Church of St James (Telč) 254
  Diana lookout tower 173
  Goat Tower 258

Holy Hill 258
New City Hall Viewing Tower 271
Old Town Hall 242
Petřín 66
Plečnik Viewpoint 57
Podyjí National Park 264
Špilberk Park 242
Vítkov Hill 111
Villa Löw-Beer 246
Villa Müller 133
Villa Tugendhat 246
Villa Winternitz 146
vineyards & wineries 20, 257, 258, 260, 264
Vinohrady & Vršovice 115-22, **116-17**
  drinking 115, 119, 120
  food 119, 120, 122
  itineraries 121, **121**
visas 276
Vltava Islands 107
Vršovice, see Vinohrady & Vršovice
Vyšehrad 25, 53, 148-53, **149**
  drinking 151
  food 151
  itineraries 152, **152**
Vyšehrad Cemetery 150
Výstaviště Exhibition Grounds 137

walking tours
  Brno 248, **248**
  Karlovy Vary 174, **174**
  Litomyšl 230, **230**
  Pardubice 233, **233**
  Prague 75, 86, 104, 121, 130, 136, 147, 152, **75, 86, 104, 121, 130, 136, 147, 152**
Wallenstein Gardens 74
Wallenstein Palace 74
water 289
weather 32-3
Wenceslas Square (Olomouc) 267
Wenceslas Square (Prague) 25, 53, 100-1, 103
West Bohemia, see South & West Bohemia
wi-fi 276
winter sports 42, 43

Žďár nad Sázavou 224
Žižkov & Karlín 109-14, **110**
  drinking 110, 114
  food 113
Žižkov Highline 113
Zlín 250-1
Znojmo 29, 241, 262-4, **263**
  drinking 264
  food 264
  travel within 262
Znojmo Castle 264
Znojmo Underground 262-3

'Linking the south and west of Czechia (p164) are endless forests and mountains, an unbroken string of virtually uninhabited, thickly forested peaks and valleys.'

MARC DI DUCA

'Spending an evening in the pub (p285) may be Czechia's quintessential experience. The pub is more than a bar and means more than the beer. It functions as the country's collective living room.'

MARK BAKER

All rights reserved. No part of this publication may be copied, stored in a retrieval system, or transmitted in any form by any means, electronic, mechanical, recording or otherwise, except brief extracts for the purpose of review, and no part of this publication may be sold or hired, without the written permission of the publisher. Lonely Planet and the Lonely Planet logo are trademarks of Lonely Planet and are registered in the US Patent and Trademark Office and in other countries. Lonely Planet does not allow its name or logo to be appropriated by commercial establishments, such as retailers, restaurants or hotels. Please let us know of any misuses: lonelyplanet.com/legal/intellectual-property.

THIS BOOK

Commissioning Editor
Sandie Kestell

Production Editor
Claire Rourke

Book Designer
Compton Sheldon

Cartographer
Bohumil Ptáček

Assisting Editors
Michael Mackenzie, Karyn Noble, Maja Vatrić, Clifton Wilkinson

Cover Researcher
Hannie Blackie

Thanks
Ronan Abayawickrema, Melanie Dankel, Alison Killilea, Kellie Langdon, Saralinda Turner

LEFT: INESSA HAJEK/SHUTTERSTOCK ©
RIGHT: VIEW APART/SHUTTERSTOCK ©

Paper in this book is certified against the Forest Stewardship Council™ standards. FSC™ promotes environmentally responsible, socially beneficial and economically viable management of the world's forests.

Published by Lonely Planet Global Limited
CRN 554153
14th edition - Jul 2025
ISBN 978 1 83869 178 3
©Lonely Planet 2025 Photographs © as indicated 2025
10 9 8 7 6 5 4 3 2 1
Printed in Malaysia